Utopia and the Dialectic in Latin American Liberation

Studies in Critical Social Sciences Book Series

Haymarket Books is proud to be working with Brill Academic Publishers (www.brill.nl) to republish the *Studies in Critical Social Sciences* book series in paperback editions. This peer-reviewed book series offers insights into our current reality by exploring the content and consequences of power relationships under capitalism, and by considering the spaces of opposition and resistance to these changes that have been defining our new age. Our full catalog of *SCSS* volumes can be viewed at https://www.haymarketbooks.org/series_collections/4-studies-in-critical-social-sciences.

Utopia and the Dialectic in Latin American Liberation

Eugene Gogol
and Latin American Colleagues

Chicago, IL

First published in 2015 by Brill Academic Publishers, The Netherlands.

Published in paperback in 2017 by
Haymarket Books
P.O. Box 180165
Chicago, IL 60618
773-583-7884
www.haymarketbooks.org

ISBN: 978-1-60846-707-5

Trade distribution:
In the U.S. through Consortium Book Sales, www.cbsd.com
In Canada, Publishers Group Canada, www.pgcbooks.ca
In the UK, Turnaround Publisher Services, www.turnaround-uk.com
All other countries, Ingram Publisher Services International, intlsales@perseusbooks.com

Cover design by Jamie Kerry of Belle Étoile Studios and Ragina Johnson.

This book was published with the generous support of Lannan Foundation and the Wallace Action Fund.

Printed in Canada by union labor.

10 9 8 7 6 5 4 3 2 1

Library of Congress Cataloging-in-Publication Data is available.

Contents

PART 2
The State and Social Movements in Latin America

Acknowledgements

For translation assistance, I would like to thank Douglas Brown, Carol, Anna Holloway, Theodoros Karyotis; for technical assistance, Hector Sanchez.

A special *saludos y gracias* to the many Latin American *compañer@s* who contributed their time, energy and knowledge to write of liberation struggles in their various countries. *Un abrazo fuerte.*

Introduction

> Utopia, contrary to what current usage suggests, is characterized by its relation to present historical reality... Utopia necessarily means a denunciation of the existing order... But utopia is also an annunciation, a annunciation of what is not yet, but will be; it is the forecast of a different order of things, a new society... [Utopia is] the driving force of history and subversive of the existing order. If utopia does not lead to action in the present, it is an evasion of reality.
>
> GUSTAVO GUTIÉRREZ, *Theology of Liberation* (1988)

> *The Time of the No, the Time of the Yes*... We defined the "*no*," we still haven't fully delineated the "*yes*"... "Could it be another way?" This question could be the one that sparks rebellion and its broader acceptance. And this could be because there is a "*no*" that has birthed it: *it doesn't have to be this way*... We have gotten to this point because our realities, histories, and rebellions have brought us to this "*it doesn't have to be this way.*" This and also because, intuitively or by design, we have answered "yes" to the question, "could it be another way?" We still need to respond to the questions we encounter after that "yes." What is that other way, that other world, that other society that we imagine, that we want, that we need? What do we have to do? With whom? If we don't know the answers to those questions we have to look for them. And if we have them, we have to make them known among ourselves.
>
> ZAPATISTA COMMUNICATION, *"Them and Us, Part V—'The Sixth'"* (*Feb. 2013*)

I Utopia and the Dialectic as Contested Terrain

December 21, 2012. (*Mayan calendar, the end of an era and the beginning of a new one*)—In a disciplined, silent outpouring, 45,000 Indigenous Zapatistas (Tzeltales, Tzotziles, Tojolobales, Choles, Zoques, and Mames) occupied the streets of five cities in Chiapas: "*Did you listen?* It is the sound of your world crumbling. It is the sound of our world resurging. The day that was day, was night. And night shall be the day that will be day. Democracy! Liberty! Justice!" read their communique. The occupation was followed by a series of communications from Subcomandante Insurgente Marcos and others in the name of the Clandestine Indigenous Revolutionary Committee—General Command of the Zapatista National Liberation Army (EZLN).

Among those documents was "The Sixth," (referring to the Sixth Declaration from the *Selva Lacandona*, Zapatista Army of National Liberation 2005), quoted in the epigraph of this Introduction. In referring to "the time of the *No* and the time of the *Yes*," the Zapatistas speak to the dual rhythm of uprooting social transformation—the destruction of the old and the creation of the new—that has characterized humanity's fight for freedom for generations, centuries, indeed millennia. In this sense the Zapatista project and utopian vision is aligned, as well, with the *dialectic*, the philosophic expression that gave word to the emancipatory struggle of women and men throughout history. The absolute negativity of the dialectic was a revolution in thought that G.W.F. Hegel forged under the impact of the great French Revolution, and that Karl Marx transformed into a philosophy of revolution—*revolution in permanence*. Whether the Zapatistas actively discerned liberatory threads implicit between their ideas and actions and those of Hegel and of Marx is not the crucial question. *The dialectic is in life and not alone in books*.

However today, it is crucial to make *explicit* these threads between the rebellions and revolutionary beginnings of the here and now and the philosophy of human emancipation that Hegel and then Marx forged. When we grasp and practice this dialectic of absolute negativity, negation of the negation—the positive (the "yes") inside the negative (the "no")—we can reach toward new human beginnings, the creation of a world that contains within the place/space for the many worlds that humanity *is* in its very being.

This dialectic is not a static entity, imposed externally as "the answer." Rather, it is a way of thinking and doing, "the power of negativity" that comes alive again and again, when human beings, rebels and revolutionaries, the vast social movements from below, re-create it in their practices and thinking. Working out for our day such a historically grounded world view of freedom goes hand in hand with having our eyes and ears, our energies and efforts, on the ongoing movements from below. It is their voices and actions that are the source of emancipatory change, as it is the methodology of the revolutionary dialectic that gives us the ability to comprehensively grasp the significance of the movements from below. The two labors of discerning the meaning of philosophy and of action are not two separate tasks, but one and the same.

To recover and recreate the dialectic is to root ourselves in what has been the *praxis* of humanity throughout history. It is this practice, this method, which the rulers, strive to keep hidden from us. As well, many activists seeking revolutionary change have, unfortunately, ignored, or mystified emancipatory philosophy. To become practicing dialecticians, is not to possess "the word" in any elitist, vanguardist manner. Rather, it is to bring together as one, humanity's historical struggles for freedom expressed as method and the here and now of our determination to uproot the old and create the new: Utopia and the dialectic in fusion.

The Zapatistas, and many, many others, are the ones who make the dialectic alive for our day. Our obligation is to join them in thought and action. Creating dialectical philosophy anew in thought and in life is the challenge for all.

•

Gustavo Gutiérrez's formulation above, on the meaning of utopia for Latin American reality forms another important point of departure for our discussion of utopia and the dialectic. Following from his view, I read an authentically emancipatory utopia as a historically rooted denunciation of the present that compels action toward a future new society. If such a utopia is, as Gutiérrez notes, both a denunciation and an annunciation, then it resonates powerfully with the Hegelian concept of negativity (dialectics) that expresses that dual rhythm: an opposition to/destruction of the old (negation) inseparable from the emergence of a positive within, a construction of the new (negation of the negation). Hegel's view in the Preface to *Phenomenology*—

> [O]ur epoch is a birth-time and a period of transition. The spirit of man has broken with the old order of things hitherto prevailing, and with the old ways of thinking, and is in the mind to let them all sink into the depths of the past and to set about its own transformation.
>
> HEGEL, 1964: 75

—while perhaps not a full call to the barricades, does signal this two-fold movement of humanity's emancipatory development as Hegel discerned it at the dawn of the 19th century.

Following Hegel, Marx in mid-19th century, recognized the dialectic's relation to the movement of actual history—

> ... because Hegel has conceived the negation of the negation, from the point of view of the positive relation inherent in it, as the true and only positive, and from the point of view of the negative relation inherent in it as the only true act and spontaneous activity of all being, he has only found the *abstract, logical, speculative* expression for the movement of history, which is not yet the *real* history of man as a given subject, but only the *act of creation,* the *history of the origin* of man.
>
> MARX, 1975, *"Critique of the Hegelian Dialectic"*

—and forged it anew. Marx both rooted himself in the Hegelian dialectic of negativity and transcended it by aligning with the living revolutionary subjectivities of his epoch. Marx was not rejecting that dialectic. Rather, he recreated it in his historic moment via the proletariat.

Historically, other crucial plunges into the dialectic—most notably Lenin at the time of the First World War, and Raya Dunayevskaya in the post-World War II world—would pose moments of emancipatory thought within 20th century revolutions.

While dialectical thought and action is a central strand of this book, the aim is not an imposition of the dialectic—be it from Hegel, Marx, Lenin, or Dunayevskaya—"for" Latin America, or "upon" a Latin American concept of utopia. Rather, the thrust of this study is an exploration of strands of the dialectic *as they emerge from within Latin America itself* in these first decades of 21st century: (1) How does a dialectic of freedom, of revolution, arise and express itself on indigenous Latin America ground today? (2) Are there living threads which connect a concept of utopia found in many of today's Latin American movements and the dialectic as found in Hegel, created anew in Marx, and by others? (3) What is the responsibility of Latin America radical intellectuals, of thinker-activists, to explore and help work out such a relationship between utopia and the dialectic in Latin American liberation? (4) What is the role of revolutionary organization—mass organizations and movements arising below, often spontaneously, and small organizations of radicals and revolutionaries seeking to unite with mass movements—in relation to the dialectic and to utopia?

More than a quarter of a century ago Dunayevskaya posed the challenge to revolutionaries as follows:

> Only live human beings can recreate the revolutionary dialectic forever anew. And these live human beings must do so in theory as well as in practice. It is not a question only of meeting the challenge from practice, but of being able to meet the challenge from the self-determination of the Idea, and of developing theory to the point where it reaches Marx's concept of the philosophy of revolution in permanence.
>
> DUNAYEVSKAYA, 1982: 195

How does such a problematic speak to Latin America today? We enter this discussion from two vantage points: (1) *Philosophically-theoretically*, we want to explore how a Latin American-constructed concept of utopia might find a resonance in a Hegelian-born, Marxian-concretized dialectic of liberation. (2) *Concretely in practice,* we want to examine how the activities of Latin American movements—of Indigenous, of women, of peasants, of youth, of workers—are expressed as project (*proyecto*) in multiple-forms of organization/community constructed from below (*desde abajo*).

The categories Utopia and the Dialectic are contested ones. In Latin America there has been a long, difficult struggle to construct concepts and practices of utopia different from, indeed, in opposition and resistance to, European and US concepts. "The Right to One's Own Utopia," (*El derecho a su propia utopía*), and "Utopia as a Space of Social Resistance," (*La utopía como espacio de resistencia social*) are crucial categories that have emerged from that struggle, and which will be central to our study. Even more contested, has been a view of the dialectic as a dialectic of liberation. Many commentators have focused on Hegel's conservative political conclusions as in his *Philosophy of Law*, or his problematic views of history in his *Lectures on World History*. Though a critique of Hegel's problematic work in these areas is necessary, this cannot divert us from a study of the dialectic in and of itself—a dialectic of liberation—found in his major writings. We intend to explore aspects of this dialectic of liberation in Hegel's *Phenomenology of Spirit, Science of Logic,* and *Philosophy of Mind.*

While utopia and the dialectic are contested terrain, we see then as encompassing crucial elements for the construction of an emancipatory vision of Latin American liberation; for aiding Latin American masses in reaching for an emancipatory reality here and now.

II The Present Moment

The creative power of social movements from below has been one of the defining characteristics of Latin America in recent decades. Faced with the repressive, exploitative regimes of neo-liberalism—often under police-state and military boot-heel structure—most often subservient to the Behemoth of the North—these social movements have nonetheless wrought impressive, if only partial, transformations within Latin America's terrain. The Indigenous dimension, as with the Zapatistas in Chiapas, the Amayra, Quechua and others who overthrew the old regime in Bolivia, are perhaps the most powerful manifestation of this. Crucial to these movements have been the role of Indigenous women. To these Indigenous emancipatory manifestations can be added such movements as students undertaking massive strikes in Chile, the unemployed workers who became *piqueteros* in Argentina, preceded by the Mothers of the *Plaza de Mayo*, the landless *campesinos* seizing land in Brazil. There is a rich diversity of movements, large and small, throughout much of Latin America.

As important as these challenges to the ruling powers have been, the most profound transformations have been *within the social movements themselves.*

In movement upon movement, masses have found their own voice, issued demands, undertaken liberatory activities, developed ideas of the kind of society they wished, constructed their own forms of organization. These movements and autonomous organizations arose primarily from below: spontaneous in that no one planned them, but full of thought and creativity that had been gestating well before rebellion and revolt became manifest. Not only have these movements arisen in opposition to the ruling state-party-military, but they often have done so independent of older forms of opposition, whether of Left parties or trade union organizations. These movements have brought down the old political forms, particularly neo-liberal regimes backed by police-military structures. In their place, primarily through elections, though principally after important upheavals, have come more progressive governments. We can mention among others, Venezuela, Argentina, Bolivia, Ecuador, Uruguay, and Brazil. Many of these new regimes in fact have come out of the social movements themselves, or at least, many government functionaries had been leaders within one or another social movement.

Whereas before, there were direct confrontations between neo-liberal state-party-military regimes and social movements—and this still occurs in a number of Latin American countries—today, a new problematic has emerged. One finds forms of party-state rule continue, but now with Left parties-progressive governments at the helm in a number of countries. The social movements that had brought down the old neo-liberal, authoritarian regimes are now often co-operating with the new governments. A dependency has developed, with some movements *co-opted* into the logic of the progressive governments' rule, a logic still within the sphere of capital. This is not true of all the movements, witness Bolivia, where important parts of the Indigenous masses in El Alto and in the TIPNIS region (*Territorio Indígena y Parque Nacional Isiboro Sécure*), have continued an independent, non-governmental role.

This is not to say that there have not been important changes, particularly improvements in social programs under progressive governments. However, the most perverse aspects of neo-liberal capitalism—intensification of commodity-producing abstract labor, domination of exchange-value over use-value, expansion of extractive-based production for a global-based market—remain in place, but now with the state as an active partner and even dominant force. State-capitalism, statist "socialism" is being posed, even promoted, as a supposed radical alternative to neo-liberalism. Some social movements are now found, not in opposition to, but entangled within, the web of progressive governments' involvement in an extractive, value producing, economic system that is capitalism, even if often veiled in anti-neo-liberal rhetoric combined with "socialist" phraseology.

In a certain sense this returns us to old debates (and authoritarian practices) of the Left on forms of revolutionary organization—spontaneity vs. vanguard party—that led to transformed-into-opposite revolutions. This is not to say that we are in a blueprint repetition of those incomplete revolutions of the 20th century: the "Communist" regimes in the Soviet Union and China; in Latin America the 1952 Bolivian Revolution, the 1959 Cuban Revolution, and the 1979 Nicaraguan Revolution.

There are significant differences from that earlier period. One difference is that those were revolutions that in one way or another actually took power with arms. Today's progressive regimes in Latin America have not taken power with arms in hand. However, as those transformed into opposite and incomplete revolutions of the 20th century have shown, the crucial question cannot be reduced to "taking power." We have had considerable "taking power" in the 20th century, only to witness transformation into opposite, with capital reasserting its domination in state as well as private forms. "What happens after" taking power (the Revolution), or in today's terms, after progressive parties win elections, is a key question. It is not that taking power should be dismissed as unimportant, though such an ideology has important adherents.

A number of social thinkers in Latin America and elsewhere, arguing from the viewpoint of social movements, pose the need for non-hierarchal, horizontal forms of organization in opposition to party-statist forms, whose heritage resides in the vanguardist concepts of "orthodox," dogmatic Marxism. One can certainly be in kinship with their strong alignment towards movements emerging from below. Here, the practice of everyday resistance, forms of organization from below, *horizontalism* as the particular organizational form, have become close to *a* universal in the mind of some social analysts.

And yet, is the question of movements from below vs. vanguardism, taking power vs. not taking power, anti-systemic movements vs. centralized authority, even of "progressive" governments, *the* defining framework we need to consider? Is the debate going to be confined to *forms* of organization—anti-systemic movements vs. state-party temptations and realities? It is not that form of organization is not an important question. It is. However, the question cannot be limited to *form of organization*—hierarchical vanguard party vs. horizontal, autonomous movements from below. Missing from such a formulation is what *philosophy of organization* is going to be developed, is going to be the basis for emancipatory organizations, including their form?

How can we defend and extend Latin America's revolutionary new beginnings of the most recent period? I would argue that we need to shift the terms of debate, find a fuller revolutionary ground for our dialogue. More precisely, how can we make these new beginnings grow into revolution-in-permanence in

Marx's sense of the concept? Here the dialectic enters. Dialectic philosophy, I would argue, can help us find the needed revolutionary space for our debate and work. There is a necessity to work out a dialectic of organization and philosophy.

This cannot be an imposition from outside Latin America. Neither Hegel, nor even Marx, has the answer for us. But they do have a revolutionary methodology, an emancipatory vision. However, even this is not enough. For dialectics to be alive today, it must be as *re-creation*: Dialectics as a concrete universal *arising from within Latin America.* How does that happen? What is the responsibility of revolutionary intellectuals, thinker-activists within Latin America in this process? The development of dialectical thought from within Latin America, in fusion with Latin America's struggles from below, is decisive. The richness of a Latin American concept of utopia can be a crucial part of such creation and development.

III Origins—Dunayevskaya and the Dialectic of Organization and Philosophy

This present study, *Utopia and Dialectic in Latin American Liberation,* was original conceived as part of *Toward a Dialectic of Philosophy and Organization* (Gogol 2012). In the process of writing that book, the section on organization and philosophy in relation to Latin America kept expanding, and finally, it was decided to create this second study, focusing directly on Latin America. This study can be considered volume II of that work, and the reader can consult the former to follow the argument in the fullest manner. At the same time, *Utopia and Dialectic* is the second book I have written directly on Latin American liberation, following *The Concept of Other in Latin American Liberation* (2002), and can as well be considered Volume II of that work.

At the same time, I am using origins here in a deeper sense, referring to my indebtedness to the labors of the Marxist-Humanist philosopher-revolutionary Raya Dunayevskaya, (1910–1987), in particular her final, uncompleted writings on "Dialectics of Organization and Philosophy: The 'Party' and Forms of Organization Arising from Spontaneity." In *Toward a Dialectic of Philosophy and Organization* I discussed these last writings in some detail, using the framework of her studies in my book. Here, I want to focus on the significance of the title of her work—"Dialectics of Organization and Philosophy: The "Party" and Form of Organization Arising from Spontaneity"—both as she conceived it, and in relation to the problematic of Latin American liberation we face today.

Dunayevskaya spent a lifetime in revolutionary movements and organizations. As a youth in Chicago in the 1920s she was active in the Black movement, working on the radical newspaper *Negro Champion*. Decades later, she would write *American Civilization on Trial* (1963) on the history of the Black movement for freedom in the United States. In the Depression years she was involved in labor battles, including the 1934 San Francisco General Strike. With a Black auto worker, Charles Denby and other colleagues, Dunayevskaya would found a labor and civil rights Marxist-Humanist newspaper in 1955. An activist on women's issues before there was the modern Women's Liberation Movement, she later published a collection of essays and presentations, *Women's Liberation and the Dialectics of Revolution* (1985), as that movement developed.

At the same time she was also a member of Marxist organizations, from the Young Communists in the 1920s to Trotskyist organizations in the 1930s and 1940s, to the founding of an independent Marxist-Humanist group, News and Letters Committee in 1955. As against the classical concept of the Marxist "vanguard" party giving "consciousness" to the masses, Dunayevskaya began to search out different ways of conceiving the relation of the mass movement from below and revolutionary organization. News and Letters, was not "a party," but a decentralized committee form of organization. She continually aligned herself with mass movements from below, and distanced herself from vanguardist concepts of organization. She saw how the vulgarization of the Party had been part of the process of the transformation of the Russian Revolution into what she had characterized as a state-capitalist society. And, she had seen that much of the anti-Stalinist Left, primarily Trotskyist, still retained the vanguard party form of organization. During these decades she witnessed and participated in the continuous emerging of new forms of organization from below, often spontaneous and decentralized, exhibiting great creativity.

However Dunayevskaya did not view the sharp contrast between vanguard party forms and spontaneous forms from below as the final word on the question of revolutionary organization. Rather, she began to explore the question of organization, not alone in practice but also in theory, that is, in relation to the dialectic: "I am concerned only with the dialectic... of that *type* of grouping like ours, be it large or small, and *its* relationship to the mass" (Dunayevskaya, 2002: 16). Organization was not alone a question of the mass movement from below and the Party supposedly directing from above (a concept which she rejected). Rather, she was asking what was the role of activist-thinkers in a small group, who were trying to work out a different, non-hierarchal basis for working with the mass movement? Was there a different way of posing the relation of theory to practice than the ossified vanguard party basis that had helped lead to the transformation into opposite of the Russian Revolution, and to still-born revolutions in the 20th century?

In News and Letters Committees, the organization Dunayevskaya founded, she practiced a different kind of organization, one that had the dialectic concretized as a philosophy of revolution rooted in Marx as its foundation. At the same time, Dunayevskaya became more and more convinced that the theoretical-philosophical basis for such *praxis* needed to be explored explicitly within the revolutionary movement:

> [U]nless we work out the dialectic in philosophy itself, the dialectic of organization, whether it is from the vanguard party or that born from spontaneity, would be just different forms of organization, instead of an organization that is so inseparable from its philosophic ground that form and content are one.
>
> DUNYEVSKAYA, 1981: VOL. XII

This was the project, "Dialectics of Organization and Philosophy: The 'Party' and Forms of Organization Arising from Spontaneity," which she undertook in the last two years of her life. As against posing the question only as *form* of organization—spontaneity versus the vanguard party—she saw working out a dialectic of organization and philosophy, finding *the dialectic in philosophy* that would bring forth a revolutionary *dialectic in organization*, as the crucial task. She died before having the opportunity to draft the chapters of this work. "How does Dunayevskaya's concept of revolutionary organization and its rootedness in dialectical philosophy speak to the present moment in Latin America?" is a key question I am posing in *Utopia and Dialectic*.

IV Structure of the Present Study

Part One, Philosophic Foundations, begins by briefly exploring a Latin American concept of utopia: its difference from European origins and its rootedness in emancipatory practice post the Conquest. Specific moments of the dialectic as developed historically from Hegel to Marx to Lenin to Dunayevskaya that I see speaking to today's unfree reality are examined. Finally, how the strands of utopia and the dialectic might intertwine is discussed.

Part Two, The State and Social Movements in Latin America, analyzes and critiques developments that have occurred in a number of countries. The role of the state in what have been termed progressive states (Venezuela and Bolivia) is examined in relation to social movements. The development of a liberation movement in a repressive state (Haiti) is taken up. The Zapatistas are discussed, not alone in relation to Mexico, but as having significance for Latin America and, indeed, a global dimension.

Part Three, Revolutionary Processes in Latin America—Voices from Below. With the exception of an essay on Oaxaca written by myself, this part is composed of essays written specifically for this book by colleagues from Latin America, or appendices written by others that I chose to include because they touch upon themes in the book. In addition to a chapter specifically on Argentina, I have gathered the essays and appendices under three chapters: Chapter 9: *Indigenous Struggles for Territory, Autonomy and Natural Resources*; Chapter 10: *Women as Force and Reason of Social Transformation*; and Chapter 11: *Youth, Popular Education, Teachers.*

This was done because it was possible thematically to arrange the material under these headings. But perhaps more significantly, the categories of Indigenous, autonomy, territory and natural resources; of women in social transformation; and of youth, education and teachers; are categories of particular importance in the struggle for Latin American liberation. Thus:

- The primitive accumulation, begun shortly after Columbus's original voyage—led by Spain and Portugal's search for gold and silver—resulted in the despoliation of much of South America, the genocidal decimation of its original peoples, and the importation of millions of enslaved African men and women. At the end of the 20th century and within the first two decades of the 21st, the Indigenous population can no longer be openly decimated. Slavery has been outlawed. Yet in terms of the despoliation of the Latin American continent, wholesale destruction of fauna and flora, the poisoning of the soil, the water, and the air, *extractive capitalism* has reached new heights of destruction: a previously unreached commodification of every aspect of nature. Today, the lives of millions of those seeking to live their lives in a harmonious, productive way in concert with nature have been under sustained, murderous attack. Technology is so advanced that the despoliation of the earth has grown exponentially. The struggles of Indigenous peoples and others for autonomy, for territory, for the preservation of national resources, is a concrete fight against 21st century extractive capitalism and for a different way of life. The complex struggles of a group of Triqui from San Juan Cópala, Oaxaca is presented in one essay. The long history of *Nasa* people in Colombia is discussed in another essay together with two interviews of *Nasa*.
- The title given to Chapter 10, "Woman as Force and Reason of Social Transformation," comes from the work of Raya Dunayevskaya in her studies

on Women's Liberation in relation to Marx's Marxism. She saw women's liberation not alone as an idea whose time had come but as a force to transform society. In my earlier work on Latin America, *The Concept of Other in Latin American Liberation,* I have written on the Mothers of the Plaza de Mayo in Argentina and on Rigoberta Menchu's autobiography as dimensions of Women's Liberation, even when that specific category is not invoked by the participants. In the present study, two original essays speak directly to the question of women's liberation from a Latin American geography. Francesca Gargallo, a Latin Americanist and feminist, writes on "Feminisms and Liberations in Our America," arguing for the specificity and creativity of Indigenous feminisms in Latin America. Raquel Vázquez, a Mexican feminist, social activist and poet, who worked for several years with Zapatista women in Chiapas, takes up Zapatista women and Indigenous women in Cherán in "The Fight for Autonomy in Mexico: The Role of Women."

- The year 2013 witnessed explosive massive teacher protests in Mexico. Faced with a repressive, anti-teacher proposed and then implemented law misnamed "Educational Reform," the teachers organized marchers, boycotts, protests in state after state in Mexico. Marches came to be centered in Mexico City where the protesting teachers occupied and encamped in a *planton* on the central plaza, the Zocalo. While unfortunately we do not have an essay on their important struggle, essays and appendices take up education, youth and teaching from a number of different perspectives. From Bolivia, Benito Fernández writes of "The TIPNIS March—New Horizons for Popular Education." From Colombia, Edison Villa Holguín discusses "Urban Resistance and the Medellin Youth Network—Formation of Subjects for Emancipatory Action." In appendices, students directly speak of their struggles both in Mexico and in Chile. A special appendix presents the Zapatistas compañer@s who created the books of their Little School.

Part Four—Battle of Ideas and Practices; Conclusions. Here, I return to discuss different theoretical and practical expressions of pathways for liberation in Latin America. In Chapter 12, I write ""Horizontal-ism, State-ism, Marxism and the Indigenous Dimension: Raul Zibechi, Álvaro García Linera, Hugo Blanco." An important appendix presents an essay of Rubén Dri, "The Organization and Building of Mass Power: Horizontalism and Verticalism, Utopia and Project." Chapter 13, "The Zapatistas and the Dialectic," explores how the Zapatistas, in my view, are creating dialectic anew in their practice and thought. My work ends with Chapter 14, "Marx, Hegel and Dunayevskaya—Toward a Dialectic of Philosophy and Organization in the Context of Latin American Liberation."

PART 1

Philosophic Foundations

∵

CHAPTER 1

The Meaning of Utopia in Latin America

I "The Right to One's (Latin America's) Own Utopia"[1]

The concept of utopia we wish to take up—what has been found within Latin America at the end of the 20th century and is being developed and created anew in the first decades of the 21st century—differs first, from the literary and historical utopian tradition found in Europe beginning with Thomas More's *Utopia*, and second, from the utopian socialism Marx felt compelled to critique and sharply separated himself from in the mid-19th century.[2] In sharp contrast, Latin America utopias of the present moment are born of resistance

---

1 Horacio Cerutti Gulberg's formulation encapsulates the long, continuing struggle of Latin America to control and determine its own present and future. For more than two decades Cerutti has written extensively on the concept of utopia in Latin America. Many of these writings can be found in his collections of writings, *Ensayos de utopia I, II, III, IV, V*. (See Cerutti Gulberg in the bibliography.) While we will not rehearse his and other important studies, we will adopt two of his categories—"The Right to One's Own Utopia" and "Utopia as a Space of Social Resistance"—in our presentation, though the discussion of each concept is our own.

2 As early as 1843 Marx wrote of his opposition to any imposition of a "ready-made system," such as a communist utopia upon a movement. (See letter to A. Ruge, September, 1843, https://www.marxists.org/archive/marx/works/1843/letters/43_09-alt.htm). In the 1848 *Communist Manifesto* Marx and Engels wrote of the utopian socialists of the 1840s, praising their critique of existing society while critiquing their limited view of the proletariat: "In the formation of their plans, they [the utopian socialists] are conscious of caring chiefly for the interests of the working class, as being the most suffering class. Only from the point of view of being the most suffering class does the proletariat exist for them". These utopians failed to see the proletariat as active subject of social change. They "corresponded to the first instinctive desires of the masses to *reorganize* society. Their continued existence when the masses moved in another direction could mean nothing but a reactionary movement *in opposition* to the actual movement of the proletariat." (Dunayevskaya 2000, 49). In the *Civil War in France* (1871), Marx would note: "The working class did not expect miracles from the Commune. They have no ready-made utopias to introduce *par decret du peuple*". If something new was to be created it would be out of the Commune's "own working existence." For Marx, the key was not a blanket opposition to the liberatory ideas of utopia(s), but a critique of the failure of the utopian intellectuals of his day to forge meaningful links with the activities and ideas of the subject(s) of social transformation, particularly the proletariat.

and concrete dreams. As the epigraph to the Introduction noted, Gustavo Gutierrez has formulated a rich concept of utopia as it is found in Latin America:

> Utopia, contrary to what current usage suggests, is characterized by its relation to present historical reality... Utopia necessarily means a denunciation of the existing order... But utopia is also an annunciation, a annunciation of what is not yet, but will be; it is the forecast of a different order of things, a new society... [Utopia is] the driving force of history and subversive of the existing order. If utopia does not lead to action in the present, it is an evasion of reality.
>
> GUSTAVO GUTIERREZ, 1988: 233

What has characterized Latin America's concept of utopia(s) has been its *difference with, opposition to*, the historical European notions of utopia. The actual manifestations of European (and later U.S.) utopias with respect to Latin America centered on occupation and domination. Far from being utopian dreams, they were the living nightmare of exploitation, destruction, and decimation of Indigenous peoples and enslaved Africans. These dystopias that Europe imposed on the New World annihilated millions.

For survival of body and spirit, the peoples of the Americas continually resisted European notions and practices that treated Indigenous peoples and enslaved Africans as objects to be worked as sweated labor for the enrichment of Spain, Portugal and then other nations. The construction of *other* utopias, the *historical utopias* of the Americas as well as present-day creation of utopias—will be a crucial theme we wish to follow. The idea of their own utopia(s) (*sus proprias utopías*), and the attempts to build them, fueled a permanent resistance.

Among the crucial sources for these utopias indigenous to the Americas were: (1) the pre-Colombian, pre-Hispanic cosmos-visions of the original peoples of the Western Hemisphere, and the African peoples' pre-enslavement memories and stories; and (2) the Indigenous peoples' historic memory of resistance and rebellion post-Columbus, such as Túpac Amaru and Túpac Katari, as well as the history of Black revolt in the Americas, most especially in Haiti.

These cosmos-visions and historic memories, stories, renderings of *Nuestra América* (Our America), became interwoven with the creation of new utopias—desires, visions, hopes, plans for a different society: Utopia as "the driving force of history and subversive of the existing order." Liberation as utopian vision and as project (*proyecto*) became fused—idea and act. The struggle for "the right to our own utopia" has been an important dimension of the Americans ever since "the discovery" and Conquest interrupted Indigenous cosmos-visions, while subsequent colonialism, with its military-economic-cultural imperialism, worked to destroy such visions. Today, utopias continue to be forged anew. They have become a place/space of social resistance.

II "Utopia as Space (Place) of Social Resistance"[3]

In contrast to the abstractness of 19th century European utopian socialist visions, present-day Latin American utopias are more closely welded to the ongoing resistance to oppression and exploitation: "Utopia as a space (place) of social resistance." In looking at the idea of utopia in Latin America we are not following any "ready-made" fixed visions. Rather, our focus is on the challenge of holding as one, project, which we read as concrete action, and utopia, the idea/vision. How does resistance and struggle in present-day reality fuse with the emancipatory hopes and ideas that many social movements are putting forth? To examine this question will be the primary focus of Part III on *Revolutionary Processes*. Here as introduction, we want to briefly sketch out this theme with reference to the Zapatista experience in Mexico and Indigenous struggles in Bolivia.

A *Zapatistas and the Autonomous Indigenous Communities: Constructing Concrete Utopias*

We have previously written of the Zapatistas in *The Concept of Other in Latin American Liberation* (Gogol, 2004: Chapter 10), and they are the subject of further discussion in Chapter 6 and in Chapter 13 of the present study. To summarize briefly: When the Mexican government refused to honor the agreements of autonomy negotiated at San Andrés Laranza in 1994, the Zapatistas and the Indigenous communities, who were demanding autonomy, decided to implement the agreements independently of the government. A process of autonomous development began to be carried out. Breaking from the corrupt party-state system that dominates Mexico, each community in Zapatista areas independently chose their own representatives. The entire Zapatista region was divided into five sub-regions, and in each, the group of communities in support of Zapatismo came together to establish a *Junta de Buen Gobierno* (*JBG*, Good Government Council). The representatives to the *JBG* were neither

3 This is also the subtitle of the Cerutti Guldberg and Mondragón (2006) book.

permanent nor paid. Rather, they were rotated so that as many members of the communities as possible had the experience of becoming representatives.

There was the work to construct an educational system independent of the government's education—a system that was bilingual, in native languages and Spanish. The schools used *promotores de educación* (promoters of education), who came from their own ranks. Formerly, the communities had state government teachers who did not respect their indigenous languages and culture. They began to work out a system of education that was not alone in the classroom with books, but as well, practical, that is, experiential. They saw this as a unification of mental and manual. The communities had to construct their own school facilities. They first began with primary schools, eventually constructing secondary schools. They had the assistance of professors and students from UNAM (the National Autonomous University of Mexico) in developing curriculum, but within a framework of the communities' desires and autonomy.

The communities began the construction of their own health and sanitation system. This meant the development of *promotores de salud* (promoters of health), involving again members of the community learning about health and sanitation, and then promoting that knowledge to the entire community.

There was also the creation of special commissions/committees on women to elicit their participation in the entire life of the community, and in the Zapatista movement as a whole. A collective manner of working in the fields involved neither individual wages nor work on private plots of land, but a communal sharing of work, resources and remuneration.

The Zapatista autonomous Indigenous movement was creating their own kind of communities. To be sure, these had limitations, particularly that of being restricted to only part of the state of Chiapas, surrounded by hostile forces of the State, including paramilitary ones. They were and are trying to survive at the same time that they are surrounded by a Mexican economic structure based on value production and a market economy. Nonetheless, these Indigenous Zapatista communities in resistance have themselves become catalysts for a different way of thinking that reaches beyond Chiapas and beyond Mexico.

B *Bolivia—Historic Memory, Project, Utopia as "Organization for Life"*

As significant as the 1952 Bolivian Revolution was, the leaders and parties involved had pushed the Indigenous dimension aside, seeking to submerge it within a worker-peasant alliance, where all were "citizens of Bolivia," as if the Indigenous dimension itself had not been crucial to the construction of a revolutionary mineworker-peasant unity. The concrete result of this continuing *colonialization* within the revolution contributed to its incomplete nature. In the decades that followed, resistance to this marginalization was found in new expressions of Indigenous creativity. The *Katarista* movement of the 1980s, particularly in relation to young *Amaryas* in the cities, was one of the points of departure (see Gogol 2002).

This new beginning, in turn, has not been separate from *utopía histórica* (historical utopia)—resistance history remembered—reaching back to 18th century rebellions and revolutionary leaders. The resistance of Tupac Katari, Tomas Katari, Tupac Amaru II, Bartoina Sisa, became important symbols in the development of new Indigenous resistance post-1952. It is a two-way road: The new moments of resistances brought the *utopía histórica* to the here and now; in turn, the historic memories served as part of the framework for the ongoing struggles, new utopian moments rooted in history.

Concepts of utopia are not fixed, but changing over time: utopia as self-developing. The *utopias historicas* become one with a reaching toward the future, toward an "organization for life," a utopia-in-the-making in today's struggles. The concept of *Pachakuti*—an overturning of time and space out of which a new phase of history comes forth—is one manner of expressing this. As well, the Aymara expression, *quip nayr untasis sartanani*, "To walk ahead while looking back," helps to capture this two-way road between the historical utopias and a reaching for the future.

Utopias are defended, realized, in projects. The project is the manner by which the historical utopias become re-born, concretized in the present moment. In the Cochabamba Water War of 2000 (*guerra de agua*), one can see the threads between utopia and project. The Cochabambans launched the war to preserve their historical communitarian collective water system, in which water as a use value was the focus—divided between agricultural use and use by the residents of Cochabamba (not without difficulties, tensions, contradictions, but communal nonetheless). The water concession was suddenly given to a private company and its users found themselves faced with the transformation of a natural resource into an exchange value. The price of water skyrocketed to impossible rates. A campaign of massive demonstrations and confrontations forced the government to cancel the privatization of water, returning water to the community. In the struggle to protect water as a community right, an organizational form developed—the *Coordinadora*—which led the struggle. In the Water War, a project to preserve water as a communitarian right, became an "*organization for life*," an important catalyst in the Bolivian revolutionary process of 2000–2005—a struggle for a realization/concretization of utopia.

How did the *Coordinadora* become, not alone a form of resistance or reaction to oppression, but a way of reaching for the future, a *proyecto* or program in concert with a full expression of organization for life? We will examine this in looking at Bolivia's revolutionary process 2000–2013 in Chapter 7.

III Utopia and Latin American Thinkers

One sees the uniqueness of a Latin American concept of utopia in the way Latin American thinkers have responded to ongoing social movements. A number of them have developed new points of departure on the meaning of utopia in Latin America today. In addition to the important work of Horacio Cerutti are contributions from Álvaro B. Márquez-Fernández in Venezuela; the Argentine social thinker Rubén Dri; Augusto Salazar Bondy of Ecuador; Aníbal Quijano of Peru.[4] Here we will take up Márquez-Fernández, Quijano and Salazar Bondy. In Chapter 3 we discuss Dri's contribution.

•••

The Venezuelan philosopher Álvaro B. Márquez-Fernández writes of the need "to philosophize from a utopian praxis":

> Philosophy, thought and realized from a utopian praxis in Latin America, requires an alternative thought and critique that emerges from the social base of the population understood in a communitarian and popular sense, that is, from those conditions of life from which people fight for their primary rights. To do this, they need a philosophical orientation for their political practices. To act from a utopian practice permits us to develop not only political ideologies but revolutionary utopias. Lacking this, the proper political ideologies appear in a disarticulated and ephemeral manner. Precisely this is the focal point of utopian practices as instances of imaginary social development and cultural representations of original and plural philosophic thought. Without this possibility from a utopian base, the utopian ideal from each person who forms part of the society and the world of political life would not emerge.
>
> The full importance of this manner of utopian thought can only project itself from the present when the desires [of such thought] recognize themselves as the means to realize a shared end in an ideological context. Ideology [as false consciousness] situates utopia in an order of domination of the powers who direct society and who traditionally are in opposition and

4 My comments on Salazar Bondy and Anibal Quijano were first developed in (Gogol, 2002).

damage the historical realization of citizens. Philosophy refers to a utopia in the field of human values related to the possibility to be different from the imposition of the hegemony of rationality in an anti-utopian, neo-liberal way of thinking. In this sense, utopia, utopianism and utopians are necessary conditions for a philosophical reflection, for the philosopher and philosophies that continually grow themselves and develop in the interior of diverse modern societies. Thus, the relation of utopia with cultural and historical practices of thinking philosophically is inherent in the possibility to make from philosophy a realizable thought that starts from the life conditions of the people without discriminating against any.

MÁRQUEZ-FERNÁNDEZ, 2005: 5, 6

•

In the early 1990s Anibal Quijano, a Peruvian social thinker wrote of a Latin American concept of utopia: "a new utopia is beginning to be formed, a new historical meaning, a proposal for an alternative rationality"—"an alternative rationality" to the modern rationality originating in the Enlightenment, European modernity. (Quijano, 1990: 144, 145) In another writing, "Recovering Utopia," (Quijano, 1991) he briefly developed this concept. He refused to make a division between the private and the state. He exposed "actually existing socialism," as no real alternative:

> One blind alley into which the instrumental rationale leads is the conflict between private and state ownership of productive resource... It has become clear that 'neoliberalism' and what could be called 'neodevelopmentalism' are two sides of a dead-end street. (35, 36)

Instead, Quijano looked to a "'socially oriented' form of private activity, differentiated from self-seeking types of private endeavor... let's take the Andean community as an example." He mentioned its environment as one characterized by reciprocity, solidarity, and democracy. But, "I am in no way proposing a return to an agrarian communal life." (Quijano, 1991: 36) Rather, he pointed to Peru, but other Latin American countries as well, where there are *barriadas*—neighborhoods of the urban poor. In these *barriadas* there is an alternative form of social and cultural experience, socially oriented private activities that coexist with the predominant form of capitalist private enterprise. Quijano contents that while capitalism alters these forms, they, in turn, as part of "a capitalist-dominated sea... alter its [capitalism's] logic." (Quijano, 1991: 36).

He argued that: "A new utopia is, after all, a project for the reconstitution of the historical meaning of society." Quijano ended his "Recovering Utopia":

> After 500 years of false modernization, the question before Latin America is not to choose between statism and control, on the one hand, and the freedom of the market and profit-making, on the other. In the final analysis, both paths lead to the same thing: vertical corporate structures which become, or are closely linked to, the state. The private state dichotomy is no more than a distinction between two aspects of the same instrumental rationale, whose ascendance has brought us an extremely protracted crisis, disorder and confusion.
>
> The socially-oriented private section and its non-state public sphere shows us a way out of the blind alley into which the ideologues of capital and power have led us. The liberation of society is more than an enlightened vision of utopia; in Latin America, its weft is already apparent in the threads of our daily life. The tapestry may be unraveled, perhaps even destroyed, but new hands will return to the ancient loom.
>
> QUIJANO, 1991: 38

•

In the 1950s, the Peruvian philosopher Augusto Salazar Bondy wrote on what would be needed to create an authentic philosophy for Latin America, a philosophy of liberation. In Salazar Bondy's view, such a philosophy could only be constituted if it took into consideration the Latin American reality of dependency, of being dominated from without. Such a philosophy would have to be constructed in relation to the resistance of those being dominated.

Salazar Bondy is perhaps most known for his *Does there exist a philosophy for our America?*, [*Existe una filosofia de nuestra America?*] (1976), where he argued that there was a lack of original Latin American philosophic thought: "Philosophy, which in an integral culture is the highest form of consciousness, cannot help but be an artificial and insubstantial expression in a defective culture." (Salazar Bondy, 1969: 17) The non-authenticity of Latin American philosophic expression was one with the condition of

> other communities and regional groups of nations, belonging to what today is called the Third World... We must utilize the concept of underdevelopment, with the correlative concept of domination... As dependents of Spain, England or the United States we have been and continue to be underdeveloped... under these powers, and, consequently, countries with a culture of domination.
>
> SALAZAR BONDY, 1969: 17

The havoc wreaked by the external domination of a community and its consequences for philosophic thought was of deep concern to Salazar Bondy. Earlier he had written in regard to Peru:

> I want to insist on this thesis: [T]he frustration of the historical subject in Peruvian life has been especially serious for [the development of] philosophy until our times... [For] an alienated existence cannot overcome the mystification of philosophy; a divided community cannot generate a genuine and productive type of reflection.
>
> SALAZAR BONDY, 1965

Salazar Bondy was writing in the 1950s—before the explosive creativity of social movements from below came to the fore. And with this development, philosophic thought in Latin America has undergone an important growth and flowering.[5] In writing in this earlier period, Salazar Bondy, in important ways, anticipated some of the key philosophic labors that would be necessary, and which have been developing in recent years. Salazar Bondy sought a way out of the labyrinth of domination and its impact on the culture of Latin America:

> Our thought is defective and unauthentic owing to our society and our culture. Must it necessarily remain so? Is there an alternative to this prospect? Indeed there is, because man, in certain circumstances rises above his present condition, and transcends in reality toward new forms of life, toward unheard-of-manifestation. These will endure or will bear fruit to the degree that the initiated movement can expand and provoke a general dialectic and totalization of development. In the socio-political field that is what constitutes revolutions.
>
> SALAZAR BONDY, 1969: 19

In working out the philosophic responsibility for such a project, Salazar Bondy posed a role for philosophy that brought him in concert with Marx's concept of a philosophy of revolution. This role extends philosophy beyond Hegel's view of the Owl of Minerva taking flight only at dusk, thus giving philosophy the character of a theory that elucidates the meaning of facts already accomplished. In distinction Salazar Bondy wrote:

---

5 See Gogol (2002), especially Chapter 2, and part III for a discussion of some of these developments in reality and in thought.

> It is not always so. Contrary to what Hegel thought, we feel that philosophy can be, and on more than one historical occasion has had to be, the messenger of the dawn, the beginning of historical changes through a radical awareness of existence projected toward the future.
>
> SALAZAR BONDY, 1969: 20

The commitment among a number of Latin American thinkers to create a "philosophy of the dawn" is what compels one to dive into the project of Latin American thought. It makes Latin American philosophy an authentic, creative possibility. I would add that despite Hegel's expression of philosophy spreading its wings only at dusk, a tracing of his philosophic creation post-Hegel would reveal how much the dialectic is a philosophy of the dawn as well as the dusk.

Salazar Bondy was arguing that philosophy in Latin America can become authentic, "in the midst of the inauthenticity that surrounds and consumes." To do so, "it must be a mediation about our anthropological status and from our own negative status, with a view to its cancellation." (Salazar Bondy 1969, 57).

Salazar Bondy refused to accept any condition of domination, or underdevelopment as a permanent status: "But there is still the possibility of liberation. While this is so, we are obligated to choose a line of action that will materialize this possibility. Philosophy also has this option" (ibid., 60). He insisted on the integrality of the act of liberation and the creation of a philosophy of liberation. Attempts to created philosophy outside the context of liberation are doomed to non-authenticity:

> If we want to look at things truthfully, the only possibility of liberation is open for the first time in history with the Third World, the world of the oppressed and underdeveloped, who are liberating themselves and at the same time liberating the other, the oppressor. Then, for the first time, there can be a philosophy of liberation. In the concrete struggle of classes, of groups, and of nations, there is another who oppresses me, whom unfortunately I must displace from... the machinery of domination. Philosophy must be involved in this struggle for otherwise it [only] constructs an abstract thought, and then, on the pretext that we are going to liberate ourselves as philosophers, we do not liberate anyone, not even ourselves.
>
> Ibid., 61

Because Salazar Bondy wrote of the need for philosophic creativity, a discussion of his thought leads us to Chapter 2 on dialectical thought. Does dialectics play a role in the construction of such a philosophy of liberation?

CHAPTER 2

Dialectical Thought—from Hegel to Marx, from Lenin to Dunayevskaya. What is the Power of Negativity for Our Day?

1 Moments in the Hegelian Dialectic

> If to be aware of the Idea—to be aware, i.e., that men are aware of freedom as their essence, aim, and object—is a matter of speculation, still this very idea itself is the actuality of men—not something which they have, as men, but something which they are.
>
> —HEGEL, *Philosophy of Mind* (1972: para. 482)

> In my view, everything depends on grasping and expressing the ultimate truth not as Substance but as Subject as well.
>
> —HEGEL, *Phenomenology of Mind* (1972: 80)

Under the impact of the Great French Revolution Hegel undertook a revolution in philosophy,[1] bringing forth dialectic thought in a new, emancipatory form that carried within dimensions of a liberatory future. It is true that when Hegel brought history into philosophy, it was in the form of a history of thought, *attitudes to objectivity*.[2] Yet, so profoundly did the dialectic in life become posed philosophically, re-conceptualized in the Hegelian dialectic, that in Hegel's

1 Did this include writing the famous "Lordship and Bondage" section of *Phenomenology of Spirit* under the impact of the world-shaking Black slave Haitian Revolution at the end of the 18th and beginning of the 19th century? For a provocative discussion of this possibility see Buck-Morss (2009). See also Chapter 4 "Haiti, 1986–1993: The Uprooting (*Dejoucki*), the Flood (*Lavalas*) and the Repression" in this present study.

2 We are here speaking of the dialectic proper, not to either Hegel's problematic, Eurocentric, at times, racist *Lectures on Philosophy of World History*, or to his conservative political conclusions as in *Philosophy of Right*. Elsewhere I have discussed Hegel critics whose focus has been to reduce the Hegelian dialectic to his political conclusions, as well as those who have sought to conflate Hegel's political and philosophic writings, or even to argue that the dialectic *per sec* was only an apologia for bourgeois society. Though Hegel's political views and problematic reading of certain aspects of history need to be critiqued, to focus solely on these writings is to close off the possibility of an exploration of the Hegelian dialectic in relation to today's contradictory, yet emancipatory-reaching reality. See Chapter 2 in Gogol 2002, and Chapter 12 in Gogol 2013.

abstract, idealistic, even, at times, miss-shaped form—catching the *spirit* of an *age* of revolution(s) in its categories of self-development, self-movement, of negation, and negation of negation—this dialectic of *absolute negativity* was able to transcend the moment of its intellectual birth to speak to other historic moments throughout the 19th and 20th centuries. Revolutionaries deeply indebted to the Hegelian dialectic, from Marx, to Lenin, to Dunayevskaya, felt this to be true.

Can this dialectic speak to today's unfree reality, today's search for an emancipatory future, including in Latin America? And if so, what is the manner by which absolute negativity becomes expressed in life and in thought at this moment?

To explore the Hegelian dialectic as such is not the project here. Rather, I wish to briefly take up moments within the dialectic that I see speaking to Latin America, particularly to a Latin American concept of utopia. Hegel's concept of spirit, of negation, and negation of the negation, his absolutes as found in the final chapters of his major philosophic works, his crucial categories of Individual, Particular and Universal found in the *Science of Logic* are among such moments.

A *Spirit*

At its core Hegel's revolution in philosophy is an exploration of *Spirit*. As *Phenomenology of Spirit* shows us, there are numerous manifestations of spirit—from consciousness through self-consciousness, through reason and beyond, to absolute spirit. Hegel's exposition begins with expressions of spirit that are necessarily incomplete, partial appearances, often at war with one another. What unites them, even at contradictory moments, is Hegel's view of the aim, the drive of spirit toward its full development: spirit's potentiality striving to become expressed as its actuality. This potentiality is not alone what one sees, for instance, in the seed of a plant, where the various stages of development are the unfolding of what is encapsulated *a priori* in the genome, with the environment (water, sunlight, etc.) serving as catalyst. In contrast, potentiality in Hegel's concept of Spirit is not what exists *a priori*, ready to make its appearance. Rather, spirit comes into being and into fullness, precisely *through* its journey from consciousness and self-consciousness to absolute spirit. The "voyage of discovery" that spirit undergoes *is* its potentiality which becomes expressed/concretized as spirit's journey, as it experiences life over time (history as individuals, as peoples). This journey is spirit's becoming.

Such development, such a way of voyaging, is why, for Hegel, spirit is synonymous with *Freedom*—not as a possession, but as what spirit is seeking to express/become in fullness. Freedom is the very *spirit* of Spirit. Despite the abstractness of Hegel's tracing of Spirit, when, at times, he seems to conceive of Spirit in a non-human manner, the fact that at its core it is a journey of *liberation* can only mean the humanness of the Hegelian concept. (We will examine this more fully when we discuss Marx's critique of Hegel below.)

Initially, Spirit cannot be realized as the expression of full-blown freedom. In fact, both in the history of thought and in actual history, it is most often *un*freedom that is found/experienced: humanity in chains. *Contradiction,* in the Hegelian sense, is the unfree existence that runs contrary to humanity's liberatory potential. From this contradiction arises the drive to *negate* barriers to freedom's full expression, to spirit's realization in its totality. In so doing we arrive, in Marx's words, at humanity's "absolute movement of becoming," wherein "human power... is its own end." This is not a single act, but a revolutionary process. Through this process, freedom is found to be, not a possession of human beings, but the fullest expression of their humanness: what it means to be human.[3]

B *Negation, and Negation of the Negation*

How does spirit undertake this journey of its own becoming? As noted above, humanity finds itself in a state of unfreedom, that is, in *contradiction* with its authentic self. Contradiction(s), and the need to overcome it/them, as well as the method for their overcoming, are key differentiating elements between the original Greek concept of dialectic—as *dialogue* involving a unity of differing elements to reach a new level—and the Hegelian concept of dialectic, which centers on the opposition of different elements, their existence in contradiction, and thus the need to *negate* the contradiction(s). If spirit is the becoming of freedom, and there are barriers that need to be transcended, then *negation,* not simply dialogue, becomes a key element of the Hegelian dialectic. Hegel's dialectic is a *dialectic of negativity.*

Following from this, the dialectic at first glance seems to be composed of a series of no's, negations. And certainly, this is a crucial part of the dialectic of negativity. One meets barrier upon barrier, contradiction upon contradiction. At the same time, Hegel recognized that if his dialectic remained only at the level of

---

3 Elsewhere, I have traced Spirit's Hegelian journey as a discovery of and exploration of Other/Otherness. Spirit discovers who it is, becomes what it is, out of its relation to Other, both as substance, and most profoundly, as Subject. For a discussion of the relationship of Spirit and Other in Hegel see "A Liberating, Negating Concept of Other in the Hegelian Dialectic," Chapter One in Gogol 2002. A reading of Hegel's concept of Spirit as a rejection and negation of Other as put forth by Derrida and others, as well as by Dussell in Latin America, cannot, in my view, withstand the scrutiny of a more nuanced examination of the concept in Hegel.

such a negation, such a series of negations, then one's freedom would be seen only in negative terms, defined only by what one is rejecting, opposing. The result of such a single negation, or series of single negations, what Hegel terms first negation, would be that, far from being free of the contradiction, of overcoming the barrier, one was continually being defined by what one was *not* or at least by what one was resisting. *Not* a sexual object of certain men, *not* a commodity in one's laboring, *not* an Other for a dominating culture to objectify and demean. Such a view, limited to first negation, has often been present in our reality.

However, as necessary, and indeed revolutionary, as this first negation is, it cannot by itself move one to full liberation. First negation, simple negativity, cannot be the full pathway forward because one is continually being defined, even in revolt, by what one is opposed to: not this or that; against this or that. And on that account one is never free from what one is opposing.

Hegel, in discerning dialectic of negativity as an historical phenomenon even if in the history of ideas more than from actual history, put forth a fuller concept of negation: a concept of *negation of the negation*, or second negativity. That is, after, or simultaneously with, or through the process of that first negation comes the necessity of a second negation beginning on new ground. A negation of one's first negation—not in the mathematical sense of a minus followed by a negation of that minus, thus returning to the original position—but a negation of one's original negation in the sense of reaching a self-development of spirit, a fuller concept of freedom that is beyond one's initial opposition, beyond the initial contradiction(s). Thus, we have a development *on its own ground, its own potentiality*; a humanism beginning in and from itself. This is what one can term the positive in the negative. In Marx's words from the 1844 *Economic-Philosophic Manuscripts*: "positive humanism beginning from itself." (Marx, 1975) In speaking of revolution, even if Hegel only wrote of a revolution in thought, *we* can express revolution as having a dual rhythm—the destruction of the old (first negation) and the construction of the new (second negation, the positive within the negative). Hegel's method of absolute negativity is thus a concept of movement through double negation, negation of the negation that, at one and the same time, negates contradictions and reaches toward new beginnings.

A word of caution is needed here. We are not here trying to schematize either the dialectic or revolution. This is not meant as a "formula" or "framework" for either. Rather, we seek to put forth certain concepts of dialectical thought, certain moments of the dialectic that can aid us in grasping the dialectic in Hegel and in life. There is no recipe intended. Dialectic is not a question of application, but of re-creation, dialectic born anew in ongoing revolutionary moments, and as new developments in philosophic thought.

Hegel's master–slave dialectic in *Phenomenology of Mind (Spirit)* (Hegel, 1966) speaks to this fuller concept of negation as double negation by first tracing out the dialectic of the slave's confrontation with the master (at first, a fight to the death; later through laboring, forming a thing,) whereby the slave gains "a mind of his own" (the movement from consciousness to self-consciousness). Here, Hegel does not stop. The slave's "gaining a mind of one's own," (first negation), as magnificent as that is, will only be another "attitude of bondage," unless the whole of objective reality is faced by the slave's newly freed mind (second negation) and the slave begins to build on new ground. This is not an automatic process. Incomplete attitudes to objectivity—stoicism, skepticism, unhappy consciousness—follow the master–slave dialectic. It is a long hard process—a labor of the negative—which reaches, after many stages, Absolute Knowing at the end of *Phenomenology*. Even this does not stop the process, the "absolute movement of becoming." Absolute Knowing is thus not the end. Instead, the Golgotha of Spirit that Hegel poses at the very end of Absolute Knowing means there is the need to enter a new sphere. This will be found first in Hegel's *Science of Logic*.

C *Science of Logic:* Universal, Particular, and Individual

Science of Logic does not have the concrete presence of humanity found in *Phenomenology*. The categories of "pure" thought in the three major divisions, Being, Essence and Notion or Concept, seem to move outside of human history. Yet within, one finds profound stirrings that put into doubt such a reading, as with the section on "Life," where Hegel treats first "the living individual," then "the life process" and finally "the genus process."

Most crucially, if one explores the central categories of the third, culminating book of the *Logic*, Notion—*Universal, Particular, Individual* (*U-P-I*)—what is revealed are Hegelian categories so in constant movement and development that a *human* view of their meaning is demanded, and when undertaken, yields crucial insights on humanity's dialectical development not alone as Hegel traced it in thought, but as living history, past *and contemporary*, reveals it to us.

What follows is not some kind of a "Hegelian" or "correct" reading of these categories, as if such a thing could actually exist. Hegel's categories, created painstakingly in his labor of negativity, yield a variety of rich interpretations as history unfolds post-Hegel. How could it be otherwise for his philosophy of absolute negativity? The only test, "proof" of the Hegelian dialectic, lies in how life itself forges the dialectic anew. Dialectical philosophy is simultaneously the *summation as well as the anticipation* of what occurs in life. Here, we wish to present one possible reading to help us think about these categories, U-P-I, in relation to the world we live in, with focus on Latin America.

For Hegel, these categories make their initial appearance in the final "Absolute Knowledge" chapter of *Phenomenology*:

> The object as a whole is the mediated result [the syllogism] or the passing of universality into individuality through specification, as also the reverse process from individual to universal through cancelled individuality or specific determination.
>
> HEGEL, Baillie translation, 1964: 790

The categories come to full fruition in the *Logic*. They are not interchangeable, yet they only become fully dialectical in their relation to one another. The Universal in Hegel, particularly at the level of the absolutes, is often interpreted as devoid of humanity, the end of history, an absolute idealism, a conversation with God. However, we see the Universal as being the new society, an idea of socialism. By itself, even if we interpret the Universal in these human-related terms, it *is* abstract. Its revolutionary power and meaning as a Universal only comes forth in its relation to the Particular and the Individual.

The Particular is not "the" particular in any singular sense, but a multitude of particulars depending on the historic moment. It can be the Soviet, the form discovered by the Russian workers in the first 1905 Russian Revolution, or the Zapatista uprising begun in 1994 in Chiapas. It can be a strike, a radical newspaper, a revolutionary organization, and on and on. Care needs to be taken to not substitute the particular for the universal. A particular is but one pathway to reach towards the universal. Equally crucial, is the movement from universal to particular. The particular becomes a way of realizing, *concretizing* the universal. Otherwise the universal remains as an abstraction.

The universal takes on a corporeal presence, flesh and blood, as it becomes realized. The concept of the universal here undergoes transformation. What is one concept of the universal before a particular or series of particulars occur becomes quite different under the "trial by fire" of actual events. But the original vision of the universal is important as well. Not as static and unchanging, but as a vision of the future, as encompassing humanity's vision, or a group's vision or an individual's vision up to a particular moment. It is thus an energizing principle, a motor for humanity's hopes and desires towards the future. The dialectic is humanity's history captured as philosophic categories, becoming the point of departure for emancipatory moments.

At the same time, the particular is *not* the universal, but the pathway to arrive there. If one becomes fixed on a particular, and falsely transforms it into the universal, one risks substituting a particular moment in a revolutionary process for the whole, and thereby halting the negativity that is the motor of transformation. For instance, to make nationalized property after the Russian Revolution, not only a crucial particular of the Revolution, but *the* universal proof of the revolution, as Trotsky did, means that one becomes blind to the possibility of transformation-into-opposite—of Russia from a workers' state into a state-capitalist entity.[4]

What becomes crucial is the inter-relationship, the *movement* between the universal and the particular(s). What is that movement? It is negation, negating contradictions, negating barriers toward reaching for a universal, barriers standing in the way of concretizing a universal. Negativity lies at the heart of the transformation. It is necessary to emphasize that this is a two-way road, movement in both directions, negation in both directions between the Universal and the Particular.

We are not speaking of entities *sans* humanity. The universal is a human creation. The particular involves the participation of women and men in movement. We see this most explicitly in the third category, Individual. For us, the Individual in the categories Universal, Particular and Individual is the *social* Individual, the *Subject* that is at the heart of dialectical transformation. An individual decides to join a demonstration, to participate in a strike, to become part of a revolutionary movement. An individual (hundreds, thousands, millions of individuals) has related to, joined together in a Particular. That individual is no longer the same individual s/he was before joining. The experience of doing and thinking within an activity has transformed that individual into a *social individual*, into a different person, relating to other social individuals, perhaps even a revolutionary subject, masses as reason. At the same time that participation in a Particular—a strike, demonstration, revolutionary organization—has transformed that individual, the Particular itself has become transformed by the individuals who have joined, who have participated with their ideas and actions. There is thus a two-way movement between the Individual and the Particular. Here again, what is the nature of that movement? Again it is *negation*. The individual(s) say(s) *No* to the situation s/he lives within. The particular can become transformed under these "no's" in a revolutionary manner. The particular can thus be driven to reach towards the universal and transform it. New questions, new ideas, new desires from below, from social individuals, enrich the particular and the universal. In turn, the concretization of the universal through the experience of the particular transform(s) the individual(s).

4 See "The Nature of the Russian Economy, or Making a Fixed Particular into a New Universal" in "Leon Trotsky as Theoretician," Chapter 4, in Dunayevskaya (1973).

What we have arrived at is a two-way road not alone of negation, but of negation of the negation. We can picture it as follows:

Universal «--- ---» Particular «--- ---» Individual
negation *negation*
[movement of 1st and 2nd negation in both directions]

Again caution, this is not a scheme for application, only a picture image to assist us in working through moments of the dialectic.

D *Concrete Universals*

What we have witnessed above is the creation of concrete universals. This is a lynchpin in dialectical thought. Without the creation of concrete universals we vitiate the power of negativity. We are left forever with abstractions, with universals that were concrete for certain historical moments but are exhausted for new moments, for new dualities. The need for concrete universals is to express the need to create the dialectic anew. As we quoted Dunayevskaya in the Introduction:

> Only live human beings can recreate the revolutionary dialectic forever anew. And these live human beings must do so in theory as well as in practice. It is not a question only of meeting the challenge from practice, but of being able to meet the challenge from the self-determination of the Idea, and of developing theory to the point where it reaches Marx's concept of the philosophy of revolution in permanence.
>
> DUNAYEVSKAYA, 1982: 195

One of the often stated objections to seeing dialectical thought as revolutionary is that Hegel sought not negation of the negation—revolutionary transformation—but reconciliation. Certainly an argument can be made that politically that is what Hegel thought and indeed worked for. However, what we are dealing with is the *objectivity* of the dialectic, no matter Hegel's personal concerns or the political conclusions he sought. Surely there are elements of reconciliation in the dialectic. At the same time, the key is the thrust of the dialectic as a totality, and here reconciliation is *not* the determinant strand. This is true because objectively-subjectively the authentic, revolutionary spirit of the dialectic is Freedom. When we arrive at Hegel's absolutes, it is not reconciliation, but, as we will see, "absolute negativity as new beginning" (Dunayevskaya) that prevails. However, before taking up Hegel's Absolutes we want to probe the dialectic as Marx propounded it, 1843–1883, and as Lenin rediscovered it in the midst of the First World War and concretized it in the Russian Revolution.

II Marx-Hegel—from "Critique of the Hegelian Dialectic" to *Capital*

> The outstanding achievement of Hegel's *Phänomenologie* and of its final outcome, the dialectic of negativity as the moving and generating principle, is thus first that Hegel conceives the self-creation of man as a process, conceives objectification as loss of the object, as alienation and as transcendence of this alienation; that he thus grasps the essence of *labour* and comprehends objective man—true, because real man—as the outcome of man's *own labour*.
>
> MARX, 1975: *"Critique of the Hegelian Dialectic"*

> The mystification which dialectic suffers in Hegel's hands, by no means prevents him from being the first to present its general form of working in a comprehensive and conscious manner. With him it is standing on its head. It must be turned right side up again, if you would discover the rational kernel within the mystical shell.
>
> MARX, 1909: "Afterword to the Second German Edition of *Capital*"

> You cannot abolish philosophy without making it a reality.
>
> MARX, 1975: "Introduction to Critique of Hegel's *Philosophy of Right*"

"How do we now stand as regards the Hegelian *dialectic*?" asked the young Karl Marx in his untitled manuscript, later called "Critique of the Hegelian Dialectic," a key writing in his *1844 Economic-Philosophic Manuscripts*. While Marx's question was initially directed to the Young Hegelians of his day, the greater truth was that Marx chose to explore the question for himself. This marked the beginning of Marx's profound four-decade long exploration of the dialectic—as critique, as the deepest of thought-dives that led to Marx's profound re-creation of the dialectic in concrete, human terms.[5]

Though we will focus on "Critique of the Hegelian Dialectic," it is important to note that the *1844 Manuscripts* were of whole cloth. The topics in the *Manuscripts* were together in one notebook, written at times in columns side

5 Marx had earlier explorations of Hegel in his doctoral thesis and in his Critique of Hegel's *Philosophy of Right*. However, it was his 1844 probing of the dialectic in and of itself, part of Marx's "philosophic moment," that set the trajectory for his revolutionary life.

by side. "Private Property and Communism," "Alienated Labor," "Critique of the Hegelian Dialectic" and other notebook manuscripts form a totality that encompassed Marx's "triple break"—a critique of classical political economy, of narrow materialism and vulgar communism, and his complex critique of Hegelian dialectics.

Marx's thoroughgoing critique was inseparable from his forging of a new philosophic point of departure—"thoroughgoing naturalism or humanism [that] distinguishes itself both from Idealism and Materialism, and is, at the same time, the truth uniting both." (Marx, 1975: *1844 Economic-Philosophic Manuscripts*) In turn, these writings of 1844 can only be understood in the context of Marx's discovery of and alignment with an emerging revolutionary subject, the proletariat. Marx attended workers gatherings in Paris, writing to Ludwig Feurebach "You have to have participated in one meeting of the French workers to be able to believe the virgin freshness and nobility among these work-worn men" (11 August 1844). He hailed the Silesian weavers revolt of 1844—"The wisdom of the German poor stands in inverse ratio to the wisdom of poor Germany… The Silesian uprisings began where the French and English insurrections ended, with the consciousness of the proletariat as a class," (quoted in Mehring, 1918)—separating himself sharply from other radical intellectuals, who failed to recognize this revolutionary subjectivity arising from within industrial capitalism.

Raya Dunayevskaya would designate these *1844 Economic-Philosophic Manuscripts,* "a new continent of thought and revolution," (Dunayevskaya, 1982: 115), "Marx's philosophic moment," (Dunayevskaya, 1981: Vol. XII) that she viewed as the determinate of the philosophic-organizational-revolutionary trajectory of his life, 1844–1883. The self-clarification of "Critique" meant a critique of the dehumanization of ideas in Hegel's hands:

> For Hegel the *human being—man*—equals *self-consciousness.* All estrangement of the human being is therefore *nothing* but *estrangement of self-consciousness.* The estrangement of self-consciousness is not regarded as an *expression*—reflected in the realm of knowledge and thought—of the *real* estrangement of the human being. Instead, the *actual* estrangement—that which appears real—is according to its *innermost,* hidden nature (which is only brought to light by philosophy) nothing but the *manifestation* of the estrangement of the real human essence, of *self-consciousness.*
>
> MARX, 1975: *1844 Economic-Philosophic Manuscripts,* "Critique of the Hegelian Dialectic"

At the same time, Marx grasped the revolutionary kernel of Hegel and thus the ground for his transcendence and re-creation of that dialectic:

> [B]ecause Hegel has conceived the negation of the negation, from the point of view of the positive relation inherent in it, as the true and only positive, and from the point of view of the negative relation inherent in it as the only true act and spontaneous activity of all being, he has only found the *abstract, logical, speculative* expression for the movement of history, which is not yet the *real* history of man as a given subject, but only the *act of creation*, the *history of the origin* of man.
>
> [T]he outstanding achievement of Hegel's *Phänomenologie* and of its final outcome, the dialectic of negativity as the moving and generating principle, is thus first that Hegel conceives the self-creation of man as a process, conceives objectification as loss of the object, as alienation and as transcendence of this alienation; that he thus grasps the essence of *labour* and comprehends objective man—true, because real man—as the outcome of man's *own labour.*
>
> MARX, 1975: *1844 Economic-Philosophic Manuscripts,* "Critique of the Hegelian Dialectic"

We need to hold before us, perhaps in tension, two central dimensions of the Marx-Hegel relation: (1) It would not have been possible to have Marx without Hegel, and yet, (2) Marx's dialectic is Marx's alone, not Marx's and Hegel's.[6] One cannot conceive of Marx without Hegel and Marx's exploration of that dialectic. If Marx had not had Hegel, he most certainly would have had to "invent" him in terms of methodology. And yet, we need to probe further into the nature of Marx's transformation/re-creation of the Hegelian dialectic, which became and remains the revolutionary point of departure for ourselves. It was neither a simple inversion of Hegel from standing on his head to standing on his feet (putting materialism forward), nor alone the "addition" of the proletarian subject to the dialectic—as crucial as both of these labors were. Marx's labors were not solely the addition of materialism in the form of the objective world and in the form of a living Subject, as opposed to following Spirit. Rather, Marx was reformulating, re-conceiving, dialectic at its source. The Subject would be a living one, the corporeal presence of freedom in action and thought, and not alone the Idea of freedom in seeming isolation as Hegel conceived it. However, Marx was not dismissing the dialectical development of the Idea of freedom. Rather he was finding it/re-creating it anew as concrete

6 The 20th century has been full of sharp debate and disagreement on the Hegel/Marx relation. We will not enter a polemic on this here, though a recent study *Marx & Alienation: Essays on Hegelian Themes* (Sayers 2011) is of interest. See as well, the important recent work, *Dialectics of Human Nature in Marx's Philosophy* (Tabah 2012).

universals in the world within which he lived—the need to comprehend the nature of capitalism so as to overcome it, the focus on revolutionary human subjectivity as the motor for uprooting transformation. Though Marx's view was born in the *1844 Economic-Philosophic Manuscripts,* one can see this most fully in *Capital,* the apex of Marx's labors.

In *Capital,* one can see at one and the same time, Marx's indebtedness to Hegel and his transcendence of the Hegelian dialectic. Take Chapter 1, "Commodities." In a straight forward manner, Marx moved from the appearance of commodities, with their two factors of use-value and value, to what lies behind this two-fold appearance: the two-fold character of the labor that is embodied in commodities, concrete labor as the creator of use value; abstract labor (which becomes measured as socially necessary labor time) as the creator of value. Thus Marx moves from appearance to essence, labor and production as the heart of industrial capitalism. We can discern here that same movement of categories in Hegel's *Science of Logic*. Further, when we move to the final section of Chapter 1, "The Fetishism of Commodities and the Secret Thereof," we move beyond appearance and essence to discover the notion or concept. The concept or "spirit" of capital, of capitalism, is precisely this fetishism of commodities. And what lies behind it is the type of labor, production, accumulation, one finds in capitalism, which Marx called "production for production's sake, accumulation for accumulation's sake." The fetishism comes, says Marx, "clearly from the form itself." That is, precisely because labor under capitalism has this two-fold nature of concrete labor and abstract labor, fragmenting the human being who labors, the products of such a way of laboring can only assume the form of commodities with their two-fold value: use value and value. Here, we have moved from being, with its commodity appearance, through essence (the two-fold nature of labor under capitalism) to notion, the fetishism of commodities (production for production's sake), in a way that "parallels" Hegel's being, essence and notion in the *Science of Logic*. However, now we have a "rupture," or transcendence of Hegel in Marx's re-creation of the dialectic. He does not stop with the fetishism of commodities, but within this section turns to its opposite, to what can strip the fetishism off of capitalist production—freely associated labor. Marx thus posed the notion or concept arising from a living revolutionary subject—the proletariat—of a totally different way of laboring, confronting capitalist production with its absolute opposite. In a dialectical manner, he put forth the movement from being to essence to notion, but now the notion is not of capitalism alone, but embedded within is its opposite—freely associated labor negating capitalist production, a negation of the negation birthing a completely different manner of laboring—the human force/creativity that can both strip the fetishism from commodities, breaking the law of value, and move through second negation to reach toward a new society. This is the revolutionary dialectic that transcends the Hegelian one and is Marx's own dialectic. Dunayevskaya posed Marx's dialectic for the whole of *Capital*:

> *Capital*... is the Great Divide from Hegel, and not just because the subject is economics rather than philosophy [I]t is that Great Divide because, just *because*, the Subject—not subject matter, but Subject—was neither economics nor philosophy but the human being, the masses. Because dead labor (capital) dominates over living labor, and the labor*er* is the 'gravedigger of capitalism,' all of human existence is involved. *This* dialectic is therefore totally new, totally internal; deeper than ever was the Hegelian dialectic of Consciousness, Self-Consciousness, and Reason. Marx could transcend the Hegelian dialectic not by denying that it was 'the source of all dialectic'; rather, it was precisely because he began with the source that he could make the leap to the live Subject who is the one who transforms reality. *Capital* is the work in which—as Marx works out the economic laws of capitalism, not apart from the actual history of class struggle—historic narrative becomes historic reason.[7]
>
> DUNAYEVSKAYA, 1981: 143

III Lenin-Hegel—Philosophical Preparation for Revolution?

> It is impossible completely to grasp Marx's Capital and especially its first chapter, if you have not studied through and understood the whole of Hegel's Logic. Consequently, none of the Marxists for the past half a century have understood Marx!!
>
> LENIN, *Philosophic Notebooks*

This justly famous quote from Lenin's notes on Hegel's *Science of Logic* has caught the attention of many a Marxist thinker. Yet surprisingly few have viewed Lenin's Hegel explorations of 1914–1915 as rising to the level of philosophic preparation for what followed—the 1917 Russian Revolution. There were strong objective reasons for Lenin's return to Hegel shortly after the outbreak of the First World War. The war brought about the collapse of the socialist/

7 To see how Dunayevskaya reaches this conclusion we can follow her extensive studies on the "Humanism and Dialectic of Marx's *Capital*" found in the all three of her major works: *Marxism and Freedom* (1958), *Philosophy and Revolution* (1973), and *Rosa Luxemburg, Women's Liberation and Marx's Philosophy of Revolution* (1982).

Marxist organizations of the Second International, with the German Social Democracy and other socialist organizations taking sides in the "defense of the Fatherland." The shock of this betrayal sent Lenin to search far beyond the question of mere "selling out."

> What were the *objective* causes for such total *ideological* collapse? The fact was overwhelming, totally unforeseen, incontrovertible. Confronted with the appearance of counterrevolution *within* the revolution, Lenin was driven to search for a philosophy that would reconstitute his own reason. He began reading Hegel's *Science of Logic*.
>
> DUNAYEVSKAYA, 2000: 168

That reluctance to explore threads between Lenin's philosophic exploration of the Hegelian dialectic under the impact of the collapse of the Marxist 2nd International at the outbreak of World War I and his revolutionary political practice 1915–1917, 1917–1923, has been part of the problematic legacy of "orthodox" Marxism throughout the 20th century. The separation of the revolutionary Hegelian-Marxian dialectics from radical politics as well as revolutionary organization has been the history of post-Marx Marxism, even by the "best" of Marxists.[8]

It is the threads between Lenin's dialectical probing and his political practice that can be of assistance in looking at Latin America liberation today. To discover these threads, we need to clear away a host of 20th century interpretations of Lenin. Anti-Leninists have often reduced him to "evil genius." A number of so-called Leninists have not been particularly helpful. One attributed his greatness to "uncanny intuition." (See Tony Cliff's three volume biography of Lenin, particularly 2004.) A recent painstaking analysis of Lenin's early political thought provides a view of his *What Is to Be Done* that sweeps away a number of problematic assumptions, but does not continue to the period of the First World War and after. (See Lih, 2006) In general we have been left with Lenin as "practical fighter," with silence or dismissal on his World War I Hegel Notebooks.

A brief look of some of the principal strands of Lenin's Hegel Notebooks will help to situate our discussion. The Notebooks were a combination of Lenin

8 See in particular Dunayevskaya's Chapter 10 of *Marxism and Freedom* and Chapter 3 in *Philosophy and Revolution*, and Kevin Anderson's *Lenin, Hegel and Western Marxism*. But also see Dunayevskaya on the *limitation* of Lenin and the Hegelian dialectic with regard to revolutionary organization in her extensive writings found in "Dialectics of Organization and Philosophy," Vol. XII of the *Raya Dunayevskaya Collection* (1981). As well, see my *Towards a Dialectics of Philosophy and Organization*, Chapter 11.

copying numerous excerpts from the *Logic*—often accompanied by marks of emphasis including underlining, capitalization, exclamation marks, and short notations such as *N.B.* (*nota bene* or note well)—together with more extensive commentary, including Lenin's "definitions," "materialist translations," references to other thinkers and works, including to Marx's *Capital*, and various Russian thinkers.

After excerpts and brief commentary on Hegel's Prefaces and Introduction, Lenin took up the first book of the *Logic*, the Doctrine of Being. Here we encounter Lenin's initial wariness about Hegel's idealistic framework, his references to the absolute, God, the pure Idea:

> Nonsense about the absolute. I am in general trying to read Hegel materialistically: Hegel is materialism which has been stood on its head (according to Engels)—that is to say, I cast aside for the most part God, the Absolute, the Pure Idea, etc.
>
> LENIN, 1976: 104

Lenin's determination to read Hegel "materialistically" was prominent in his early notations, though later he will comment on the materialism *within* Hegel as opposed to the need to give it such a reading from the outside. However, Lenin never abandoned this framework of the need to read Hegel materialistically. In the initial section of the Doctrine of Being on Quality, Lenin wrote his first "definition":

> Dialectics is the teaching which shows how Opposites can be and how they happen to be (how they become) identical,—under what conditions they are identical, becoming transformed into one another,—why the human mind should grasp these opposites not as dead, rigid, but as living, conditional, mobile, becoming transformed into one another. (109)

It is such definitions or "translations" that yield some of Lenin's richest commentary "*en lisant* (while reading) Hegel." The question of movement, of the identity of opposites continued to be of importance in Lenin's readings:

> Hegel analyzes concepts that usually appear to be dead and shows that there is movement in them. Finite? That means moving to an end! Something?—means not that which is Other. Being in general?—means such indeterminateness that Being = not-Being. All-sided, universal flexibility of concepts, a flexibility reaching to the identity of opposites,—that is the essence of the matter. This flexibility, applied subjectivity = eclecticism

> and sophistry. Flexibility, applied objectively, i.e., reflecting the all-sidedness of the material process and its unity, is dialectics, is the correct reflection of the eternal development of the world. (110)

This movement was recognized by Lenin to not be an externally imposed movement, but a self-movement. He quoted Hegel: "the negative in general contains the ground of Becoming, the unrest of self-movement," (113) and emphasized the concept of self-movement in his marginalia. In his notes on the last section of the Doctrine of Being, Measure, that movement will be seen as "leaps," as opposed to mere gradualness in the dialectic, as Lenin wrote "leaps" several times in the margin next to his Hegel excerpts, and even drew an illustration of the concept.

In turning to the Doctrine of Essence, we again will only give the barest indication of Lenin's probing of Hegel, a hint of the rich wealth of his philosophical discoveries. In the first section on Essence as Reflection Within Itself, Lenin excerpted a number of paragraphs on the Law of Contradiction. Amidst the excerpts he inserted the following comment:

> Movement and "*self*-movement" (this NB! Arbitrary (independent), spontaneous, *internally-necessary* movement), "change," "movement and vitality," "the principle of all self-movement," "impulse" (Trieb) to "movement" and to "activity"—the opposite to "dead Being"—who would believe that this is the core of "Hegelianism," of abstract and abstruse (ponderous, absurd?) Hegelianism?? This core had to be discovered, understood, rescued, laid bare, refined, which is precisely what Marx and Engels did. (141)

Lenin was again emphasizing the self-movement, internally necessary that he found within the dialectic. He immediately followed this by noting that,

> the idea of universal movement and change (1813 *Logic*) was conjectured before its application to life and society. In regard to society it was proclaimed earlier (1847) [*The Communist Manifesto*] then it was demonstrated in application to man (1859) [Darwin's *Origin of the Species*]. (141)

Dunayevskaya in lecture notes she prepared in the 1970s would comment on this section of Lenin:

> From now on, Lenin shows the highest appreciation of idealism in dialectical philosophy. Thought has its own dialectic and what is crucial is that

> Lenin is not merely saying: Let's read Hegel materialistically... By now he has taken that for granted philosophically as well as in life, and instead stresses that the *idea* of universal movement came first with Hegel, then with Marx, and finally with Darwin.
>
> DUNAYEVSKAJA, 1981: "Notes on a Series of Lectures," #3894

Lenin continued his excerpting on contradiction, and in his own commentary proceeds to link contradiction, thinking reason, negativity and self-movement:

> Thinking reason (understanding) sharpens the blunt difference of variety, the mere manifold of imagination, into essential difference, into opposition. Only when raised to the peak of contradiction, do the manifold entities become active and lively in relation to one another,—they acquire that negativity which is the inherent pulsation of self-movement and vitality. (143)

Both in the second section on Appearance and the third on Actuality, Hegel's conception of "moment(s)" drew Lenin's attention. Under Appearance he wrote:

> The essence here is that both the world of appearances and the world in itself are moments of man's knowledge of nature, stages, alterations of deepening (of knowledge). The shifting of the world in itself further and further from the world of appearance—that is what is so far still not to be seen in Hegel. NB. Have not Hegel's "moments" of the concept the significance of "moments" of transition? (151)

In the section Actuality, Lenin will comment: "The unfolding of the sum-total of the moments at actuality NB = the essence of dialectical cognition." (159) After excerpting and commenting upon Hegel's discussion of causality, Lenin ended his commentary on the Doctrine of Essence by noting and emphasizing Hegel's expression "the Notion, the realm of Subjectivity, or of Freedom": "NB Freedom = Subjectivity ('or') End, Consciousness, Endeavour NB" (164).

In turning to the Doctrine of Notion, which Lenin excerpted and commented on in a more extensive manner than for the Doctrines of Being and Essence, we will briefly comment upon his notes on the first sections, leaving the crucial section, The Idea, for separate treatment in Chapter 3. Though Lenin's notes on the Doctrine of the Notion were the richest, he was still at times wary of Hegel's idealism, commenting upon it as "mysticism" on more than one occasion.

At the same time, Lenin showed his appreciation of Hegel's dialectics viewed materialistically as against vulgar materialism. Thus he would write: "Plekhanov criticizes Kantianism (and agnosticism in general) more from a vulgar-materialistic standpoint than from a dialectical-materialistic standpoint." (179) Further, "Marxists criticized (at the beginning of the twentieth century) the Kantians and Humists more in the manner of Feuerbach (and Buchner) than of Hegel." (179) This is, as well, where Lenin will make his provocative comment:

> Aphorism: It is impossible completely to understand Marx's *Capital*, and especially its first chapter, without having thoroughly studied and understood the whole of Hegel's *Logic*. Consequently, half a century later none of the Marxists understood Marx!! (183)

There was a constant tension in Lenin, even at the highest points within his commentary on the *Logic*, between finding tremendous illumination, profoundness, a previously unimagined philosophical richness in the Hegelian dialectic, and a constant need to be giving a materialist interpretation, finding a materialist kernel, a continual presenting of an historical materialist framework. This, even though Lenin often saw or was close to seeing that materialism was itself integral to dialectal thought. Thus one finds references to "the germs of historical materialism in Hegel," and to "Hegel and historical materialism" and similar expressions at all stages. Lenin's final comments before his excerpts on The Idea read:

> Remarkable: Hegel comes to the 'Idea' as the coincidence of the Notion and the object, as truth, through the practical, purposive activity of man. A very close approach to the view that man by his practice proves the objective correctness of his ideas, concepts, knowledge, science. From the subjective Notion and subjective end to objective truth. (191)

•

In turning to the relation of Lenin's *Philosophic Notebooks* and his political practice post 1914, we are not claiming a one-to-one relationship between the two. Lenin was a creative, practicing revolutionary before his exploration of Hegel in 1914–1915. However, in two areas—self-determination of nations and revolutionary subjectivity in 1917 and beyond—there were indications of important self-development in Lenin post-1914 in relation to dialectics.

Lenin's position on self-determination of nations in the midst of World War I sharply differed from his Bolshevik colleague Bukharin. Bukharin elaborated the following thesis:

> The imperialist epoch is an epoch of the absorption of small states... It is therefore impossible to struggle against the enslavement of nations otherwise than by struggle against imperialism... *ergo* against *capitalism* in general. Any deviation from that road, any advancement of 'partial' tasks, of the 'liberation of nations' *within* the real of capitalist civilization, means diverting of proletarian forces from the actual solution of the problem... The slogan of 'self-determination' is first of all *utopian* and *harmful*... as a slogan which *disseminated illusions*.

Lenin called such an attitude "Imperialist Economism": "The scornful attitude of 'imperialist economism' toward *democracy* constitutes one of these forms of *depression* or *suppression*, of human reason by the war." Lenin did not have any illusions about the power of imperialism, including ideologically: "Capitalism in general and imperialism in particular transform democracy into an illusion... At the same time [it] generates democratic tendencies among the masses."

Dunayevskaya commented on Lenin's position: "As opposed to Bukharin's and Pyatakov's counter posing the existence of imperialism and the non-existence of democracy, Lenin stressed the *co-existence* of imperialism and democratic tendencies among the masses." (Dunayevskaya, 2000: 173) This was not alone a theoretical debate. In spring 1916, the Irish masses took on British imperialism:

> Lenin hailed the rebellion and accepted it as the real test of his thesis. In summing up the discussion on self-determination, he concluded: "The dialectics of history is such that small nations, powerless as an *independent* factor in the struggle against imperialism, play a part of one of the ferments, one of the bacilli, which help the *real* power against imperialism to come to the scene, namely, the socialist proletariat."[9]
>
> "Discussion on Self-Determination Summed-Up," Vol. 19, *Collected Works*, quoted in DUNAYEVSKAYA, 2000

9 For a fuller discussion of Lenin, the dialectic, and self-determination see Dunayevskaya 2010 (Chapter X: "The Collapse of the Second International and the Break in Lenin's Thought").

During and after the Russian Revolution, it is Lenin's dialectic point of view that one sees in action. His insistence on "All power to the Soviets" in the midst of the revolution—when not only the Mensheviks and others adhered to the Provisional government, but many of his fellow Bolsheviks as well—argued for his view of subjects of revolution, of changes from below.

After the Bolsheviks took power, the 1920–1921 Trade Union Debate within the Communist Party helps illuminate the methodology of Lenin's political practice. The role of the workers and their organizations, the trade unions, in relation to the Soviet State and the Communist Party was the central theme, revealing the tensions and dangers lying *within* this new "workers' state."[10]

Trotsky, who had headed a militarized absorption of the water workers' and rail workers' unions during the emergency situation of the Civil War, and wanted to universalize that position after the war ended, argued that since the Soviet Union was a workers' state, there was no need for the workers to have these organs independent of the state. Rather, the unions should be absorbed within the state—"state-tification" of the trade unions.

Shlyapnikov, as well a Bolshevik and a member of what was known as the Workers' Opposition, also arguing from the position of the Soviet Union as a workers' state, called for eliminating the role of the state and substituting producers' congresses—"trade-unionize" the state. (The Workers Opposition formulated this as follows: "The organization of the management of the national economy is the function of an All-Russia Congress of Producers organized in industrial unions which shall elect a central body to run the whole of the national economy of the Republic.")

Lenin stood on entirely different ground from both of them:

> Ours is not actually a workers' state but a workers' and peasants' state. And a lot depends on that... Ours is a workers' state *with a bureaucratic twist to it*. ... A workers' state is an abstraction. What we actually have is a workers' state, with this peculiarity, firstly, that it is not the working class but the peasant population that predominates in the country, and, secondly, that it is a workers' state with bureaucratic distortions.

Answering Trotsky, Lenin sharply critiqued his "administrative mentality," as a way of solving problems: "bureaucratic projecteering." "The sum and substance of his policy is bureaucratic harassment of the trade unions." In answering

10 See Dunayevskaya 1958 for a fuller discussion of the significance of this debate. See also Gogol, 2004.

Shlyapnikov, he hit out against his syndicalist-anarchist "deviation," arguing that it would be suicide for the new state:

> It is syndicalism because—consider this carefully—our proletariat has been largely declassed; the terrible crises and the closing down of the factories have compelled people to flee from starvation. The workers have simply abandoned their factories; they have had to settle down in the country and have ceased to be workers. Are we not aware of the fact that the unprecedented crises, the Civil War, the disruption of proper relations between town and country and the cessation of grain deliveries have given rise to a trade in small articles made at the big factories—such as cigarette lighters—which are exchanged for cereals, because the workers are starving, and no grain is being delivered? Have we not seen this happen in the Ukraine, or in Russia? That is the economic source of the proletariat's declassing and the inevitable rise of petty-bourgeois, anarchist trends.

The difficulty in fully grasping the dialectical framework of Lenin's political positions is that he did not spell out and share with his Bolshevik colleagues this philosophic foundation. (This is what Dunayevskaya would term Lenin's "philosophic ambivalence." See Chapter 3 of Dunayevskaya, 1973) Methodologically, it left them rudderless post his death.

In what has become known as his Will, Lenin critiqued a number of his fellow Bolsheviks—calling for Stalin's removal as General Secretary, praising Trotsky as the most capable but critiquing his preoccupation with "the administrative side of the work." His only remark on the dialectic came in relation to his commentary on Bukharin: "Bukharin is not only a most valuable and major theorist of the Party; he is also rightly considered the favorite of the whole Party, but his theoretical views can be classified as fully Marxist only with the great reserve, for there is something scholastic about him (he has never made a study of dialectics, and, I think, never fully appreciated it)." In Chapter 3 below, "Utopia and the Dialectic," we will discuss a significant limitation of Lenin's reading of the dialectic.

IV Dunayevskaya-Hegel—Reading Absolute Negativity "As New Beginning"

> This new world, which Hegel calls Absolute Knowledge, is the unity of the real world and the notions about it, the organization of thought and

> activity, *which merge into the new*, the whole truth of the past and the present, which anticipates the future.
>
> DUNAYEVSKAJA, 2002: "Notes on Hegel's *Phenomenology*"

The prevailing reading of Hegel's Absolutes by Hegelians and Marxist Hegelians alike has been that the Absolutes are grand summations, recapitulating the vast philosophic journey Hegel undertook in each of his major philosophic studies—Absolute Knowledge (Knowing) in *Phenomenology*, Absolute Idea in *Science of Logic*, Absolute Mind (Spirit) in *Philosophy of Mind* (*Spirit*)—but with no new points of departure for the future to be found within. The Hegelian Marxist Herbert Marcuse viewed the Absolutes as representative of a pre-technological age. The Marxist philosopher George Lukács in his *Young Hegel*, saw *Phenomenology's* final chapter, Absolute Knowledge, as swallowing up history, and not ground for new discoveries of dialectical thought. From academia, Hegel scholars often viewed the absolutes as the rarefied air of Hegel's idealism, a place to explore the dialectic's relation to theology.

In contrast to these readings, Dunayevskaya came to view the absolutes as important points of departure for today's reality. She saw them speaking concretely to our age in a manner that they did not speak to Marx's or Lenin's ages, and expressed this as "Hegel's Absolutes As New Beginning." How did she come to this view? What did she mean by Absolute Negativity As New Beginning?

To explore this we begin by briefly following Dunayevskaya's development within the Marxist movement. With the transformation of the Russian Revolution from an early, incomplete workers' state into a state-capitalist monstrosity under Stalin, (See Dunayevskaya's writings in *The Marxist-Humanist Theory of State Capitalism*) Dunayevskaya asked: If Russia was not a workers' state, but a state-capitalist one, what was a workers' state? The majority of the anti-Stalinist Left (Trotskyism) did not accept state-capitalist theory and confined their critique of the Soviet Union to the political realm, continuing to defend it as a workers' state even if deformed. In sharp disagreement, Dunayevskaya based her critique and analysis of the changed economic structure in the Soviet Union on categories from Marx's *Capital*. Asking how to begin anew in the revolutionary Marxist movement, her development of state-capitalist theory led her to writings on the Hegelian dialectic of both Marx and Lenin. Marx's "Critique of the Hegelian Dialectic" from what became known as his *Economic-Philosophic Manuscripts of 1844* and Lenin's *Philosophic Notebooks on Hegel's Science of Logic* showed Dunayevskaya that a new beginning for revolutionary Marxism was not alone a question of economic and political analysis. She came to see the need for an intense probing of Hegelian dialectics in the post-World War II era, in the manner Marx and Lenin had undertaken in their time.

In the mid-1940s and early 1950s, Dunayevskaya, together with colleagues, undertook studies of the dialectic in Marx, in Lenin, and directly in Hegel's major philosophic writings. The goal was to restate theoretically-philosophically Marxism anew and to seek to practice it in revolutionary organization. She would translate Lenin's Hegel Notebooks into English, and later Marx's "Critique of the Hegelian Dialectic," both of which became important points of departure for her development of Marxist-Humanism.

In her studies of Hegel's major philosophic writings—focusing on his Absolutes in each of his major philosophic works: Absolute Knowledge (Knowing) in *Phenomenology of Spirit*, Absolute Idea in *Science of Logic*, Absolute Spirit or Mind in *Philosophy of Spirit* (*Mind*)—she worked out a philosophic breakthrough on the dialectic. She would come to call her initial May 1953 Letters on Hegel's Absolutes "the Philosophic Moment of Marxist-Humanism."

What did she discern in Hegel's Absolutes? *Philosophically*, as against the interpretations of many Hegel scholars and Hegelian Marxists such as Marcuse and Lukács, she did not see the Absolutes as being only summaries, or only idealism, though Hegel was certainly an idealist philosopher. She argued that negativity, the negation of negation that was at the heart of dialectical movement, did not cease in the Absolutes. Rather, it came to full fruition—an absolute negativity. The Hegelian absolutes were not end points, the "end of history," or the exhaustion of thought. Rather, the "ending" of each absolute led to the need to continue the dialectic, the power of negativity, in a new realm. The "self-determination of the Idea" did not cease with *Phenomenology's* final chapter, Absolute Knowledge, but led to the *Science of Logic*. In turn the Absolute Idea chapter of the *Logic* did not signal a stopping of the dialectical movement. Rather, Hegel posed the need to go to Nature, (*Philosophy of Nature*), and most crucially to Mind, (*Philosophy of Mind* (*Spirit*)).

Her reading was both a *philosophic* dialogue—probing the self-determination of the Idea itself—and an exploration of *dialectical philosophy's relation to reality*, to the objective world. The inseparability of the development of dialectical philosophy and the relation of the dialectic to reality has continually been at the heart of Dunayevskaya's labors. She was a practicing revolutionary who saw the dialectic both as emancipatory philosophic expression, and as a reaching towards/emerging from humanity's revolutionary moments historically, including ones she witnessed and/or participated within.[11]

---

11 See her activities on 1949–1950 Miners' General Strike, her writings on the Negro question in the 1940s, on Stalin's death and the subsequent revolts in Eastern Europe in the 1950s, all of which occurred in the period of her studies on dialectic in Marx, Lenin and Hegel. The most complete documentation of her work can be found in *The Raya Dunayevskaya Collection* (1981).

In sum, Dunayevskaya's reading/practice of Hegel's absolutes was two-fold: the dialectic in and of itself inseparable from the dialectic in relation to life, including within revolutionary Marxist organization. Her point of departure for discerning the absolutes resonated with Marx's expression of Humanism:

> We see here how thoroughgoing Naturalism or Humanism distinguishes itself both from Idealism and Materialism, and is at the same time the truth uniting both. We see, at the same time, how only Naturalism is capable of grasping the act of world history.
>
> MARX, 1975: "Critique of the Hegelian Dialectic"

She saw the absolutes neither as only idealist nor only materialist, though important threads of both were within her view. Her reading was as a revolutionary humanist seeing a unity of materialism and idealism. It was this which brought forth her breakthrough on Hegel's absolutes, and the birth of Marxist-Humanism.

How was this revolutionary humanist reading she gave to Hegel's absolutes manifest concretely for each of his major philosophic works? *Phenomenology of Mind* traces stages of the Mind, from consciousness to self-consciousness to reason, and on to spirit with its divisions in art and religion till we come to absolute knowledge (knowing). It is important to grasp that absolute knowledge is not a question of knowing absolutely everything, a closed totality. Hegel certainly had an encyclopedic knowledge (though not always a correct one). However, merely a quantitative concept of totality was not the aim of the Hegelian dialectic. Rather, his "voyage of discovery," was seeking to arrive at *the method of knowing*, the dialectical method as the proper method for grasping reality. The dialectical attitude as against other attitudes from faith and superstition, to empiricism and Kantianism, to intuitionism, was what he was presenting. "Against" is not quite correct, for Hegel saw the necessity, though incompleteness, of these other attitudes, as they were representative of certain historical stages of humanity expressed as stages of thought. The dialectical attitude was not a rejection of these attitudes. Rather the dialectical attitude pointed to the partiality and insufficiency of these attitudes, and thus the need to transcend them.

When Hegel arrives at Absolute Knowing in *Phenomenology* he proceeds to look back over the journey undertaken. However the chapter is not solely a question of recollection. In Absolute Knowledge, spirit becomes fully conscious of what it is and how it came to that result. The dialectic of absolute negativity does not cease with this consciousness. (For a discussion of this see "The Dialectic in Philosophy Itself" in my *Towards a Dialectic of Philosophy and Organization*. Gogol, 2012) Rather, in the final paragraphs of the Absolute

Knowing chapter, the dialectic does not cease, but proceeds to enter a new realm. The final section of the last paragraph of Absolute knowledge reads:

> The goal which is Absolute Knowledge or Spirit knowing itself as Spirit finds its pathway in the recollection of spiritual forms as they are in themselves and as they accomplish the organization of their spiritual kingdom. Their conservation looked at from the side of their free existence appearing in the form of contingency is History; looked at from the side of their intellectual comprehended organization it is the Science of the ways in which knowledge appears. Both together or History (intellectually) comprehended form at once the recollection and the Golgotha of Absolute Spirit the reality, the truth, the certainty of its throne, without which it were lifeless, solitary, and alone.
>
> HEGEL, Baillie translation, 1964: 808

> The *goal*, Absolute Knowing, or Spirit that knows itself as Spirit, has for its path the recollection of the Spirits as they are in themselves and as they accomplish the organization of their realm. Their preservation, regarded from the side of their free existence appearing in the form of contingency, is History; but regarded from the side of their [philosophically] comprehended organization, it is the Science of Knowing in the sphere of appearance: the two together, comprehended History, form alike the inwardizing and the Calvary of absolute Spirit, the actuality, truth, and certainty of his throne, without which he would be lifeless and alone.
>
> HEGEL, Miller translation, 1977

There is an extraordinary Hegelian moment here. Spirit knowing itself as Spirit recalls the various Spiritual forms in two ways: (1) "free existence appearing in the form of contingency is History"; (2) as "their intellectually comprehended organization it is the Science of the ways in which knowledge appears." History and intellectually or philosophically comprehended organization are the two manifestations of Spirit. Hegel immediately unites them: "History (intellectually) comprehended." It is a unity of theory and practice, and seems far away from any idealism without a sense of the actual. But then the real shocker comes: "the Golgotha of Absolute Spirit"!! After the 800-page journey of the *Phenomenology*, Absolute Spirit has reached an end. Or has it?

Hegel was not declaring the end of history, but the end of Absolute Spirit *in the form he had put it forth in Phenomenology*. The knowing that he had traced in humanity's development until Absolute Knowledge now needed to be developed in a different sphere, first in the *Science of Logic*. Golgotha of Absolute Spirit was not an absolute end, but a death that brought forth a new life. Hegel, in his Preface to *Phenomenology,* written after he completed the book, took up the death of Absolute Spirit:

> [*T*]*he life of the mind is not one that* shuns death, and keeps clear of destruction; it endures death and in death maintains its being. It only wins to its truth when it finds itself utterly torn asunder. … [M]ind is this power only by looking the negative in the face, and dwelling with it.
>
> *Phenomenology,* 1966: 93

Before turning to the form of the absolute in the *Science of Logic,* we want to briefly follow Dunayevskaya's reading for this last paragraph of *Phenomenology of Spirit,* not only as philosophic movement, but in one interpretation when she was probing dialectic philosophy's relation to reality. In this case she was seeking to understand Hegel's referring to two types of organization in this final paragraph:

> I turned back to Hegel's *Phenomenology* focusing fully on the last page with its very difficult, abstract climax that leads, at one and the same time, to the Absolute and its Golgotha. For the first time, I abbreviated that whole page (p. 808 in Baillie's translation, p. 492–493 in Miller's) into two sentences and suddenly saw that in Hegel's use of the word Organization, twice in the same paragraph, something that could be considered the actual ground for our concept of the relationship both of spontaneity and the party *and* its inseparability from organization of thought. Read it for yourself and see what you can work out, but here is what I saw, precisely because I'm working on a book on Dialectics of Organization and Philosophy: The two types of organization Hegel has in mind are, first "as free existence" in its varying "historic forms," what we would call the movement from practice at historic turning points. Secondly, Hegel is defining "intellectually comprehended" organization and concludes, "the two together, or History intellectually comprehended form as at once recollection and the Golgotha of Absolute Spirit." My point is that it was no accident that Marx judged the *Phenomenology of Mind* as the most creative act of all of Hegel's works, and where he began not just a critique of the Hegelian Dialectic, but the finding of a new continent of thought and revolution; both indeed had become the ground for what we are working out on the Dialectic of Organization and Philosophy.[12]
>
> DUNAYEVSKAYA, 1981: #10727

12 For my commentary on Dunayevskaya's reading of this last paragraph see Gogol (2012).

Science of Logic: How to begin anew after the 800-page *Phenomenology of Spirit*? Being, nothing, and then *becoming* are its opening categories. The movement is of the Idea in its "pure" movement through three books of the *Logic,* the Doctrines of Being, Essence, and Notion, with Notion culminating in the Absolute Idea. (For my discussion of the Absolute Idea see "The Dialectic in Philosophy Itself" in Gogol, 2012.) However the Absolute Idea is not absolute in the sense of a closed totality, or a resolution. In the first paragraph of this final chapter we read: "The Absolute Idea... contains within itself the highest degree of opposition" (825) (466). The whole chapter is an outpouring of second negativity, absolute negativity, the methodology of the dialectic. Hegel expressed this as follows:

> The method is both soul and substance, and nothing is either conceived or known in its truth except in so far as it is completely subject to the method; it is the particular method of each individual fact because its activity is the Notion. (468)

When Dunayevskaya *philosophically* explored negation of the negation, absolute negativity, she, at the same time, had before her *dialectical philosophy's relation to reality*. Despite Hegel's idealistic dehumanization of the idea (at times), Dunayevskaya grasped the profoundly historic origin of his philosophic labors:

> Hegel can reach these anticipations of the future because a very truly great step in philosophic cognition is made only when a new way or reaching for freedom has become possible, as it had with the French Revolution.
>
> DUNAYEVSKAYA, 2002: *Power of Negativity* (PON), 77

At the same time, as world-shaking as Hegel's philosophic labors were, they were not an ending but an opening: the challenge of constructing a new beginning:

> The negation of the negation will not be a generality, not even the generality of a new society for the old, but the specific of self-liberation, which is the humanism of the human being, as well as his philosophy.
>
> DUNAYEVSKAYA, "Rough Notes on Hegel's *Science of Logic,*" PON, 73

Let us see how this is concretized in terms of the ending of the Absolute Idea chapter and Dunayevskaya's probing of Absolute Mind (Spirit) in Hegel's

Philosophy of Mind. We will focus on the dialectical method as seen in the ending of the Absolute Idea. What transpires with Absolute Idea at its culmination? The final lines of the chapter read:

> The Idea *freely releases* itself in its absolute self-assurance and inner poise. By reason of this freedom, the form of its determinateness is also utterly free—the *externality of space and time* existing absolute on its own account without the moment of subjectivity. In so far as this externality presents itself only in the abstract immediacy of being and is apprehended from the standpoint of consciousness, it exists as mere objectivity and external life; but in the Idea it remains essentially and actually the totality of the Notion, and science in the relation to nature of divine cognition. But in this next resolve of the pure Idea to determine itself as external Idea, it thereby only posits for itself the mediation out of which the Notion ascends as a free Existence that has withdrawn into itself from externality, that completes its self-liberation in the *science of spirit,* and that finds the supreme Notion of itself in the science of logic as the self-comprehending pure Notion.
>
> HEGEL, 1976

What does "the idea freely releases itself" signify? It argues for an absolute negativity, the absolute movement of becoming. Why? Because the Idea does not cease its self-movement. Its free release is first "to determine itself as an external Idea," that is, manifest as Nature (Hegel's *Philosophy of Nature*). At the same time the Idea manifests itself "as a free Existence that has withdrawn into itself from externality, that completes its self-liberation in the *science of spirit"* (Hegel's *Philosophy of Spirit*). The free release of the idea comes first in the world, nature, and then returns from that experience and "completes its self-liberation" in *Philosophy of Spirit.* Hegel has thus not left Absolute Idea as an absolute end, but found new spheres for its development—the continuance of absolute negativity. The "self-comprehending pure Notion," "the pure Notion which forms a Notion of itself," further manifests itself in nature and in spirit.

Lenin, in his Notebooks on the *Science of Logic,* proceeded to "translate" nature as practice and wrote: "The transition of the logical idea to *Nature.* Stretching a hand to materialism." This practicing revolutionary saw in Hegel's thought threads to the material world. Actually, Lenin had even gone even further. In commenting on the Idea of Cognition chapter just before the Absolute Idea, he had written "Man's cognition not only reflects the objective world, but creates it." Thus, he saw a two-way road between thought and reality. However in his comments on the Absolute Idea chapter, Lenin ended his commentary after noting the idea's turn toward nature (materialism) and chose *not* to follow or comment on Hegel's further release of the Idea to the *Philosophy of Spirit.*

Could Lenin have developed in a more comprehensive way his powerful expression "Man's cognition not only reflects the objective world, but creates it," if he had following Hegel to *Philosophy of Mind*? Dunayevskaya evidently thought so, for after exploring Absolute Idea, she went to Absolute Mind in *Philosophy of Mind* in following Hegel's absolute negativity in the third of his major philosophic works. There, her commentary would center on this question of objectivity and subjectivity. She would find a two-fold movement in the Hegelian Absolutes—a movement from theory to practice and a movement from practice to theory. We will follow her in *Philosophy of Spirit* (*Mind*) below.

However, we need to pause and ask where we stand with Lenin before passing to *Philosophy of Mind* with Dunayevskaya. There is no doubt of the great leap Lenin had taken in seeing the Hegelian dialectic as alive in the world he faced of World War I and socialist betrayal, of self-determination of nations as bacillus of revolution, and the coming Russian Revolution. Lenin saw materialism *within* the dialectic itself and not the need to externally impose materialism upon the dialectic. And yet he did not go further. He chose not to follow Hegel to *Philosophy of Mind* with its Absolute Mind. One might say the need was not concrete for him in the historic moment he lived. Dunayevskaya, living at a different historic moment, with a workers' revolution being transformed into a state-capitalist society and the anti-Stalinist Left (Trotskyism) unable to find new revolutionary ground, felt compelled to explore the dialectic in the realm of *Philosophy of Spirit*, focusing on Absolute Mind.

•

In the Introduction to *Philosophy of Spirit* (*Mind*) Hegel wrote of the need of mind to "become conscious of freedom as *its* very being, i.e. to become fully *manifested*." He then posed that liberation in three stages: "finding a world presupposed before us, generating a world as our own creation, and gaining freedom from it and in it" (paragraph 386). The three divisions of *Philosophy of Mind*—Mind Subjective, Mind Objective, and Absolute Mind—pose the pathway of these stages. Philosophically, "gaining freedom from it (the world) and in it," is the labor of Absolute Mind.

Dunayevskaya in her studies, focused primarily on Absolute Mind's final paragraphs, 574, 575, 576, 577. (See especially her May 20, 1953 Letter on Hegel's Absolute Mind in *Philosophy of* Mind. Dunayevskaya 2002: 15). What happens to Hegel's Absolute Mind at the very end of the *Encyclopedia of Philosophical*

Sciences? Here is how I discussed this in *Raya Dunayevskaya: Philosopher of Marxist-Humanism* (Gogol, 2004) with minor modifications:

Paragraph 574 began "This notion of philosophy is the self-thinking Idea, the truth aware of itself and certified in concrete content as in its actuality." At first glance, the concept of "the self-thinking Idea" seems strange. Naturally it is human beings who have ideas, and who think, not ideas in themselves. Is this Hegel as pure idealist? A more helpful reading is that Hegel is focusing on the *logic* of an Idea, that ideas have consequences. We think not alone sequentially, but consequentially. Dunayevskaya wrote in her May 20, 1953 letter that this reminded her of Hegel's Introduction to the *Encyclopedia Logic* where, "the Idea is not so feeble as merely to have a right or an obligation to exist without actually existing." She 'translated' this for her age as "Socialism 'is not so feeble as merely to have a right or obligation to exist without actually existing.' Quite the contrary, the new society is *evident* everywhere, *appears* within the old."

In paragraph 575, the self-thinking Idea would make its first appearance in the form of a syllogism, Logic-Nature-Mind: "The Logical principle turns to Nature and Nature to Mind." Dunayevskaya, after quoting from the opening sentences of the paragraph, expressed her reading of this first syllogism: "The movement is from the logical principle or theory to nature or practice *and* from practice not alone to theory but to the new society which is its essence."

This reading of paragraph 575—stating that within Hegel's Absolutes there is a movement from theory to practice, *and* a movement from practice that reaches out to theory and to the new society—would come to have enormous implications for the development of Marxist-Humanism both theoretically/philosophically and in organizational practice.

Following Lenin, Dunayevskaya 'translated' Nature as practice. But whereas Lenin had done so at the beginning of the last paragraph of the Absolute Idea chapter of the *Science of Logic*, and had not followed Hegel to the end of the chapter or into *Philosophy of Mind*, Dunayevskaya was doing so within the final paragraphs of Absolute Mind. Thus, Nature was not outside the Idea, an "answer" in the revolutionary practice of the masses alone. Rather, Nature was the mediation: "Nature is essentially defined as a transition-point and negative factor, and as implicitly the Idea" (paragraph 575). As such, Dunayevskaya noted, "that practice itself is 'implicitly the Idea'" (28). And such practice not only expressed theory, but reached toward a new society. This conception made philosophically explicit that the practice of masses was not only muscle of revolution, but Mind as well.

At the same time, Dunayevskaya noted, "[L]et us not forget that this is only the first syllogism," and proceeded to quote the second syllogism in which the form is Nature-Mind-Logic:

> [T]hat syllogism is the standpoint of the Mind itself, which—as the mediating agent in the process—presupposes Nature and couples it with the Logical principle. It is the syllogism where Mind reflects on itself in the Idea: philosophy appears as a subjective cognition, of which liberty is the aim, and which is itself the way to produce it. (paragraph 576)

With Mind now "the mediating agent in the process," Dunayevskaya's 'translation' became:

> I cannot help but think of Marx concluding that the Commune is "the form at last discovered to work out the economic emancipation of the proletariat," and of Lenin in Vol. 9 [*Selected Works*] saying that the workers and peasants "must understand the whole thing now is *practice*, that the historical moment has arrived when theory is being transformed into practice"... And so I repeat Mind itself, the new society, is "the mediating agent in the process."

Dunayevskaya now moved to "where Hegel arrives at Absolute Mind, the third syllogism":

> The third syllogism is the Idea of philosophy, which has self-knowing reason, the absolutely-universal, for its middle term: a middle, which divides itself into Mind and Nature, making the former its presupposition, as process of the Idea's subjective activity, and the latter its universal extreme, as process of the objectively and implicitly existing Idea.

She summered up the dialectical movement she had discerned:

> No wonder I was so struck... with the Syllogism which disclosed that either the Universal or the Particular or the Individual could be the middle term. Note carefully that the "middle which divides itself" is nothing less than the absolute universal itself and that, in dividing itself into Mind and Nature, it makes *Mind* the presupposition "as process of the Idea's subjective activity" and *Nature* "as process of the objectively and implicitly existing Idea."

Dunayevskaya's recognition that *either* the universal *or* particular *or* individual could be the middle term--the mediation, a "middle which divides itself" and thus "the absolute universal itself"--released the Absolute as an absolute movement of becoming. There was nothing static about the categories Universal,

Particular and Individual—all was movement, self-movement through double negation, second negativity, both forward and rearward. Each of the terms, universal, particular, individual—the new society as cognition and reality, the particular (specific) forms of practice and thought to get there, the social individual striving for liberation—could be the middle, the mediating agent, and thereby implicitly the whole. She now quoted the last sentences of paragraph 577:

> The self-judging of the Idea in its two appearances (paragraph 575, 576) characterizes both as its (the self-knowing reason's) manifestation and in it there is a unification of the two aspects:—it is the nature of the fact, the notion, which causes the movement and development, yet this same movement is equally the act of cognition. The eternal idea, in full fruition of its essence, eternally sets itself to work engenders and enjoys itself as absolute Mind.

In these final sentences of the last paragraph of Absolute Mind one has the two manifestations of the self-thinking idea: "the nature of the fact," (I again read this as the unfolding of history, the movement from practice) *and* "the same movement is equally the action of cognition" (I read this as the science of philosophy). I see these manifestations as *two expressions of revolutionary subjectivity*. In 1953, Dunayevskaya ended her letter on Absolute Mind's final three syllogisms, "We have entered the new society." As for the final sentence of paragraph 577, Dunayevskaya in 1987 'translated' "the eternal idea" as Marx's concept of "revolution in permanence."

In "entering the new society," we have arrived at one way of expressing the profound concordances of the Hegelian-Marxian dialectic(s), even with their profound differences: *The concept of "revolution in permanence" in Marx resonates with the dialectic of absolute negativity in Hegel.*

What is the significance of this Hegelian-Marxian dialectic of absolute negativity/revolution in permanence for Latin America? How can the concept of utopia in Latin America as emancipatory vision and as project find common ground with the dialectic? To explore these questions we turn to Chapter 3 on Utopia and the Dialectic.

CHAPTER 3

Are There Emancipatory Threads between Utopia and the Dialectic in Latin America?

A crucial function of dialectical philosophy is to make *explicit* what is implicit in the emancipatory activity and thought of masses overcoming an oppressive, exploitative reality as they construct and concretize their utopias in Latin America. When philosophy is able to do that, when it can express itself, not as an imposition, but as indigenous to the masses' activities, then it becomes an energizing power in their hands. There is nothing automatic in such a process. It doesn't occur by spontaneity alone. Rather, it takes the active participation of revolutionary thinker-activists, including intellectuals indigenous to the struggle, who recognize both the creativity of the masses *and their own responsibility* to work out theory anew for their age: a unity of *praxis*, utopia and the dialectic. I wish to suggest some threads between utopia and the dialectic that can assist in such a unity, as well as point to incomplete pathways, traps along the way.

1 Preliminary Note: The Dialectic of *Universal-Particular-Individual* Reaching toward *Utopias-Projects-Masses*

In Chapter 2 we developed the relation between universal, particular and individual as follows:

Universal «--- ---» Particular «--- ---» Individual
negation *negation*
[movement of 1st and 2nd negation in both directions]

When we examine how utopia is *practiced* in Latin America we see *utopia* concretized as *project* (*proyecto*) by masses, individuals in collectivity (social individuals), as an *organization for life* (*organización para la vida*). For instance, a territory, and with it the right to autonomy of a group—their *utopia*—is defended by occupation of the land, and/or a march—their project—against the government, the state, which wants to give a nature-destroying concession to a mining company, or build a road through a natural reserve. In working out the project (of resistance) they have created *organization*, an organization for life.

Utopia «--- ---» Project «--- ---» Masses (in self organization, communitarian)
(Organization for life)

Without arguing for any one-to-one relation between Utopia and the Dialectic, we can see important parallels. This is so because the dialectic is not only in the thought of a Hegel or a Marx, but is in life itself. In fact, life itself is the only "proof" of the relevance for the dialectic today.

That said, we want to examine two key moments in the Hegelian dialectic that can help us approach the question: *How Do a Latin American Concept of Utopia and the Dialectic of Absolute Negativity Speak to Each Other*? First, is *the transition between the Practical Idea and the Absolute Idea* in *The Science of Logic*. We would argue that this speaks to the relation of practice and theory within Latin American social movements. Second, are *the final three syllogisms* in the *Philosophy of Mind* (*Spirit*): Here, following Dunayevskaya, who saw in these final paragraphs of Absolute Mind (paragraphs 574–577) a dual movement—the unification of the movement from practice that is itself a form of theory with the movement from theory that is itself rooted in philosophy—we would ask, where is the manifestation of this dual movement in Latin American reality, that is, Latin America's "entrance into the new society"?

II The Challenge in Practice and in Theory: Will Latin America Arrive Only on the Threshold of a New Society, or Enter into the Realm of Absolute Liberation?

The Hegelian journey of Spirit is a determination to unite Notion (the Idea) and Reality—a journey toward absolute liberation. When there is a contradiction between Notion and Reality, Hegel argues that reality is not authentic, but is only Appearance. He is not privileging the Idea over Reality; rather he is holding forth the power of the Idea because the Idea (Notion) in the dialectic is Freedom. Hegel critiqued the view that "true thoughts are said to be only ideas," that is, only subjective, and wrote of the Idea as the objective or real Notion. It is Appearance that is "the untrue being of the objective world," (Hegel, 1969: 756) while the Idea is "the unity of the Notion and objectivity" (756). Our reality in Latin America is unfree, full of contradiction, and in this sense not authentic; not in concert with the fullness of what it means to be human, to be in human liberation. The power of utopia in America Latin as Idea, as Notion, is in its relation to objectivity, in its ability to move people, be transformative in determining their actions, its potential to bring into unity the utopian vision (the idea) and reality.

What Hegel was searching for in the two final chapters of *Science of Logic*, "The Idea of Cognition" and "The Absolute Idea," was the manner whereby the Notion and Reality, subjective and objective, can be united. The movement from the Idea of Cognition to the Absolute Idea was a striving to unite reality and the idea. At times, Hegel idealistically claimed an objective-subjective identity. However, that need not concern us here. We can reject this idealism without throwing out the concept that Notion and Reality strive towards each other. We begin with a brief discussion of how Hegel developed the transition between the Idea of Cognition and the Absolute Idea.

A *The Movement from the Idea of Cognition to the Absolute Idea: The Dialectic within the Practical Idea*

1 Hegel on the Idea of Cognition

Hegel writes on the Idea of Cognition: "There are still two worlds in opposition, one a realm of subjectivity in the pure regions of transparent thought, the other a realm of objectivity in the element of an externally manifold actuality that is an undisclosed realm of darkness" (Hegel, 1969: 820). The practical idea is faced with the gulf between its goal and the limitation of actuality—an unresolved contradiction.

We have a situation in which both the theoretical idea and the practical idea, because of their respective one-sidedness, fail in their relation to the objective world. The Theoretical Idea feels it must sublimate itself and fill itself with the content of the external world, but a content it sees as mere datum. The Practical Idea sees the objective world as viable only when it is sublimated by the Theoretical Idea, the Theoretical Idea must give it its true determination. How to solve this dual one-sidedness?

> What is still lacking in the practical Idea is the moment of consciousness proper itself; namely, that the moment of actuality in the Notion should have attained on its own account the determination of *external being*... The *practical* Idea still lacks the moment of the *theoretical* Idea... [I]t separates itself from cognition, and external reality for the will does not receive the form of true being; the Idea of the good [the practical idea] can therefore find its integration only in the Idea of the true [the theoretical idea]. (821)

Hegel argued that, "it [the idea of the good] makes this transition through itself" (821). That is, the practical idea can find *within itself* the theoretical idea. It does so through a double negation, and thus not through immediacy, but through mediation. That is, the solution is not found just through immediate action. Rather:

> [T]he realization of the good in the face of another actuality confronting it is the mediation which is essentially necessary for the immediate relation and the accomplished actualization of the good. For it is only the first negation or the otherness of the Notion, an objectivity that would be

> a submergence of the Notion in the externality; the second negation is the sublating of this otherness, whereby the immediate realization of the end first becomes the actuality of the good as of the Notion that is for itself, since in this actuality of the good as of the Notion that is for itself, since in this actuality the Notion is posited as identical with itself, not with an other, and thus alone is posited as the free Notion. (822)

If the practical idea does not go through this mediation, if it continues only in a first negation in which actuality is presupposed as "intrinsically worthless," then it is only a "spurious infinity," a would-be absolute. So the Practical Idea's authentic confrontation is not alone with the actuality of the world, but against itself, against its attitude toward the actuality of the world.

> In the result the mediation sublates itself; the result is an *immediacy* that is not the restoration of the presupposition, but rather its accomplished sublation. With this, the Idea of the Notion that is determined in and for itself is posited as being no longer merely in the active subject but equally an immediate actuality; and conversely, this actuality is posited, as it is in cognition, as an objectivity possessing a true being. (823)

We have reached the proof or demonstration of the Notion. Actuality, the real world, has within it the Notion, and thus the proof of the objectivity of subjectivity. The movement is within objectivity. Cognition is within reality, and thus the objectivity of cognition. The Notion absorbs objectivity not as datum but as objectivity which itself contains reason. Instead of actuality "as an objective world without the subjectivity of the Notion, here it appears as an objective world whose inner ground and actual subsistence is the Notion. This is the absolute Idea" (823).

2 Lenin on the Threshold of the Absolute—The Pull of the Practical Idea

We turn to Lenin who explored the Practical Idea in the Chapter "The Idea of Cognition" in his *Philosophic Notebooks*. As we saw in Chapter 2, Lenin, that most "practical," organization man, felt compelled to plunge into a study of the Hegelian dialectic to find new revolutionary ground in philosophy to meet the challenge, not alone of total capitalist crisis in World War, but of established Marxism in complete disarray. Lenin was drawn to the "Idea of the Good," that is, the Practical Idea in his 1914–15 Philosophical Notebooks on the *Science of Logic*, as resolving the division between the theoretical idea and the practical idea. Lenin brilliantly expressed the *potential* of the practical idea to resolve the one-sidedness of both the theoretical and practical when he wrote: "Man's cognition not only reflects the objective world but creates it." Herein lay the pathway for resolving the gap between Notion and Reality.

However, argued Dunayevskaya, Lenin did not develop this insight philosophically with his exploration of the Absolute. Philosophically, Lenin remained on the threshold of the Absolute Idea. In particular, he failed to subject the party, his Bolshevik vanguard party, to the dialectic in philosophy, found in its fullest form as the Absolute Idea. For Lenin, the turn toward practice became concretized in the Russian Revolution of 1917. Surely no one can critique a turn to the practice of revolution. Rather, the crucial question with regard to Lenin was whether his revolutionary practice, 1917–23,—which was immersed in Hegelian dialectics, reached fully into Hegel's Absolutes, that is, in resolving the duality of the practical idea and the theoretical idea? In truth, when it came to *revolutionary organization*, Lenin continued in the truncated form of the elitist party—the practical idea *not* finding the theoretical idea within—thus unable to meet the test of revolutionary transformation. Instead, the Soviet Union post-Lenin became a revolution transformed into its opposite, ruled by the Stalin-led vanguard party-dictatorial state—a state-capitalist society. Revolutionaries, including independent anti-Stalinist ones, facing the challenge of "What Happens after the Revolution?" were philosophically/theoretically unarmed, and instead sought resolution within one or another form of the vanguard party. Lenin, of course, cannot be held responsible for the transformation of the Bolshevik/Communist Party after his death. However, not subjecting that party fully to dialectical philosophy while he lived left a void in dialectics of organization that has had huge consequences.

B *Latin America and the Practical Idea*

In Latin America today, the *appearance* of the problem seems miles away from the question of Lenin and the Party. The two decades since the collapse of so-called Communism have led to the rejection of the party-to-lead form of organization in much (though by no means all) of Latin America. The movements from below (*desde abajo*) have stayed away from hierarchical party forms and stressed horizonalism in organization. They have questioned the role of the state in emancipatory social change.

And yet, we need to ask, *philosophically*, are these powerful movements from below theoretically caught in the same Practical Idea within the Idea of Cognition that Lenin was within? Not on the question of "the Party," but on the question of practice. Are they only on the threshold of the Absolute Idea, and thus not yet able to make the leap to a new society and full freedom? In their important rejection of vanguard parties to lead, is there, at the same time, a failure to move beyond first negation, and reach an explicit recognition of the need for second negation? Are the social movements, and primarily the radical thinkers that accompany them in Latin America, remaining in the Practical Idea, *practice alone as the resolution of the contradictions*, the pathway to an alternative to neo-liberal capitalism? Do we end up in a situation where once again form of organization becomes the "answer,"—not the vanguard party, rather, in this case a decentralized, non-hierarchical form, horizontalism? Does the dialectic in philosophy itself, and with it, working out the dialectic of revolutionary organization, remain the missing dimension, the unexplored terrain?

In Latin America, the movement from below *as practice* has become *the* focus for creating a new society. There is recognition that the masses are more than muscle of social transformation. This certainly is a great leap forward from the vanguard party as the bearer of consciousness. However, by itself, even a revolutionary movement from practice is still one-sided. In Hegel's Absolutes, Dunayevskaya discerned a *dual movement*: a movement from practice that was itself a form of theory, and a movement from theory that reached to meet that movement from practice and was itself rooted in the fullness of a philosophy of revolution. *What are the implications of Dunayevskaya's concept of the dual movement in the Absolutes?*

For revolutionaries, it would mean asking: What is the responsibility of thinker-activists to meet that movement from practice to theory with a movement from theory that is itself rooted in philosophy, and that must meet the fullness of theory coming from below?

Put differently: Is the creativity of the movements from below in Latin America recognized in its fullness? If so, this would compel thinker-activists to undertake *their* difficult responsibility of becoming one with such a movement by creating revolutionary philosophic ground to help propel the movement forward. This has nothing to do with "giving" philosophy to the masses in the way that the vanguard party supposedly "gave" consciousness to the masses. Rather, it focuses on how philosophically we find the revolutionary ideas that explicitly unite with the self-activity (in action and thought) of the mass movement.

The answer *does* lie with the practical idea, but not in practice alone. Rather it lies in the practical idea in the sense that the practical idea is compelled to realize that the theoretical idea *lies within itself*. The persistence of the Notion, not alone as activity but as theory, philosophy, lies within that objective world. To repeat: "[the idea of the good] makes this transition through itself." Thus the practical idea *has the elements to move beyond itself into the absolute*.

It is precisely here that a crucial focal point for activist-thinkers, theoreticians within Latin America, is found. Can they make a contribution by laboring with the social movements in the needed, urgent task of finding the revolutionary theoretical idea within the masses' own practice, striving to make explicit what is implicit within? What might that mean concretely for Latin America? To probe this further, we need to turn to the second Hegelian moment: the ending of Absolute Mind (Spirit) in *Philosophy of Mind (Spirit)*—particularly paragraph 577.

III How Do a Latin American Concept of Utopia and the Dialectic of Absolute Negativity Speak to Each Other?

A *What is the Significance of Hegel's Ending of Absolute Mind for Latin America Today?*

Without attempting to rehearse our discussion of the final syllogisms from Chapter 2 we want to return to the ending of *Philosophy of Mind*. The final paragraph of Absolute Mind reads as follows:

> The third syllogism is the Idea of philosophy, which has self-knowing reason, the absolutely-universal, for its middle term: a middle, which divides itself into Mind and Nature, making the former its presupposition, as process of the Idea's subjective activity, and the latter its universal extreme, as process of the objectively and implicitly existing Idea. The self-judging of the Idea in its two appearances (paragraphs 575, 576) characterizes both as its (the self-knowing reason's) manifestation and in it there is a unification of the two aspects:—it is the nature of the fact, the notion, which causes the movement and development, yet this same movement is equally the act of cognition. The eternal idea, in full fruition of its essence, eternally sets itself to work engenders and enjoys itself as absolute Mind.

In this final development of the self-knowing reason (self-thinking idea), what is the meaning of Hegel's concluding remarks? No definitive answer is intended here, only a suggestive reading. In putting forth both "subjective activity" and "as process of the objectivity" Hegel is once again arguing for the power of the Idea, the power of negativity to hold as a unity Reality and the Concept. Reality and Concept may have been in opposition, in contradiction, from the very beginning, not only in *Philosophy of Mind*, but as well in *Phenomenology of Spirit* and in *Science of Logic*. But the opposition has never been static, fixed. Rather it has been in constant movement, negation, negation of the negation. This has been true even as Hegel reached the Absolute in each work. A new beginning in a new realm was posited. Furthermore, this constant movement, absolute negativity, is a *self*-movement. No outside force, no external hand, even that of the philosopher is needed. The movement toward resolution comes from *within*, an overcoming of any opposition to the fullest expression of the Idea, that is, freedom. That freedom is not an *a priori* possession, not a "having," but a *being* that self-develops, comes to be expressed, becomes the crucial dimension of humanity, in the very history (unfoldment) of humanity's development.

Hegel now argues that self-knowing reason's manifestations—its movement and development—as seen in the two previous paragraphs, 575 and 576, are in fact a unification of the notion in Reality and the notion in Cognition. Can we not here suggest that in Dunayevskaya's concept, the drive for liberty is expressed, at one and the same time, as a movement from practice that is a form of theory (found in history, reality) and a movement from theory that moves to meet the movement from practice and is at the same time connected with profound threads to dialectical philosophy (the concept or notion as expressed from Hegel, through Marx to our day)?

What is the significance of this for Latin America? It means first, that the rejection of the vanguard-party-to-lead is absolutely crucial. No external giving of consciousness to the masses is necessary. However, it also means that we need be cognizant that a new society is not alone a question of spontaneity or practice alone. The needed, revolutionary movement from practice is one sided if it cannot find the theoretical idea within itself. Finding the theoretical idea within itself is the labor of dialectical philosophy, wherein it assists in opening the door to a new society.

Hegel's final sentence in Absolute Mind reads: "The eternal Idea, in full fruition of its essence, eternally sets itself to work, engenders and enjoys itself as absolute Mind." Whatever Hegel may have meant by this expression, the interpretation Dunayevskaya gave to "the eternal Idea" was that of *Permanent Revolution*. This in turn brings us to the moment of Marx and his concept of revolution in permanence. Today, does it not bring us as well to Latin America's permanent confrontation with its unfree reality, and thus to the construction and concretization of utopia(s)? Is it not in this manner, with this methodology, that we can enter the new society in reality?

B *Rubén Dri: Reading Utopia, Project, and Organization via Hegelian Categories*

In an important essay, "The Organization and Building of Mass Power: Horizontalism and Verticalism, Utopia and Project," the Argentine social thinker Rubén Dri (Dri 2006) viewed the mass eruption that took place May 20–21, 2001 in Argentina as an "all revolutionary Utopia,": a "step in Hegel's *Phenomenology*, the leap from independence to freedom," wherein "the negative reality" against which Utopia was formed could be found in the cry "*¡Que se vayan todos!*" ("All of them must go!"), while the "positive" "supersession of that negative reality" could be seen by "Everyone simply represented themselves":

> The utopic moment is that moment that has moved individual and collective Subjects since the origins of humanity. It is the driving force of all the new moments in culture, science, literature, philosophy, economics, politics, and society. The Subject is always more than itself; it is always beyond.

However,

> Utopia cannot come about immediately, or completely, because that would signify the end of the Subject who essentially constitutes the utopic space. Utopia is wide open and demands, pushes forward a realization of itself. If that is to be, another moment is required, and that moment is that of the project.

The project itself involves organization. Dri points to the danger of bureaucratization, but at the same time argues that "not organizing is impotence. Whether the organization is that of a family, a club, a union, a school, a church, or a group of friends. Otherwise, being merely 'the multitude' they are doomed to the aforementioned impotence." Dri saw this as the dilemma of being "Between Scylla and Charybdis":

> It is necessary, then, to flee from bureaucratization. But often the escape from Scylla can drive you right into the arms of Charybdis. Charybdis is found below, sucking and vomiting the "dark waters," poisonous and lethal to those who fall in. This is horizontalism, pure multiplicity, individuals dispersed and atomized. Vertical bureaucracy and inarticulate horizontalism; both will spell the end of the Subject. He either becomes frozen in the rigid structure of bureaucracy, or disappears in an anthill of atomized individuals. Where, then, is the way out of this conundrum? Even better, is there an out?

For Dri, organization is a necessity, but "organizational criticism of all phenomena that might lead to bureaucratization within the organization" is crucial. In a section entitled "Horizontalism, organization, collective will, and leadership" Dri began asking what is a Subject: "To be a Subject is to make it so, to 'subjectify' one's self. To subjectify one's self is to potentialize one's self, to apply one's self." This he saw as a dialectical "self-bringing-forth." For this to happen, Dri argues, "The Subject requires organization and leadership."

Here Dri opened the debate with "horizonalism": "For the Subject to set out, he requires an organization of the tendencies that will serve to overcome the contradiction between horizontalism and verticalism, democracy and leadership." His view is that there are ways to overcome this contradiction:

> People don't just exist: they are self-made, self-constructed, self-created. To self-construct the subjectivity of a group of people is to construct a collective will. This isn't simply a mere "will" but the supersession of the collective's potentials. It is a magnificent and enlightening will. It is a will that, to be such, necessarily begs to be expressed by a leader or leaders. They are the measure of the true expression of the collective will.
>
> Here is where we again see the contradiction between horizontalism and organization. Leadership carries an inherent impulse toward domination, full power, and self-perpetuation. This is inevitable. This contradiction can only be overcome if it is clear to all that power truly lies in the base of the group, of the people. The organization has to exercise the will to truly make this part count.

To not grapple with these contradictions, to rely alone on horizonalism, on anti-power or not taking power, is, in Dri's view, to be trapped without a way forward. He characterizes it as Hegel's "Beautiful Soul," doomed to be crushed. In contrast he argues:

> Utopia and project, horizontalism and verticalism, direct democracy and representation, are moments in the dialectic of totality that is the Subject, whether individual or collective. Utopia without the project is the self-consumed Beautiful Soul, smoke that vanishes into thin air. Project without Utopia is a closing-off, the death of the Subject. Utopia demands its own realization by way of the project and the project demands the contents of Utopia.
>
> Utopia is the impossible. The project is the possible. Wanting the impossible, strongly needing it, is how the possible is realized. Only with grand Utopias can magnificent projects be realized. By wanting a just society, one of brotherhood, we can bring to existence a new society, one in which the inhuman inequalities and oppression that characterize our

society today disappear. (Dri's full essay appears as appendix in the final part of our present study.)

C *Revolutionary Organization, Utopia and the Dialectic*

1 Marx's Concept of Organization

Though Marx had no explicit "theory of organization," from the 1840s to the end of the 1870s he participated in and wrote about numerous revolutionary organizations. In the 1840s there were the organizational forms created by the nascent workers' movement reaching to rebellion and revolution, as well as tendencies such as the League of the Just that, with the writing of the *Communist Manifesto*, became transformed into the Communist League.

Even after the defeat of the Revolutions of 1848–49, and Marx's exile to England together with his withdrawal from the querulous exile movement of the refugees of 1848, he still referred to "our Party" when he was writing of himself and Engels as representative of a body of thought in the decade of the 1850s.

When new objective-subjective moments began to develop in the mid-1860s—working class struggles in Europe including Polish and Irish movements for self-determination, the growth of a trade union movement in England, and the Civil War in the U.S. involving Northern white labor's relation to the Black southern slave labor in rebellion—Marx was instrumental in the formation, development and work of a new organizational form, the International Workingmen's Association (First International). He saw no separation between his theoretical labors in completing *Capital* and his organizational labors in the International.

When the self-organization of the Paris Commune erupted in 1871, Marx followed those "heaven-stormers," chronicling their revolutionary *praxis*, proclaiming its greatest moment to be "its own working existence," and made important additions to the French edition of *Capital* under the impact of the Commune's creativity. As the repressive, bitter period that followed the Commune's bloody destruction, manifested both pusillanimous behavior on the part of some British trade union leaders who wished to separated themselves from the revolutionary Communards, and an intensification of factionalism in the International, particularly on the part of the followers of Bakunin, Marx was prepared to let the First International's center be relocated in America where it would later die.

This did not end Marx's involvement in organizational questions. When he found that his would-be followers in Germany were so awed by Lassalle's shadow, (and especially his organization), that they were prepared for organizational unity based on a program that moved far away from the principles Marx had striven to work out over three decades, he issued his *Critique of the Gotha Program* (1875) against an erroneous *organizational* program of would-be revolutionary socialists. Revolutionary organization without an organizational of thought based on emancipatory principles would be a dead-end.

At each historic moment, Marx strove to present a concept of organization born out of the proletarian and other mass struggles of his day, *and* out of the organization of thought that we know as Marx's Marxism. In a letter to Ferdinand Freiligrath (29 February, 1860), a German poet and original member of the Communist League, Marx distinguished between two kinds of organization: "The *party*, [the Communist League] therefore, in this wholly ephemeral sense, ceased to exist for me 8 years ago… By party, I meant the party in the broad historical sense." These two senses of organization (the Party) *ephemeral* and the *historical* were at the heart of Marx's concept of organization.

Post-Marx, beginning with the Second International, the intertwining of Marx's organization of thought and actual Marxist organizational life was deeply frayed, and indeed, rent asunder. Much of the 20th Century Marxist organization suffered deeply under this separation. (See my *Toward a Dialectic of Philosophy and Organization*. Gogol: 2012.)

2 Dunayevskaya's "Dialectic of Organization and Philosophy"

Raya Dunayevskaya, in breaking with Trotskyism in mid-20th century was determined to restore Marx's intertwining of revolutionary organization of thought and actual radical organizational life. As we saw in Chapter 2, she rooted her organization of thought in both the Hegelian dialectic and Marx's radical transformation and re-creation of that dialectic. She concretized that in actual organization, News & Letters Committees. (See my *Raya Dunayevskaya: Philosopher of Marxist-Humanism* (Gogol: 2004) and *Toward a Dialectic of Philosophy and Organization* (Gogol: 2012) for a detailed discussion of her labors.)

Here, we want to briefly take note of her searching out the relation between dialectics and organization. In 1953, in studying the Absolute Idea Chapter of Hegel's *Science of* Logic, she commented: "I am concerned only with the dialectic… of the type of grouping like ours, be it large or small, and its relation to the mass." (May 12, 1953 Letter on Absolute Idea, Dunayevskaya, 2002: 16). Two years later, she and colleagues would found News and Letters Committees, seeking to base themselves on the unity of the Hegelian and Marxian dialectics in fusion with a movement from practice, from masses in motion that Dunayevskaya viewed as itself a form of theory.

After a quarter of a century of non-vanguardist organizational *praxis*, founded on ongoing restatements of Marxist philosophy—*Marxism and Freedom* (1957), *Philosophy and Revolution* (1973), and *Rosa Luxemburg, Women's Liberation and Marx's Philosophy of Revolution* (1982)—she turned to develop a work on the relation of organization and philosophy. Tentatively titled "Dialectics of Organization and Philosophy: Forms of Organization Arising from Spontaneity vs. the Vanguard Party," the worked remained unfinished at her death (1987). In one of her last writings she had returned once again to the question of revolutionary organization in terms of a small group of Marxists:

> [W]hat happens to a small group 'like us' who know that nothing can be done without the masses, and are with them, but [such small groups of] theoreticians always seem to be around too. So, what is the objectivity which explains their presence, as the objectivity explains the spontaneous outburst of the masses? In a word, I was looking for the objectivity of subjectivity. (Dunayevskaya, "Presentation on the Dialectics of Organization and Philosophy," June 1987, commenting on her May 12, 1953 Letter.[1])
>
> DUNAYEVSKAYA, 2002: 7

3 Latin America's Revolutionary Organizations and the Idea of Freedom as Utopia and as the Dialectic

In recent decades, Latin America has given birth to a vast array of forms of organization from below: To the Mothers of the Plaza de Mayo in Argentina, the EZLN and the autonomous communities in resistance in Chiapas, Indigenous groups in Bolivia, including recently in the TIPNIS region—among the most known—can be added dozens upon dozens, hundreds and more of self-organizations that have emerged in recent times. To mention only a few: the important student movements in Chile and most recently in Mexico, the mothers and families of the disappeared, including migrants traveling across Mexico to the US who have organized protest organizations and searches, the women organized against femicides and other violence against women. Without such movements/organizations (sometimes referred to as organization for life) no uprooting social transformation would be possible. They have emerged spontaneously, but often linked to historical memory and radical tradition. (We will discuss a number of these emerging forms in parts II and III of the present study).

1 For further discussion of her writings on *Dialectics of Organization and Philosophy* see Gogol (2012).

These new organizations have often emerged in separation from and even as a break with some aspects of other organizational traditions, including political parties, union organizing and formal protest. It part, today's changed movements have been rooted in the changing nature of capitalism which has broken the power of unions in certain areas. See for example the enormous change in mining in Bolivia since the time of the 1952 Bolivia Revolution. In part, it has been the bankruptcy of "progressive" political parties, who even when "in power" have only initiated limited change at best. Guerrilla warfare too—whether as seen in Cuban *focoism* in other Latin American countries, the Nicaragua Revolution after taking power, or El Salvador's armed attempt in the 1970s and 1980s—suffered defeat principally via U.S. counter-insurgency warfare, but as well, exhibited internal contradictions and limitations.

Within the new forms emerging, the Zapatistas hold a special place: Not so much because they have obtained an important place in the consciousness of movements globally, though this is important. Rather they have become a beacon principally because their forms of struggle—army, Indigenous communities in resistance, councils of good government, emancipatory forms of education, freely associated communitarian form of work, their struggle for autonomy, etc.—have been inseparable from a radical organization of thought. In their Declarations from the *Selva Lacandona*, in their revolutionary laws on women, land and other aspects of struggle, they have sought to put forth a unity of ideas and action, theory and practice. Indeed, perhaps it is this unity that has been the energizing principle to thrust them to prominence in the consciousness of global social movements. They have, perhaps to a greater extent than any of the other movements, united the word and the deed. "The true arms of the Zapatistas is the pen of Marcos" read an early graffiti expression on a wall at the National Autonomous University of Mexico (UNAM). This is not to say that the Zapatistas and the Indigenous communities in resistance in Chiapas have connecting threads directly to Marx's concept of organization, to the necessity of uniting organization of thought and actual organization. But important beginnings have been made. How can they be further developed today?

•

Let us return to our original question: *What is the relation between the concept of utopia as found in many of today's Latin American social movements and the Hegelian concept of the dialectic of negativity? And let us add the dimension of revolutionary organization as we have just taken it up into the discussion.*

The unification of project (freedom activity, including organization) and utopia (the dreams, desires, hopes of the masses) is how Hegel's expression, "[the idea of the good (the practical idea)] makes this transition through itself [to the absolute idea]," can take on flesh and blood in the reality of today's Latin America. The Latin American concept of utopia, as historical and as concrete ongoing project, has important elements for being able to make the transition through itself toward the Absolute of a new society. It has this possibility if thinker-activists within the Latin American social movements engage in creative labor to fuse the active concept of utopia (movements from practice that are themselves forms of theory) with the Hegelian-Marxian dialectic of absolute negativity (the movement from theory toward practice which is at the same time rooted in the fullness of dialectical philosophy).

We can find implicit in the activities and ideas of the autonomous Indigenous communities in resistance in Chiapas, and in the creativity of the primarily Indigenous social movements in Bolivia of the last decade, a relation to the dialectic of absolute negativity. This is *not* to say we have arrived fully in the absolutes, on the threshold of a new society. The challenge is to work out the relationship between a Latin American concept of utopia and the dialectic; to make explicit what is implicit in today's liberatory social movements; to concretize the universals of the dialectic within the reality of the practice and theory in Latin America. Put differently: There is a need to demonstrate that within the reality of practice and theory in Latin America, its *praxis*, is a manifestation of the Hegelian dialectic of negativity. This is so, *not* because the movements "know" the Hegelian dialectic, but because absolute negativity is objective, is indigenous to freedom struggles in the real world.

Revolutionary organization enters into this exploration of the threads between utopia and the dialectic because, at certain times organization—both as mass organization from below *and* as a small group of activist-thinkers (theoreticians)—becomes the carrier or the concretization of a certain body of ideas, a motor towards a fullness of an "organization for life" that is utopia, and is, thus, an organizational expression of dialectical thought.

How do we see the relation of organization, project, utopia, and the dialectic in Latin America today? The *project* is the concrete work of the moment, including the motor of *organization* carrying out the project, moving toward a realization of a *utopia*. The *dialectic* embraces this concreteness, indeed cannot express/fulfill itself without it. At the same time, the dialectic brings forth the historically-created methodological form of this work: *emancipatory philosophy's role of making explicit what is implicit in the movements from practice.* At one and the same time, the dialectic allows for the most concrete expression, or real-time explicitness, or meaning of the struggle, *and* the most universal manifestation of it—*a universalization of the particular*. The dialectic is able to realize this universalization of the particular because it itself is the expression of previous human experience (history) presented in the form of thought.

Because the Latin America concept of utopia is rooted in the concrete, that is, in both the historic practices of masses and in the ongoing actions, ideas, desires of the masses, this concept of utopia can be read, following Dunayevskaya, *as a movement from practice that is itself a form of theory.* Such a reading sees in the activities of the Indigenous, the workers, the women, the Afro-Latin Americans, the youth, a type of practice that is reason as well as force, mind as well as muscle. To a greater extent than perhaps any other region of the world at the present moment, there is a realization in Latin America—including on the part of intellectuals, thinker activists, philosophers—that this movement from below is the source, the wellspring, for a new society.

At the same time that there is this realization that to philosophize in a radical manner is to do so from the perspective of the masses own social emancipatory struggle, there is often a silence or void on the need to philosophize as well from the perspective of the Hegelian and Marxian dialectic of negativity.

It is here where an exploration of Dunayevskaya's concept of "absolute negativity as new beginning" can be of great assistance within Latin American reality. What she found in Hegel's absolutes was a dual movement: a movement from practice that was itself a form of theory, *and* a movement from theory that both met the movement from practice and was itself rooted in/reached for the fullness of emancipatory philosophy. For Dunayevskaya, this meant a new way to look at and work out revolutionary organization: Not only was there the mass, often spontaneously-created organization from below that was the genuine motor of social transformation, but as well, there was another form of revolutionary organization, the small group of thinker-activists, who felt compelled to take responsibility for working out theory anew in response to these movements from below. These thinker-activists could do so because their labors were rooted in the fullness of the dialectic of Hegel and of Marx. Dunayevskaya's concepts were a million miles away from any vanguard party-to-lead that the revolutionary movement had been burdened with for much of the 20th century. Rather, there was recognition of the necessity to be rooted in dialectical thought if revolutionaries were to aid in bringing to fruition the task of uniting theory and practice, thus reaching toward a new society. This was the absolute challenge she saw for her age. I would argue it remains the same absolute challenge for Latin America today.

PART 2

The State and Social Movements in Latin America

∴

CHAPTER 4

Haiti, 1986–1993: The Uprooting (*Dejoucki*), the Flood (*Lavalas*) and the Repression

> The history of the abuse of Haiti, which in our lifetime has become a tragedy, is also the story of Western civilization's racism.
>
> EDUARDO GALEANO

1 Haiti was the First: A Brief Note on the Significance of the Haitian Revolution, 1791–1804

It is often forgotten or deliberately obscured that there were not two but three great revolutions in the last decades of the 18th century: the American, the French and the Haitian.[1] Haiti's revolution shook the slavery-driven colonial world at its very foundations. Prior to the 1790s, the Santo Domingo colony was France's precious jewel, at the heart of its primitive accumulation with racist roots, a manifestation of the slave origins of capitalism's accumulation, the richest colony in the world. With the slave revolt-become-revolution, the world of slavery, colonialism, and primitive accumulation, which had been imposed in the Western Hemisphere following Columbus's voyages, could no longer continue in its original form.[2] With the founding of this Black republic by former slaves, the slave trade was on its last legs. Napoleon's unsuccessful attempt to take back France's former colony led to the abandonment of the Louisiana Territory to the United States. It is true that with the development of the cotton gin at the end of the 18th century, accumulation via slave-capitalism intensified in the U.S. in the first half of the 19th century. However, the Haitian Revolution struck great fear in the mind of the slave-holding South, and served as a significant catalyst for the emergence of a powerful Abolitionist movement of white New England intellectuals, Black runaway slaves and free Blacks in the North.

1 "The Haitian Revolution was one of the three defining revolutions of the 1700s, and as much as the American and French Revolutions, it has shaped the world we all live in. It destroyed the era's economy of slave capitalism; it wrecked the global ruling powers' dreams of eternal colonialism" (Wilentz 2013).

2 "If we have become accustomed to different narratives, ones that place colonial events on the margins of European history, we have been seriously misled" (Buck-Morss 2009, 39).

Haiti was Latin America's first revolution. Its beginnings came two years into the French Revolution, and no doubt the winds of 1789 reached the shores of Saint-Domingue. At the same time, the dozen years of slave rebellion-revolution that, against enormous odds, transformed the slave colony of France (coffee and sugar) into the Black republic of Haiti had its own dialectic, which we cannot trace here. (See for instance C.L.R. James, *Black Jacobins*, original published in 1938, and Laurent Dubos, *Avengers of the New World—The Story of the Haitian Revolution* 2004.)

If the American Revolution "sounded the tocsin" (Marx) for the French Revolution, the Haitian Revolution served as a catalyst for Latin America's wars of independence. However, Haiti's Revolution brought forth a double-edged legacy. Yes, it helped open the door to Latin America's wars of independence as Haiti's internationalism meant concretely aiding Simon Bolivar. Haiti's only request was for the abolition of slavery in those wars, a request not fully honored. However, at the same time, the revolution so struck fear into the slavery-based United States that its slave-owning President Jefferson refused to recognize Haiti as a nation, working hand and glove with the European powers, who were intent on isolating Haiti internationally. It would not be until the time of the Civil War and slave emancipation in the United States, that President Lincoln finally granted recognition.

Even more ominous, Haiti was faced with immediate isolation and threat of war from France, to whom it had to promise to pay millions of dollars over decades and decades for the loss of its "property" (the slaves), thereby crippling any opportunity for economic development and sustainability, making impossible truly independent existence, and with it, genuine self-determination.

Nor can we here follow the onerous U.S. occupation of Haiti (1915–1934) (See *Haiti: The Aftershocks of History* by Laurent Dubos), which once again denied self-determination for the Haitian masses, and would set the stage for Duvalier-ism (father and son).

Rather, we wish to examine the period mid-1980s through the beginning of the Aristide presidency. For it is here where we can see a new beginning in the struggle for self-determination. What were its great leaps and its limitations?

II Haiti in Books and in Life[3]

When Jean-Claude Duvalier was forced to leave the country in 1986, nobody expected that after 30 years of repression, the first 15 of which

3 To try and have one's pulse on the popular movement from afar, and by someone who does not speak Creole, the language of the Haitian masses, presents difficult barriers. And yet,

were sheer terror, that there would be this profound movement within the Haitian population that would turn into thousands of grassroots organizations. It was this movement that was the origin of the Haitian saga of the last 20 years. It was this movement rather than the political parties that stood up against the return of dictatorship. It was this movement that confronted the military government when it tried to control the election in 1987 and this movement that swept Aristide into power in 1990... And I think that this movement that literally exploded onto the scene in 1986 preceded what we've seen in Venezuela, in Bolivia, and what may be appearing in Mexico and maybe it is the wave of the future for countries like Haiti in Latin America... [W]hat Haitians are trying to do.

PATRICK ELIE, interviewed by LINDSAY REED (2006)

Women's voices gained volume with the political opening of 1986. One of the first events of the post-Duvalier uncorking was a boisterous march of almost two thousand women in the remote village of Papaye. Immediately thereafter, on April 3, 1986, over thirty thousand women from all social sectors took to the street throughout Haiti, rhythmically chanting their demands and carrying strongly worded posters.

BEVERLY BELL, Walking on Fire—Haitian woman's stories of survival and resistance

On our main road we planted fruit trees and flowers. When you come into our area and you feel the wind blowing on you, you'll know that here we are, we women who planted these little trees. We're always here and we're joined together.

CLAUDETTE PHENE, Artibonite Valley, Haiti, quoted in BELL

---

there is a crucial need to do so, especially when there has been so much demonization and vulgarization of the thought and activities of ordinary Haitians. I have relied on a number of studies of others who have had their eyes and ears attuned to Haiti's masses from within. I found the writings of Amy Wilentz helpful as well as the article by Aristide and Richarchson: "Haiti's Popular Resistance" (1994). A truly remarkable contribution to grasping the reality of Haiti, particularly its peasant and urban women, has been the crucial work produced by Beverly Bell, *Walking on Fire—Haitian Woman's Stories of Survival and Resistance* (2001). In the life-stories, the *istwa* (meaning both story and history) of many Haitian women, and from Bell's own perspective in the Introduction and commentaries throughout the book, a window on Haiti seen from below has been presented. It is rare to find a work that authentically gives voice to those so often unseen and unheard. If I have borrowed too much from her work, I apologize. It is not meant as any substitute for an interested reader to explore the whole of this work.

I will try and give a sense of the Haitian movement gained from my readings. Crucial dimensions include the *Ti Legliz* (the little church), the peasant dimension, the demand for Creole to be the language in use, working out ways to communicate particularly through the radio, and in all of this, the participation of women.

A *Ti Legliz*

The Haitian popular movement that emerged in the mid-1980s was multidimensional, with no single point source. Rooted in opposition to Duvalianism, perhaps its most important initial motor was the *Ti Legliz*—the little church—of liberation theology and base communities. It would be from within *Ti Legliz* that the Catholic priest Jean Aristide would develop his profound relation to the Haitian masses.

Ti Legliz came to Haiti in the mid-1970s out of theology of liberation that was taking hold in Central and South America. By the mid-1980s just before Jean Claude Duvalier's ouster there were *Ti Legliz* groups throughout Haiti. Bob Corbett, a teacher and political activist involved in Haiti in the 1980s and 90s, described his experience of observing base communities:

> A meeting begins with some prayers and religious songs, followed by a reading from scripture. These meetings are almost invariably led by a lay person, not a priest or minister. The reading done, the leader would ask about the reading and some general discussion would follow. However, after a while, 15 minutes to 1/2 hour the leader would shift the topic to: What does this reading mean in our lives?... People would then respond to these questions of what does this passage of scripture mean to us. Sitting in meeting after meeting in those early days I can attest this was very grass roots local democracy being born. No talk of "Haiti" or "the nation" or any of that. It was stuff like: How can we grow more food for us (as opposed to the land owner) so we do not suffer hunger? How can we get schools for our children and our selves, so that we aren't so uninformed of what's going on? (Basic literacy was invariably understood by the simple peasants as indispensable to the growth. There was only ONE language ever mentioned or used in any meeting I ever attended, Creole, their language.) How can we get safer water to drink that isn't so distant from our village and home?
>
> The emphasis was not on how do I, the individual get this, but how do WE, the community achieve this. And the central notion was that by putting our heads together we could achieve this. The Haitian nation had held for nearly two centuries that union creates force and that by joining

> together would make light work of the heavy. But it had never really translated these notions into a democratic ideal of people of equal worth working together to achieve these goals. That's what made it so democratic in my eyes, eyes that were often moved to tears by what I was seeing and hearing in the work of these *Ti Legliz* groups.
>
> The exciting next stage, which didn't really come until after the fall of Jean-Claude in that short euphoric time of hope before the disastrous elections of Nov. 29, 1987, was that these small groups began meeting with other small groups and the ante was upped to not only the problems of OUR village, but of our ZONE, our region. That was so dramatic and earth-shattering to the consciousness of the peasants that I was often sitting there with skin tingling listening to the drama of democracy growing not in talk of intellectuals, but in the lives, dreams and commitments of ordinary people, changing an entire history of their nation.
>
> BOB CORBETT

Beverly Bell noted:

> Public revolt burst forth in the mid-1980s sparked by *tilegliz*, the liberation theology-inspired 'little church' or church of the poor. The mobilization of Christians who believed that justice is God's will galvanized the population into action. Among the clergy and laity, women were more central and vociferous than ever before. (2001: 11)

Bell interviewed Louise Monfils, a Haitian activist on women's and peasants' issues, who spoke of religion and its importance in her work:

> If I need to meet Jesus, I meet him in my brothers and sisters. I meet him in the work I am doing, in helping them live as human beings. In my everyday life what does living the gospel mean? Not praying, singing, clapping, making a lot of noise. That's not it. It means that those around you can know that a brother or sister has come into their midst. It's answering a cry for help by someone in the night... You're taking a better communion that way. It's not opening your mouth and taking the host, answering 'Amen' to 'The Body of Christ,' while being mean and a nuisance to your neighbors...
>
> Do I need to kneel in front of somebody to confess my sins? No, I need to work together with my friends, my family, my brothers and sisters so that we can fight together for change. It's going for a taste of the water and letting the river carry you away. So when I went with the tide of the *tilegliz*,

> the church of the poor. I left Port-au-Prince and went to the mountains. I started forming groups without a penny. I didn't have any money, and I wasn't paid for my work. My friends and I climbed up and down the mountains, through the briars, to bring the gospel and to help people work together. I was responsible for *tilegliz* in a rural zone. Each Sunday I celebrated mass for the group. It didn't matter that I was a woman, because the spirit of God was in me to send the good news to the poor. I was helping people in solidarity with each other... We were collecting information from the peasants so we could use it to help them understand their situation better. You synthesize what they've been told with what you saw yourself, and analyze it to understand the situation better. You extend the consequences to the whole country since all the peasants have the same problem. Then the peasants can use that information to analyze important questions, like: How can they protect their land? From there we would organize peasant groups... We studied the chapter in the Acts of the Apostles where the disciples put their goods together. And the people realized they need to work together. They build a collective silo to store seed and grains.
>
> BELL, 2001: 127, 128, 129

B *The Peasantry*

Marx V. Aristide and Laurie Richardson writing in the mid-1990s on "Haiti's Popular Resistance"[4] described the emergence and resistance of peasant groups:

> The seeds of Haiti's peasant movement were planted in the late 1960s in the form of farming cooperatives, or *gwoupman*. Consisting of ten to 15 members, *gwoupman* gave peasants a collective base of resistance against the rural structures of exploitation and repression. By 1986, *gwoupman* had become widespread and extremely politicized. After Duvalier's fall, they developed into a myriad of local and regional peasant organizations. Relying on tactics such as marches and land takeovers, peasant groups demanded agrarian reform, elimination of the repressive section chiefs, repopulation of Creole pigs eradicated by U.S. AID between 1981 and 1983, tax reform, and promotion of Haitian Creole. Founded in the early 1970s and operating in semi-clandestinely until 1986, the Peasant

4 While their article is an important synthesis of the popular resistance in Haiti, they fail to single out or even mention the role of women.

Movement of Papay (MPP) is Haiti's oldest peasant organization. In March, 1987, the MPP formed the National Peasant Movement of the Papay Congress (MPNKP), which reported 100,000 members before the 1991 coup d'etat. Another national movement is Tet Kole Ti Peyizan (Heads Together Little Peasants), which has its roots in meetings held by peasant delegates starting in September, 1986. Tet Kole has *gwoupman* in each of Haiti's nine departments, and is strongest in the northwest town of Jean Rabel.

MARX V. ARISTIDE, and LAURIE RICHARDSON, 1994

Many of the women Beverly Bell interviewed were peasants or had a peasant background:

Gracita Osias: My mother and father are peasants. Well, what can I say? I am a peasant too. It's in my blood... Oh you find so many strong people among peasants. But they're a category of people that's always ignored. There's been no cultural value placed on them, and there's so much richness and capacity lost... The country's culture means all our habits, our customs, our language, our way of seeing life, our music. The reserve of culture, where it's strongest, is found in the middle of the peasants. The peasants are full of the capacity to resist and to continue expressing their culture... The gifts peasants have to express themselves—a people who don't know how to read and write—are so strong. These people can sit and compose music that other people, who've gone to school to study it, could never do... But little by little peasants are beginning to establish their value bring up their morale, express themselves. We need to lift up the peasants, each one, by supporting them and giving them the strength they need to continue...

I work in a peasant organization, especially with women. The hard lot of women in the country has always struck me. We found the women's organizations always had to get a man to come and take notes because the women couldn't read and write. So I made it a priority to give them a high level of training... There was a period when people couldn't even do literacy. Under Duvalier, if the state learned you were teaching people to read and write, they could arrest you. The same thing during the coup [against Aristide]... The elite that know how to read and write, that have this intellectual knowledge, they traumatize the peasants, scare the peasants. As soon as the peasants know they have a right to learn, to gain understanding, to speak, they won't bow down before the rich anymore.

BELL, 2001: 83, 84, 85

C *Creole and the Radio*

Language, incontestably, reveals the speaker. Language, also, far most dubiously, is meant to define the other—and, in this case, the other is refusing to be defined by a language that has never been able to recognize him.

JAMES BALDWIN, "If Black English Isn't a Language, Then Tell Me, What Is?" *New York Times,* July 29, 1979

I'm living in a Creole country. I must speak the way I speak.

ALINA 'TIBEBE' CAJUSTE, quoted in BELL

[T]he spreading use of Creole on radio, beginning in the 1970s, gave millions of people who did not know French access to news—also for the first time. In moments of political upheaval, each rare transistor radio became a convergence point for a small crowd eager for news.

BELL

The dual struggle for Creole and for Creole-language radio stations with the voice of the people was an important strand of the liberation struggle from the 1970s through the post-coup period. A number of women in *Walking on Fire* spoke of these battles:

> Those who can't speak are those who can't eat. They can't live, they can't drink, they can't breathe. They don't have a right to anything because they are not considered people in our country. These are the people I feel it's necessary to stand with, work with, be their spokesperson, give them a microphone, help them speak out so they don't suffocate with what is inside them... My awareness increased when there were huge movements of mobilization to crush Jean-Claude Duvalier's regime during the 1980s. We saw the necessity of helping out through the microphone. At that time, you know, there were no radio stations working with the poor... There was an urgency for people to spread information by whatever means possible, whether by tracts or radio or newspaper. So after my studies, when Radio Cacique called me in '85, I went without thinking twice. It was different than other radio stations; it was a station of struggle. I gave a hand to this radio station, which was both young and full of youth... Through this radio station we waged a battle for the poor, for the factory workers in Cite Soleil, in all the shantytowns. We went to all corners of the country to collect speech from the mouths of

those who didn't have the right to speak for themselves. Of course the radio station was later destroyed, but the work is still being done.

We won a brief victory on February 7, 1986, when Duvalier fled Haiti. I think you know there was a wonderful outburst. Everyone could talk. Everyone could express themselves.

LELENNE GILLES, quoted in BELL

Under the dictatorship, there wasn't a lot people could do when their eyes began opening, when they were angry. Then you could just go around the edges of a problem. It was during school that my will to change the country took off. I felt there must be a battle. So I started working in the movement for Creole. The issue of Creole was really taboo at the time. In school we weren't allowed to speak Creole; we were forced to speak only French. When they told us not to speak Creole in school, it was like saying to the people: do not speak... We built student organizations to really launch the fight. It was an act of resistance to say you weren't going to speak French in school. Struggling inside the school to incorporate Creole was resistance against the whole social structure... The whole population was marginalized by the requirement to speak French, since most speak only Creole and don't go to school.

This was a period when Radio Haiti was broadcasting in Creole when the battle for *Haitiennite,* Haitianicity, was taking off. *Haitiennite* was a search for identity within a system dedicated to controlling how we could express ourselves... The struggle to speak Creole was an important step in our lives. Most of my generation of activists started off between 1970 and 1980 with that as their first involvement. That's where it started this struggle to allow, little by little, an unblocking so that the people could resist the dictatorship.

YANIQUE GUITEAU DANDIN, quoted in BELL

III Theology of Liberation in Concrete Practice: Aristide's Sermons and Actions

The base ecclesial communities—*ti kominite legliz* (in Creole), (TKLS)—that formed the concrete practice of theology of liberation came to Haiti in the 1970s. It meant a major transformation of the Church, whose hierarchy had been appointed by Francois Duvalier. Against the formalism and estrangement of the official Church from large segments of the population, the TKLS were able to tap into existing indigenous self-help groups, and to form many new TKLs. "The TKLs brought the young and the desperate back into the Church in Haiti because the community groups gave these people a new understanding of the possibility of change." (Amy Wilentz, 1990: xi)

Jean-Bertrand Aristide, a young priest of the Silesian order, returned to Haiti from study abroad in 1985, and quickly threw himself into activity in the *Ti ligliz*, giving sermons in St. Jean Bosco, a church at the edge of the Le Saline barrio in Port-au- Prince, and

> helped initiate a number of TKLs, for young people, for students, for young women, and the church, for years sparsely attended by older women and little children, was suddenly full of young people. Every Tuesday evening, there was a youth Mass, in which these lay people took over, and Aristide ministered only nominally... The young people were always engaged in heated political debate; they were always drawing up plans for one project or another; they were developing literacy programs; there was a sense of excitement and potential in their lives.
>
> Aristide worked with them, but he drew his spiritual strength from—and breathed into—a wider congregation. His Sunday sermons, full of Creole wordplay and biblical invective against the dictatorship, were famous in Port-au-Prince in the months and weeks before Jean-Claude Duvalier fell.
>
> WILENTZ, 1990: xi–xii

Within Haiti, Aristide's sermons in public and often on the radio, were not discourses on the universal of liberation theology, but powerful, even at times inflammatory, political speeches in religious language—religious metaphors, references to the bible. [See Aristide, *In the Parish of the Poor* for a small selection of his sermons.] This is not to say religious discourse was only a cover for radical thought and action. Rather, for Aristide and especially his followers, particularly the youth, the question was one of concrete thought and action of the little church, *Ti ligez,* in relation to the masses. Aristide was making an absolute demand, first, for bringing down the dictatorial regime of Jean-Claude Duvalier, and then later, against the military dictators that followed.

> To my sisters, my brothers, to all my brothers and sisters in the Good Lord who raise their voices together with us, to the valiant youth of Haiti, to the peasants—whether Catholic, Protestant, or Vodouisant—to the Haitians abroad, to the courageous Haitians here in Haiti and to all of you who have achieved a legal general strike in spite of the declarations of an illegal general: Hats off to you, congratulations on your courage...

What luck for the Haitian church, rich, thanks to the poor, in a country that is poor because of the rich. The church is rich thanks to us, the poor, who ceaselessly demand the truth from every corner...

Alone, we are weak. Together, we are strong. Together, we are the flood [*levales*]. Let the flood descend, the flood of poor peasants and poor soldiers, the flood of the poor jobless multitude (and poor soldiers), of poor workers (and poor soldiers), the flood of all our poor friends (and all the poor soldiers) and the church of the poor, which we call the children of God! Let that flood descend! And then God will descend and put down the mighty and send them away, and He will raise up the lowly and place them on high (cf. Luke 1:52).

To prevent the flood from the children of God from descending, the imperialists of soutane have conspired with the imperialists of America. That is why we Haitians must say to one another what Jesus declared (Mark 2:11): Arise! Go Forth! Walk!

Yes, arise and go forth. Walk. Arise and go forth so the Tontons Macoutes will stop walking in ways wet with our blood. Arise and go forth so that the criminals will stop walking upon us. Arise and go forth so that the assassins will stop waking us in our beds with rounds of gunfire. Too much blood has been spilled! Too many innocent have fallen! This is too much for us...

One coup d'etat. Another coup d'etat. One general goes. Another takes his place. And then? And then, nothing! ...

The matter is in your hands. The people will write their own fate. The blessing of God is upon them. Thus, grace will descend until the flood brings down all Duvalierists all Macoutes all criminals forever and ever. Amen.

Excerpts from "Let the Floor Descend," message delivered on Radio Haiti-Inter November, 1988. Found in Aristide, *In the Parish of the Poor*, 1990: 101

At crucial as Aristide was in the events from 1985 forward, it is important to recognize that,

> Aristide did not create the mass movement but rather was created by it. That is, the popular movement against the neo-Duvalierist forces created the conditions for a charismatic persona like Aristide to rise to the occasion and capture its essence like no one else could. Through his sermons at Saint Jean Bosco church and his radio broadcasts, Aristide inspired his followers, the poor, and the population at large, gave them hope, explained to them the nature of the system that imprisoned and impoverished

> them, and galvanized them into action against the neo-Duvalierist forces. His attacks were not limited to the Duvalierists and *makout* system only but were also directed at the United States (which he referred to as 'the cold country to the north'), the Catholic Church hierarchy, and the bourgeoisie for their collaboration with the dictatorships and their roles in the exploitation and oppression of the people.
>
> ALEX DUPUY, 2007

The military certainly was aware of Aristide's profound relationship with the Haitian masses. Three times in the late '80s they tried to assassinate him. In one attempt they destroyed Saint Juan Bosco, the church where Aristide preached, murders more than a dozen parishioners:

> From the fall of the hereditary Duuvalier regime in February 1986 until March 1990, Haiti experienced an unparalleled political crisis marked by the rise and fall of four military dominated governments and an unrelenting popular struggle for a democratic alternative.
>
> DUPUY, 2007: 57

Election attempts were marked by violence. Finally, after the last military strongman could not continue due to mass protests, a new presidential election was set for December 1990, and in October Aristide decided to participate. It transformed everything. From the moment of its announcement, hundreds of thousands of unregistered Haitians, decided to register.

We should note that within the progressive opposition movement there were sharp divisions on whether to participate in the elections. What would an election mean if Aristide was without real power to initiate social transformation? This discussion was not so much about taking power with arms. Few thought that was a real alternative given the army and the remnants of the murderous *Tontons Macoutes* in different guises.

What overruled these important doubts was the tremendous outpouring of the Haitian masses in support of Aristide, who won decisively with 67% of the vote. Because Aristide rode the wave of a massive movement that would take the organizational name of *Levales* (the flood)—hundreds of thousands of Haitians participated in the inauguration—he felt emboldened to try and begin the transformation of the government. Aristide removed a number of the army's top commanders, lowered the price of food, modestly raised the minimum wage, implemented a literacy program, and began to take steps to redistribute fallow land. Hardly a radical socialist agenda, but a few steps to begin moving Haiti's masses from living in misery to living in poverty.

Even these steps were unacceptable to Haiti's ruling elite and the army that had been pushed aside with Aristide's election. Just eight months into his presidential election, a military coup forced him out of office and into exile. A reign of terror was instituted against his *Levales* supporters.

We will not here follow all the compromises and manipulations that allowed Aristide to return to the Presidency. Suffice it to say that the return of Aristide *not* via a movement of the masses, but via the U.S.'s controlling imposition, and even his second election in 2000, again followed by a coup three years later—all meant that the crucial relationship between Aristide and the creative mass movement of the Haitian masses was irreparably damaged, particularly because the grassroots Haitian movement was subject to extreme repression. At well, Aristide's second presidency was enveloped in weakening compromises imposed by the U.S. and at times agreed to by Aristide. The decomposition of the popular movement was not alone the result of a murderous terror of the elite and their troops, but as well due to the connivance of the U.S., which bears a heavy responsibility for the terrible blows that the Haiti popular movement suffered post-1991.

Patrick Eli, a member of the Aristide government, noted that in 1991, "Aristide came to power too early and too fast. We were not ready. We came to power through a *coup de pueple*; the mobilization of the people was strong enough to bring us to power, but not strong enough to keep us there." (Quoted in Peter Hallward *Damning the Floor—Haiti, Aristide, and the Politics of Containment*, 2007.) Whether one agrees with this statement or not, what was clear is that the relation of a charismatic leader and creative movement from below was not sufficient to transform Haitian society under these terrible, repressive conditions.

Revolutionary organization, in this case *Lavalas,* was very late in developing, certainly due to the extreme conditions of repression. Later, it would be joined by opportunists, and soon deep divisions occurred within. Aristide in his relation to the Haitian masses was a powerful proponent and spokesperson for direct action. At the same time, he did not attempt to develop a theoretical basis for Haitian liberation in his interchanges with the mass movement. In his sermons and presentations, he chose to present a concrete reading of theology of liberation, which called for action. But Aristide did not work out a unity of theory and practice that might have been able to reach beyond the immediate moment and provide a theoretical basis for continuing the movement in a new form.[5]

5 Elsewhere, I have written on the power and the limitations of theology of liberation's theoretical expression to confront Latin America's unfree reality. See Gogol 2002, Chapter 5.

IV Epilogue: Post-the Jan. 12, 2012 Earthquake

(Below I reproduce my essay written after the January 12th earthquake.)

The Meaning of Haiti: Tragedy, History, Culture, Philosophy

The profound depth of the Haitian tragedy seems boundless. It is impossible to get an accurate count of the dead, but it is surely well above 100,000. Tens upon tens of thousands injured, many still barely treated, others treated so late that amputation of infected limbs became the only possible treatment. They died and were injured as tens of thousands of homes in Port-au-Prince's shantytowns collapsed, not only from the might of the earthquake, but as well from the reality of Haiti's devastating poverty.

Vulnerability to natural disasters is almost a direct function of poverty. "Impacts are not natural nor is there a divine hand or ill fate," noted Debarti Guha Sapir, director of the World Health Organization's Center for Research on the Epidemiology of Disasters. "People will also die now of lack of follow-up medical care. In other words, those who survived the quake may not survive for long due to the lack of adequate medical care."

Poverty is the principle reason for the poor construction of Haitian homes. People who make on average $2 a day can't afford to build something that can withstand earthquakes and hurricanes. Cement is expensive and often mixed with excessive sand to keep the cost down. Steel reinforcing is barely used. Lumber isn't used in most construction because of the vast deforestation, as Haitians have cut down trees for charcoal used in cooking. The environmental disaster that is Haiti has been created over decades.

Poverty, in turn, isn't a home-grown fact of Haiti, but an imposed condition brought about by dozens of countries' complicity with or indifference to the deplorable conditions of life and labor (or lack of opportunity to labor) that Haitians' masses face every day of their lives.

The unnaturalness of this natural disaster cannot become buried with the vast loss of life, and the devastation of Haiti. It is certainly true that no such powerful earthquake has hit Haiti for over 200 years. However, the conditions of human life that have made the Haitians particularly venerable to the consequences of this massive earthquake are not "natural." They have been present and growing for decades and decades.

It is a tribute to the vast majority of Haitian people that, as opposed to scare stories of looting and potential violence, their resilience, dignity and simple humanity has been continually present. In the immediate aftermath, they quickly acted to save one another in the collapsed rubble and sought to take the injured to where they could possibly be treated. In the days that followed, they fought starvation, not by hoarding, but by communally sharing whatever food they can obtain.

This is no accident. The Haitians are a proud people. They have endured much, not only in this most recent moment, but for decades: natural and man-made ecological and human devastation, dictatorial repression, imperialist military occupation, neo-liberal exploitation and abandonment. They have resisted foreign occupation and overthrown native-born oligarchies. That resistance, rebellion, and indeed revolution, began centuries ago.

Before the island of Hispaniola's division into Haiti and the Dominican Republic it was "discovered" by Columbus in 1492, and claimed for Spain. The indigenous population, *Taino*, were put to work in gold mines, and died off in vast numbers due to mistreatment, malnutrition and lack of immunity to European diseases.

The Spanish began importation of Africans as slaves in 1517. At the end of the 17th Century, the island was divided between France and Spain with France taking over the Western third and naming it Saint-Domingue. By 1790, Saint-Domingue was the richest colony in the Western Hemisphere. Half a million enslaved Africans worked its plantations, supplying Europe with vast quantities of sugar and coffee. So brutal were the conditions that tens of thousands of African had to be continually imported to replace those killed off.

The brutality of the conditions, the creativity of the African-born slaves, and the winds of the French Revolution "conspired" to launch a massive slave revolt in 1791:

> In an immensely complex decade-long conflict, these African slave-soldiers, commanded by legendary leaders like Toussaint Louverture and Jean-Jacques Dessalines, defeated three Western armies, including the unstoppable superpower of the day, Napoleonic France. In an increasingly savage war—"Burn houses! Cut off heads!" was the slogan of Dessalines—the slaves murdered their white masters, or drove them from the land.
>
> On Jan. 1, 1804, when Dessalines created the Haitian flag by tearing the white middle from the French tricolor, he achieved what even Spartacus could not: he had led to triumph the only successful slave revolt in history. Haiti became the world's first independent black republic and the second independent nation in the Western Hemisphere.
>
> MARK DANNER, "To Heal Haiti, Look to History, Not Nature," *New York Times*, Jan. 21, 2010

If the winds of the French Revolution reached the Caribbean, the great fear of the rulers and plantations owners in the United States was that the winds of the

Haitian Revolution would reach the Black slave laborers of the southern states. It was thus no accident that the U.S., under of the author of the Declaration of Independence, but slave-holder presidency of Thomas Jefferson, refused to recognize Haiti (the nation's name) as a legitimate state. It would be in the midst of the Civil War that would abolition slavery, before Lincoln gave recognition to Haiti.

However, who did recognize Haiti's slave rebellion/revolution *philosophically* was G.W.F. Hegel. In the first half decade of the new century, he was at work on his first monumental work, *Phenomenology of Spirit* (1807), as the Haitian conflict proceeded. One of its crucial sections was Lordship and Bondage, the struggle for recognition, or the master-slave dialectic. There, Hegel wrote of how initially the master was "the power dominating existence," holding the bondsman in subordination. However, in labor, "in fashioning the thing, self-existence [of the slave] comes to be felt explicitly as his own proper being." "[T]he bondsman becomes aware, through this re-discovery of himself, of having and being a 'mind of his own'." Hegel wrote of two self-consciousnesses, master and slave, of two worlds that became a struggle of life and death. The risk of life taken to destroy the other is "self-activity," for "it is solely by risking life that freedom is obtained."

When in the past, Hegel historians asked, what was the source of this master-slave dialectic, they looked to philosophic sources in Greek philosophy, or saw it as an abstract construction with no historical antecedents. However recently, the work of Susan Buck-Morss, has cast an important illumination on its origins within the contemporaneity of the Haitian Revolution and Hegel's writings of the *Phenomenology*:

> No one has dared to suggest that the idea for the dialectic of lordship and bondage came to Hegel in Jena in the years 1803–5 from reading the press-journals and newspapers. And yet this selfsame Hegel, in this very Jena period during which the master-slave dialectic was first conceived, made the following notation: "Reading the newspaper in early morning is a kind of realistic morning-prayer. One orients one's attitude against the world and toward God [in one case], or toward that which the world is [in the other]. The former gives the same security as the latter, in that one knows where one stands."
>
> "HEGEL AND HAITI," *Critical Inquiry*, Vol. 26, No. 4, Summer, 2000: 821–865. See her *Hegel, Haiti and Universal History*, 2009, where she as well explored the question of writing, or failing to write, history as a universal history.

Buck-Morss documents how the news of the Revolution appeared in the French and German papers and journals of the period, of which Hegel surely was aware. This intertwining of Haiti and Hegel, an unexamined subject, can lead us to explore further the relation of freedom struggles and dialectical thought. The peoples of Haiti not only entered decisively into the history of revolution at the turn of the century, but entered into Hegel's revolutionary dialectic of negativity.

The aftermath of this second revolution in the New World was both profound and contradictory. Not only did the United States refuse to recognize the new nation, but France attempted to invade Haiti twice. This threat only ended when France demanded and obtained reparations—payments for the loss of territory, property (the slaves), and the slave trade. Under the threat of invasion and blockade, Haiti was forced to pay France over many decades, greatly crippling any possibility for its economic development.

The new Haitian nation had an important relation to what would become the Latin American Wars of Independence. Simon Bolivar was first given refuge, and then given financial and military assistance for his fight to liberate Venezuela, on condition that he free whatever slaves he encountered in his military campaign for South American independence. However, within Haiti, a new form of exploitation arose:

> [T]he slaves had become soldiers in a victorious revolution, and those who survived demanded as their reward a part of the rich land on which they had labored and suffered. Soon after independence most of the great plantations were broken up, given over to the former slaves, establishing Haiti as a nation of small landowners, one whose isolated countryside remained, in language, religion and culture, largely African.
>
> Unable to replace the whites in their plantation manors, Haiti's new elite moved from owning the land to fighting to control the one institution that could tax its products: the government. While the freed slaves worked their small fields, the powerful drew off the fruits of their labor through taxes.
>
> DANNER, op. cit.

In the 20th century, Haiti was subject to a series of invasions and occupations. The most prominent in the first half of the century was the U.S.'s military occupation beginning in 1915 and lasting until 1934. Withdraw did not mean the end of U.S. domination, only its presence in a different form, most especially its acquiescence to and support of the dictatorship of the Duvaliers, first father and then son.

It was only in the 1980s and the 1990s that a powerful movement for self-determination took root under the leadership of a former priest, Jean-Bertrand Aristide, who spoke of and practiced a theology of liberation. In 1991 he won the presidency, winning more than two-thirds of the vote, in the only free democratic election in Haiti's history. This movement, principally of the Haitian poor, became known as the *Lavales*, (the flood or torrent). For both the rich families that controlled much of the wealth within Haiti and for the United States, an Aristide presidency and the powerful movement from below that it represented and released became intolerable. Therefore it was no surprise that Aristide was overthrown and murderous attacks took place on *Lavales* members and supporters.

There is no need to follow the back-room deals and maneuvers, the murderous gangs and terrible immiserating conditions that characterized the rest of the 1990s and first decade of the 21st century. It resulted in terrible blows against the movement of the Haitian people to determine their own destiny. On top of this destruction of authentic self-determination, there has been the layering upon—and at times an imposition upon—Haiti's poor, an incredible number of "aid" organizations—humanitarian, religious, ecological, medical, United Nations, and on and on—all with their different agendas "to help" the Haitians. Such aid began as early as the Duvalier dictatorship and reached almost unaccountable numbers in the most recent period. It is sure to obtain new heights in this post-earthquake world. Haitian-born photographer Daniel Morel spoke of encountering this aid scene in the first days after the quake:

> Since day one of the earthquake, I have everything. I'm on the street covering what other people don't cover. I'm covering the people. I want their voice to come out. Massive aid is coming every day. Big cargo plane is landing every 15 minutes at the airport. What happened to that aid? Why do people still have to buy their own prescription at the hospital? That's the question I'm asking myself and the world... They're playing with people here. CNN is playing with people... They're doing show business here... All I want to say is: stop playing with my people. Stop playing with my people. If you want to help, help. Don't come here for show business... They're playing with the Haitian people again... The press is playing with them. The government is playing with them. The U.N. is playing with them. That's the reason I'm not so excited when they talk about rebuilding Haiti.
>
> *New York Times*, Jan. 27, 2010

It is against this onslaught—economic, military, humanitarian—that we need to again focus on the Haitian masses, on their long history of resistance and revolt, and on what they will do now. Their future will in part be determined by their past as history, as culture, with their roots in Africa and their permanent manner of resistance and revolt. In the Haitian Revolution, "most of those half-million blacks had been born in Africa, spoke African languages, worshipped African gods" (Danner). Even when, in the intervening centuries, some of the original traditions have faded, new modes of resistance have appeared, rooted in the ongoing cultural development of the Haitian people: religion of their own creation and not that of their oppressors; language, not of the occupiers, whether French or English-speaking, but Creole, related to French, but distinct to Haitians.

The question is: With the unprecedented destruction from the earthquake, combined with the huge influx of needed aid—but aid controlled by the outside or by powerful elites within—what will happen, what is the future of Haitian culture—the creative resistance and self-determination of the Haitian people?

Maggie Steber, who has worked on Haitian projects, photographing and documenting their lives and travails for more than 20 years, wrote a short essay in the immediate post-earthquake period, "A Culture in Jeopardy, Too":

> PORT-AU-PRINCE—Ten days after the earthquake. Where to begin and what to say? ... Devastated by the loss of its people and its places, Haiti stands on the precipice of losing something more precious—as audacious as that sounds amid all this death—because it is transcendent. *Haiti stands to lose its culture*. Culture describes a people more than anything. It stems from history. It is the glue that holds a nation together when all else fails. But now that, too, may be lost, in the well-intentioned rebuilding efforts by the international community. In Haiti, culture is something ephemeral that floats just above the fray of daily life. In it is embedded an identity with ancestors who must be served; a history marked by unimaginable violence and a resounding victory over slavery; a character that might seem eccentric elsewhere but works very well here; a tradition of incredible art and music and story-telling and even voodoo which—despite the claims of missionaries—is perhaps the single most important aspect of life for peasants and slum dwellers... All around me, I see a greater loss. And Haitians see it, too. Haitians had their culture, if nothing else. If the world is going to rebuild Haiti, Haitians must have a say. And not just the bourgeoisie, who would most likely want to see Port-au-Prince become a modern city without character.
>
> *New York Times*, Jan. 21, 2010

The question is, who decides in Haiti?—for culture, for the life and labor of the Haitian people, for the Haitian nation? That Haiti needs a huge amount of assistance is undeniable. But the history of assistance to Haiti, not only in recent decades, but for its entire history is abysmal. Exploitation, racism, military invasion and domination—all brought in from the outside; repression, corruption, more exploitation, murderous gangs created and manipulated by dictatorial rulers and the rich elites within; the foreign powers and the native rulers often working hand in hand to close any doors to self-determination, to real development in material and human terms. All of this is the real history and true reality of Haiti.

It is time for another reality, another history-in-the-making—new human beginnings—rooted in the Haitians masses own ideas and actions. No other pathway is a viable one.

January 31, 2010

CHAPTER 5

The Revolutionary Process in Venezuela—Advances, Contradictions, Questions

1 The Passing of Hugo Chavez

For Latin America and, most crucially, for Venezuela, Hugh Chavez's presence at the end of the 20th century and beginning of the 21st represented a significant moment. At a time when the U.S. strove (and continues to strive) toward single power domination globally, Chavez's anti-imperialism, particularly his aid for a number of countries in Latin America, his establishment of a regional alternative to neo-liberal domination, were important efforts in seeking an alternative to U.S. hegemony. Within Venezuela, his labors to redistribute the oil wealth toward the poor in housing, health and education changed the lives of millions. At the same time, we need to be aware of the limitations and contradictions in his attempt to construct "socialism for the 21st century."

Chavez's anti-imperialism was often quite narrowly focused. "The enemy of my enemy is my friend" was a significant strand of his view, as could be seen in his support for the President of Iran, Mahmoud Ahmadinejad, who, while anti-U.S., actively repressed his own people. On this, Chavez kept a deep silence.

Within Venezuela, the focus on *re-distribution* of wealth derived from that crucial commodity oil, oil capitalism imposed an economic straitjacket on constructing "21st century socialism." Redistribution of wealth, as important and needed as it is, is not changing the mode of production that is crucial to the construction of socialism. As well, extractive capitalism in the name of socialism at times meant running rough-shod over Indigenous demands for autonomy and non-development in their territories.

Important as well, socialism directed from above under a single leader, rather than constructed from below, put a huge question mark on how to construct an authentic socialism, that is, from below with participation of the masses. And now, after Chavez's death, what? These advances, contradictions and questions will be explored below.

II Preliminary Moments: The Oil Addiction; The First Period of the Chavez Government

The early 20th century discovery of oil decisively shaped (or distorted) the Venezuelan economy. With the exploitation and exportation of oil that quickly became the dominant source of wealth for the country, agricultural production—cocoa, coffee, cotton, sugar, tobacco—was no longer a central focus of accumulation. Neither a landed elite nor a business elite were dominate, as neither a reliance on agro-export nor the development of domestic industries were points of economic focus. An addiction to oil revenues meant an abandonment of the countryside and an intense urbanization. Importation of goods took precedence, and Venezuela became non-self-sufficient in food production.

At first, control of the wealth was in the hands of foreign oil companies. When oil was nationalized in the mid-1970s, it became the property of the state. As Gregory Wipert noted, "the real center of Venezuela's power was based in the state itself." (*Changing Venezuela by Taking Power*, (11) Times of boom and bust followed, tied to the price of oil. From the late fifties to the end of the seventies, the Venezuelan state and sectors of its population benefited from relatively high oil prices.

However, that changed in the last two decades of the 20th century: "Real per capital income suffered a massive and steady decline for a period of twenty years, from 1979 to 1999, declining by as much as 27% in this period. No other economy in South America experienced such a dramatic fall. Along with this drop, poverty increased from 17% in 1980 to 65% in 1996." (Wilpert, 2007: 13).

Under this economic/social onslaught of the 1980s, the pact of Punto Fijo, a 1958 agreement between the major bourgeois political parties to share power and exclude others, began to come apart. In February 1988, the state under Carlos Andres Perez, brutally suppressed the *Caracazo,* a mass protest in Caracas against the imposition of neo-liberal economic shocks, leaving hundreds dead.

Chavez, who joined the military at an early age, observed this disintegration of the state and its institutions. In 1983, he with others in the military founded the *Ejercito Bolivariano Revolucionario*. Three years after the *Caracazo,* Chavez and his comrades launched a military rebellion against Perez. Their failed attempted led to Chavez's imprisonment, but also meant a gathering of support and recognition of his efforts, especially among Venezuela's poor. Released from prison in 1994, Chavez turned to political organizing, and in December 1998 was elected president with more than 50% of the vote, including support from much of the Left.

The first period of the Chavez presidency was characterized by an anti-neoliberal, but not anti-capitalist, agenda, write Lander and Navarrete (2009: "The Economic Policy of the Latin American Left in Government: Venezuela"):

> This mixed nature of the economy is repeated in Chávez's campaign platform entitled, *A democratic revolution: Hugo Chávez's proposal to transform Venezuela.* While it criticizes the path that the Venezuelan economy has taken, it does not question capitalism as a system. Rather, it seeks a 'humanist, self-managing and competitive' economic model that is summarized by the phrase 'as much market as possible and as much state as necessary.' Significantly, in the political field the document emphasizes the need to transform the existing political-juridical framework through the Constituent Process in order to 'give way to an authentic participatory democracy.'

It would be the Constitutional Assembly and subsequent ratification of a new Constitution (December 1999), with its provision for "participatory and protagonist" democracy, that opened the space for economic changes. However in the first years these changes would be limited. "Economic freedom" and private property were guaranteed. The state would control the oil activities, and would be responsible for the development of sustainable farming and food security. There was a consciousness of the need to break from complete dependency on the oil economy. However, the solution was seen, *not* in breaking from export dependency, but in the state providing a stimulus for *developing an export economy in additional sectors of the economy.* The limitations of these plans for re-orienting the economy could be seen in their assigning, as Lander and Navarrete noted, "a minor role to co-operative and self-managing activities" (15). A "democratizing capital," as opposed to any challenge to the role of capital, was the view presented.

It was not that the Chavez government did not wish to have a social-economic policy that began to change the conditions of extreme poverty. However, initially it would be a government-military plan from above.

> The first major social program of the Chávez government was *Plan Bolívar 2000*, (1999–2001), a civil-military emergency program to repair public infrastructure in the barrios, schools, clinics and hospitals; provide medical attention; repair and build housing as well to distribute food to remote areas of the country...
>
> Public spending as a percentage of GDP went from 23.7% in 1998 to 31.6 % in 2001... Social spending as a percentage of public spending went from 34.6 % in 1998 to 2038.3% in 2001. (16, 17)

As important as these initial efforts were, it was not until the passing of 49 Enabling Laws in November 2001 that a legal framework to implement the new Constitution was created, thus confronting the neo-liberal direction of the Venezuelan economy. The most crucial of these laws was the General Hydrocarbons Law, which increased the royalties paid by foreign oil companies to the state. Subsequent confrontations were as much with the Venezuelan state oil company as with the foreign companies. Though the oil resources had been nationalized for more than two decades, the state company which ran the oil industry, the PDVSA, was more like a state within a state. It had its own rules, its own control of the oil revenues, not for the benefit of the Venezuelan people, but for the benefit and development of the state oil company. This is what Chavez moved to change.

The enabling laws on hydrocarbons, fishing, (protecting the rights of "artisanal" fisherman), and agriculture, (which called for the redistribution of idle lands greater than 5,000 hectares), catalyzed opposition among the business/ownership class. The aborted coup attempt of April 2002, and the failed "business-oil strike/sabotage" of December 2002–March 2003 followed. It would be the radical response of the Venezuelan poor to these events, which created the *social* framework to go beyond anti-neoliberalism and thus move the revolutionary process forward.

III Under the Whip of the Counter-Revolution a Revolutionary Process Begins

Though Chavez was certainly popular among the poor for his initial attempts to redistribute social wealth and partially alleviate poverty, it was the response of the masses to the coup of April 2002 that both reaffirmed his substantial support among the Caracas poor and began the deepening of the social process. After the aborted coup, Chavez spoke of this:

> What happened on April 12 had never happened before in this country: hundreds of thousands of unarmed Venezuelans, many of them without political organization or party affiliations, without a preconceived plan, headed through the streets to the barracks and surrounded them en mass. They sang the national anthem. They spoke to the soldiers and yelled to them *"Soldado, consciente, busca a tu presidente!"* [Soldier, with conscious, go find your president!] and *"Soldado, amigo, el pueblo esta contigo!"* [Soldier, friend, with the people to the end!] Not only did they go to Fort Tiuna, but they also went to barracks all over the country. Nothing

> like that had ever happened before in Venezuela, and it wasn't because I was in those barracks. In fact, the masses that surrounded Fort Tiuna on the third day, when it was already publicly known that I wasn't there, were impressive: 300,000 people or more... This popular uprising would not have happened without the profound contact and cooperation between the army and the people.
>
> QUOTED IN HARNECKER, 2005: 81, 82

The devastating December 2002–March 2003 business-oil strike/sabotage that followed was defeated, as retired workers, foreign contactors and the military eventually returned oil production to near normal levels. But the cost was enormous, particularly for the poor, as the unemployment and poverty rates skyrocketed.

It was after the defeat of the oil strike, combined with a sharp increase in oil prices and thus oil revenues—which the Chavez government could finally have direct control over—that a host of

> new social programs, known as "missions," to address the desperate needs of the country's poor was introduced. The first missions Chavez initiated between late 2003 and early 2004 were for literacy training, (Mission Robinson), high school completion (Mission Ribas), university scholarships (Mission Sucre), community health care (Mission Barrio Adentro), and subsidized food makers (Mission Mercal).
>
> WILPERT, 2007: 23

Mission Barrio Adentro proposed primary and family health care at the grass roots, including the participation of hundreds of Cuban doctors. Mission Mercal was to supply low-cost food to low-income sectors and to try and have alternative production and commercialization channels. "In the agricultural sphere, the Zamora Mission proposed providing peasants with land, training, technical and marketing assistance as well as infrastructure, services and financing." (Lander and Navarrete, 2009: 24). Other Missions followed. These programs were introduced directly by the government in conjunction with the military, and avoided some of the bureaucracy found in lower government levels. It meant the programs could be implemented quickly. However, it also meant that the initiative came primarily from the state above and not from a mass movement from below.

In dividing the period of Chavez's government in two, Lander and Navarrete called the period December 2001—June 2003, "the Battle for State Control." They termed the period after the strike July 2003 to June 2006 (the end of their writing),

"The Beginning of the Social Offensive." It was in this second period that the question of the construction of "21st Century Socialism" came to the fore.

IV Chavez's Call to Build "21st Century Socialism"—What is Its Meaning? How Can It Move "Beyond Capital"? Who are the Social Subjects of Revolutionary Change? What is the Role of the State? The Unions? The Party?

At the end of 2005/beginning of 2006, Chavez declared his Bolivarian Revolution's intention to build "socialism for the 21st century," as a constitutional/electoral project. Words of caution are needed here. The tragic history of the 20th century has shown us that the construction of 21st century socialism must of necessity extend beyond the boundaries of a single nation. It would need the fullness of a Latin American context as a minimum. Indeed, confronting the global nature of capitalism, its needed uprooting, is central to any such project. Furthermore, after the incomplete, failed and transformed-into-opposite experiences of "socialism" and "communism" in the 20th century, the *meaning* of 21st socialism cannot be left as an unexamined category. We will return to these questions in the final section of this chapter, and more fully in the concluding chapters of this study. We can begin probing 21st century socialism through the lens of Venezuela's revolutionary process, focusing on the challenges posed by three crucial factors:

(1) A crucial capitalist commodity—oil—is at the center of the Chavez project of building 21st century socialism in Venezuela: This is both an important resource—the country's oil wealth is being invested in important social programs—and the gravest danger/contradiction for such a project. How can one move beyond capital when the Venezuelan economy is so fully dependent on this commodity?

(2) Venezuela faces only the *partial* presence of two crucial social subjects for its revolutionary process due to the oil-distorted economy of the last half of the 20th century: (a) The substantial oil revenues meant that it was cheaper to import food than to support and develop a peasantry/farm worker base. The peasantry was pushed off the land and into the cities. No substantial group of farm workers/peasants survived to provide food security. (b) What was true with food was also the case with manufactured goods. There was no substantial development of a Venezuelan working class, as manufactured goods and industrial production had no priority in the economy. It was cheaper to import goods than develop a

manufacturing base. Thus, there is a lack of a substantial proletariat. How to construct socialism in face of the lack of a substantial proletarian and peasant base? Who are the subjects of revolutionary social transformation in Venezuela today?

(3) A structure of class society—the state and its leader, not to mention a bureaucracy—stood at the head of this project. Does this open the door to uprooting social transformation, or only lead to statism/state-capitalism? A fierce debate raged on this question within Venezuela. As we focus on these three factors we need to keep in mind two crucial points of departure in looking at Venezuela today:

- *There are masses in motion,* perhaps not proletarian and peasant in the classical sense, but crucial to Venezuela's present moment. Time and again they have demonstrated their desire to defend and participate in the process of social transformation, to resist living under neoliberal, free-market manacles, to move beyond present-day capitalism in Venezuela and toward an emancipatory human future.
- *There is the power of revolutionary ideas to draw upon,* and thus the urgent need for a deepening and concretizing of emancipatory ideas in facing the contradictory reality that is Venezuela today.

These two *subjectivities*—revolutionary human subjects and emancipatory ideas: the power of negation—are profoundly interrelated. In Marx's words, "It is not enough for thought to strive for realization, reality must itself strive toward thought. ... Theory becomes a material force when it seizes the masses." (Marx. 1843. *Contribution to the Critique of Hegel's Philosophy of Law: Introduction.*) These two subjectivities are central to our entire text.

A *Oil as Commodity*

At the present moment there can be no doubt about Venezuela's reliance on oil. As opposed to the difficult conditions of economic underdevelopment faced, for instance, by Cuba and Nicaragua in their revolutionary processes, Venezuela's possession of *the* capitalist commodity of the 20th-21st century has meant a certain breathing space for its revolutionary process. In the period since Chavez was first elected there have been important steps in taking control of oil by the Chavez government from the state oil company's "private use" of its revenues, much of it outside the country in purchase of gas stations, etc. Chavez, particularly after the oil sabotage strike, was able to take control of the oil revenues, and to focus on a redistribution of the money toward a vast array of social programs. There was an important shift of the oil profits toward the Venezuelan poor.

However, a redistribution of wealth by itself is not the building of socialism. At most, it can open up the door for more fundamental social changes. Furthermore, as we noted earlier, Venezuela's capitalist-imposed 50+ years' reliance on oil has stunted the development of the very proletarian and peasant forces that could catalyze the needed social transformation toward socialism. If, at one and the same time, oil as commodity has historically distorted the development of crucial class forces, and presently is allowing a *temporary* moment free from direct imperialist economic control, then how can Venezuela move forward to building a socialist society? One claim is that it needs to be done through the intervention of a "progressive state"—changing Venezuela by taking power.

B *The Venezuelan State*

Debates have raged about the nature and role of the state in Venezuela as well as globally. Against the concept of *Change the World Without Talking Power* (Holloway, 2002) comes *Changing Venezuela by Taking Power.* (Wilpert, 2007) These are not alone titles of books, but different concepts of social transformation.

We need to keep in mind another difference of Venezuela from the social process of Cuba (1959) and to some extent Nicaragua (1979). The Cuban revolution destroyed the old state power and uprooted its private capitalist economic base. Nicaragua's revolution overthrew the political power of the Samozas even if it did not significantly uproot the economic base. Venezuela's change was not an armed destruction of the old state, but began with a change of leadership through an election. The process then turned to writing a new Constitution in attempting to transform the state through changing the law rather than through arms. Here, we will not rehearse the activities to write and implement the new constitution. Rather, we are asking what is the nature of the Venezuela state today, particularly in relation to its attempt to initiate economic transformation?

To tackle this question we need first to return to Marx, and his *Critique of the Gotha Program* (1875). There, Marx took up the Lassallean proposal for the establishment of cooperatives with state aid as the manner for building socialism in Germany in the 1870s. In quoting from the Gotha Program—

> The German Workers' party, in order *to pave the way to the solution of the social question,* demands the establishment of producers' co-operative societies *with state aid under the democratic control of the toiling people.* The producers' co-operative societies *are to be called into being* for industry and agriculture on such a scale *that the socialist organization of the total labor will arise from them.*

—Marx gave a scathing critique:

> Instead of arising from the revolutionary process of transformation of society, the "socialist organization of the total labor" "arises" from the "state aid" that the state gives to the producers' co-operative societies and which the *state*, not the workers, "calls into being." It is worthy of Lassalle's imagination that with state loans one can build a new society just as well as a new railway!

Marx was clear: It is not the state aid from above but the revolutionary process of transformation of society from below that is the determinate. It is not the state but the workers, who seize the initiative to form producers' co-operatives.

There is of course no one-to-one relationship between the Prussian state of 1875 and the Venezuelan state in the first decade of the 21st century. In the last decade, Venezuela has undergone important social changes, involving mass participation, and not alone a prescriptive program. However, Marx's sharp warning of where social transformation originates and the human forces who carry forth such transformation, does speak to the debates occurring in Venezuela in relation to changes originating from below (*desde abajo*) via the masses, and those initiated from above (*desde ariba*), from a state and its leader. Of course it is not a question of either/or, but the relationship between the movement from below and "its state," and whether, or how, a state could become or even be the masses' state. Can one have an ongoing revolutionary process that is both *desde abajo* and *desde ariba*? What would that look like? What emancipatory ideas would allow such a process to be fruitful?

Much of the initiative to form producer's co-operatives, to have co-management in enterprises, has come from the state. The question remains: To what extent are Venezuelan workers taking the new forms of organization into their own hands, putting their own stamp of ideas and action upon them?

What is clear is that state initiative alone cannot be the answer. We need to focus on the activities and thought of the masses, Venezuela's social subjects. How are they faring in this new Venezuelan state? What organizational forms are there for these social subjects to express and carry out their will?

C *Venezuela's Social Subjects—Proletarian? Peasant? The Mass of Urban Poor? Venezuela's Organizational Forms for Social Transformation—Unions? Community Councils? The Party?*

How does one construct socialism without a strong proletarian and peasant base? The attempt to construct socialism initially focused on redistribution. But if the concentration is on a radical redistribution rather than an uprooting of social relations of production, is there really socialist construction? And if one wants to transform production, how does one develop a proletarian and peasant base to do so?

1 The Proletariat

How will the working class, the Venezuela masses, assert their control over the state, and society? Through the party? Through workers' co-operatives? Through the state-owned factories? Through the unions?

As we noted earlier, an oil-dependent economy has meant the lack of a significant proletarian base. And yet without a significant worker input into questions of production, into changing the very nature of work, it is illusionary to believe one is constructing socialism. One way the Venezuelan state has sought to build a new proletarian base is through the establishment of co-operatives. In an almost hot-house fashion, Venezuela has seen the establishment of 100,000 plus co-operatives in the last decade. However, this raises many questions. Among them: How many were instituted from above rather than from below? Are co-operatives—operating in a capitalist environment, and thus seeking to turn a profit, with the workers' salaries and possible bonuses dependent on how they produce (speed-up?, overtime?), and finding a market—building socialism in the 21st Century? Or do they turn workers into seekers of profit for their individual enterprise?

One observer-participant in the Venezuela events, Michael Lebowitz, warned that focusing upon the self-interest of the workers in individual enterprises is not the same thing as focusing on the interest of the working class as a whole. Even a focus on the working class as a whole has to be with recognition that this needs to encompass the mass of Venezuelan poor, working and unemployed. Indeed, the majority of workers in Venezuela are non-wage workers, most trapped in the informal economy. How can production be seen as production for the needs of communities?

Another form of work involves state-owned enterprises. There seems to be recognition in Venezuela that state-owned enterprises without worker input in their management is only the state-capitalist form of capitalism. However, what form and what amount of direct workers' control remains a hotly-debated topic. The slogan that came forth by the May Day demonstrations of 2005 stated, "Without co-management there is no revolution!" However, the meaning of co-management is quite unsettled. Some Venezuelan anarchists have argued that when you look at some state-owned factories—the Alcasa aluminum factory and Invepal, a paper factory—co-management is a myth. They argue that the workers in these plants have not really had genuine control of their workplaces. And that working conditions are not significantly different than earlier. (*El Libertario*, Venezuela, October 2007).

Another view is put forth by Alcides Rivero, a spokesperson for the Alcasa factory. He spoke of high worker participation in the elections setting up co-management, but as well critiqued the unions within the plant, who "have a monetarist view," and are having very polarizing fights among themselves. He spoke of the "culture" within the workplace: "Every workplace has its own culture. In ALCASA there was a culture where workers only worked to get money, and didn't have a vision of creating a new society." (Quoted in "Without Workers Management There Can Be No Socialism" report by Kiraz Janicke, Oct. 30, 2007). Perhaps we can see these differing views as a small slice of a rather large debate taking place in Venezuela today.

When one looks at what organizational forms the workers have for expressing their will, the question of the unions comes to the fore. Before Chavez, the union leadership supported the neo-liberal governments of the 1980s and 1990s. The Confederation of Venezuelan Workers (CTV) supported Democratic Action (AD), the social democratic party. The election of Chavez meant the emergence of a new layer of union activists. New laws enabled workers to have referendums at the workplace. The CTV leadership collaborated with the right-wing anti-government protests and participated in the coup attempt of April 2002. At first, pro-revolution unions stayed within the CTV umbrella. But with the management strike that began in December of 2002, in which an attempt was made to shut down the state oil company as well as a shutdown of factories, workers moved to take control of their factories and to help break the bosses' strike. This resulted in a definitive break with the CTV and the formation of a new labor federation—the National Union of Workers (UNT)—beginning in April 2003.

The UNT quickly outdistanced the CTV is obtaining collective bargaining agreements. It should be remember that only about 20% of the formal workforce is organized, and that some 47% of Venezuela's workers are presently in the informal sector. At its highest point in the May Day 2005 march, some one million participated under slogans such as "co-management is revolution" and "Venezuelan workers are building Bolivarian Socialism."

But the next three years left a deeply fragmented labor movement. There are a number of factions inside the UNT, and at least one union current chose to remain outside of that federation. The UNT's attitude toward the vast informal sector of the economy has at best been ambiguous, with little or no effort at organizing this group. The union movement and the vast numbers of Venezuela's poor, who have, in significant ways, been a catalyst of the Bolivarian revolution, seem to inhabit two different worlds. Lebowitz speaks of an "aristocracy of labor," particularly in the fact that the union movement is not organizing the informal sector.

What is the relationship to the unions to the United Socialist Party of Venezuela (PSUV)? Most of the union currents decided to join the party. When we ask, "How will workers exert control over the economy and the state?" the answer is conflictive, partial and contradictory. First, it appears that significant parts of the union movement do not have such a question on their agenda. The leadership narrows the view to only traditional trade union demands centering on wages, and does not leave a space for their members to pose wider questions.

Second, when workers try to assert themselves vs. the state in terms of co-management/workers' control, they find themselves in sharp conflict with a state bureaucracy. Thus at the state-owned CADAFE electricity company:

> After a long struggle, winning the right to workers participation in their collective contract, and establishing workers committees to make it a reality, management moved to crush any real participation, limiting it to decisions over what Christmas decorations would fill the halls of administration offices.
>
> JANICKE and FUENTES, 2008

This question of conflict with the state bureaucracy is not an isolated question, but is found in many work situations. The state bureaucracy and how to overcome it—including this "Bolivarian Revolution State"—is a crucial question not alone for labor but for society as a whole. Thus, even when the state with its new Constitution is supposed to represent and carry out the Bolivarian Revolution, only the action and demands of Venezuela's masses can break a stranglehold of bureaucracy hiding under "revolutionary" verbiage.

An important manifestation of the conflict involving the workers, the unions and the state were the events that transpired at the SIDOR steel plant. The nationalized plant had been privatized in 1997, prior to the election of the Chavez government. After a workers' struggle, the plant was renationalized in April 2008.

> After more than a year of struggle for a collective contract the SIDOR workers found themselves in a situation of open confrontation not only against management but also with the policies of the local 'Chavista' governor, Francisco Rangel Gomez, and the labor minister [Jose Ramon Rivera, a member of one union current] who tried to impose a referendum on the company's final pay offer. At one point the workers were brutally repressed with teargas and rubber bullets by the National Guard and the local police.

> The labor minister also slandered the SIDOR workers, claiming they were "counter-revolutionary" and falsely alleged they had supported the boss's lockout of Dec 2002, when in fact, they had heroically seized control of the plant to help break it. Chavez eventually overrode Rivera and sent in Vice-President Ramon Carrizalez to settle the dispute and announced on April 9 the government's decision to nationalize the plant.
>
> ... One important question will be what happens in SIDOR: Will the creative spirit of the SIDOR workers in struggle be unleashed through active participation in the running of the company, or will they be relegated back to simply fighting for a better collective contract, like the electricity workers before them?
>
> "VENEZUELA'S LABOR MOVEMENT AT THE CROSSROADS"

In SIDOR we can see both the power of the workers and the deep obstacles to workers' power that characterize Venezuela today.

2 The Peasantry

As we noted above, Venezuela's oil addicted commodity has led to a deformed economy that is highly urbanized. Only an estimated 12% of the population is rural, with agriculture economic activity in 1999 accounting for just 6.1% of GDP, the lowest in all of Latin America. "Venezuela is Latin America's only net importer of agricultural products" (Wilpert, 2007: 110). Some 75% of Venezuela's food is imported. Can this extreme imbalance in food production, and lack of food security, be overcome?

A campaign of "Vuelta al Campo," (Return to the Countryside) under the Law on Land and Agricultural Development began in November 2001, two years after Chavez was elected. Before, it is estimated that 5% of the people owned 80% of the private land. Redistribution of land began with state-owned land, not private land. Overall, the government has taken over several million acres of land and has resettled tens of thousands of landless peasants, primarily on state lands. Only since 2005 has some underutilized private land (*latifundias*) been appropriated. State-financed cooperatives have been formed, a number of "communal towns" have been started. Cattle ranches and farms have been appropriated by peasant collectives. Lands taken over by the state have been settled by landless poor peasants and unemployed from the cities. A National Land Institute (INTI) was set up, and in 2003 Plan Zamora was set up to help peasants on the land, including marketing.

In Urachiche, peasant squatters arrived with machetes and arms, surrounded a sugarcane field, burned and occupied the land. They established Fundo Bella Vista, a farming community on the outskirts of Urachiche. They have planted crops like manioc, corn and beans to replace the sugarcane. (See "Clash of Hope and Fear as Venezuela Seizes Land," *New York Times*, May 17, 2007).

How much of the land reform in the country-side is a top down state initiative, and how much involves peasant decision making from below? Where are the *campesinos* own organizations? In July 2005, some 6,000 *campesino* members of the National Agrarian Coordinator Ezequiel Zamora (CANEZ) (named after a 19th century peasant leader) marched in Caracas, demanding an end to the assassination of activists in the land reform movement by *sicarios*, hired killers.

A report from the first national congress of the National Campesino Front Ezequiel Zamora, (F.N.C.E.Z.), held in September 2005, indicated that many *campesinos* felt frustrated with agricultural reform. They were having difficulties forming cooperatives and felt there was neither adequate training nor political education. (See Federico Fuentes "Venezuela: Land Reform Battle Deepens" *Green Left Weekly*, October 12, 2005). Fuentes' article concludes:

> Numerous *campesinos* and cooperative members at the F.N.C.E.Z. congress denounced problems they have had with some of the state institutions. One story was that of Carlos Perez. He spoke on behalf of 1,527 graduates of Mission Vuelvan Caras, who had formed themselves into 36 cooperatives, of which 21 were agricultural cooperatives. Six months after doing so, they still had no decent land to work on and were unable to get any loans for technical equipment because of this lack of land.
>
> The Sept. 24 *Diario Vea* quoted Minister for Popular Economy Elias Jaua as saying: "By the end of this month, 2140 cooperatives will still be waiting for land in order to commence productive activities."

The question isn't whether there are difficulties and contradictions within the land reform movement. Certainly this is to be expected. The question is how will they be resolved? Can peasant voices and organization from below have a real influence? Will the tension between state institutions and peasant demands yield a more radical, thorough-going reform? What is the role of the state, of a developing *campesino* movement in doing so? And crucially: Is it possible for Venezuela to move toward greater food self-sufficiency, to the growth of a *campesino* dimension, in its oil dominated market-economy?

3 The Urban Masses

Ninety-percent of Venezuelans live in urban areas, the majority in poverty. If the country has an underdeveloped working class due to its oil economy, it also has a vast population of unemployed and those working in the informal economy. How does this massive urban population assert itself within the Bolivarian Project? What organizational form does their participation take? Within the short history since Chavez's first election there have been a number of organizational forms:

- Bolivarian Circles, were neighborhood councils of discussion and action, linked to and supportive of the government.
- Another experiment in popular organizing, established in the period leading up to the Venezuelan opposition's push for a recall referendum against Chavez in 2004, were the Units of Electoral Battle (UBEs) and the Urban Land Committees (CTUs).
- Local Public Planning Councils were also formed. They were composed of urban citizens, politicians and government bureaucrats who were supposed to work together at the city level to address specific problems.

These vehicles for popular mobilization and participation flourished to varying degrees in the early years, as the Bolivarian revolution developed. Later, there were intensive organizational activities in relation to the vote on the new Constitution, to a new presidential election, to a recall election, and finally, in relation to the closely defeated Constitutional initiatives.

These various organizational forms aimed at greater citizen participation. However, the initiative has often been from the government more than from the Venezuelan masses. In some ways it stands apart from the revolutionary process that began under the whip of the counter-revolution in the form of the attempted coup and the bosses' oil-strike. Responding to those attempts to overthrow the government is what brought forth mass urban participation, a defense of the revolution, on an unprecedented scale. The hundreds of thousands of Venezuela's poor who poured into the streets demanding Chavez's release, together with military units that remained loyal, halted the coup. This mass protest began to deepen what had been a nationalist/populist movement into one that has taken steps along a more radical path. In a country where much of the direction and stimulus for action had been coming from above (*desde ariba*) through the initiative of Chavez and his government, the possibilities of catalyzing the process from below (*desde abajo*) opened. The activities and ideas of Venezuela's masses—proletarian, unemployed, youth, women, Indigenous, *campasino*—have at times been together with, and at other times, in tension with and in contradiction to what has been happening from above.

The various organizational forms post the anti-coup mass urban outpouring, need to be examined and critiqued in relation to their authenticity in giving expression to, developing the movement *desde abajo,* as opposed to a bureaucratic channeling and control of it.

Two important organizational forms that involve the urban masses (not to the exclusion of the rural population) are the communal councils (*Consejos Comunales*), and the formation of Chavez's political party, the United Socialist Party of Venezuela (*PSUV*).

a *Consejos Comunales*

The *Consejos Comunales* (*cc*) are citizen assemblies on a much smaller scale than local public planning councils:

> By 2005 most of the Local Public Planning Councils had become mired in bureaucracy and dominated by politicians [thus] paving the way for communal councils. These new councils are organized at a much more local level, usually a few blocks.
>
> "COMMUNAL COUNCILS IN VENEZUELA: CAN 200 FAMILIES REVOLUTIONIZE DEMOCRACY?" JOSH LERNER, *Z Magazine*, March 6, 2007

The CCs are supposed to consist of from 200 to 400 families in urban areas and closer to 20 families in rural areas. They were set up to break the power of governors and local authorities, providing a direct relation between the state and the population. The councils apply directly to the government for financial support of local projects. Thousands of grants have been awarded for community improvement projects. Originally up to $14,000 per project. Chavez called for a "revolutionary explosion of communal power," and there certainly has been that:

> Eight months after the law was passed, over 16,000 councils had already formed throughout the country—12,000 of them had received funding for community projects. That's $1 billion total, out of a national budget of $53 billion. The councils had established nearly 300 communal banks, which have received $70 million for micro-loans. The government plans to transfer another $4 billion in 2007." (Can 200 families...)

The state provides funding for a wide range of projects: street paving, sewage and water systems, medical centers. Decisions are made at a local level, bypassing some bureaucracies. The idea is for the community councils to replace the decision making of governors and mayors. At the same time however, such an arrangement augments the development of a centralized state as the final decision maker. The local councils do involve important mass participation, but in *local* projects, *local* decision-making. Direct mass participation in the fundamental development of the economy and the state on a national level is not at hand. Lower level bureaucracies at the state and municipal level may be avoided, but a centralized state, not *consejos comunales,* holds the ultimate decision-making power.

This is not to dismiss the participation of tens of thousands of Venezuelans in this important mass organizational form. Their participation is authentic and has concrete ramifications in their communities and lives. Questions of proper sewage disposal, clean water, and medical centers are not minor matters. Rather, it is to note the parallel increase in the power of a centralized state, and thus not to have illusions that this transforms the direction of the economy or marks a shift in state control.

b *The United Socialist Party of Venezuela: Will the Masses Authentically Have It as Their Own?*

In December 2006, Chavez called for the founding and building of the United Socialist Party of Venezuela (*psuv*). Between April and June, 2007, some 5.7 million people registered to be part of the party. Twelve thousand local battalions (branches) were formed mostly on a geographic basis, with seven to fourteen battalions coming together in socialist circumscriptions (districts). The battalions met on week-ends the second half of 2007 to discuss and debate party structure and program. Radical political groups and trade unions joined. Intellectuals, Indigenous groups, students and others participated. Other political parties dissolved and joined, becoming factions within.

From January to March, 2008, a founding congress was held with 1,600 delegates, (selected from the socialist circumscriptions), who approved a program and declaration of principles. At the same time Chavez was not only elected president of the party, but given the power to appoint five vice-presidents.

Following the Congress, when it came to voting for the election of a national directorate, neither the five million who registered for the party, or the close to a million who participated in the local battalions could vote. Rather, 90,000 spokespeople were selected to elect the 15-person national directorate, as well as 15 alternative delegates. In the end, Chavez consolidated the leadership by proceeding to appoint a total of nine territorial vice-presidents and seven national commissions for the new party.

Thus one ended up with a party that elicited the participation of a million or more, but at the same time, a top-down appointment of the vast majority of the leadership. Is this an authentic elicitation and expression of mass participation, or a channelizing of hopes and desires in narrow political ways? The question remains open.

•

The Venezuela revolutionary process has thrown up a rich variety of organizations. One cannot say *a priori* which one or ones can become full pathways for social development. There is no reason to think there is only *one* organizational form anymore then there needs to be only a single-party form for this process.

The crucial question is not so much which particular form or forms will speak to or manifest the historic moment. Rather, the question becomes what philosophic-theoretical developments, (an emancipatory view), can in a concrete way, help release the creativity of the masses in its chosen organizational expression(s)?

V The Venezuelan Debate on 21st Century Socialism: Relation of Party and Mass Movement; What Kind of Party? What Kind of Leadership? The Role of the Intellectual: Excerpts from Forum on "Intellectuals, Socialism and Democracy"

There is not a lack of debate in Venezuela on the possibilities and direction of socialism. Far from it. It is not alone Chavez who put forth a concept of socialism for the 21st century. Many intellectuals within Venezuela as well as Left intellectuals from other countries have taken part in ongoing discussion and debate on this concept. A forum was held at the Centro Internacional Miranda, June 2009, with the theme "Intellectuals, Democracy & Socialism." We can look briefly at some of that discussion:

(http://venezuelanalysis.com/analysis/4539; http://venezuelanalysis.com/analysis/4610)

The debate covered several important topics: the relationship of party and mass movement; what kind of party is needed; leadership as collective and as hyper leader; bureaucratization, the role of intellectuals.

Vladimir Acosta, a professor of sociology at the Central University of Venezuela, spoke of several weaknesses in Venezuela today: (1) the lack of a clear political program; (2) the lack of a collective leadership arising alongside Hugo Chavez; (3) the absence of a revolutionary party. He asked why there should not be more than one revolutionary party as a way of fighting against bureaucratization. After speaking of important achievements of the Venezuela social process that have allowing financing of important social projects he noted that "these achievements [were] obtained without having touched a single hair of the bourgeoisie, without having touched a single hair of the dominant class. . . . The fact is that the bourgeoisie continues in control here." He argued that there was

> a lack of ideological training, of education, and cadres. There's a weakness in generating a constructive vision, constructing, step by step, this Socialism of the 21st Century, on the basis of understanding that this implies a real revolution in the minds of each and every one of us. Including those of us who believe we are really revolutionary, and who sometimes forget that we also have some of this rubbish in our heads.

There was "the lack of popular revolutionary organizations":

> We have a serious problem: that our revolutionary process does not have a truly independent, class conscious and organized workers movement. And the attempts to organize one have ended up bringing the workers movement closer to the policy of the state, which should not always be the policy that the workers movement should take because the workers movement has to go much further beyond this.
>
> Nor do we have a peasant movement that is sufficiently strong and a student movement; we have been trying to build one but it also is not sufficiently strong. These are great weaknesses of our process, because you cannot build socialism without workers, without peasants, without well-organized popular sectors that can push towards more radical situations or positions.

In the ongoing discussion and debate at the forum, Juan Carlos Monedero, who divides his time between Spain and Venezuela and one of the founders of the Centro Internacional Miranda, continued on the question of leadership:

> The first spectrum is hyper-leadership... it has the advantage of articulating the unstructured and uniting the fragments, in a way that Gramsci called 'progressive Caesar-ism,' that helps us to retake the path of the revolution in moments of political vacuum or of ideological confusion.
>
> But this leadership also comes with problems. Hyper-leadership ultimately deactivates a popular participation that trusts too much in the heroic abilities of the leadership.

Roberto Lopez, a longtime militant, noted:

> [T]he need to construct a collective leadership of the revolutionary process is undeniable, the necessity of a rectification of President Chavez himself, who should allow the construction of this collective leadership, who should allow a type of vanguard. I don't see this possibility in the current leadership of the [United Socialist Party] PSUV, because there are

> personalities in the PSUV who weren't even elected and, however, are vice-presidents of the party. They were co-opted by President Chavez himself despite the fact that the bases of the PSUV didn't vote for them.

Javier Biardeau, a radical sociologist and frequent commentator:

> Chavez has taken up political space and if he continues doing this he's going to generate problems: One of the observations that has been made from the beginning is the theme of hyper-leadership. Others have called it progressive Bonaparte-ism, others Caesar-ism with the positivist reading by Vallenilla Lanz about democratic Caesar-ism. I think it's a big mistake. What Gramsci said is basically that in moments in which a collective political leadership structure isn't well established, a big political personality takes, under the weight, the dialectics of the revolution or the dialectics of the restoration. And I think that Chavez has occupied a political vacuum, an important political vacuum that if he continues to occupy, he can create knives for the very throat of the Bolivarian revolution.
>
> For the tasks, for the functions, for the advance of the Bolivarian Revolution a political structure is required, we're going to call it an intellectual collective. It doesn't require intellectual individuals, it requires critical thinking and it requires a recuperation of the vehicle between socialism and democracy that the right has constantly tried to obscure, creating a dilemma in which socialism is totalitarianism and representative democracy is precisely the end of history and the last path that remains for us.

Santiago Arconada, an activist who works on water problems, spoke on the relationship between political organization and grassroots social organizations:

> I think there is currently a risk that the PSUV will crush the forms of organization at the base, which have to exist independently. I'm convinced that political organization can't orchestrate nor colonize the grass roots organizations. The grassroots social organizations have the right to count on all the diversity possible and they can't be pigeonholed.
>
> The appropriate relationship between political organization and the grassroots organizations constitutes a problem that we have yet to confront. This would be one of the rectifications, in my opinion, that is most necessary right now.

Michael Lebowitz, a Canadian Marxist writer who serves as an advisor in Venezuela, spoke on the role of the intellectual:

> The party should guarantee spaces for intellectuals: Once, someone asked Victor Serge if the seeds of Stalin were present in Lenin. Serge responded, 'There were a lot of seeds in Lenin.' I believe that the responsibility of the intellectual revolutionary is to take care of the revolutionary seeds—and to do it anywhere possible. It is to communicate the vision of socialism of the twenty first century to the masses because, as we know, ideas become a concrete force when they grab the minds of the masses. The responsibility [of the intellectual] also consists in trying to convince the leadership of the process of these ideas and visions.
>
> If the party really wants to advance the process of construction of twenty-first century socialism, it should guarantee space where revolutionary intellectuals can fulfill their revolutionary commitment. To not offer this space and to not encourage the caring of the revolutionary seeds is to allow the weeds to grow.

Gonzalo Gomez, a co-founder of the Venezuelan internet journal *Aporrea* ("Popular Communication for the Construction of 21st Century Socialism") and a member of the Regional Political Committee of the PSUV spoke of the problems of the Party:

> I was at the founding conference [of the PSUV]. A good part of the leadership did not participate in the founding conference as such, and there we voted on some principles and on a program that isn't referred to and that doesn't guide politics with its orientation. Politics is being characterized essentially by electoralism. It's an appendage to public management and removed from the concrete struggles of the popular sectors, and this needs to be resolved.
>
> It has to do with problems of [ideological] formation and it has to do with problems of composition, including [the PSUV] leadership. This is a party where the government bureaucracy dominates in an exaggerated way... but there's very little impact on the workers movement and on workers and their organizations, which is starting to reverse with the creation of the fronts. There's no working class in the leadership of the party, there are no rural worker leaders in the leadership of the party. There is a government bureaucratic sector that monopolizes the management and therefore the process of the social movements, its aspirations, its worries,

its struggles, can't be reflected how they should be reflected. If this party doesn't change, it could be difficult to be on top of the challenge of the revolutionary process.

Luis Britto, a Venezuelan writer, also spoke of the relation of social organization and the political party:

> With the nominations of candidates, the criteria of the grassroots aren't respected. In many cases it's said that there is no consultation at the base that little by little in some places a political class has been crowding out what should be the work of popular representation. Apparently, in many cases, candidacies have been lost because there was one candidate that had been elected by the bases and another was imposed, who hadn't enjoyed the support of the bases, so that the revolutionaries were divided in the electoral process and for that important points were lost.
>
> They say to the social organizations, organize yourself, meet, unite, and later when they do that, they aren't given any kind of role, their postulations are rejected, they aren't paid attention to, etc. etc.

VI Is There a Missing Ingredient in Venezuela Today?

> Yet the revolutionary situation did not develop into a full revolution. And while the counter-revolution is mobilizing both visibly and clandestinely, the revolutionary forces are in disarray, not because they were defeated, but because they lacked the unifying cement of a philosophy of revolution. It is no accident that it was in East Europe, precisely because their struggle was *directly against* Communism in power, that this was expressed most clearly by Danilo Pejovic in [Eric Fromn's] *Socialist Humanism*: "'Philosophy and Revolution' is only another way of expressing Marx's well-known catch phrase about the 'realization of philosophy,' beginning as a revolution in philosophy in order to end as a revolutionary philosophy in the form of the philosophy of the revolution." *This is the missing ingredient in France today.*
>
> DUNAYEVSKAYA, "On France 1968"

The crucial question is not a lack of debate in Venezuela. The difficulty lies in the parameters of the debate. On the one hand it is situated in concrete questions and problems of the present moment, as it should be. But on the other hand, these questions are seen in isolation—"leadership," "bureaucracy," "grassroots social movements and the party"—without linking them to the construction of, or being rooted in, an emancipatory philosophic vision. The debate appears unmoored, rather than related to the meaning of constructing socialism in the 21st century. It lacks a rudder of dialectical philosophy. Philosophy not as an abstraction—there is no need to genuflect before the dialectic in general. Rather, there is the need to work out *concrete universals*. And for that a dialectical framework in needed. "Leadership" is not alone the question of a single leader verses a collective leadership, not alone the question of *desde abajo* (from below) verses *desde ariba* (from above). But *what ideas, what philosophy* is the foundation of leadership? What is at stake here is the needed philosophic preparation so that the social process in Venezuela becomes revolutionary social transformation. Philosophy cannot by itself make a social transformation. However, Marx's *"'realization of philosophy,' beginning as a revolution in philosophy in order to end in the form of the philosophy of the revolution."*—seems to be a missing dimension within the Venezuelan debates.

If there are not live human beings working out the dialectic of philosophy in an emancipatory social process, then can there be the full development of the masses own organizations—be it mass party, unions, peasant organization or mass urban community organizations? Can there be a dialectic in revolutionary organization without the revolutionary dialectic in philosophy expressing itself in organizational form?

There is as urgent a need to work out the dialectic in philosophy as there is the need to create new organization forms. Such new organizational forms cannot fully manifest themselves without rooting themselves in revolutionary philosophy. Otherwise, we are going to lose ourselves in the small coin of the particular, and not in concrete universals that form the basis of a new society. Are there revolutionary intellectuals who see this as their responsibility, as an urgent, needed task within the Venezuelan revolutionary process? The *praxis* of the masses and the *praxis* of revolutionary intellectuals are not in two separate worlds. But they are not automatically joined. Only sustained theoretical and practical labor forges their unity.

We simply cannot allow these questions be reduced to the proper form of the movement from below or a new manifestation of the proper form of the party from above—and thus think we are grappling with the problem. No, dialectical philosophy is not the luxury of a summary *post-festum*. It is the urgent need of the dawn, of the now—the moments of preparation and execution as they unfold. The task of *doing* dialectical philosophy is an action.

Who sees *this* praxis as necessary and crucial to the praxis of the masses? Who sees dialectical thought as related to the forms and content of revolutionary organization?

As I wrote earlier in the chapter, "*There is the power of revolutionary ideas to draw upon,* and thus the urgent need for a deepening and concretizing of them in facing the contradictory reality Venezuela today." We will return to this problem in the concluding part of this book.

CHAPTER 6

Mexico's Revolutionary Forms of Organization: The Zapatistas and the Indigenous Autonomous Communities in Resistance*

> There is another element… the force from below. And its rebellion is in organization… It speaks of a feeling or a rebel subjectivity.
>
> MARCOS, interview in *Rebeldía* magazine, May 20, 2006

1 Indigenous and Zapatista Organizational Praxis—The Building of Autonomy in Rebel Lands

As inspiring as has been the Zapatista Rebellion for Mexico as a whole, as well as for social movements and activists internationally, its deepest impact has occurred within Indigenous communities aligned with the Zapatistas in Chiapas. Despite the fact that President Zedillo refused to implement the San Andrés Accords on Indigenous rights negotiated in 1994, and the Congress passed a measure subverting their meaning, for the rebel Zapatista Autonomous Municipalities they remained very much alive. Their implementation over the past decade has been the difficult, creative labor of the autonomous communities in resistance together with the EZLN (*Ejército Zapatista de Liberación Nacional,* Zapatista Army of National Liberation).

A *December 21, 2012: A New Revolutionary Moment of the Zapatistas—Focusing on Practice, Developing Theory—Living Praxis*

A crucial manifestation of their creative labor has been the outpouring of forty-thousand plus Zapatistas (*Tzeltales, Tzotziles, Tojolobales, Choles, Zoques,* and *Mames*) on December 21, 2012, (in the Mayan calendar the beginning of the *13th Baktun*), in five municipalizes of Chiapas: San Cristóbal de las Casas, Ocosingo, Altamirano, Las Margaritas and Palenque. This was followed by a powerful series of communications, December-March, 2012–2013, from Subcomandante Marcos and new Subcomandante Moisés, a *Tzeltal* Zapatista. (See

---

* For my discussion of the first years of the Zapatista Rebellion and the beginning development of autonomous communities in resistance see Gogol 2002, chapter 11. See also chapter 13 of the present study, "The Zapatistas and the Dialectic."

Enlace Zapatista, http://enlacezapatista.ezln.org.mx/ for the texts in Spanish and English), As well, there has been the production of a series of "textbooks" on the Zapatista way of working and living featuring the voices of the Indigenous communities which are being used in schools for adherents to the Sixth Declaration of the Lacandón Jungle.

The massive march followed by the communiques was a manifestation of the unity of practice and theory that characterize the Zapatista work. There was not a separation of their action and their thought. The first communication on the day of the march read:

> Did you listen? It is the sound of your world crumbling. It is the sound of our world resurging. The day that was day, was night. And night shall be the day that will be day. Democracy! Liberty! Justice!

Ten days later, they issued a second communique: "Ours is not a message of resignation. It is not one of war, death, or destruction. Our message is one of struggle and resistance." They continued:

> We, who never went away, despite what media across the spectrum have been determined to make you believe, resurge as the indigenous Zapatistas that we are and will be. In these years, we have significantly strengthened and improved our living conditions. Our standard of living is higher than those of the indigenous communities that support the governments in office, who receive handouts that are squandered on alcohol and useless items. Our homes have improved without damaging nature by imposing on it roads alien to it. In our communities, the earth that was used to fatten the cattle of ranchers and landlords is now used to produce the maize, beans, and the vegetables that brighten our tables. Our work has the double satisfaction of providing us with what we need to live honorably and contributing to the collective growth of our communities. Our sons and daughters go to a school that teaches them their own history, that of their country and that of the world, as well as the sciences and techniques necessary for them to grow without ceasing to be indigenous. Indigenous Zapatista women are not sold as commodities...
>
> Our culture flourishes, not isolated, but enriched through contact with the cultures of other peoples of Mexico and of the world. We govern and govern ourselves, always looking first for agreement before confrontation. We have achieved all of this without the government, the political class, and the media that accompanies them, while simultaneously

> resisting their attacks of all kinds. We have shown, once again, that we are who we are. With our silence, we have made ourselves present.

The majority of the documents came under the title of "Them and Us." The first three were strong critiques of those from above and their lackeys. The fourth "Them and Us" turned to "The Pains of Those Below." [*Los dolores de abajo*] It spoke of the pains not alone in Mexico, but of those from below throughout the world, an internationalism of pain if you will. After mentioning many parts of the world, different kinds of pain felt below, and concretely naming a few of those who have felt such pain, including death, Marcos ended the communication by writing: "... although neither you nor we know it yet, we are part of a 'we' that is even larger and yet to be built." This was followed by a most remarkable document, *Them and Us, Part v.—Sixth*:[1]

> We have ended one phase in the path that we call the Sixth, and... we think that we must now take another step. ... *The Time of the No, the Time of the Yes.*
>
> We defined the "*no*," we still haven't fully delineated the "*yes*." ... This isn't the only thing, as we also need more answers to the "*how*," "*when*," "*with whom*." ... All of you know that it is not our intention to build a great big organization with a central governing body, a centralized command, or a boss, be it individual or a particular group... We think that yes, something is wrong, very wrong. But that if in order to save humanity and the badly damaged house it inhabits someone has to go, then it should be, it must be, those above. And we aren't referring here to banishing those above. We're talking about destroying the social relations that make it possible for someone to be above at the cost of someone else being below.

In these brief passages from the document, (See Appendix 1 to this Chapter where major excerpts are published.) one dimension that comes forth is the Zapatista concept of time. Karl Marx had written, "Time is the space (place) of human development." The Zapatistas have practiced that concept of time for two decades and more. They have refused to let others set their calendar for them. When the federal government betrayed the original Agreements on Indigenous rights negotiated in San Andrés Larráinzar, the Zapatistas with the

---

1 The "Sixth" referred to the Sixth Declaration of the Lacandón Jungle (*La Selva Lacandona.*) For the complete text see Enlace Zapatista. For my discussion of the original 6th Declaration of the Lacandon Jungle see *II. Anti-Capitalist and From the Left: The 6th Declaration and La Otra Campaña* below.

Indigenous communities began their own implementation. In writing the 6th Declaration of the Lacandón Jungle and then launching the Other Campaign (*La Otra Campaña*) at the time of the presidential electoral campaign of 2006, the Zapatistas were insisting on their own time, their own calendar. After that fraudulent election, the EZLN maintained a "silence" toward civil society and the government authorities. As the years passed this silence became "the topic" of rumor, speculation and lies about the Zapatistas.

In fact, the Zapatistas were anything but silent *in their thought and action in relation to the Indigenous communities in resistance in Chiapas.* There, a rich, creative "communication" in the development of those communities independent of the government took place. In health, education, government, a communal manner of work, there were important steps of autonomy and self-development.

In their new series of communications, December 2012-Janaury 2014, the Zapatistas set forth their view of that would be needed in this new moment:

- A sharp attack on those above—the Mexican rulers and exploiters.
- A strong critique and separation from much of the "official" Left, including the parties of the "progressives."
- A separation from those who formerly were part of the movement, but who in recent times had criticized the Zapatistas or remained silent in face of government repression of Zapatista communities and individuals.
- The language of the Zapatistas in these communications is crucial. It is not a language about "civil society," but *class*: those above and those below. The Zapatistas speak very specifically about *those from below*: youth, women, Indigenous people, workers, etc.
- The discourse of the Zapatistas is a focused one. In a number of communications we have the words of women and men living in the Zapatista communities in resistance: their experiences in recent years. The words, the ideas, the experiences of those from below are central to who the Zapatistas are.
- The fact that an Indigenous person, Moisés, is now a *subcomandante* and writing communications is an important development. He is the rector of the Zapatista Little School. (See Appendix 2 of this Chapter for one of his communications.)
- Finally, what we see in the Zapatista Communications is, in my view, the dialectic of action and thought of the Zapatistas. The communication titled 'the Sixth,' in which Marcos develops the concept: "The time of the 'no' and the time of the 'yes'," is key to understanding not only these recent communications of the Zapatistas but illuminates the trajectory of the Zapatistas

from 1994, and indeed the period before the uprising. Thus, the Revolutionary Law of Women, written before the 1994 uprising, is a "no," against sexism and machismo, *and* at the same time a "yes," the right of Indigenous Zapatista women to decide their life, their future.

- In sum, the Zapatistas labor of more than two decades is profoundly dialectical, dialectic as a force of life.

•

To more fully understand this new moment in the Zapatista rebellion for liberty and democracy, we need to trace developments of the last decade. Indigenous communities have had a long tradition of practicing self-organization. What has been new post the January 1994 rebellion, is, first, the Zapatista autonomous Indigenous communities have been practicing self-organization in opposition to the Mexican government at the federal, state, and local levels. Or perhaps better stated—they have created an autonomous practice in face of the *active opposition* of the Mexican government at all levels. Second, these communities are united with the Zapatistas, i.e. they are supporters of the EZLN ideas and actions, (some are active members of the EZLN), and are in turn assisted by the EZLN. Third, the communities began to have the support of "civil society" in Mexico and internationally, what Marcos would designate as the "third shoulder" (See "Reading a Video," Sub Comandante Marcos, August 2004, *La Jornada*, Mexico).

The communities have taken responsibility for what Mexican governments have continually failed to provide in an adequate manner: health care, education, the administration of justice, care of the land. They have been doing so through cooperative decision making, collective action, and communal labor:

- With the help of Mexican civil society and the international community, Indigenous communities in autonomous municipalities have built clinics and pharmacies, trained health workers and carried out campaigns for community health and disease prevention. Where possible, the Zapatista clinics do not charge for consultations or for medicines.
- In relation to education, the autonomous communities "build schools, trained education promoters, and in some cases, even created their own promoters, accompanied by 'civil societies' who know about those subjects In some areas they have managed to see to it that girls—who have been traditionally deprived of access to learning—go to school" (Chiapas: The Thirteenth Stele" part five: A History, Marcos, July 2003). Education is free and education committees work to see that each student has his/her

notebook and pencil available. In mid-2003 the educational effort was principally in the area of primary education. One region developed an autonomous secondary school, graduating both Indigenous men and women. The Rebel Autonomous Zapatista Educational System of National Liberation operating in Los Altos teaches the following themes: humanism, sports, arts, reflection on reality, social sciences, natural sciences, reflections in the mother language, communication, mathematics and production and services to the community.

- Autonomous councils are in charge of administering justice in the communities. It has not been an easy road. A Zapatista report from 2003 indicated the results were erratic, "full of contradictions" between the Autonomous Councils and communities, and "doubt and confusion" in relation to interchanges with non-government human rights organizations, and with "*denuncias*" against Zapatistas. However, what is as well clear is the transparent manner whereby Marcos and the Zapatistas are willing to discuss not only the advances, but the problems with building autonomy in rebel lands. This has been a continual way of functioning on the part of the Zapatistas.

If the key to autonomous development has been the work of the Indigenous communities themselves, at the same time, it has not been done in isolation from civil society and from the EZLN. These relationships have aided the communities, and yet, at the same time, have been the source of difficulties that the Zapatistas have worked to overcome.

In relation to civil society, there was a decision by July 2003 to let the "*Aguascalientes,*"—constructed in different rebel territories in the first years of the rebellion—"die," and a new organizational form, the *Caricoles*, whose heart would be the Councils of Good Government, come into being. This was no mere change of names, but a different manner of functioning—a revealing decision in trying to resolve problems that characterized the relationship of Indigenous communities to civil society.

The *Aguascalientes* had been constructed by the Indigenous communities to build a relationship with civil society: "We wanted a space for dialogue with civil society. And 'dialogue' also means learning to listen to the other and learning to speak with him... spaces for *encuentro* and dialogue with national and international civil society... the place where 'civil society' and Zapatistas met every day."

However, this only happened with difficulty: "I told you that we tried to learn from our *encuentros* with national and international civil society. But we also expected them to learn. The Zapatista movement arose, among other things, in demand of respect. And it so happened that we didn't always receive respect. And it's not that they insulted us. Or at least not intentionally. But for us, pity is an affront, and charity is a slap in the face" (Marcos, "The 13th Stele"). What the communities wanted was political support, not charity.

In terminating the *Aguascalientes*, the Zapatistas "will no longer be receiving leftovers nor allowing the imposition of projects" without consultation. In place of the *Aguascalientes*, a new form of organization and a new level of governing was created in the autonomous regions. The *caracoles* were born in August 2003. The *Juntas de Buen Gobierno* (Councils of Good Government) were at their heart. Five juntas have been set up, one for each of the rebel regions. One or two delegates from each of the autonomous councils of the region were sent to be part of the *juntas*. One job for the *juntas* was to work out a way of coordinating and taking charge of donations and help from civil society nationally and internationally. The communities as a whole wanted to make sure that material and help went to the individual communities that were most in need.

A year after their initiation, the functioning of the Juntas were examined by Marcos in a document, "Reading a Video," published in *La Jornada* in August, 2004. Here again, the Zapatistas publicly presented a self-examination, and a self-critique. Among the points taken up was the fact that the composition of the Good Government Juntas, JBG, changed continually with "rotations" of delegates every eight to fifteen days. "Those who are there then return to their work in autonomous councils, and other authorities come to run the JBG. ... The plan is that the work of the JGBs should be rotated among the members of all the autonomous councils of each region. This is so that the task of governing is not exclusive to one group, so that there are no 'professional' leaders, so that learning is for the greatest number of people, and so that the idea that government can only be carried out by 'special people' is rejected. ... If this is analyzed in depth, it will be seen that it is a process where entire villages are learning to govern. ... We are aware that this method makes it difficult to carry out some projects, but, in return, we have a school of governance that will, in the long run, bear fruit in a new way of doing politics."

Marcos wrote of "two flaws" not yet corrected: the place of women in governing structures, indeed in Indigenous society, and the relationship between the political-military structure (the EZLN) and the autonomous governments:

> One flaw which we have been dragging along with us for some time has to do with the place of women. The participation of women in the work of the organizational management is still small, and it is practically non-existent in the autonomous councils and JGBs.

> While the percentage of female participation in the Clandestine Revolutionary Indigenous Committees is between 33 and 40%, in the autonomous councils and the Good Government Juntas it is less than 1% on average. Women are still being ignored in the naming of *ejidal* commissioners and municipal agents. Government work is still the prerogative of the men. And it's not that we're in favor of the 'empowerment' of women, which is so fashionable up above, but that there are still no spaces for women who are participating in the Zapatista social base to be reflected in government positions.
>
> And not only that. Despite the fact that Zapatista women have had, and have, a fundamental role in the resistance, respect for their rights continues, in some cases, to be just words on paper. Domestic violence has decreased, it is true, but more through the limitations on alcohol consumption than through a new family and gender culture.
>
> It is a shame, but we have to be honest: we still cannot give a good report regarding women, in the creation of conditions for their gender development, in a new culture which acknowledges their capacities and aptitudes that have purportedly belonged exclusively to men.
>
> Even though we are aware that it will take a while, we hope someday to be able to say, with satisfaction, that we have achieved the disruption of at least this aspect of the world.
>
> Only in that way will it all have been worthwhile.

The second flaw was in regard to the relationship of the political-military structure to the autonomous civil government:

> The idea we had originally was that the EZLN should accompany and support the peoples in the building of their autonomy. However accompaniment has sometimes turned into management, advice into orders... and support into a hindrance.
>
> I've already spoken previously about the fact that the hierarchical, pyramid structure is not characteristic of the indigenous communities. The fact that the EZLN is a political-military and clandestine organization still corrupts processes that should and must be democratic.
>
> In some juntas and caracoles the phenomenon has arisen of CCRI [Indigenous Clandestine Revolutionary Committee] *comandantes* making decisions that are not theirs to make and involving themselves in problems with the junta. "Govern obeying" is a tendency that continues to run into those walls which we ourselves have erected.

•

To follow the building of autonomy in rebel lands is to take an important journey. It is not simply the struggle of everyday existence under conditions of harsh poverty in the presence of indifferent and often hostile state and federal government. The decade of practice in autonomous Indigenous communities and Zapatista lands has been the struggle to fuse a developing vision of a different life with the concrete labors to make it real—an emancipatory praxis—even as this takes place in a small, vulnerable area, something the Zapatistas and the autonomous communities realize. The Zapatistas recognized the need to sum-up their experience as ground for a new projection and practice. The 6th Declaration of the *Selva Lacandona*, was the result, as was the Other Campaign (*Otra Campaña*). In June 2005, almost a dozen years after the initial rebellion of 1994, the Zapatistas issued the Sixth Declaration of the Lacandón Jungle. The Sixth was the Zapatistas most crucial document since the early days of the rebellion. It declared their movement to be anti-capitalist and from the Left, and set the stage for *La Otra Campaña*, a Zapatista-initiated project for developing an emancipatory alternative to the corrupt politics of the Mexican state.

II Anti-Capitalist and from the Left: The 6th Declaration and *La Otra Campaña*

> To our way of thinking, and what we see in our heart, we have reached a point where we cannot go any further, and, in addition, it is possible that we could lose everything we have if we remain as we are and do nothing more in order to move forward. The hour has come to take a risk once again and to take a step which is dangerous but which is worth-while. Because, perhaps united with other social sectors who suffer from the same wants as we do, it will be possible to achieve what we need and what we deserve. A new step forward in the indigenous struggle is only possible if the indigenous join together with workers, campesinos, students, teachers, employees... the workers of the city and the countryside.
>
> *Sixth Declaration of the Selva Lacandona*

A *The Sixth*

The 6th Declaration was a retrospective that was at the same time a perspective. It looked back to the origin and development of the *Zapatismo* in Chiapas, analyzed and critiqued the neoliberal manifestation of capitalism globally and within Mexico, and laid out notes for the beginning of an alternative emancipatory project that would be anti-capitalist and from the Left.

In the years immediately prior to the 6th Declaration, the EZLN together with Indigenous communities that were in agreement with them, began to construct an alternative to the Mexican government, which, on both the state and national level, was governing by supporting exploitation, enforcing it with repression, disrespect for the culture of Indigenous peoples, and marginalization through inferior education facilities and lack of basic health care—all within the context of a neoliberal capitalist economic structure.

The Zapatistas never viewed their work as building an alternative Mayan or Indigenous nation. Rather, at each stage of their struggle, they viewed themselves as integral to the Mexican nation. For them, the question was how to build an authentic relation with the whole of Mexico that took into account the rights, the full recognition of Indigenous peoples. If the first negotiations of the San Andrés Accords were made with the hope that "official Mexico" of those in power would listen, negotiation in good faith and carry out the agreements, then, with the rejection of the accords by the government and all the major parties (PRI, PAN *and* PRD) in the National Congress, it became clear to the Zapatistas and the autonomous Indigenous communities that there was no possibility for working out an agreement with "official Mexico." The Zapatistas broke off any relation with that Mexico, deciding to develop their alternative manner of living and governing in Chiapas. The autonomous municipalities and the Councils of Good Government were the result of the years 2001–05.

Breaking with official Mexico did not mean breaking with an "Other Mexico" from below that the Zapatistas saw as suffering from and opposed to official Mexico. It was clear from early on, when the Other Mexico poured out to the streets in the first days after the January 1, 1994 rebellion to halt the government's attempt to eliminate the Zapatistas by force of arms, that there was a crucial relation between the Zapatistas and this Other Mexico.

What became clear to the Zapatistas out of more than a decade of struggle was the manner by which they wanted to relate to the Other Mexico. First, after the experience of official Mexico with regard to the San Andrés Accords, the Zapatistas were determined to say a strong NO to electoral politics. There saw no authentic Left among official Mexico, including in the PRD (Democratic Revolutionary Party).

This rejection of official Mexico was not only in relation to the experience with the San Andrés Accords and electoral politics. It was as well tied to their analysis of the neoliberal model of global capitalism, which they presented in the 6th Declaration. They saw each of the major political parties accepting the neoliberal model, accepting capitalism. This, the Zapatistas saw as the death of Mexico as a country.

The rejection of electoral politics was as well tied to the Zapatista philosophy of not taking power. They saw fundamental change as taking place outside the confines of elections and mere changes of governments, and thus, that a reach for power was a false road for fundamental social change. (This need not be interpreted as a philosophy of anti-power, as some have done, as much as a questioning of how power is constituted, and whether the *social power* of change from below is the more fundamental question, the crucial pathway.)

Second, the Zapatistas saw the necessity to not be isolated, to not have the struggle be limited to Chiapas, and only involve the Indigenous of Mexico. They could not hope to obtain their full rights if the Other Mexico—of workers, women, youth, intellectuals, homosexuals, religious people, the elderly and others—were not brought into the construction of a different Mexico. As the Zapatistas wrote in the 6th Declaration:

> To our way of thinking, and what we see in our heart, we have reached a point where we cannot go any further, and, in addition, it is possible that we could lose everything we have if we remain as we are and do nothing more in order to move forward... A new step forward in the indigenous struggle is only possible if the indigenous join together with workers, *campesinos*, students, teachers, employees... the workers of the city and the countryside.

The 6th Declaration called for a new way to relate to civil society: *La Otra Campaña* (the Other Campaign), launched at the beginning of 2006 and continued into 2007.

B La Otra Campaña: *Lessons, Contradictions, Challenges, Questions*

> We are watching. We are looking below. There is still fear, and there is still rage.
>
> Above all there is rage, more rage than fear. But now the extra element is organization.
>
> MARCOS, interview in *Rebeldía* magazine, June 2006

La Otra Campaña paralleled the electoral campaign for president. However, it sharply separated itself from what occurs every six years in Mexico: political maneuvering, empty promises and demagoguery. The fact that the Zapatistas began their campaign in a completely different direction than the "progressive" PRD upset many on the Left, who believed that the candidacy of

Lopez Obrador represented a chance for an authentic change in Mexico. The Zapatistas did not believe that to be true.

La Otra Campaña had a different, deeper meaning than an electoral campaign. It was meant to be a campaign of the Other—of those without voice, the marginalized, the despised, the rejected, the invisible—in the countryside among *campesinos* and Indigenous communities, and in the city, especially the behemoth that is Mexico City, with its hundreds of thousands in factories and small workshops, its Indigenous peoples organized in their own neighborhoods, its countless millions struggling in the informal economy of selling commodities in the street, its tens of thousands of women who do domestic work for pitiful compensation, its multitude of youth who find a closed door to meaningful employment, and who often end up spending their days selling pirated CD music in subway trains, or risking their lives to cross the Arizona desert in search of employment in *el Norte*. It was to this Other Mexico and to Mexican Left intellectuals as well as human rights and social activists—that *La Otra Campaña*, and its heart, the 6th Declaration from the *Selva Lacandona*, were aimed.

The Other Campaign began officially on January 1, 2006 when Marcos (Delegate Zero) and other Zapatistas began traveling from state to state in Mexico. What became clear for the Zapatistas in the opening months of the campaign—"getting to know each other and listening to each other"—was the powerful and complex response elicited.

The Zapatistas had expected to discover "pain and sorrow." The amount they found was far more than they had imagined: "small communal farmers, indigenous communities, small merchants and street vendors, sex workers, workers, domestic servants, teachers, students, youth, women, children, and the elderly" were subject to displacement, exploitation, and repression, as well as acts of intolerance, exclusion, sexism, homophobia and racism. Stories were told of how nature was being destroyed in place after place, and of how there was the selling of peoples' history and culture. But at the same time,

> if the Mexico from below that we were encountering exuded an indignant pain, the organized (and sleep-deprived) rebels who were appearing, and united, revealed "another" country, a country full of joy, struggle, and the work of building their own alternatives.
>
> "Pedestrians of History," September 2006

One could see this fusion of pain and rebellion in the stories told to the Other Campaign by Indigenous youth forced from countryside to the city to survive, working on the assembly line, which Marcos summed up:

Because all these people that are today in the sweatshops are indigenous people that because of the looting of their lands, leave—above all youths—to find work and they begin with this reality. Now they have arrived from the countryside to the city, as the saying goes, but in the most brutal form that can be imagined. In this sense we identify with the roots, the common denominator, and I think that, one way or another, when we met them it was easier for us than with the traditional workers, because we have the same roots, the same origin.

And at the hour that they explained this, they explained it like we explain ourselves. And we have said it again and again: these people go there because they are expelled. They don't go to find better living conditions, but rather to survive. Because there is no other option. And this is what allows for such brutal conditions of exploitation: workdays of 14 to 16 hours, very minimum wages of 45 or 50 pesos [less than five dollars a day]; and a high cost of living because in the city you have to scratch yourself with your own fingernails.

We think that with this proletariat, with this new proletariat, there is an almost immediate identification. The indigenous roots give it strength and clarity, at least for us. And in the workers' gathering it was very clear that the workers from this sector and with this tradition came saying this is about a system, not a union. In spite of what have been struggles to gain recognition for unions and for better working conditions, the presence of the boss is so immediate and brutal: almost the same as the presence of a plantation owner in the times of *porfirista* hacienda... Very combative, very radical, very ready to confront capital right there, at the place of work. We strike, we strive, we rebel on the same assembly line, a line that has today, almost no employment on this side.

Since the current workers' movement—we are speaking of that which is most known—is not found on the assembly line, but rather, it is seen outside through the union or through mobilizations. I don't know. I am very ignorant about this, but there are very few workers' struggles on the assemble line. And they are coming forward here. Here is where the rebellion is being fought. At least that's what they were telling us. At the hour when the sweatshop workers send the assembly line to hell or rise up, or strike, then all the repression will follow. We believe that we have here an important teacher that on their part they still don't have the notion that they have a lot to teach; maybe that is made opaque by their own will and the radical nature of their struggle.

Marco, interview in *Rebeldía* magazine, May 2006

The Zapatistas extraordinary listening to voices from below, characterized the first several months of *La Otra*. Then in the first week in May, supporters in San Salvador Atenco, who were aiding flower venders in a nearby community, were brutally attacked, beaten, and even raped by local police ordered in by the PRD mayor. The community refused to remain passive and fought back. There were deaths and many were imprisoned. Atenco became a turning point because reaction to it demonstrated the difficulties and contradictions in building an alternative movement in Mexico.

In Atenco, the population chose to fight against the brutality of the police in the midst of the presidential electoral campaign. Parts of the Left and many Mexican intellectuals, who were already disturbed that Marcos was sparing no critique of Lopez Obrador and the PRD during his travels in the Other Campaign, suddenly found that this "messy," rude interruption of the electoral campaign by the Atenco events threatened the chances of their progressive candidate. Atenco were greeted with silence and looking in another direction by far too many. Marcos and the Zapatistas fought against media distortion of events, suspended travels of *La Otra Campaña* to concentrate on building support and protest in relation to Atenco.

In the end it was not Marcos and *La Otra*, or the Atenco resistance to oppression that determined the results of the Presidential election. Lopez Obrador most likely won the vote, but so corrupt and incestuous is the Mexican ruling class, that they could not accept his limited victory as the manager of neoliberal capitalism. Massive fraud was performed to take his victory away. The outrage in Mexico City produced massive protests, but no changed results.

Meanwhile the Zapatistas with their 6th Declaration and *La Otra Campaña* stood on different ground. They proceeded to carry on the campaign, and to share even more openly the process of their work in building autonomy in rebel lands through a remarkable *encuentro*.

III Once Again, the Building of Autonomy in Rebel Lands: The Second *Encuentro* of the Zapatistas and the Peoples of the World—The Power of Indigenous Voices in Rebellion

In July 2007, the second *encuentro* between the Zapatistas and the Peoples of the World, held in the rebel territories of Oventic, Morelia and La Realidad. I was able to travel and observe. Below are excerpts from my notes.

> There was an important difference between this *encuentro* and the majority of earlier ones. It centered on the powerful participation of the Indigenous

communities in resistance. These communities had, of course, always participated in the previous *encuentros*, however rarely speaking. This now changed in a dramatic way.

The *encuentro* was to report on the 10+ years of building autonomy in rebel lands after the betrayal of the San Andrés Accords followed by the decision of the autonomous Indigenous communities in resistance to implement them unilaterally. The focal point of the gathering was a series of presentations delivered by the Indigenous themselves to "the peoples of the world." For our benefit they spoke in Spanish, though for the vast majority of speakers it was not their mother tongue. What came through was a powerful discourse of ideas, actions, and spirit. The presentations were from Commissions on education, health, production, governance, and women, which had been created in various autonomous municipalities in each of the five *Caracoles* that have been set up in different regions of Chiapas. The *Caracoles*, are more than administrative regions. They are forms of organization and practice of the Indigenous communities. Municipalities within each *Caracole* set up commissions to concretize how authentic autonomy—a transformation of life and labor in the communities—could be implemented. At the *encuentro* there were oral reports from commission members within each of the five Caracoles.

The Commissions on Education faced the challenge of starting from the beginning. They did not wish the government of Mexico at the state or federal government to be involved in their education. This, after years of *miss*-education, disrespect for the native languages, ways of teaching which did not relate to their needs, hierarchal in nature. We heard reports from the autonomous municipalities on how their commissions had to start by introducing educational promoters. But this meant that *they* themselves had to learn to be the new teachers, to develop the materials to teach in the schools, to teach in native languages as well as Spanish. To attain this, they worked with students from universities and others to begin to develop a new kind of curriculum, one which developed learning not only from books but concretely in practice, a method for a different kind of education, practical and theoretical together. As one of the woman commission members noted: "We wanted to end the division between mental and manual labor in our way of teaching and learning."

Their curriculum included their true history ("including from our grandfathers and grandmothers"), questions of collectivism, of how to practically relate to nature in their communities. They had to physically build schools beginning with the primary level. More recently they have begun establishing secondary education. The educational promoters do not receive a salary. It is a work of consciousness. One evening during the cultural part of the *encuentro* we were treated to the activities of students from secondary education.

The health commissions had to begin by learning and teaching what the Mexican government had often never bothered with. This included the building of clinics; the teaching of personal hygiene, going from house to house, family to family; how to preserve food properly, have clean water, construct latrines. Teaching how to have kitchens which did not have excess smoke so there would not be so many respiratory infections, how to use less wood, to keep animals separate from living quarters, were part of the work of the health commissions. The health of women took special priority during pregnancy, at birth and after birth. To do all of this whether in education or health meant teaching the promoters, who then would teach others.

There were reports on production. The great majority of the work is agricultural labor—beans, corn, animal products. It is for the most part a communal collective labor. It involves becoming stewards of their lands with discussions and decisions on how to use the land, how to preserve it and restore it. It is for the most part production for use within their communities or simple exchange with other communities.

It is when these communities face the need to exchange outside their communities that there is the barrier of the world market, even if here it presents itself on a small scale. We heard reports in relation to coffee production and with artisan goods. Zapatista communities are trying to work out a way to export their coffee outside Chiapas without the need of middlemen who take a big cut while the Indigenous communities receive very little. The communities are seeking outlets for their coffee with co-operatives who will give a fair price.

A woman from the Oventic *Caracole* reported on the women who collectively produce artisan goods, but when trying to sell them in San Cristobal de las Casas they face stores that give them little for their goods. The women opened a co-operative store, but it is small and cannot sell all that is produced. And they are lacking other markets outside of the region.

Even the Zapatistas in this tiny corner of the world are shackled in some sense to the world market. They realize this, and are aware that their activity alone cannot free them. *La Otra Campaña* and reaching out for international solidarity are part of a search to break the power of capital.

A number of reports centered on governance: how the commissions in the various municipalities and the Good Government Councils (*Juntas de*

Buen Goberno) undertake governance in their communities and regions. First, it is governance without a costly bureaucracy—no one receives a salary for their work. Second, there is no separate governing group. Governing is not a professional specialization, but the responsibility of the community. People serve on commissions of governing on a rotating, immediately replaceable term. For the good government councils, terms are for 30 days, so that everyone experiences how to govern. Anyone can be immediately removed for doing improper things.

There is the job of serious accounting and administering, but not one limited to a quantitative question. Rather it is a *qualitative* one: the administrating and accounting are in relation to the entire community, its needs, rather than simply individual remuneration for labor preformed.

There were reports from the Women's Commissions. Everywhere in this *encuentro* was the presence of women. They were half or more of the speakers. They spoke of the condition of Indigenous women before the 1994 uprising and after, noting important changes. But they also spoke of difficulties and problems in relation to the condition and treatment of women in Indigenous communities at the present moment. The 6th Declaration had written a self-critique of the failure to have a sufficient participation of women. By the time of this *encuentro* two years later, the voice and participation of the women was strong. It does not mean they have fully solved the problem.

To sum up in a few paragraphs the experience of building autonomy in rebel regions is of course impossible. Perhaps we can recall Marx's words in writing of the Paris Commune, in which ordinary women and men in their daily revolutionary practice under the most extreme conditions of deprivation and danger, strove to create a new world: *its greatness was its own working existence*. Without trying to make any one-to-one parallel, we can certainly say that the greatness of the Zapatista autonomous Indigenous communities in resistance over these past dozen years has been their own working existence.

•

IV The Zapatistas and Mexico's Left Intellectuals

Let us turn to the Zapatistas' concept of the relation of theory and practice, as seen in a critique of Mexican left intellectuals posed by Marcos. Earlier we wrote of *La Otra Campaña's* attitude to the presidential campaign, including the candidacy of Lopez Obrador, which a significant segment of the Left intellectuals supported. The stand of the Zapatistas—with Marcos as a particularly strong spokesperson—separating themselves from Lopez Obrador and the PRD, was quite unpopular among these Left Intellectuals, as well as among some radical activists, who saw the Lopez Obrador candidacy as an opening and qualitative change from PRI-PAN.

Marcos in an interview in *Rebeldía*, a magazine closely associated with the Zapatistas, commented on how the Zapatistas viewed a segment of the Mexican Left, including academic intellectuals and the manner by which these intellectuals theorize:

> We say that there is a problem in the intellectual sector, not in just the part you talk about but among the entire intellectual sector—including on the radical left—which is the separation or detachment of intellectual action and political action. At the hour that you are producing theory or theoretical reflection, not linked to a movement, in this species of outsider that the intellectual poses himself to be, he is spontaneously taking a concept from reality and that concept is what permits him to edit reality and choose: "this is what is most important." It is the idea that, well, if spontaneously—not as a product of a social movement but spontaneously—of what I see in reality—that what you see in reality is what other intellectuals say, what the media says, what is said in the cultural circles: which is imperialism, or the Empire, or the new correlation of forces—that is what allows them to say: "this is what is important" and it allows them to construct theories like those of the currents and different tendencies that say, "this is reality." And yes, if you begin with this concept, yes, you are able to obtain elements of reality that confirm your thesis and also the contrary. But they never get to that part.
>
> We say that theory, in this sense, over there, above, is always going to stumble with that. Because the saying—I don't remember who said it—that the problem of theory is that praxis, fundamentally praxis, is not taken into consideration. And praxis is not teaching a class. It is not writing an article. It is connecting yourself directly with a social or political movement. Now, inside of that sector, this is what is called comfort in the cultural code. Anything that alters my position as an intellectual; that which puts it in crisis or which questions it, is something that the intellectual spontaneously rejects. If there are elements of reality or of movements that in reality are proposing a radicalization of society that means that the intellectual loses his space of safety from which to produce theory.

> The elements precipitate and don't rise to produce theoretical reflection. What is the fundamental complaint by the intellectuals of the left and of the right with respect to the interruption by the Sixth Commission beginning in Atenco? It messes up the scenario. We already have here two elements: the political parties and the [Federal Elections Institute]... And soon—from where? Through what window?—there appears and enters this band of plebes that not only do I not control them but I don't know what they are about, I don't want to understand them, and they mess up the entire panorama for me. And that is the desperation that turns into hatred and anger.
>
> What we think is that this analysis of "what is the correlation of forces" that is being made is selecting the elements that allow them [the intellectuals] to make the argument of "I am not going to do it... there is nothing to be done... don't move... don't make waves." But if we really analyze the correlation of forces, the enemy probably does continue as the more powerful force, but there is another element of which they are not conscious: the force from below. And its rebellion is in organization.
>
> This is not about what the EZLN is saying. It speaks of a feeling or a rebel subjectivity. The EZLN, at the moment that this is happening in the states, is detecting that this subjectivity is organized and has a history. This is not about spontaneous movements, nor about finding only the people who are ready. It turns out that the people already have their organizations and their history.

Marcos and the Zapatistas have begun to work out their own view of a unity of organization and theory. When they say they are rejecting looking above and are only looking below, it is not simply in praise of spontaneity. They are talking about "the extra element—organization" coming from below. They are referring to the organization of the Indigenous autonomous communities in resistance in Chiapas, and to adherents of *La Otra Campaña*, those with their own organizations, their own histories.

The Sixth Declaration of the Lacandón Jungle was written out of the experience of close to a decade of building autonomy in Chiapas through Indigenous organization from below, out of a determination to reach out to the Other Mexico outside of Chiapas, and after experiencing the imposition of neoliberal capitalism from abroad and from above. At the same time, it was written by another kind of organization, the Clandestine Revolutionary Indigenous Committee (*CCRI*). We do not know the complete composition of this organization, or the fullness of their theoretical-organizational discussions and debates. However, we do have a wide range of their statements and declarations over more than a decade. The Sixth Declaration was worked out in consultation with the autonomous Indigenous communities. Two forms of revolutionary organization coalesced—the Indigenous communities and the CCRI. The Zapatistas practice a way of theorizing, that recognizes that the movement from below is not only force but *mind* of fundamental social transformation. The CCRI's theoretical declaration is written in relation to the organization of the Indigenous communities in resistance.

The CCRI was created as a part of the EZLN, a political-military organization. It has from the beginning brought theory, ideas, to the fore. We need only recall the series of revolutionary laws which were worked out by the EZLN together with their Indigenous supporters *before* the organized uprising of January 1, 1994. The fact that students at UNAM in the 1990s could write on the university walls, "The true arms of the Zapatistas is the pen of Marcos," speaks to how central has been the role of emancipatory *ideas* in this struggle. It is clear that the CCRI saw as one of its crucial responsibilities as giving word to the thoughts, aspirations and practice of the Indigenous movement in resistance. With the Sixth Declaration, this responsibility has extended itself to the Other Mexico. This has nothing to do with the "orthodox" view of vanguardism and vanguard parties giving "leadership" and "consciousness" to the movement.

The very opposite is the case. It is a sharp break from such "orthodoxy." The CCRI, as well as the Commission for the Sixth, seem to be a different kind of "leadership group," if we would use such an expression. Marcos and the Zapatistas recognize that the source for theory in a crucial sense—perhaps they would say *the* crucial source—resides in the movement from below. Again and again they speak of looking below, listening to what is occurring below, touching it.

What I would ask here: *Is the movement from below the only source for revolutionary theory, or is there another crucial source*? When we commented earlier that the importance of the autonomous forms of organization and governing is *their own working existence*, we said we were not trying to draw any one to one relationship between the autonomous Indigenous communities and Marx's description of the Paris Commune. They were founded in different historic, political and geographic circumstances. But it is to remark: (1) That these two emancipatory moments were initiated and carried forth *by the creative mind and practice from below.* (2) That 1871 was the both the Parisian masses, *and the creative mind and praxis of Marx.* Marx met the challenge of his time by having all his senses attuned to the movement from below *and* by recreating the dialectic anew in response to that movement from below. (See my chapter "The Paris Commune, 1871: Mass Spontaneity in Action and Thought Fused with the Responsibility of the Revolutionary Intellectual: The Two-Way Road Between Marx and the Commune" in Gogol, 2013).

The challenge we face today, is in some ways the challenge faced by Marx in the period of the Commune. We are asking today, as Marx asked and strove to answer for his day: What is the meaning of these events? Marx did not limit his response to a revolutionary description of these events. Meaning meant working out a dialectical theoretical framework for these new beginnings from below, thereby helping to deepen and extend them. Marx recognized the Parisian masses as reason *and* met the challenge of working out theory anew in response. His response found its way into the revised French edition of *Capital*, 1872–75.[2] He could only do so by rooting himself in dialectical thought at the same time he rooted himself in the masses' creativity from below.

How can the revolutionary new beginnings that have taken place in the Southwest of Mexico be "summed up" in a manner which assists in reaching for a liberatory future? Is not the challenge for the Zapatistas to draw upon the rebellious critical activities, including their emancipatory organization forms, as ground for new theoretical labors, which in turn help establish the vantage point for further revolutionary organizational manifestations/concretizations?

Here I would suggest that the philosophic vantage point of Marx, the Marxian-Hegelian dialectic, including his break with the old concept of what is theory, can help to work out the continuous *two-way* road between theory and practice, the dialectic between ideas and organization for our day.

2 See Dunayevskaya (1958, especially "The Paris Commune Illuminates and Deepens the Content of *Capital*.")

APPENDIX 1

Zapatista Document: Them and Us—V

Subcomandante Insurgente Marcos

Zapatista Army for National Liberation, Mexico

January 2013
To: The compañer@s adherents of the Sixth Declaration of the Lacandón Jungle across the world.
From: The Zapatista men and women of Chiapas, México.
Compañeras, compañeros, y *compañeroas*:

… [W]e would like to communicate and explain to you some of the changes that we will make on our path. On this path, if you agree and accompany us, we will take up once again, but in another form, the extended recounting of pain and hope that before was called the Other Campaign in Mexico and the Zezta Internazional in the world, and that now will simply be known as *The Sixth*. Now we will continue further, up to…

The Time of the *No*, the Time of the *Yes*

Compañeras, compañeros:

Having defined who we are, our past and present story, our place and the enemy that we face, as laid out in the Sixth Declaration of the Lacandón Jungle, what is left pending is to further define why we fight.

We defined the "*no*," we still haven't fully delineated the "yes." This isn't the only thing, as we also need more answers to the "*how*," "*when*," "*with whom*."

All of you know that it is not our intention to build a great big organization with a central governing body, a centralized command, or a boss, be it individual or a particular group. Our analysis of the functioning, strengths, and weaknesses of the dominant system has led us to believe and to emphasize that unified action is possible if we respect what we call the "*modos*" [manner, way of doing things] of each of us.

And these things we call "*modos*" are nothing but the knowledge that each of us, individual or collective, have of our own geography and calendar. That is, of our pains and our struggles.

We are convinced that any attempt at homogeneity is no more than a fascist effort at domination, regardless of whether it is hidden in revolutionary, esoteric, religious, or any other language. When one speaks of "unity" they elide the fact that such "unity" occurs under the leadership of someone or something, be it individual or collective. On the false altar of "unity," not only are differences sacrificed, but the survival of all of the small worlds under the tyranny and injustice they suffer is obscured. In our history, this lesson is repeated time and again. And every time the world turns, our place is always that of the oppressed, the disdained, the exploited, the dispossessed.

What we call the "four wheels of capitalism": exploitation, displacement, repression, and disdain, have been repeated throughout our history, with different names up above, but we are always the same ones below.

But the current system has gotten to a state of extreme madness. Its predatory ambition, its absolute disrespect for life, its delight in death and destruction, and its effort to impose apartheid on all of those who are different, that is, all of those below, is taking humanity to the point of disappearance as a form of life on the planet.

We could, as someone might advise, wait patiently for those above to destroy themselves, without acknowledging that their insane arrogance and pride will destroy everything. In their drive to be higher and higher above, they dynamite the floors below, the foundations. The building—the world—will ultimately collapse and there won't be anyone to hold responsible.

We think that yes, something is wrong, very wrong. But that if in order to save humanity and the badly damaged house it inhabits someone has to go, then it should be, it must be, those above. And we aren't referring here to banishing those above. We're talking about destroying the social relations that make it possible for someone to be above at the cost of someone else being below.

The Zapatistas know that this great line we have drawn across the world geography is not a conventional understanding. We know that this model of "above" and "below" bothers, irritates, and disturbs some. This is not the only thing that irritates them, we know, but for now, we are referring specifically to this discomfort.

We could be mistaken. Quite likely we are. The thought police and knowledge inspectors will surely appear in order to judge, condemn, and execute us... hopefully only in their flamboyant writing and not hiding their vocation as executioners behind that of judges.

But this is how the Zapatistas see the world and its *modos:*

There is machismo, patriarchy, misogyny, or whatever one may call it, but it's one thing to be a woman above and something completely different to be one below.

There is homophobia, yes, but it's one thing to be a homosexual above and something very different to be one below.

There is disdain for those who are different, yes, but it's one thing to be different above and quite another to be so below.

There is a left that is an alternative to the right, but it is one thing is to be on the left above and it is something completely different (we would say opposite) to be on the left below.

Place your own identities within the parameters we are laying out and you will see what we are saying.

The most deceitful identity, fashionable every time the modern state goes into crisis, is that of "citizenship." The "citizen" above and the "citizen" below have nothing in common; they are opposite and contradictory. Differences are chased, cornered, ignored, disdained, repressed, displaced, and exploited, yes.

But we see a greater difference that crosses all of these differences: that of above and below, the haves and the have-nots. And we see that there is something fundamental to this great difference: the above is above on the backs of those below; the "haves" have because they dispossess those who don't. We think that being above or below determines our gaze, our words, what we hear, our steps, our pains, and our struggles.

Perhaps there will be another opportunity to explain more of our thinking on this. For now we will just say that the gazes, words, ears, and steps of those above tend to conserve this division. This does not, of course, imply immobility. Conservatism seems to be very far from a system that discovers more and better forms of imposing the four wounds that the world below suffers. But this "modernization" or "progress" has no other objective than to maintain above those who are above in the only way it is possible for them to be there, that is, on the backs of those below.

In our thinking, the gaze, words, ears, and steps of those below are determined by the line of questioning: Why this way? Why them? Why us?

In order to impose answers to such questions on us, or in order to avoid our asking them in the first place, gigantic cathedrals of ideas have been built, more or less well thought out, usually so grotesque that not only is it amazing that someone has developed them and someone believes them, but also that they have also constructed universities and centers for research and analysis based on them.

But there is always a party pooper who ruins the festivities at the end of history. And that stick-in-the-mud responds to these questions with another: "could it be another way?" This question could be the one that sparks rebellion and its broader acceptance. And this could be because there is a "*no*" that has birthed it: *it doesn't have to be this way*. Forgive us if this confusing detour has irritated you. Chalk it up to our *modo*, our ways and customs.

What we want to say, *compañeras, compañeros, compañeroas*, is that what convoked us all in the Sixth was this rebellious, heretic, rude, irreverent, bothersome, uncomfortable "no." We have gotten to this point because our realities, histories, and rebellions have brought us to this "*it doesn't have to be this way.*" This and also because, intuitively or by design, we have answered "*yes*" to the question, "*could it be another way*?" We still need to respond to the questions we encounter after that "*yes*." What is that other way, that other world, that other society that we imagine, that we want, that we need? What do we have to do? With whom? If we don't know the answers to those questions we have to look for them. And if we have them, we have to make them known among ourselves.

•

In this new step, but on the same path of the Sixth Declaration of the Lacandón Jungle, as Zapatistas we have tried to apply some of what we have learned in these 7 years. We will make changes in the rhythm and speed of our step, but also in its company. You all know that one of the many and great defects we have as Zapatistas is memory. We remember who was present when and where, what they said, what they did, what they didn't say, what they undid, what they wrote, what they erased. We remember the calendars and geographies.

Don't misinterpret us. We don't judge anyone, everyone constructs their alibis as they can for what they do or don't do. The stubborn advance of history will tell if they were correct or erroneous. For our part, we have seen, listened to, and learned from everyone.

We saw who came around only to take political advantage of the Other Campaign, who jumped from one mobilization to another, seduced by the masses, and thus revealing their incapacity to generate anything themselves. One day they are anti-electoral, another day they hang their flags in whichever mobilization is in style; one day they are teachers, the next students; one day they are indigenists, the next they are allied with landowners and paramilitaries. They clamor for the avenging fire of the masses, and disappear when the antiriot tanks arrive with water cannons. We will not walk again with them.

We saw who appear when there are stages, dialogues, good press, and attention, and who disappears when it is time for the work that is silent but necessary, as the majority of those who are hearing or reading this letter know. All this time our gaze and our ear were not directed toward those on the stage, but rather toward those who built it, who made the food, swept the floors, tended to things, drove, stuck it out, as they say. We also saw and heard those who climbed over everyone else. We will not walk again with them.

We saw who the professionals of the assemblies are, with their techniques and tactics for driving meetings into the ground so that only they, and their followers, are left to approve their own proposals. They distribute defeat wherever they appear; facilitating roundtables, sidelining the "yuppie" and "petit-bourgeoisie" who don't understand that at stake in the day's agenda is the future of world revolution. Those who think poorly of any movement that doesn't end in an assembly that they themselves run. We will not walk again with them.

We saw those who present themselves as struggling for the freedom of the political prisoners during events and campaigns, but who insisted that we abandon the prisoners of Atenco and continue the journey of the Other Campaign because they had their strategy ready and their events programmed. We will not walk again with them.

•

The Sixth was convoked by the Zapatistas. To convoke is not to unite. We don't intend to unite under a single leadership, be it Zapatista or any other. We do not seek to coopt, recruit, supplant, impersonate, simulate, trick, subordinate, or use anybody. Our destiny is the same, but the richness of the Sixth is its difference, its heterogeneity, the autonomy of distinct modes of walking, this is its strength. We offer and will continue to offer respect, and we demand and will continue to demand the same. The only requirement to adhere to the Sixth is the "no" that convokes us and the commitment to construct the "yeses" that are necessary.

•

Compañeroas, compañeros, compañeras:

On behalf of the EZLN we say:

1.- For the EZLN, there will no longer be a national Other Campaign and a Zezta Internazional. From now on we will walk together with those we have invited and who accept us as *compas*, whether they are on the coast of Chiapas or that of New Zealand. In this sense, our territory for our work is now clearly delimited: the planet called "Earth," located in that which is called the Solar System. We will now be what we are in fact already: "The Sixth."

2.- For the EZLN, to be in the Sixth does not require affiliation, membership fee, registration list, original and/or copy of an official ID, or account statement; one does not have to be judge, or jury, or defendant, or executioner. There are no flags. There are commitments and consequences to these commitments. The "no" convokes us, the construction of the "yes" mobilizes us.

Those who, with the resurgence of the EZLN, hope for a new epoch of big stages and large gatherings, with the masses peering in to see the future being made, and the equivalent of assaults on the winter palace will be disappointed. It is best they leave now. Don't waste your time, and don't make us waste ours. The walk of the Sixth is a long one, not meant for mental midgets. For "historical" and "conjunctural" actions, there are other spaces where you will surely find your place. Here we don't want only to change the government, we want to change the world.

3.- We confirm that as the EZLN, we will not ally ourselves with any electoral movement in Mexico. Our conception about this in the Sixth has been clear and has not varied. We understand that there are those who think that it is possible to transform things from above without becoming one more of those above. Hopefully the coming consecutive disappointments do not turn them into that which they fight against.

...

5.- The EZLN asks your patience while we make public the initiatives that, over 7 years, we have developed, and whose principal objective will be to put you in direct contact with the Zapatista bases of support in what is, in my humble opinion and long experience, the best way possible: that is to say, as students.

6.- For now we'd just like to let you know that those who can and want to, and who are explicitly invited by the Sixth-EZLN, should start getting together the bread, the dough, the money, or whatever it's called in whatever part of the planet, in order to be able to travel to Zapatista lands...

[W]e would like to send the best of our embraces (and we only have one best) to the men, women, children, elderly, groups, organizations, movements, or however each might refers to themselves, that all this time have not let their hearts grow distant from us, who have continued to resist and who have supported us as the compañeras, *compañeros* y *compañeroas* that we are.

Compas:

We are the Sixth. It will take a lot. Opening ourselves to those throughout the world who have pain will not lessen our own. The path will be even more treacherous. We will battle. We will resist. We will struggle. We may die. But one, ten, a hundred, a thousand times, we will always win always.

For the Revolutionary Indigenous Clandestine Committee—General Command of the Zapatista Army for National Liberation The Sixth-EZLN,

Subcomandante Insurgente Marcos.

Chiapas, Mexico, Planet Earth.
January 2013.

APPENDIX 2

Zapatista Document: Them and Us—VI

Subcomandante Insurgente Moisés

Zapatista Army For National Liberation Mexico

February 14, 2013.
To: The Adherents of the Sixth all over the World.
From: Subcomandante Insurgente Moisés.

The time has come, and its moment too. There are times that all human beings experience, good or bad; one is born, comes into the world, dies, and is gone. Those are times. But there is another time, in which one can decide in what direction to walk, a time when the time arrives to look at time. That is, when one can understand life, how life should be, here in this world, and that no one can be the owner of that which makes up the world.

We were born indigenous and we are indigenous. We know that we came into the world and that we will leave this world, which is the law. We began to walk through life and we realized that we as indigenous people were not doing so well, we saw what happened to our great great great grandfathers and grandmothers, that is, in 1521, in 1810, and in 1910, that we were always used, that we gave our lives so that others could take power, that once in power they forgot about us again and went back to disrespecting, robbing, repressing, and exploiting us.

And we encountered a third time. The third time is where we are now, for a while now we've been walking, running, learning, working, falling, and getting back up. This is important because one has to record, to fill a tape that can be reproduced later with more lives from other times. Yes, we have been left a full bag of tapes, even though some of us aren't here anymore. So others continue on and the process moves forward like that, and what is yet to come is yet to come, until we get to the end and we begin that other work of construction, where another world begins to be born, where they cannot screw us over again and where we are not forgotten as original peoples, we will not allow that again. Now we have learned. We want to live well, in equality, in the city and the countryside, where the people of the city and the people of the countryside rule and the government obeys, and if it doesn't, it gets kicked out, and another is instituted.

Yes, we are indigenous, we work mother earth, we know how to use tools to harvest the fruits that she provides. We are various peoples with distinct languages. My mother tongue is tzeltal, though I also understand tzotzil and chol, and I learned Spanish in the organization, with my *compañeras* and *compañeros*. And now I am what we are, together with my *compañeros* I have learned what it is that we want in order to live in a new world.

...

Because we believe and trust the people, now is the time to do something about the damages that we have seen and endured for so many years, now is the time to join together in our thinking and learning and then to work, to organize. After so much experience we are ready to do this, and that experience will guide us so as not to repeat the mistakes that have gotten this world to this point.

If we don't follow the thinking of the people, the people don't follow us. And we only need to look at those who came before us in order not to fall into the same mistakes. To build something truly new will take word, thought, decision, and analysis, proposed by the people, studied by the people, and finally decided upon by the people.

It is like the 10 years that we worked clandestinely, when no one knew about us. "One day they will know us," we told ourselves and that's how we kept working all those years. And then one day we decided that it was time to be known. Now that you have known us for 19 years, you can say if what we are doing is good or bad. My *compañeros* say that they live better now with their autonomous governments. They realize that real democracy happens with the people, and not just every 3 or 6 years [with elections]. Democracy is carried out in each village, in autonomous municipal assemblies and in the zone-wide assemblies that make up the *Juntas de Buen Gobierno* (Good Government Councils), when each zone that makes up a *Junta de Buen Gobierno* gets together in assembly. That is, democracy is carried out every day and in every entity of the autonomous governments, alongside the people, men and women. Democracy addresses every aspect of their lives, they know democracy belongs to them, because they discuss, study, propose, analyze, and make the final decision on each issue.

They [the people] ask us, "how would this country and this world be if we organized with other indigenous brothers and sisters, and also with those brothers and sisters who aren't indigenous?" Afterwards, they give a big smile, as if to answer this question: happiness. They already know the answer, because they hold the results, the work that they are doing, in their hands.

Yes, that's how it is, it only requires that we organize ourselves as the poor of the city and the countryside without anyone leading us but ourselves and those that we name, and without those who only want to get into a position of power and once in power forget about us. And again and again, another just like them comes and says now this time it's for real, this time it will be different, and then, the same tricks. They are not going to honor their word, we know that, it's really not even worth writing about this, but that's how it is in this country. It is desperate, exhausting, horrible.

We, the poor, know what the best way of life is for us, we know what we want, but they will not leave us be, because they know that we will get rid of exploitation and the exploiters and that we will build a new life without exploitation. This isn't hard for us to understand, because we know how things need to change, because everything we have lived needs to change. The injustices, pains, sorrows, mistreatments, inequalities, manipulations, bad laws, persecutions, tortures, prisons, and many other bad things that we have endured, we know very well that we will not repeat the ways that have subjected us to these things. As we Zapatistas say, if we make mistakes, then we had better be up to the task of correcting them ourselves, instead of how it is now, where some people make all the mistakes and everyone else pays for it. That is, those who make the mistakes now are the representatives, senators, and bad governments of the world, and it is the people who pay the price.

One doesn't have to have a lot of education, or speak good Spanish, or know how to read much. We're not saying those things aren't useful, but that we can learn enough to do our work, enough to help us organize our work. These things are like tools for the work of communicating. What we are saying is that we know how to make change, we don't need someone to come with their campaign telling us that he or she is the change, as if we, the exploited, don't know what change we want. Do you understand what I'm saying, indigenous brothers and sisters and people of Mexico, indigenous brother and sisters of the world, non-indigenous brothers and sisters of the world?

So, indigenous and non-indigenous brothers and sisters who are poor, join the struggle, organize yourselves, lead yourselves, do not let yourselves be led, or keep careful watch over those you choose to lead you, make sure they do the things that you have decided and you will see that things begin taking shape like they have for us the Zapatistas.

Don't stop fighting, as the exploiters will not stop exploiting us, fight until the end, the end that is, of exploitation. No one will do this for us, no one other than ourselves. We have to take the reigns, take the wheel and take our destiny where we want it to go. In that destiny, the people are the source of democracy, the people correct themselves and keep going. Not like now, where 500 representatives and 228 senators fuck everything up and millions suffer the deadly pestilence and toxicity that result; that is, the poor, the people of Mexico, are those who suffer.

Brothers and sister laborers, we have you in mind and all others who work, we all carry the same smell of sweat from working for the exploiters. Now that my Zapatista *compañer@s* are opening the door, if you understand what we mean, join the Sixth and learn about the autonomous government of the *EZLN*. And you also, indigenous and non-indigenous brothers and sisters of the world, we want you to understand us.

We are the principal producers of the wealth of those who are wealthy. Enough! We know that that there are others who are exploited and we want to organize with them, to fight for the people of Mexico and of the world, which belongs to us, not to the neoliberals.

Indigenous and non-indigenous brothers and sisters of the world, exploited peoples, peoples of America, peoples of Europe, peoples of Africa, peoples of Oceania, peoples of Asia.

The neoliberals are those who want to be the owners of the world, that's what we say, they want to make all capitalist countries into their own ranches, and their overseers are the capitalist governments of underdeveloped countries. And that's how they'll keep it, if all of us, as workers, do not organize.

We know that there is exploitation in the world. We should not let the distance between each of us on our side of the world distance us from each other. We should get closer, uniting our thought, our ideas, and our struggle for ourselves.

Where you are, there is exploitation, just as there is for us. You suffer repression, just like us. You are being stolen from, just like us, here they have been stealing from us for more than 500 years. They look down on you, just as they continue to look down on us.

And that's where we are, that's where they have us, and that's how things will continue if we don't join each other's hands. There are many reasons to unite ourselves and give birth to our rebellion and defend ourselves against this beast that does not want to get off of us and that never will if we don't throw it off ourselves. Here in our Zapatista communities, our autonomous governments in rebellion and their organized *compañer@s* are confronting neoliberal capitalism day and night, and we are ready for anything that comes and in whatever form it may come.

These are now facts, this is how the Zapatista *compañer@s* are organized. It only takes decision, organization, work, thought, and putting things into practice, and then we must correct and improve without tiring, and if we rest, it is in order to gather strength and go forward. The people rule and the government obeys.

It can be done, brothers and sisters, the poor of the world, here is the example of your indigenous Zapatista brothers and sisters in Chiapas, Mexico.

It is time for us to make the world that we want, the world that we imagine, the world that we desire. We know how. It is difficult, because there are those who don't want this, and they are precisely those who exploit us. But if we don't do it now, our future will be even harder and there will never be freedom. That's how we understand things, and that's why we are searching, wanting to find each other, know each other, learn from each other and ourselves. We hope you will be able to come, and if not, we will look for other ways to see and get to know each other.

We will be waiting for you here at this door that it is my job to take care of, here where you can enter the humble school where my *compañer@s* want to share the little that we have learned, to see if it is of use to you there where you live and work. We are sure that those who are part of the Sixth will come, or not, but in any case they will enter the little school where we will explain what the Zapatistas mean by freedom, they will see our advances and our failures, which we will not hide, but they will do all of this with the best teachers there are, that is, the Zapatista peoples.

The little school is very humble, it has humble beginnings, but for the Zapatista *compañer@s* it means the freedom to do what we want for what we think is a better life. We are making this little school better every day, because it is necessary to do so and because it is in practice that we learn and demonstrate how to move forward. That is, practice is the best form through which to learn how to make things better. Theory gives us ideas, but what gives us form is practice, the practice of how to govern autonomously.

It's like they say: "When the poor believe in the poor, then we will be able to sing freedom." Only we haven't just heard this, but we are doing it in practice. That is the fruit that our compañer@s want to share with you. And yes it is true, just think how many bad things the bad governments have done to us and they haven't been able to destroy us, nor will they be able to, because what is built is of the people, for the people, and by the people. The people will defend it.

There is much I could tell you, but it's not the same thing for me to tell you as it is for you to see it for yourselves and have your questions answered in person by my *compañeros* and *compañeras* who are bases of support. They may answer with difficulty because it will be in Spanish, but the best answer is the practice of the *compañer@s*, which will be visible and which they are living out.

What we are doing is very small, but it will be very big for the poor of Mexico and the world. Just like we, the poor of Mexico and of the world, are very big, that is, very many, and we need to construct the world in which we will live for ourselves. We know what it is like when the opposite happens, when it is a ruling group that comes to an agreement, and not the people. We have come to understand what it really means to represent, we now know how to do this in practice, by carrying out the 7 principles of rule-by-obeying.

We can now see the horizon, which according to us is a new world, and which you will be able to see and learn from, so as to give birth to a different world, the world that you imagine wherever it is that you might live. We can share our wisdom with each other and create our worlds differently from the way that things are now.

We want to see each other, listen to each other; this is a great experience for us, it will help us to know other worlds and to choose the best of the world that we want.

We need organization, decision, agreement, struggle, resistance, self-defense, work, practice. If there is something missing here, add it *compañeros* and *compañeras*.

So, for now, we are deciding how the little school we are making for you will be, we'll see if there will be enough space. The point is that we are getting ready. And that any *compañero* or *compañera* who we invite and who wants can come and see and feel, and even if they can't come, we'll find a way to share it.

We are waiting for you *compañeras* and *compañeros* of the Sixth.

We are preparing to receive you, take care of you, and attend to you like the *compañer@s* that we are, like our *compañer@s* that you are. And we are also preparing for our word to reach the ear of those who cannot come to our home, we will do this with your help.

And of course, we should tell you that this might take a while, but that, as our brother and sisters of the Mapuche people says: one, ten, one hundred, one thousand times we will win, we will always be victorious.

So, to finish, next time it will be *compañero* Subcomandante Insurgente Marcos' turn to talk to you, we're going to keep taking turns back and forth, he and I, to explain everything to you. Now it is time for you to hear me too, for while I have been doing this work for many years, this is the first time that it is up to me to sign the following lines publicly...

From the mountains of the Mexican Southeast.
For the Indigenous Revolutionary Clandestine Committee
General Command of the Zapatista Army for National Liberation

Subcomandante Insurgente Moisés.
Mexico, February 2013.

CHAPTER 7

Bolivia: In Revolutionary Transformation, 2000–2005; The Pull of State-Capitalism, 2006–2013*

An extraordinary series of revolutionary events unfolded in the first half decade of the 21st century in South America's most-poverty stricken land. From the Water War in Cochabamba, 2000, through the vast mobilizations of the Aymara in the Bolivian *altiplano* in 2000, 2001, and 2002, the actions of the coca growers (*los cocaleros*) in Chapare between 2000 and 2003, the First Gas War of 2003 with the powerful protests of Aymara en El Alto, and finally to the Second Gas War of 2005, Bolivia experienced a series of mobilizations, popular protests, strikes, highway blockades, confrontations with army and state. Again and again came eruptions of creative human power resisting the governing powers of capital and state: a projection of a different manner of life and labor through a uniting of emancipatory action and thought by urban masses, peasant growers of coca, Aymara and Quechua Indigenous—hundreds of thousands of Bolivian women, men, youth.

Bolivia, 2000–2005, was a period verging on full social uprooting. In October 2003, President Gonzalo Sánchez de Lozada was forced to flee after unleashing state forces, who massacred 67 demonstrators protesting his rule as hundreds of thousands marched from El Alto into La Paz. Developing a radical agenda, a Left Indigenous and popular insurrectionary movement extended from October 2003 through the Second Gas War of May–June 2005, leading to the forced resignation of Carlos Mesa, Sánchez de Lozada's replacement. As Jeffery Webber expressed it: "... Bolivian society was intensely divided along the lines of class, race, and region. Out of this context two social blocs emerged: a left indigenous bloc, constituted by worker and peasant organizations based in La Paz, Cochabamba, Oruro, Potosi and Chuquisaca, and an eastern-bourgeois bloc in the Departments of Santa Cruz, Tarija, Pando and Bendi." (Webber, 2010).

Rather than outright civil war and/or the taking of power by the left-indigenous insurrectionary force that had forcible dismissed two presidents and developed a radical agenda, the movement found itself presented with an electoral

* As integral to this Chapter the reader should consult "The Statist Marxism of García Linera," Section II of Chapter 14, "Horizontal-ism, State-ism, Marxism and the Indigenous Dimension: Álvaro García Linera, Raul Zibechi, Hugo Blanco," as well as "The TIPNIS March: New Horizons for Popular Education" by Benito Fernandez in Part III.

pathway—a December 2005 presidential election. The result was the unprecedented election of an Indigenous president, Evo Morales, breaking the old colonialist framework that had characterized Bolivia's history for centuries, and thus taking important steps toward Indigenous liberation.

However, at the same time, *the electoral road fundamentally changed the trajectory of this profoundly revolutionary half decade 2000–2005*. In this sense, we can divide the transformative process in two: the first period of 2000 to 2005, a revolutionary transformative process; and a second period of 2006 to the present, a process of *what happens after?*, after the election of Morales, a period marked by the pull of state-capitalism within the framework of what Webber terms "reconstituted neoliberalism." But as well, a period marked by Indigenous resistance to the imposition of state-ism. We wish to briefly examine and contrast key moments in these two periods.[1]

1 The Revolutionary Social Process, 2000–2005

In *Los ritmos del Pachakuti,* Raquel Gutiérrez's presentation and analysis center on three threads of the rebellion, at times acting independently with their own demands, views and actions, and at times intertwined with a strength and power that proven determinate in confronting the Bolivian state: (1) The Coordination for the Defense of Water and of Life (*La Coordinadora de Defensa del Agua y de la Vida*), which carried on the "Water War" in Cochabamba; (2) The blockades launched by the Aymara communities around La Paz, particularly under the leadership of Maliku Felipe Quispe; (3) The struggles in Chapare carried out by the coca growers under the direction of their union, headed by Evo Morales. This does not exhaust the vast, multi-dimensional participation of the Bolivian masses in this period of revolutionary transformation. It is only to single out these three most prominent currents, which, at different moments, would unite diverse segments of the population with their demands and actions.

A concurrent, complementary way of thinking about the struggle which Gutiérrez discussed, and which Hylton and Thomson put emphasis upon, is the intellectual division between the national-popular struggle, with its components of the national, the proletariat, and the state form, and that of Indian

1 This Chapter is indebted to a number of important studies on Bolivia which have detailed these social processes in a far more extensive manner then could be taken up in the present study. See in particular Gutiérrez Aguilar (2008). As well, see Hylton and Thomson (2008); Olivera (2004); Webber (2011); and, Zibechi (2012a).

struggles based on Indigenous communities, Indian peasant trade union organization and urban Aymara youth and activists. Hylton and Thomson note: "The power and depth of the transformations in present-day Bolivia, we argue, are the direct result of a historic convergence between these two different traditions of struggle" (Hylton and Thomson, 2008: xxiii).

Gutiérrez wrote of a "communitarian-popular" perspective (*communitarian-popular*) and a "national-popular" (*nacional-popular*) horizon. While Hylton and Thomson see contradictory elements between these two views, their focus is on the unity of the two in the struggles of 2000–2005. Gutiérrez, while not denying a certain coalescence, sees between the two currents a significant difference on the future direction of the Bolivian social transformation. For her, the national-popular horizon focuses on the redefinition of the relation between the state and civil society, aiming for a more inclusive and democratic relation. The communitarian popular proposal, she sees as embodying a radical reordering of the present order, involving a more throughgoing reformulation of the relation between the government and society, including a reorganization of the state relations of capitalism. While these two tendencies worked together, not without tension, in moving to overthrow neoliberal rule in the period of revolutionary transformation, 2000–2005, in the period post-2005, there has been a deepening division between the two over the pathway of Bolivia's future.

In the first half decade of the present century Bolivia underwent sweeping, rebellious changes, a vast canvas of social transformation. In the present chapter I focus on only a single aspect of this transformation—forms of organization in the Water War in Cochabamba, 2000. Following Gutiérrez's work, we will examine the *Coordinadora,* the Coalition for the Defense of Water and Life, as it sparked the Water War in Cochabamba. I will briefly also look at the blockades launched by the Aymara communities in 2000–2003. To explore the specific forms of organization and modes of thought that emerged in the Water War in Cochabamba and in the Aymara struggles in the *altiplano* seems crucial for beginning to comprehend the revolutionary transformation that occurred in Bolivia, 2000–2005.

A *Coalition for the Defense of Water and Life* (*La Coordinadora de Defensa del Agua y de la Vida*)

In September 1999, the Bolivian government, at that time headed by Hugo Banzer, leased Cochabamba's water supply to a transnational consortium, *Aguas de Tunari,* controlled by Behtel. In November and December *La Coordinadora* was founded primarily by the Federation of Regantes [water irrigators] of Cochabamba, the Federation of Factory Workers of Cochabamba and various professionals, who were activists in defense of the environment. When massive rate hikes for water were announced in January, the Coalition lead by factory-worker activist, Oscar Olivera, began a general strike which received massive support, including the occupation of the central *Plaza de 14 de Septiembre* and the blocking of numerous roads. Between the 11th and 14th of January the city was paralyzed and the government declared it would review the new rates.

However by early February, when no change had taken place, a massive urban, semi-urban and rural mobilization was called under the slogan "Take Cochabamba!" The government sought to interrupt the mobilization by intercepting protesters at the bridges which encircle the city. The crowds confronted this opposition and continued to cross the bridges, with street fighting lasting the whole day. The next day, the fighting continued over many blocks around the central plaza. Some 1,200 police and soldiers used tear gas and much force, injuring more than 175. Finally, the government was forced to announce a temporary reduction of rates.

After the vicious attacks by the government, the demands of the protesters escalated. They now called for a total rejection of the water contract, and any control of natural resources by multinationals. *La Coordinatora* called for an unlimited blockade, which began April 4th. On April 6th the protesters took the water treatment plant and the installations of the Aguas Tunari, proclaiming, "If the government did not expel them, the people of Cochabamba were going to throw them out." On April 7th negotiations began, while on the 8th, 50,000 persons proceeded to occupy the central Plaza for hours. The government called a state of siege, but was forced to retreat. The governor of the Cochabamba department announced that he would cancel the contract with Aguas de Tunari.

What was the significance of Cochabamba's Water War? One of the strengths of Gutiérrez's work was her labor to discern and present the forms of organization that were present historically, and that emerged during the protest. A number of communities had developed organizational forms to control and share an equitable distribution of water long before the government attempted to usurp control and give it to a private company. These groups became part of a new organizational form, *La Coordinadora. La Coordinadora* arose to oppose the emergence of government malfeasance—the decision to privatize the water company. New forms of discussion and decision making took place within *La Coordinadora.*

Three different groups came together to form *La Coordinadora*: (1) *La Federación de Regantes de Cochabamba*, a group of men and women from the regions in the Department of Cochabamba, who had historically coordinated the use of water in a complex way through "*usos y costumbres*" (the traditional customs and uses of communities). The Federation had been organized to unite the various water communities to reconstitute more ancient communitarian practices of water use and sharing. It was this series of agreements worked out by Indigenous communities that the government would run roughshad over with its privatization of water.

(2) The Departmental Federation of Factory Workers of Cochabamba (*La Federación Departamental de Trabajadores Fabriles de Cochabamba*), led by its executive secretary, Oscar Olivera. At a time when unions were becoming weaker under a neo-liberal onslaught, the Federation of Factory Workers, with its offices at the principle plaza of the city, became a place for organizing workshops, a space for *sindicato ciudadano* (a union of the citizens of the city). It was different from traditional unions: a place where mobilizations could by planned for and debated. "The Federation of Factory workers of Cochabamba opened its space in order that the simple worker population as a whole with a formal contract or not, affiliated with a union or not, could meet and talk." (Gutiérrez 62) Olivera and his *compañeros* of the Federation of Factory Workers had specific knowledge of the water question in Cochabamba, particularly the attempt to privatize its distribution.

(3) Committees in defense of the environment and professional colleagues. These organizations dealt with the environment and with the defense of water. As well, there were individuals who had connections with the middle class in the cities and who organized forums and diffused material explaining the law on privatization of water and the need to defend the water rights of the communities. Their work was particularly crucial in the months before the Water War.

As the Water War unfolded, *La Coordinadora* became the place where delegates from smaller assemblies "met in order to voice the concerns, perspectives and demands of their sections. In addition to workers, there were students, and young people, environmentalists, intellectuals, irrigation farmers, neighborhood water committees" (Hylton and Thomson, 2006: 103–104) Oscar Olivera explained the structure and meaning of the *Coordinadora* assemblies:

> The popular meetings, or assemblies, contained various levels of participation. They were, on the most basic level, a space of participation of the communities. The workers came together in small assemblies according to sector—all of the irrigation farmers, for example, or the business men, or the factory workers. In this way, everybody had a chance not just to air their complaints, but also to discuss ideas and advance proposals. A space was created in which people could participate in the political process by

discussing the issues and trying to reach a consensus about what the next step should be.

Next, there were the *Coordinadora* assemblies. Each small assembly of workers sent members to present the points of view of their particular sector and make proposals. These spokespeople were informal representatives, who were able to speak insofar as they accurately represented their sector. People from various interest groups such as environmentalists, intellectuals, and members of the water committees attended. Even those individuals who did not fit into one or another sector were allowed to attend these second-level assemblies, so that their concerns did not go unheard. Anyone could speak, but for you to be heard required action. There was one meeting when we were discussing whether to maintain the blockades and this group came and said that we need to maintain them. Everyone was tired and said, "You have to talk with your action, where is your blockade?' And they did not have one. This became the first requirement to speak. It was a time for talk, but not talk without action. The *Coordinadora* assemblies were where the communiques were written and strategic political analysis took place. The decisions made as a result of this process were presented for validation as the next level, the *cabildos* (town meetings).

Between fifty and seventy thousand people attend the *cabildos*, which were held in large public plazas. It was in this context that final decisions were made. At this level of assembly, though representatives addressed the crowds, there was an undercurrent of popular democratic participation and commentary. The crowd responded to different proposals by expressing noises such boos or whistles. Sometimes the leaders had to follow the people.

OSCAR OLIVERA, 2004: 37–39

Gutiérrez described,

three levels of participation [in the Water War]: the orderly and consistent action of the irrigation farmers who sustained the blockades of the roads with a system of rotations and turns similar in style they had developed in relation to the water; the massive and belligerent response of the urban population which formed the urban blockades and kept the city in a state of commotion; and the participation of the "guerrillas of water," the young students and neighbors, principally in the Southern Zone of Cochabamba who converted themselves into authentic brigades, the first line (of defense) in a self-convening manner.

GUTIÉRREZ, 2008: 69

What emerged from the Water War was a much more radical set of demands: from a roll back of water price increases to demand for nationalization of water resources; from demands on water to demands in relation to all natural resources; from opposition to the government laws on water to the call for a Constituent Assembly (*Asamblea Constituyente*) to create a new constitution.

In following the *Coordinadora* after the victory of April, Gutiérrez raised an important question: "In a certain sense, the *Coordinadora* confronted a problem very complicated for social articulations [social movements] who think of themselves as 'spaces of the confluence for the struggle,' which is the question of the permanence in time." (Gutierrez, 2008: 71) I read this to mean, How to continue the struggle in the period after the immediate battle? What happens after?

In looking at the tasks of the *Coordinadora* after April, Gutiérrez took up two in particular: (1) How will the government agency, SEMAPA [the public company in control of the water], undertake the work of water distribution? (2) How does the demand for a Constituent Assembly, which came concretely to the fore during the Water War, become developed as "la idea-fuerza" (a forceful or powerful idea)?

Once it was clear that there was no acceptance of water as a commodity, there began a discussion of water as a public right: Would access need to be considered a human right or would it constitute a common benefit? How to realize the social re-appropriation of SEMAPA, that is, how would the population of Cochabamba have authentic social control—the re-appropriation of common property under social control? This in turn opened a wider discussion of how to bring into being a "Constituent Assemble without party intermediation in order to construct the country in which we want to live." (Gutiérrez, 2008: 71).

These questions became the subject of dozens of forums, conferences, seminars. Some in small meetings with specific populations at offices of the Federation of Factory Workers, in meetings put on by environmentalists, including at the universities. As well, there were discussions in networks of communitarian radios. Within the *Coordinadora* a decision was made to form a Team of Technical Support to try and formulate some possible proposals in relation to water and SEMAPA. This team was seeking to work out what would it mean to have a public company under social control.

"How to push (impel) the social appropriation of the resource beyond a mere judicial status of companies as state institutions?" (Gutiérrez, 2008:74) This opened the door, necessitated, the discussion for a Constituent Assembly because there were not yet in place the laws needed to establish the kind of company, or relationship that the demonstrators wanted.

The discussions that followed saw the Constituent Assemble being imagined as an instance of political organization of civil society, in which working men and women would be able to recuperate the capacity to deliberate and intervene in common affairs. In this sense such an Assemble would not be understood as a form to reorganize the state relations, but as a way to be able *to break* the state relation and construct the capacity of decision making by the public based on their own practices.

In 2000, the *Coordinadora* directed the first successful uprising since the planting of liberal structural reform in 1985: the "social re-appropriation" of the municipal water company of Cochabamba. After the April success, the *Coordinadora* continued to implement a public discussion in relation to the privatization of natural resources, with the leadership promoting connections with other social forces, in particular with the Aymaras organized in the CSUTCB (*La Confederación Sindical Única de Trabajadores Campesinos de Bolivia* [The Single Trade Union Confederation of Campesino Workers of Bolivia]) and with the coca growers in Chapare:

> From the latter part of 2001 until 2003 the *Coordinadora* was converted into an intermediate articulation of the multiple forms of Bolivian social struggle, putting at the disposition primarily of the Aymarias *comunarios* and the coca growers of Chapare—their knowledge and abilities developed during 2000 [Water War].
>
> GUTIÉRREZ, 2008: 75

The *Coordinadora* was able to offer a space, El Salon Azul in the Federación de Fabriles in the Central Plaza of Cochabamba, as a non-institutional space where different social components could meet, discuss and communicate—a citizen's union. It was an unfoldment of active solidarity, a systematic activity of analysis, diffusion and discussion of the government actions: a space for full deliberation of themes important to the population as a whole.

B *A Brief Note on Indigenous* Campesinos *in Rebellion*

A second crucial strand from 2000 onward was the blockades initiated by the Aymara communities. These began the first week of April 2000, when CSUTCB (Bolivian Peasant Trade Union Confederation, *Confederación Sindical Única de Trabajadores Campesinos de Bolivia*) under the leadership of Felipe Quispe, with the participation of *campesinos* from numerous Indigenous communities, blocked highways in the Omasuyos region near La Paz simultaneously with the culminating actions of the Water War in Cochabamba. Quechua-Aymara communities in other regions—Sucre, Oruro and Potosi followed suit, as did coca growers in Chapare. In Achacachi, insurgents responding to the deaths of two Aymara, attacked army officers, called on conscripts to join the rebellion and freed prisoners from a jail. "Communal power had temporarily supplanted state authority." (Hilton and Thompson, 2008).

Further extensive road blockades occurred in September–October 2000 covering the entire *altiplano*, and included a call of an Aymara nation as opposed to a Bolivian one. Raul Zibechi briefly described the action:

> The most notable feature during the nineteen days of the uprising was establishing the "indigenous general headquarters of Oalachaka" which became the nerve center of the movement. Here 50,000 militarized communards congregate, exercising self-government in deed.
>
> ZIBENCHI, 2012a: 105

A third uprising in the countryside began in June and July 2003, lasting some two months. We will not follow further the creativity of these uprisings, nor the manifestos arising from them, such as the Declaration of Achacachi of 2000. Rather, we want to finish by pointing to the important questions and discussion that Gutiérrez raised in relation to the *meaning* of the Indigenous actions in the countryside. She asked: How did there arrive a situation of a generalized blockade of roads in April 2000, something which had been repeated time after time in a radical authentic local uprisings, and now became actions involving practically the whole country? Why were the Aymaran men and women willing to put their bodies in the road, constructing barricades of stone on so many kilometers of pavement, and maintain a blockade for days? What were they looking for? They would do this not alone in April, but again in September. And then again there would be recurrent Aymara communitarian uprisings in June–July 2001, and a generalized one in 2003. She then put forth some reasons, residing in the complex communitarian fabric of the Aymara and the long history of colonial-capitalist domination:

> In recurrent Aymara community uprisings experienced in April and September 2000, further radicalized in June–July 2001, and more widespread in 2003, we were in the presence of a profound communitarian fabric having ancient roots, often invisible and silent, under the history of colonial exploitation and domination that had been organized by the Bolivian political-economic-social structure. This profound Aymara communitarian strength, found and felt in the daily life of the rural villages—the *ayllus* and *markas* of the *altiplano* of La Paz and the valleys that form at the foot of the great glaciers as well as in the marginal neighborhoods that surround the city of El Alto—became a dazzling,

> visible power that had the force of lightening and the roar of thunder, a power that came forth in the densest clouds of social confrontation and thereby dramatically and abruptly transformed the terms of public, political discourse. This power burned in the hearts and minds of the proud inheritors of Tupac Katari and Sisa Bartolina. [Historic heroes of resistance to Spanish colonial domination.]
>
> The potential and momentum of recurring actions of uprising and rebellion by the communitarian Aymara at a certain point overflowed the channel of modern forms of representation and political organization, unions, party-forms and states, thus illuminating the possibility of *Pachakuti* [a revolutionary overturning of time and space out of which a new phase in history may issue], the substantial transformation of colonial-capitalist domination and exploitation.
>
> GUTIÉRREZ, 2008: 88

11 What Happens After? Social Movements under the Threat of State-ism and Neoliberalism in Unity, 2006–2013

> Bolivia is an extensive territory in permanent deliberation... In other words, people are always waiting to see what's going on, and I think that's a big problem for any government. This is not subordinate, submissive people; it's not a people who are indifferent to what is going on. It's a people who are always... you go to a beauty shop, stand in line at the market, people are talking politics, about what's going on. So I think the good thing is that people are searching here in Bolivia, and in the world, I would say: what do we want to be? I think that the great challenge is, as the *compañeros* here say, to be in the opposition. I think it is a process of structuring a social base that is looking for what to do in the long term. Not only for elections. Elections can be a step, but I think people have gone beyond this kind of democracy that doesn't work.
>
> OSCAR OLIVERA, 2012

The 2005 election of Evo Morales as President was an important moment in Bolivia history. He was re-elected in 2010 with an overwhelming majority. At the same time, he and Vice President García Linera, together with their political party MAS, have developed and carried out an agenda of developmentalism and state-ism that, in many ways, has put them in conflict with the social movements that brought them to power. We will look at this by briefly examining three conflicts between the state and popular movements, and by asking what is the economic-political framework operating today.

A *Three Moments in the Relation of Social Movements and the State Post 2005*

1 The Constituent Assembly: From a Demand of Social Movements to a Tool of Party-ism

Two activist-thinkers in the popular movements expressed the significance of the demand for a Constituent Assembly:

> Where is this Constituent Assembly going to come from? There is no longer going to be a Congress. There is no longer going to be a government... We will organize ourselves in a constituent Assembly where there will be workers, peasants, carpenters, shoe-shiners, women and men... We will need to define what kind of a country we want, what kind of economy we want... We are going to do these things... after a *pachakuti* as the Aymaras and Quechuas say, after a grand revolution, as the socialists and Marxists say. In our federation we say if one has an old shoe, what should one do, save it or throw it out? Obviously, throw it out brothers. This system is an old shoe, rotten and full or corruption. We have to destroy it once and for all, so that a new system can be born to take its place... If in the end we are going to struggle for this revolution, to follow through with this, we are only going to be able to do it through social movements. It will be the insurgency of the Bolivia people. —Gualberto Choque, executive secretary of the *Federación Única Departamento de la Campesinos Trabajadores de la Paz, Tupaj Katri*, speaking at an emergency assembly of the Federation of Neighborhood Councils of El Alto. May 27, 2005. (Recorded, transcribed and translated by Jeffery Webber. Webber: 2011)
>
> The Constituent Assembly... should be understood as a great sovereign meeting of citizen representatives elected in their neighborhood organizations, their urban and rural associations, their unions, their communes. These citizen representatives would bring with them ideas and projects concerning how to organize the political life of the country. They would seek to define the best way of organizing and managing the common good, the institutions of society, and the means that could unite the different individual interests in order to form a great collective and national interest. They would decide upon the modes of political representation, social control, and self-government that we should give ourselves for the ensuing decades. And all these agreed decisions would immediately be implemented... Let us be clear: Neither the executive branch nor the legislative branch, not even the political parties, can convoke the Constituent

> Assembly. These institutions and their members all stand discredited for having plunged the country into disaster.
>
> OSCAR OLIVERA, *Cochabamba! Water War*

The call for a Constituent Assembly was a revolutionary demand of the social movements 2000–2005. It centered on what would be the role of social movements in such an assembly. However, what emerged after the election of Evo Morales was the organization of a Constituent Assembly based, not on social movements, but on political parties in which Morales' MAS (Movement for Socialism) would play a dominant part. MAS' role became one, not so much of representing the popular movements that had put Morales and MAS in power, but, of channeling the popular demand into party politics, and ended up with questionable compromises that gave the neoliberal right in the country a critical voice in greatly weakening the demands for a transformative Constituent Assembly. (For an analysis of the struggles within the Constituent Assembly see Webber, 2011)

2 The Gasolinazo—Mass Protest against a Massive Increase in Gasoline Prices

On December 26, 2011, without a word of warning, the MAS government instituted the *gasolinazo*, raising the price of gasoline by 73% and that of diesel by 82%, the largest increases in 30 years. The economic shock was immediate: bus and taxi fares doubled, food prices soared and panic-buying in state-run markets ensued. Morales, who was conveniently out of the country when the announcement was made by his Vice-President García Linera, proclaimed the increase a patriotic action needed to protect the economy.

Immediately, a massive protest movement began: By December 30, strikes, demonstrations, and road blockades occurred in most major cities. In the Aymara *altiplano* and in the coca zones of Chapare collective actions were propelled precisely by those who had been the president's most ardent supporters in his sweeping reelection victory a year earlier.

Among the most powerful protests were those that occurred in El Alto, the Aymara city that had been the epicenter of the revolt of 2003, and where Morales won 81% of the presidential vote. On December 30, the headquarters of the organizations which supported the increase in fuel prices, including the Federation of Neighborhood Councils and the *Central Obrera Regional* (COR) were set upon by protesters, who, as well, burned tollbooths between El Alto and La Paz.

Plans were scheduled for a national mobilization by worker and highland indigenous groups for January 3rd. Coalitions of groups were demanding that

Morales either rescind the degree or resign. Faced with growing protest movement that threatened to become a social explosion, Morales, in a New Year's Eve announcement, abrogated the fuel degree. "With the December uprising," noted Oscar Olivera, "the people recovered their voice, their memory of struggle."

The protests exposed the hollowness of some of the government's programs, most notably, the "nationalization" of hydrocarbons, which was a mere renegotiating of contracts with multinationals. An economy based on extraction-ism and not on the construction of an alternative economic model has severe limitations. With no attempt to consult the social movements before imposing the degree, how far had the government moved from the neoliberal practices of previous governments? What had happened to the decolonialization process of this new state?

3 The Struggle in TIPNIS: Developmental-ism and the State

> The protracted conflict over construction of a highway through the Isiboro-Sécure Indigenous Territory and National Park (TIPNIS) in the Bolivian Amazon has been a defining moment for the government of Evo Morales, Bolivia's first indigenous president. It has altered the country's political landscape, rupturing the Unity Pact, an alliance among five national social movements that brought Morales to power and refounded Bolivia as a plurinational state. It has shocked the world with the spectacle of police brutally repressing lowland indigenous marchers under a leftist indigenous government, and it has called into question Morales's status as a worldwide champion of environmental and indigenous rights.
>
> EMILY ACHTENBERG, "Contested Development: The Geopolitics of Bolivia's TIPNIS Conflict," *NACLA*

The conflict over TIPNIS began in June 2011, when the Morales government began construction of a proposed 182-mile highway, whose central segment would divide the 3,860-square-mile TIPNIS ecological reserve. The TIPNIS is the home of the Moxeño-Trinitario, Yuracaré, and Chimáne peoples, and was supposed to be protected as both Indigenous land and as a national park. The highway, it was argued, would unite the Andean and Amazonian regions of Bolivia, helping coca growers, farmers, cattle ranchers, and bringing services to the Indigenous in the TIPNIS.

However, a number of Indigenous groups in the TIPNIS felt the road would open their lands to deforestation, already a serious problem, colonization by migrant settlers, and exploitation by transnational oil companies, which already had petroleum concessions in the park. They argued that there had never been a consultation with the effected communities

> as required by the constitution. Morales continued to insist that the road would be built. In August, some 1,000 residents and supporters of the TIPNIS began a 360-mile protest march from the Amazon to La Paz.
>
> Over the course of their 65-day pilgrimage, the marchers endured punishing weather and altitude changes, food and water shortages, road blockades, and brutal repression by the national police, resulting in at least 70 wounded. The police action was widely condemned, leading to a civic strike that paralyzed activities in the country's nine departmental capitals. Two government ministers resigned.
>
> Morales publicly repudiated the repression and asked for forgiveness, but denied responsibility for the attack, blaming disgruntled police for breaking the "chain of command." In a stunning reversal, after the marchers arrived in La Paz to a tumultuous popular reception, Morales agreed to cancel the road. In October 2011, he signed a law banning construction of the TIPNIS highway and protecting the reserve as an "untouchable" zone. —Emily Achtenberg, "Contested Development: The Geopolitics of Bolivia's TIPNIS Conflict"

But almost immediately, the government began new maneuvers with regard to the TIPNIS and the road, banning even sustainable activities in the TIPNIS, helping to organize groups of *campesinos*, coca growers and some Indigenous groups to demand continuing with the highway. The government submitted a new law calling for a *consulta* of the effected groups. However there were charges of manipulation of the *consulta*, with a disputed majority voting for the road.

The struggle has continued into 2014 with charges and counter-charges. Among recent developments has been the government's promise to reduce poverty in the TIPNIS before any road building beginning in 2015. The TIPNIS situation has exposed substantial divisions including within different segments of the Indigenous community. (For a detailed summary and analysis of the dispute in English, see Emily Achtenberg, "Contested Development: The Geopolitics of Bolivia's TIPNIS Conflict." https://nacla.org/article/contested-development-geopolitics-bolivia%E2%80%99s-tipnis-conflict).

TIPNIS poses fundamental questions for social transformation in Bolivia. Among them: What is the role of the state in developing the natural resources of the country? How can social movements, particularly of the Indigenous, play a fundamental role in the social-economic-political organization of the nation? Is developmental-ism under state control any different than under private ownership? Is there an alternative to extractivist economic policies that have characterized Bolivia both before and after Morales's presidential election?

The MAS government, and particularly Vice-President García Linera's substantial discourses, has made clear the intent to pursue extractivist economic policies, including the government's exploration and exploitation of oil and gas resources in Bolivia's national parks. According to Achtenberg:

> Eleven of Bolivia's 22 national parks currently include hydrocarbons concessions... Seven parks—including TIPNIS—have concessions covering at least 30% of their land area. Four parks are at least 70% consumed by concessions and are at risk of disappearing entirely once these become operational.

Using the winged expression "resource nationalism," the MAS government is intent on pursuing a capitalist development under the guiding hand of the state, soliciting the investment resources of outside capital, private and national. As against any discussion and debate of an alternative communal mode of development based on Indigenous communities in the countryside and popular urban social movements, the view of García Linera and MAS is one of state-capitalism as a long transition to "socialism." Such a concept has a deeply conflictive history, as we will discuss in the final section of this chapter.

•

This is no doubt that there have been important changes in terms of the expanded rights of Indigenous peoples in Bolivia, both in the Constitution and in concrete practice. However, the struggle for Indigenous rights without a simultaneous struggle for an uprooting economic change toward socialism—both crucial foundations for thoroughgoing social transformation—ends up as self-limiting. To explore this we turn to the economic ideas and practices of Bolivia under Evo Morales and García Linera.

B *The Economic-Political Framework: State-Capitalism and Neoliberalism—Contradictory or Opposites in Unity?*

With the Great Depression, capitalism in its private-property form could nolonger sustain itself without massive state intervention. The New Deal in the U.S., the Co-Prosperity Sphere in Japan, the extreme barbarity of Nazism in Germany, were among the various forms of this statist form of capitalism. In Russia, the transformation took on a different, extreme form. With Lenin's death and Stalin's consolidation of power, marked by the initiation of the First 5-Year State Plan in 1928, this newly-born workers' state in extreme isolation was being transformed into its opposite, a state-capitalist monstrosity. What became clear was that the seeming opposites, planless-ness of capitalism verses the planned economy of what passed for socialism, were not opposites, but rather stages in the development of, the logic of, capitalism. The great disorientation was that in Stalin's Russia, this transformation was done in the name of "Communism," using Marxist language. Marx's sharp differentiating between the vulgar communism of his day, with its focus on property-form rather than production relations, and his own concept of a "thoroughgoing naturalism or humanism" centered on new human relations beginning at the point of production, (See "Private Property and Communism" in the *1844 Economic-Philosophic Manuscripts*) took on a flush and blood reality in relation to those in state-power in Russia in the 1930s. (For a detailed analysis of state-capitalism rise in the 20th century, see Dunayevskaya's *The Marxist-Humanist Theory of State-Capitalism*, News & Letters.) The idea that state-capitalism was a supposed pathway to socialism received further impetus with the rise of Mao's China, which opened proclaimed itself as state-capitalist under the direction of a Communist Party.

The rise of state-ism has had a Latin America face as well. During the Depression, when U.S. and European capitalist countries could not sustain their investments in Latin America, there came the rise of theories of development, beginning with import substitution. Webber, in his important study, briefly traces/summarizes various stages or schools of development that have passed through Latin America: structuralism, neoliberalism, neo-structuralism and various combinations. What we witness are different forms of state intervention (or withdrawal) in the developing economics in Latin America. In differing from Webber, I see these various theories and practices of developmental-ism not alone as capitalism in private form with the help of the state. Rather, they are Latin American forms of state-capitalism, not, to be sure, in its "pure" form as manifest in Stalinist Russia or in Maoist China, but as appearing *together with* private capitalism. (State-capitalism's appearance in Cuba post the important Cuban Revolution of 1959, is still another form.)

From the Great Depression forward we have been in the era of state-capitalism, the unity of capitalism and the state, particularly the military part of the state as the enforcer. The trajectory of capitalism has been not alone its transformation from competition to monopoly and imperialist in the first part of the 20th century, but with the Great Depression followed by the Second World War, capitalism now has the state, not just as the representative of private capitalism, (though this too remains in force), but the state *as capitalist*, state-capitalism. This is missing from Webber's view, and while "reconstituted neoliberalism" is an important concept, it is incomplete, when it does not articulate a unity with the state as capitalist. In my view, "reconstituted" here involves the state as an active agent. This pull of state-capitalist (frequently with the name of "21st century socialism") is what characterizes not alone Bolivia but much of progressive left governments in Latin America.

A significant part of the Left accepts this, and views state-capitalism as a transition to socialism. Here, García Linera is the Bolivia representative of this view. (See "The Statist Marxism of García Linera" in Chapter 12.) However, far from state-capitalism being a transition to socialism, it is a fatal diversion. That is, it is the logic, not of a movement toward socialism, but of capitalism's own inner development—concentration and centralization, ultimately into the hands of a single capitalist, i.e., the state. In the developing world of Latin America, where the state often does not have the power (or the desire) to eliminate private capital, the form taken is a unity of state-ism and neoliberalism.

•

It is important to note that the door opened by Bolivia's revolutionary transformation 2000–2005 has not been closed. The social movements continue as a powerful liberatory force. At the same time, the responsibility for revolutionary transformation is not alone a challenge for social movements. It is the responsibility, as well, of thinker-activists in Bolivia and all of Latin America. Clarification of *what kind of economic uprooting is necessary* is an essential part of the task. In fullness, the task encompasses not alone economics, but working out and concretizing an emancipatory philosophy in unity with the creativity of the social movements from below. In part, we have begun a discussion of that task/challenge/responsibility in Part I of this book. It will continue in Part IV. First, however, we want to listen to more voices from Latin America colleagues in Part III.

PART 3

Revolutionary Processes in Latin America: Voices from Below

∴

CHAPTER 8

Social Movements in Argentina

Francisco T. Sobrino

1 Background

On the 19th and 20th of December 2001, a human tide flowed onto the streets of Buenos Aires and other Argentinean cities. In the best historic tradition, without planning or leadership, a community emerged that represented all the underprivileged sectors: domestic workers, housewives, employed and unemployed laborers, students, impoverished professionals, teachers—in the majority people who from a certain point of view could be called "middle class," or from another "the people."

The crisis that provoked this spontaneous protest represented the culmination of an entire decade, the 1990s, of decadence and neoliberal hegemony with its constant economic "adjustments." In reality the decade was a continuation of something that began with the 1976 military coup. The democratically elected government of Alfonsín (1983–1989) that followed the wrecked dictatorship aroused popular illusions of a democracy that by itself would manage to improve people's standards of life.

It is worth mentioning that in much of Latin America, the 1980s were also known as| the infamous "lost decade." Low-interest loans of the 1970s became unrepayable high-interest burdens, and net financial capital flowed from the South to the North (Thompson, Frank 2006). Illusions promptly vanished as weak resistance from the Alfonsín administration to IMF recipes gave way to reluctant neoliberal policies. Consequential contradictions triggered off hyperinflationary peaks and Alfonsín hurriedly left his office to newly elected president Carlos Menem, who overtly adopted the neoliberal agenda, including privatizations of state utilities, opening of the domestic market to cheaper foreign commodities, therefore liquidating many industries. In turn, Menem was replaced by the "Alliance," consisting of the *Partido Radical* (Radical Party) and sectors of the center left. It could be said that Argentina had the sad privilege of being the first neoliberal experiment at the international level. The rest of the Latin American countries suffered more or less the same process.

At the beginning, the neoliberal policies crushed all hints of emancipation. It was universally held that "there is no alternative" to neoliberal globalization, the so-called TINA effect. In Argentina, we also witnessed a slew of converts to the benefits of the market, and it is true that the major part of the population supported the massive privatization, the "deregulation" of labor laws, openness in foreign trade, and the reduction or disappearance of what remained of the Argentinean version of a "welfare state."

It must be remembered that hyperinflationary experiences in the late eighties meant hard blows to most people's standard of living, especially to wage earners, pensioners and poor people in general. The new economic and social measures, though bitter, seemed to be needed in order to alleviate past hardships. Those who attempted to confront these measures were a minority from the sectors most affected by loss of jobs, increasing unemployment and the real reduction of salaries.

But as it advanced, the neo-liberalism program created increasingly coercive measures such as cutting the pensions and salaries of government workers, the reduction of provincial, and health and education budgets, more privatizations, greater deregulation of labor legislation. Unemployment rose even more. The incipient resistance grew as the neoliberal program was increasingly unable to respond to popular demands and at the same time was forced to confront an opposition that was expressing the limits beyond which growing segments of society were not willing to go. The political regime and the state that sustained the neoliberal agenda were suffering from an accelerated process of disintegration and loss of legitimacy, while the initial indifference of civil society was being transformed into an open and active opposition.

The depth of the opposition could be perceived in the cry of "out with them all," a slogan which appeared in December 2001, and was repeated endlessly during the popular rebellion. As a consequence the hegemony of the system of bi-party representation (Peronism and the "Radical Party"), that had begun with the return of democracy in 1983, came to an end. Through its own policies the neo-liberal agenda had undermined its stability. The crisis provoked by the convertibility of the peso with the dollar (one to one) meant that vast sectors of civil society was aroused to the fact that the social breech that had been opened up during the 1990s was profoundly illegitimate. The questioning of the neo-liberal program brought together the middle classes and the *piqueteros*, who were both the victims and now the principal opposition.

II The Movement of the Unemployed

At the high point of the crisis the rate of unemployment rose above 24%, added to this was a similar rate of under-employment. Born in the last decade of the twentieth century, the first *piquetero* organizations had a troubled relationship with the government of Carlos Menem.

Toward the second half of that decade they were forced in many cases into a physical fight against the "welfare" and patronage structures organized by the state. Under the ensuing regime of Fernando de la Rúa (head of the *Alliance*, overthrown in December 2001), the independence of the *piqueteros* grew and they became an organized social movement. Finally, in 2002, the *piqueteros* became protagonists in the huge protests of that year, demonstrating their central role in the Argentinean political arena.

The cycle of protests, road and highway blockages in opposition to the neoliberal program began with a popular uprising in Cutral-Co, a small town in the far south of the country. The protest was generated by people who had been affected by the privatizing of *YPF*, a state-owned oil company, where many employees were considered "redundant" by the new owners and subsequently fired. The blockades signaled the launching of a tactic that would eventually be taken up in the majority of Argentina's provinces. What stood out in these mobilizations was the application of direct democracy by means of assemblies that were organized as the protests proceeded, the election of removable delegates, and direct action as a means of gaining access to the powers that be, and by obtaining demands that, while minimal, did help to alleviate the effects of the depression.

The majority of movements that sprang up adopted similar strategies. The *piquetero* tactics changed the common sense logic of the moment. To these characteristics were added others, born of the experience gained in the outskirts of Buenos Aires and other major cities. One of these was the incipient self-management of the employment "plans" (state subsidies), created since the year 2000. Managed at first by state institutions, groups of beneficiaries began increasingly to take a hand in it and started to promote the expansion of community works in dozens of places. Hundreds of individuals created community production projects in the most impoverished barrios; neighborhood meeting places, libraries, food kitchens and child recreation centers sprung up where once there had been garbage strewn lots.

Programs were developed and carried out on literacy for all ages, vegetable gardens, modest food kitchens and bakeries, while food cooperatives created access to better nutrition. The organization of woodworking and metalworking workshops, and collectives for construction or cement block production resulted in barrio improvements and better housing where neighborhoods were organized. All these events would be a glimpse of what would probably come: experiences of organizing work collectively, without bosses, with social relations based upon solidarity, mutual confidence and fraternity.

Numbers were an important factor in the *piquetero* presence. According to their own calculations, adding together all the organized unemployed, their capacity to mobilize was over 100,000 persons nationwide. However, the number paled in comparison to the millions of unemployed and underemployed, a fact which demonstrated that more than size, it was the actions of the "pickets" that explained the visibility of the *piqueteros*: the road blockages provided a powerful political tool whose effect was multiplied via the media. Although some *piquetero* groups limited themselves to claims for subsidies, others later directed resources towards more diverse activities, developing a much broader reach in the communities where they had become well established.

Some of the activities have already been mentioned, above all productive initiatives in which the subsidies and food obtained through mobilizations were reinvested, for example in the development of community gardens, direct sales of produce through alternative commercial networks, small scale and industrial preparation and production of agricultural products, bakeries and small scale industrial weaving, among others. In reality the road blockades represented only the tip of the iceberg, the more visible elements of a much more complex social structure.

The organization of these activities took on self-generated and cooperative forms, although among the different *piquetero* groups the initiatives had no common criteria or characteristics of viability or future development. On the other hand, there were groups of the unemployed that focused on self-generated projects intended to be sustainable over time. Centered in the rural area that supplied Buenos Aires with fresh food products, these individuals worked to develop sustainable enterprises, in which the generation of surpluses ensured the maintenance and economic expansion of production, and thus independence from official subsidies.

This generation of surplus ensured the strengthening of social and community relations and was not identified with capitalist profit. In this cycle of resistance to neoliberalism, the movements intermixed and converged with other urban sectors where new forms of organizations were also springing up: workers (especially the public sector and the growing mass of salaried workers whose employment was precarious), students and youth, and those middle class sectors impoverished by neoliberal policies.

These new experiences of "re-collectivization" began in 1999 with the redirection by the *piquetero* organizations of state subsidies or "social plans." As we noted earlier, the groups took control of subsidies and re-oriented the counterpart demanded by the state (four hours of daily labor) toward community projects in the barrios. Discussions then began about the need to redefine the notion of "work," which incorporated the lessons learned through self-management. The different positions that arose in fact represented a recreation of the classic dilemmas confronted by the workers' movement in past years. Two arguments stood out. The first asked: what is "true work?" For many, this is salaried work, while for others work was defined in terms of "dignified work," that is to say, "unexploited work," outside the field of salaried work.

The influence of the realm of salaried employment (or, if you wish, of *abstract labor*) or the manufacturing image carries great weight, and the process of marginalization was also such that a great part of organized unemployed workers only understood the first definition of work. These contradictory notions of the nature of work generated unexpected statements such as that issued in April of 2004 by one of the high level leaders of the *Polo Obrero* (an organization of unemployed workers related to the Trotskyist radical left Workers Party): "We want to return to the factories. As socialists we say to the Minister that we question private ownership of the means of production; that we struggle to form a workers state, but that we are not going wait for the revolution before going back to work. We want to go back to the capitalist who exploits us."

III The Movement of "Recovered Factories"

The movement of companies taken over by workers also began toward the mid-1990s, and grew with the recession of 1998. The crisis of late 2001 increased its momentum. As a whole, some 200,000 small and medium sized businesses went bankrupt and many large businesses operated at less than half capacity. Unemployment and under employment rose to 40% of the workforce. As the owners closed their factories down, growing numbers of workers began to take over the companies where they worked. Having initially taken over to avoid any looting, many of them now began production with the idea of reactivating the businesses. An originally defensive measure, the worker take-overs signaled the beginning of a genuine breakdown of bourgeois private property. What a few months earlier would have been considered a violation of sacred private property, after the December events could be socially considered as striving for something legitimate: work and dignity (Magnani, Esteban. 2003).

The bankrupt industries and those near bankruptcy or factories outright abandoned by their former owners were those hardest hit by imports or difficulties in exporting (refrigerators, textiles, tractors, couplings, metals, plastics, etc.). The workers had become creditors or victims, because, in general, every business affected by the crisis lead to broken work contracts, reduced salaries, in-kind payments and/or the failure of employers to comply with obligatory social security payments, etc.

The recovery of the businesses involved a transition to a new type of organization, in which workers took charge of production. A variety of new legal structures were adopted by the State in order to face this new phenomenon. The majority became cooperatives; although initially new forms were proposed, chiefly by the radical left, such as "worker controlled nationalizations," which were never fully accepted, as well as more traditional forms such as participation in public companies. But regardless of the form or wording adopted, it was the workers who took charge, which implied a redefinition of their previously dependent and subordinate role in the organization of work. As they took on the responsibility of management, a profound change in the relationship between the workers and the unions took place.

The recovery of the companies was an example of the fight for the expansion of social rights, and their impact on society went beyond their relative dimensions. The relationship between these rescued businesses and their social and cultural influence was immense, as a relatively small number of diverse businesses—around 150—which employed nearly 9.000 workers, called the entire system of labor relations into question.

Eighty percent of the rescued companies were located in the greater Buenos Aires area with the remaining 20% situated in the provinces; this relation was basically in proportion to the national distribution of businesses. The average number of workers was 64, mainly in small and medium sized businesses, although there were a few that employed greater numbers and had correspondingly greater output.

The ownership of the property belonging to the "recovered" companies then became a point of contention. Did it belong to the cooperative or to the State? If the cooperative was owner, then the venture would continue to be capitalist in character. The old employees would now simply be acting as capitalists, and the socialization of the means of production would be limited to a particular type of structure, and to a tiny fragment of the working class that had taken control of those means of production.

If the State is owner, then the population as a whole would be the formal but indirect owners. This type of socialization is only formal in the sense that the State is not under the effective control of the general population. This contradiction, where the state has political control of the operation of the cooperatives, imposing legal requirements, promoting a hierarchical structure in the interior of the cooperatives can be resolved by the labor collective that continued to use the mechanism inherited from the recovery of the company, through assemblies, pragmatically, often depending on the accommodation between State pressure and the worker's responses.

The case of *Zanón* (currently *FaSinPat*), a ceramics' factory in Neuquen, capital of a southern province, is an exception with respect to the majority of rescued businesses, because it both used leading edge technology and because the initiative was not a result of desertion by management. The workers took control before the company could be closed down.

At the end of the decade of 1990s, the internal commission elected by the workers began resisting the employers, and then went on the offensive demanding salary increases and improvements in work conditions. The owners preferred to resort to a lock-out. The result was that the workers occupied the factory, and finally the provincial justice department ruled in their favor, allowing them to maintain production. Although they had few technicians and the upper echelon employees had abandoned them, the workers were able to reorganize production thanks to the assemblies and organization by sections, and to the help provided by provincial university engineers. In early 2009, there were some 500 workers employed, producing at 40% of installed capacity. There were daily debates by section, where discussion topics range from advances in production to national political life. Although the provincial government is strongly opposed and several times has been on the point of evicting them, *Zanón* stands out as much for the direct as the indirect socialization of the means of production, carried out both inside the factory as well as outside the gates: with the university, with the indigenous Mapuche minority of the region, the unions, health centers, the population of the neighboring prison, etc.

It is probable that the biggest impact of the "recovery" of companies by their workers was the blow suffered by the unstoppable neoliberal ideological offensive of the time. Indeed, in spite of these earlier mentioned growing responses and challenges, the production environment continued to be that of the ability of capital to do what it liked and of overcoming contradictions through open competition: if companies went under it was due to the creative dynamics of capital. But when the workers burst onto the scene, over the smoking ruins of dead capital, and reactivated the means of production with real work, a new political symbol appeared. In some ways it could have been ambiguous, because although it represented a new challenge on the part of workers to the attempts to close companies, this very fact could also be considered as the "exit" of capital for its own interests, when faced with "inefficient" and obsolete productive units. But it could also be interpreted as the taking over of factories and companies, and their self-management by the workers. As such it provided a wide ranging process of social control of work in response to the outrages of workless capital (Trinchero, Hugo. 2007).

IV The Meaning of the Protests of December 2001 and the Mobilizations of 2002

We have portrayed earlier how the first year of the new millennium witnessed the rapid growth of dissatisfaction and unrest. How sectors of the exploited classes began to mobilize together with others that had until then lived calmly, and even with certain expectations, with the economic "revelry" of the Carlos Menem government (due, among other factors, to the relative stability of the Argentinean currency, after decades of chronic inflation). Ironically, most sectors of the middle class in greater Buenos Aires that would later play the major role in the *cacerolazos* [a popular protest of people creating noise by banging pots, pans, and other utensils in order to call for attention] and would discover points in common with the *piqueteros*, were people that earlier had fully supported Menem and had believed in the effectiveness of the neoliberal program, based on convertibility of the peso with the US dollar, and who would later vote for the conservative government of the *Alliance*, expecting it would maintain the same economic agenda.

The social fabric began to fray. The parliamentary polls of October 2001, when support for all the candidacies opposing the regime (among them those of the radical left) significantly grew, were a premonition of what was to come. From January 2001 to the 22 of February 2002, there were almost 1,500 marches to the Plaza de Mayo and the Plaza of the Two Congresses. A third of them took place in the short lapse of time between December 19, 2001 and the middle of February 2002. It was the most intense summer in Argentinean history.

On December 19, 122 supermarkets and small shops were plundered in greater Buenos Aires and 17 in the Capital itself. There were three national *cacerolazos* whose epicenter was the city of Buenos Aires. In the second one, there was a massive participation on the part of 32 cities and towns of the interior. Twenty-seven local *cacerolazos* also took place, many of them in towns that few people had heard of before. Twelve banks in Buenos Aires, La Plata, Rosario and Mendoza were subjected to 26 popular "deafening, popular eruptions" known locally as *escraches*. The *escrache* is a specific form of resistance begun by children of the missing during the country's last military dictatorship. Under the banner of "if there is no justice, there is *escrache*," the members of Children for Identity and Justice against Forgetfulness and Silence (HIJOS/CHILDREN) carried out surprise events in front of the houses of the former repressors that the Argentinean justice system had left at liberty, making impunity visible, and rejecting it. The *escrache* is an action outside traditional politics, and is used against those who are or have been government functionaries. It was spontaneous and self-organized by people with no affiliation to social or political organizations. (Modesto Guerrero, Modesto. 2002).

In later analyses, some scholars and social analysts have claimed in a pejorative way that wide social strata, especially the middle class, only reacted, and consequently brought about December mobilizations when they were "hit in the pocket" i.e. when the De la Rúa government's draconian measures stopped them from taking their money out of the bank. The *bancarización* was what supposedly angered them and made them take to the streets with their weapons, the saucepans. This is only partially true and when presented in black and white, is consequently false. All social and political actions are influenced by a number of causes and are driven by multiple motives, but there is always one that sets the chain of events in motion. This we know at least from the time of Hegel, who resolved the mystery of the jump from the quantitative to the qualitative. In the Marxist dialectical doctrine this has been become hackneyed discourse, but that doesn't make it untrue. At a certain undefined moment the accumulation of contradictions that a subject suffers, be it an individual or a collective, leads to a change in the environment and produces a quantum leap. That there was interest in getting rid of De la Rua or that there was a "plot" and similar such things, is simply anecdotic.

During those December days people simply over-ran all types of calls to action. The mobilizations had nothing to do with those dark palace plots in which interests of groups embedded in the political structures converge. Nobody could be said to be the owner of that potent, overflowing, noisy multitude that screamed out after so many humiliations, so many violations, so much impunity, so many lies (Dri, Rubén. 2006).

V The Local Assemblies

The most novel approach of those who opted to protest when faced with the institutional collapse of 2001, was that of organizers of the spontaneous local assemblies that cropped up in Buenos Aires, in several parts of the suburbs and in cities in the interior of the country such as La Plata, Mar del Plata, Rosario and Córdoba. The local assemblies gave witness to the capacity for self-organization of society. They built and regenerated social units unrecognized at the upper levels of the political system, where they were seen as a factor of instability due to the difficulty of controlling them and channel the mobilizations within the operating institutional framework. These new forms of appropriation of public civic space, driven by the utopia of a direct democracy that questions the forms of representative democracy, contrasted vividly with the privatization of public space carried out in the nineteen nineties. The new modalities of social protest suggested other forms of occupation of that space and of access to public services.

As with the December protests, no one could claim ownership of the assemblies. They sprang out of the morass of demands, rage and unsatisfied complaints. In the local assemblies, direct action measures linked to questions of general political issues and complaints against public authorities combined and established a tension with local issues and needs. They meshed with issues such as the provision of supplies for health centers and hospitals, with community purchases or with the creation of organic vegetable gardens, small businesses and work markets for the unemployed. The local assemblies began generating autonomous productive activities, fixing their action horizon through objectives that transcended the political-institutional plan. The activities were aimed at intervening in the economic and social plan through the development of experiences of a new embryonic economy that looked for new answers to solve the crisis in the educational and health systems, amongst others.

They were an important factor in the development of a would-be social and solidarity economy, as in the politicizing of the sphere of the social reproduction, and of the consumption and distribution of goods and services. They were a factor that was also present in the companies taken over by their workers and in the activities of the *piquetero* groups. But while in the latter their needs prevailed above all else, in the assemblies the incentive to create worker-managed businesses was the product of an ideological choice. The assemblies were subjects whose primary objective was to become subjects. There is no other way to become a subject than becoming one, because if someone else does it, they do not do it as a subject but as an object. (Dri, 2006).

This politicization was accentuated in the exploration of the solid articulations of the assemblies with other social movements, designed both to defend positions gained and to redefine alternative economic activities. For example, a march of almost 15 thousand *piqueteros* to the Buenos Aires downtown was received by the members of the local assemblies along the route with the shout of "Picket, Pots and Pans: the fight is one." The city was transformed into a huge stage for a historical drama, albeit one without director or script. The only thing that was known was where the work began.

There was no need to call people together, or to dream up slogans, or to announce events. The thousands that rushed time and again onto the streets did so as if moved by a powerful magnetic force which drew them out to vent their anger. Social happenings, usually slow to get moving, began to accelerate. The resigned acceptance of the daily fight for survival, prevalent until the previous day, gave way to the vertigo of the protests and the *cacerolazos*. In the chants, the accusations, the repudiations, the hate, and the rejection of everything that was questioned, all came together. Out of those events a new social actor emerged: what in general was called the "middle class": semi-employed professionals, the new services workers, teachers, bank employees, the unemployed, impoverished small traders, students, housewives and even lower level managers threatened by ruin.

The employees and workers that participated in those days of mobilizations did so fundamentally on their own, not as part of the non-existent mass of organized union workers. In the main they were the new poor or those threatened with very soon being so. Suddenly, they were taking on a political role they had never imagined. The new subjects, abandoning their previous personifications, their masks, now became "neighbors." People that on the night of December 19th left their homes individually or in small family groups or groups of friends, were now much more than mere individuals, although they did not know it at the time.

The neighborhood was the starting point, the neighborhood assembly the organism of militancy, the square the space, the word the instrument, and politics a necessity of their existence. (Guerrero, Modesto Emilio. 2002.) A small fringe of that mobilized mass, around 10.000 people, then began to meet weekly in some 100 neighborhood assemblies in the city of Buenos Aires. From there came the idea of "inter- neighborhood" coordination of the assemblies, that during its short and tumultuous existence, during the Sunday park meetings, brought together some 2.000 to 3.000 people. In those meetings, people went to share local flags and to listen to or give small reports of around two to three minutes, and to vote on some 50 chants every week. It was a versatile, informal, and even contradictory movement, and in that, a faithful reflection of the assemblies that fed it. The most activist sector of the assemblies was composed of the new militants of the *cacerolazos*, where the unemployed and low-income professionals predominated, and which had a large female contingent whose presence could also be felt in the marches and in the responsibilities that were undertaken, as well as by their initiatives in the assemblies and commissions that were formed there.

Argentina had been transformed into a factory for the production of new self-organization experiences, and quickly became one of the most original "social al laboratories" of the global periphery. While the new experiences seemed to multiply sharply (neighborhood assemblies, savers' groups, cooperative of cardboard recyclers, factories managed by their workers, countercultural collectives etc.), those already in existence (the *piquetero* groups) became even more highly visible. The urban character of the mobilizations also inevitably implied a quick connection with the anti-globalization movement, and a new presence in the multi colored social landscape of Latin American, dominated up until that point almost exclusively by *indigenist-campesino* movements (Mexico, Bolivia, Ecuador, and Brazil). And so, the country that for years had been the model of behavior and of the orthodox application of the neoliberal recipes imposed by the international financial organizations, was transformed first into a model of civil disobedience, and with the passage of a time, into an illustration that "another possible world," predicted by so many anti-globalization activists, which could appear in and through the most varied forms of self- organization "from below" (Svampa, Maristella. 2004).

VI Attempts by the New Government and the Dominant Classes to Resolve the Crisis

In the last few years, devices and strategies aimed at stemming the loss of hegemony suffered by neoliberalism had been put into place by the ruling class hoping that this would lead to the reconstruction of the governance of the system. One of these strategies involved the change of the government team. This tactic was designed to recover the legitimacy of the State by reestablishing, with a new government and programs replete with anti-neoliberal rhetoric, politics understood as the exclusive attribution of the State and political party representations as the only legitimate mediations through which popular sovereignty should be delegated. The Kirchner government, elected in October 2003, began the transition. One of its first measures was to negotiate with creditors a 75% reduction in a foreign debt that in practical terms had become un-payable. Although explicable in the international political context, even this was a too generous an offer. This re-legitimization of the State was aimed at taking back control of the public sphere at the expense of the capacity for action and the autonomy of the popular movements.

The exercise involved, on one hand, a process of political integration of factions or sectors of the subordinate classes, and on other the direct or indirect co-optation of its leaders. The fragmentation and de-politicization of a large part of those who were backbone of the movements in the initial years, something that can be clearly seen today, is probably a result of this maneuver. The new policy skillfully used methods that proved effective in "taking the *piqueteros* off the streets."

It is worth pointing out that there was no one single *piquetero* movement, but rather a conglomerate of different movements with common goals, and different styles. Some of the movements were incorporated into the State apparatus, playing down the complaints and the *protagonism* of popular protest, and assuming a new attitude: hoping for solutions from above. Other movements remained on the streets, repeating the same slogans, and using the same tactics, making the same complaints. But these methods, slogans and complaints were losing the social legitimacy they had once possessed, with the result that these forces were further fragmented, into thousands of small initiatives. The situation was illustrated quite clearly by the small groups dependent on left wing parties that developed a triumphalist rhetoric, without noticing that the call for insurrections and uprisings, as had already happened with the slogan "out with them all," had gradually lost its meaning and had become a sort of repetitive twitch.

This is not to say that nothing remains of that entire period of mobilization and effervescence, as some analysts strive to affirm. Seeing it in modest and realistic terms, it can be said that what has crystallized in terms of both new organizations and the consolidation of those already extent, is no small thing. There has been a retreat, but like the river Nile, when the waters subside they leave behind a great deal of fertile ground.

The economic recovery, and the consequent recovery in the levels of consumption of the middle classes, also had an effect, including the incorporation of an immense number of unemployed into the labor market. The drastic devaluation of the peso in December 2001 (from one to three pesos to the dollar) brought as a consequence a notable improvement in external trade. Imports diminished and exports increased, aided by high prices on the world market for the main commodities that Argentina exports. This new relation encouraged increased goods and services output. The unemployment index dropped to less than 10%. But possibly more important was that the mobilized actors, the members of the assemblies and the *piqueteros*, in the face of this new situation, were not able to insert precise contents into the demands for the creation of a new institutional structure which would be embedded in civil society.

As time passed, it became evident that there was a new context, and to this was added the hope for change, all of which might bring a certain measure of well-being, or at the very least, a respite in the fight for the life style that so many yearned for. The government's assault was also carried out in the context of an increasing indifference to the protests of the lower social strata on the part of a wide range of the upper social sectors, including broader middle classes. The space that had been opened and the resonance created between the *piquetero* movements and the demands of the progressive middle classes quickly began to be reduced. There was a growing demand for "institutional normality," that could even be heard in the voices of those that some few months previously had accompanied the demonstrations, demanding that "they all go home." And in spite of the bad reputation of the traditional political parties, a level of saturation with street blockades and protests began to once again dangerously reduce the threshold of tolerance toward social protest. The state of the public opinion was changing.

VII The Cooptation of Sectors of Intellectuals, Human Rights Organizations and a Part of the Left

The ambivalence of this new 'governance' was reflected in the fact that the Kirchner government openly recognized the fundamental role of the social movements, while at the same time placing them, right from the outset, in a traditional position, assigning them the role of making demands to which only the traditional political representative system could provide the answers. As a result, the creative dimension, the potential of devising new solutions, new ways of living, and even new social institutions, that had characterized the movements of the previous years, was drastically reduced. There has not been, up to now, the capacity to extend or consolidate the constructive potential of the autonomy represented by the movement that arose in the final years of the 20th century. In addition, the new strength of the government has been complemented by the co-optation of the intellectuals of the subordinate classes. A considerable number of social and political leaders, reference points and personalities connected to human rights, culture, some left wing parties and the critical thought that had formed part of the broad coalition that for many years lead the resistance to neoliberalism, have now become part of, or have allied themselves with the new government, now considered a "disputed land" (meaning that an antagonist struggle between a right wing and a left wing was taking place within the government) by its more critical sectors. In office, the Kirchner version of Peronism has assumed as its own the agenda of the human rights organizations. Some earlier measures, such as the decapitation of the military high command, which was still permeated by former dictatorship remnants, the complete renovation of a Supreme Court that had been a docile instrument in the hands of Menem administration, a position of relative autonomy—often more a matter of words than action—in diverse areas of foreign policy, the reduction of the foreign debt, the open opposition to forming part of the Free Trade Area of the Americas (FTAA) with the United States, and the rescue by the State of some privatized companies that were on the edge of bankruptcy, as well as the re-nationalization of the pension's funds which had been privatized by Menem administration, have all served to give the government an image clearly contrary to the characteristic neo-conservatism of previous administrations.

The resurrection of a Peronism that had been considered virtually lifeless, the transformation of certain state functions and a recovery of cultural values that neoliberalism had buried under the forces of the market, the illusion of a new development of industrialization and the internal market, recreating as by magic a "new national bourgeoisie," encouraged a considerable number of progressive intellectuals of a left wing or Peronist tradition, to dream of a return to the policies of the decade dating from 1945, that is, of the initial presidential period of Juan Domingo Perón, characterized by a nationalist and developmentalist policy, sponsoring a higher standard of living for the working classes, and sometimes confronting the United States strategy in Latin America.

In the eighties, after the fall of the military dictatorship, many intellectuals had jumped onto the democratic bourgeois bandwagon, renouncing their "subversive" past. They were rewarded with the control of a large part of the cultural apparatus and the state universities. This volte-face was influenced by an important number of the exiles that returned after the fall of the dictatorship. Many of them were burdened with a generally statist and positivist education, a result of time spent in the Communist Party or guerrilla movements, which now eased their adaptation to the government of Alfonsín and neoliberal politics. The new round of co-optation, resulting from the events of 2001 and 2002, meant that their horizon continued to be the horizon of bourgeois democracy, seen as the only possible way to think and to do politics.

The political swing that took place in those final years of the 20th century was ambivalent. On the one hand it expressed the dislocation of broad sectors of the population and channeled them towards a new vision, one that broke with the concepts and consensus forged in the decade of the nineties. The impositions of the International Monetary Fund (IMF) and warlike politics of the United States and the fire sale and handing over of state companies were now rejected in favor of a more active state role in economic regulation, attached to important democratic and anti-repressive convictions. Priority was given to employment and social justice, to the recovery of public heritage and the progressive distribution of wealth. It could be said that the Argentinean people heralded, in this respect, the new vision that has erupted at global level, since the world capitalist crisis that erupted in mid-2008.

However, in addition to all these progressive moves was added the new government's political maneuvering with its "anti-neoliberal" rhetoric, instilling the idea that the way to achieve these ends is by means of the state structures, from above, and not through direct action and political confrontation, not through struggle from below. The result is greater passivity and an increasing lack of action on the streets, an expectation of state measures, and an abandoning of the social movements born in 2001 and 2002 in favor of action on the part of the government and the rest of the dominant classes.

VIII Other Measures Used by the Ruling Classes in order to Solve the Crisis of Legitimacy

Another measure used to solve the crisis of legitimacy has been the criminalizing of protest and poverty as a way to overcome the democratizing dynamic of the popular leadership. It is a process that has taken place, albeit with different levels of intensity, throughout the continent. The state apparatus began to assail the mobilized social actors, expelling them from spaces recovered by the neighborhood assemblies and the worker-managed factories, in some cases by means of prosecutions and even the imprisonment of known *piquetero* leaders from the country's interior. The purpose of the repressive actions was to reinforce the notion that with the general elections a particular social and political cycle had come to a close and, at the same time, to erase the visible "symbols" of the self-organization and self-management of society.

Lastly, the third and most recent measure consisted of the disputing of street spaces and social mobilizations by the elites and dominant sectors. The latter had even pointed to the current government as responsible for evil policies, say, demagogic and patronage practices. Actually, what the upper classes seek is to recover their lost privileges they used to enjoy in the nineteen nineties. In the last few years the popular movements have been confronted by a challenge in which the street and the mobilization that was called street democracy, is now an area under dispute. The dominant sectors and classes, aided by the major media, now hope to appropriate the power of occupation and protest in public spaces, and consequently to speak for and integrate other social groups, for example the urban middle classes and even segments of the subordinate classes. The same situation can also be seen in other Latin American countries, mainly where more progressive processes of post-neoliberal transformations are under way, such as in the experiences of Venezuela, Bolivia and Ecuador.

IX In a Way, a Provisional Conclusion

The complex challenges noted above oblige us to ponder the problems we have pointed out, and to initiate a deep examination of the social forces and the strategies in play, where the urgency of the present is judged in the light of medium term perspectives and objectives. As we can see, reality has developed with much greater complexity than that supposed by the debates inaugurated at the end of 2001. The major themes of those debates have become intertwined in a frantic dance since the initiation of the Kirchner government. New problems and new contradictions have arisen in the building of popular movements, with both advances and setbacks. In the last few years, the social movements have often lacked answers to the new challenges, while the splits and fragmentations have been accentuated. The relationship of the social with the political has been shown to be more complex and more difficult to solve than imagined. Equally, the fertile ground left behind by the retreat of that once powerful river, are still with us. In that fruitful terrain we must stimulate debate. Above all we must recover and rethink the emancipator possibilities that arose out of the popular movements and social struggles of last decade and a half in Latin America. Starting from there we should ponder the challenges faced today by those of us who seek to build a new society, and a new way of life.

Appendix

Excerpts from an interview with Paula, an Argentine feminist and member of the Gay, Lesbian, Transvestite, Transgender, and Bisexual (GLTTB) Collective. Reprinted from: Horizontalism—Voices of Popular Power in Argentina. *Edited by Marina Sitrin. Original Spanish edition:* Horizontalidad—Voces de Poder Popular en Argentina. *2005.*

"We're Trying to Take Charge of our Own History"

No one expected what happened on the nineteenth and twentieth. It was a complete surprise. I remember that on the nineteenth, I went to my department at the university to hand in my students' grades, and when I left, the front of the supermarket in my neighborhood of *Paternal* was full of police. So I asked them, "What happened here?" That was the day of the looting. It was that night that everyone went out in the street—the nineteenth. And well, the twentieth we know what happened, right?

For me, the twentieth was very strange. It was as it something took hold of me. I'm not a person who is very... I don't know, really I don't have much courage; I'm not very brave. When I see the police, I run away in terror. Repression is something I've always been very afraid of. I see a policeman and I split. The police terrify me. Early on the night of the twentieth, I was home watching television with my sister, where we saw the police repression the Madres of the Plaza de Mayo—using horses and everything. Despite my fear of police, I was seized with such a powerful indignation that I said, "Come on, we're going." It was crazy because we knew they could kill us—they had killed someone the night before. We headed first to the *Congreso* area, downtown, but the police were using teargas nearby, so along with another friend, we took a different street to get to the Plaza de Mayo. We could see what was happening. We saw the police kill someone right in front of us. I can't tell you how horrible that was, but it still didn't deter us. It was something unconscious, you know? We needed to be there. (25)

•••

Political participation was nonexistent in Argentina before the nineteenth and twentieth. We came from a decade of Menem, a horrifying situation. In a way we're trying to take charge of our own history. (32)

•••

I have thinking about [*horizontalidad,* (*horizontalism*)] for years, since I first read gender theory. It was then that I began to read feminist theory, but not just feminist, theories of social construction, and the rest of it—reflecting on relationships to or with other people without thinking about the differences between them. What is it that makes a person different from me? If I only think about difference, then I am sort of pigeon-holing them and making a separation. *Horizontalidad* permits us to think not solely in terms of difference, but rather to live with other people and be able to have political discussions with them, without trying to define them. This is really important to me. I had a very powerful and important political experience in the GLTTB movement, which is pure *horizontalidad.* That's where I first experimented with *horizontalidad,* before my experience with the neighborhood assemblies. The GLTTB movement functioned horizontally, though they didn't use that term. It wasn't important if you were lesbian, transvestite, gay, heterosexual, or whatever. It wasn't important. The question was not asked, and that's interesting—no one asked, how do you identify yourself? The discussions were about people and politics, and that is fundamental for me. It was not about the creation of divisions.

In my opinion, horizontalist practices began developing in Argentina in December of 2001, because of the social demands that emerged at that time, demands that couldn't be resolved by either leftist political parties or the bourgeois parties. The left-parties' discourse is correct, but is very abstract for people. Abstract, in that it does not refer to new identities like gender, race, sexuality, or ethnicity. Abstract, in that the only problem the left sees is capitalism, and the only way to resolve problems is to get rid of capitalism.

Horizontalidad is a new way to think about political action, based in the acceptance of the other—of course in a democratic context. For example, if the "other" is Nazi, then no, we're not talking about *horizontalidad.* To have *horizontalidad* you need to have an emancipatory base.

In December, there were all sorts of conflicts—not just economic, but many types. People reacted against everything they knew. *Horizontalidad* appeared as a new and massive system because it addressed the very political necessities that the parties couldn't hear and weren't dealing with. Also, *horizontalidad* permitted the emergence and acceptance of differences. The party structures are very macho, and there's a division between manual and intellectual work. The parties reproduce the very things that they claim to be critical of. *Horizontalidad* gives voice to women, gays and lesbians, transvestites (here there are many), and immigrants. It permits the debate of ideas and acceptance of differences. (45)

•••

I haven't voted in years. In Argentina, elections are mandatory, but I don't give a shit. Make sure to translate it that way in the book I don't give a holy shit about the elections and the obligation to vote. I have not voted in a very long time. I have absolutely no faith in parliamentary representation. I don't believe in anything that's ever elected in this way. It's a total political farce. It's an enormous problem that Argentina has had military governments, because one of the supposedly progressive discourses insists that we take advantage of our ability to vote, since there were periods in history when we couldn't. This is absolutely ridiculous and false, because our vote today doesn't have the same weight that it had when voting wasn't permitted. When voting wasn't allowed, the vote would have resulted in the election of a parliament that people might more or less agree with. I've never believed in bourgeois institutions, but it isn't the same to have a fascist government as having a democratic guy. Nowadays, the vote means nothing. Voting legitimizes perverse functions of the political and economic system. In other words, when someone goes out to vote, the only thing he/she accomplishes is the legitimization of this perversion.

There's no longer a middle ground, because capitalist society is very complex. Things aren't necessarily clear, but in this case, it seems to me that the decadence of Argentina's political system stems from the fact that you, when you vote, are only legitimizing a political system that is absolutely perverse. This is why I oppose elections. For me they have no meaning whatsoever, and I know that many people who voted think exactly as I do. (122)

•••

New social practices, in general, when they're new, need new forms of articulation. For example, I have an experience that relates to language and the practices that come along with queer movements. In the LGTTB movements, we speak using the feminine. The Spanish language has articles that are not neutral like in English. In Spanish, you've got, "*el*" and you've got "*la*" right? In English, you don't. The language is neutral. Generically speaking, I mean. Here it isn't. Therefore, in the LGTTB movement, we would never say to each other, "*nosotros*" [the masculine form of "we"], we always say "*nosotras*" [the feminine form of "we"]. This is because we understand that language signifies lots of things, it isn't just the way for people to communicate with each other. It's infused with social relations, gender and otherwise. It seems to me that people who participate in assemblies, recuperated factories, and the MTDs [Movement of Unemployed Workers] also realize that language is a social experience. That it's not a convention. It's a social experience. And if the social experience changes, a different language is needed. I believe that the fact that new words appear in a movement... excuse me, in a certain historical moment, in a certain place, and that cannot be translated to other languages—that this has to do with what's happening there and not happening in other places. So there aren't certain words in English, because those same things are not happening in English-speaking countries. What's happening in Argentina is happening in Argentina, right? And in Argentina it happens that lots of groups suddenly are living new experiences that aren't immediately translatable into the language produced by previous experiences. (157)

•••

I have an idea of power, but it is a critical one. The concept of power, at least in the leftist tradition, has always meant that to transform society it's necessary to take power. That means to take political power, to take over the means of production, which is the class vision. I had to laugh because after December 20th, when there were still many *cecerolazos*, which my friends and I always participate in, there was one that was particularly violent, with a lot of police repression. To escape this, we ran and jumped the fence to the Pink House [government building] and went inside. I was on television. They said that I was encroaching on the Pink House, that I was taking over the Pink House. I had to laugh. It's especially funny because at the time, my friend said, "We can go there, but we're not taking power." To us power didn't exist any more. The concept of taking power is archaic. What does it mean to take power? Power over what?

The social movements are thinking of a different kind of power that's distinct from the power of dominance, the power of transforming daily relations. We need to build different social relations in the present, and then later think about a future society. That's what the left doesn't understand. The left has a structural view, not very Marxist, not very dialectic, no? It has retained the least dialectical concepts within Marxism. For me, I must define power in terms of building an alternative power. What does building an emancipating, liberating power mean to me today? It means building, as much as possible, distinct social relations in the present. Of course, there are things that can be eliminated only if capitalism ends. Exploitation is exploitation, and can't be eliminated until the means of production are socialized. But machismo, violence, all the things that transform daily life, these much be changed because without such changes, how can we build a new society? It's contradictory. It's theoretically impossible to construct a new society if we don't first imagine new social configurations. I believe that the idea of power isn't homogeneous now, it isn't the same everywhere. The MTD isn't the same as the recuperated factories or the neighborhood assemblies, but a large part of the spirit of these groups is the same.

I learned many of these political ideas with my friends in the GLTTB movement. I met with many groups of people who were terrible persecuted in their daily lives because of their sexual orientations and their sexual identities. To be lesbian in Argentina isn't easy. It's more difficult than being gay, which isn't accepted. And transvestites? Don't ask. In these groups, there's such a profound respect for other people, and such a real need to change social relations today, because their suffering is yesterday and today. I learned that it's necessary to change the present in order to think of future change. It's not that I'm not thinking about future change, but for me, it isn't possible to construct an image of a different society without simultaneously reconstructing society. For me, that's a Marxist dialectic. I still consider myself a Marxist, and of course, a revolutionary. (161)

•••

Repression within a capitalist system, as we all know, can be economic as well as political. The eviction of popular assemblies represents both of these types of repression. On the one hand, the government is taking back the buildings that the assemblies had taken, which are private property. The neighborhood assembly, Cid Campeador, even took over the Mayo Bank. A bank! Can you imagine a better symbol of capitalism? So, on the one hand there's this: under capitalism, the law must protect private property, and this law must not be broken. On the other hand, this is political repression, since people were using the space for an assembly, in order to create new forms of doing politics.

Capitalism does allow for some political play, in regards to the representation of the bourgeois through the political parties. Anything that's outside of this kind of politics is a threat to capitalism. For example, I don't think that any government, no matter how right-wing it is, wouldn't support the Workers' Party participating in elections. I think that this is part of the accepted political game. Now, an assembly is a very different thing, because there is no institutionalized control mechanism. Therefore, this is something new and threatening. According to the government and the state in general, the MTDs are a big threat. The unions in Argentina maintain a disciplinary control over the working class. It's been years since there has been a general strike in Argentina. However, the MTDs are different. MTDs block streets, argue about politics, propose a different kind of society, and the MTDs are based in every marginalized and poor zone. They really are a threat. (189)

•••

The best part about assemblies is that they let people do politics is a different, non partisan way. This new relationship has given way to very deep changes in people's subjectivity.

The way people get together in their neighborhoods now and talk about things, the way they listen to each other and value every person's opinion equally, are profoundly important. In political parties, it's not like this. In political parties, some people's opinions are valuable and some aren't. I believe that we are constructing a new way of being political which is really positive.

If the assemblies disappeared, it wouldn't be so terrible. I say this because there's something happening to people right now—a real change. And this is really important for building whatever kind of future—it doesn't matter what kind exactly. I think the most important thing, with respect to the neighborhood assemblies, is that they've created a profound change in people's subjectivity. People who believed they were never going to do anything again, all of a sudden did. This is especially important considering our society, which teaches us that nothing done collectively matters, and that the only important thing is the individual. Just the fact that people have started to realize they can do things collectively is really important. They feel like if they can gather ten, twenty or thirty people together, they can do something—they can change something, even if it's small. This, just this, is really important. This change is an extremely deep subjective change, because people are questioning this individualism that has been so entrenched in us since the end of the last century. While the neighborhood assemblies aren't everything we'd like them to be, I believe much of this change is related to them. (217)

CHAPTER 9

Indigenous Struggles for Territory, Autonomy and Natural Resources

∴

The Meaning of Autonomy in Mexico: The Case of the Autonomous Municipality of San Juan Cópala

Brenda Porras Rodríguez and Fernando Alan López Bonifacio

On the first of January 1994, with the armed uprising of the Zapatista National Liberation Army (EZLN), a new phase of the struggle began in Mexico. With its universal demands,

> the EZLN burst onto the military-political stage to demand of the bad government *work, land, shelter, food, health, education, independence, freedom, democracy, justice and peace*, which was reflected in the 11 points of the *Declaration of the Lacandona Jungle*. In addition to that, they protested and condemned the coming into force of the FTA with the United States and Canada signed by Salinas with the support of transnational corporations and the Mexican bourgeoisie.
>
> ADRIAN SOTELO, "The disastrous six-year term of Calderon and the emergence of the new liberalism of the PRI" [Spanish], *Rebelión*

These demands are summarized in the slogan *"Democracy, Freedom and Justice for Everyone!,"* an idea that determinedly propels the struggle for indigenous autonomy. The above must be mentioned because it is the background, the basis and source of inspiration for the Mexican and Latin American indigenous movement to set in motion their own processes in the struggle for autonomy. However, we will not discuss the EZLN here. Rather we will present one of the most difficult and complex indigenous struggles that have ever taken place in Mexican territory: the case of the Autonomous Municipality of San Juan Cópala in Oaxaca.

Our goal is to examine the meaning of the struggle for autonomy in Mexico, not from the perspective of academic interpretation, but from the depths of the struggle itself, from the voices of those who made possible the materialization of this utopia with their actions and ideas, with the practice and the experience they handed down to us, leaving a message in history from which those of us that are in struggle can learn a lot.

1 Autonomy and Counterinsurgency

DEFEND THE AUTONOMY OF THE TRIQUI INDIGENOUS PEOPLES.
Banner displayed in the inauguration of the Autonomous Municipality of San Juan Cópala, Oaxaca.

> Starting on the first of January 2007 the autonomous municipality of San Juan Cópala has been constituted, comprising all communities and districts that have broken or are going to break with the subordination to the government and the organizations linked to it.
>
> Declaration of Autonomy, San Juan Cópala, January 20, 2007 (Extract)

> Autonomy means self-governing ourselves, we are autonomous in our community, we are the ones who will decide what our people need, how we will do it, how we are going to work; the decision lies with everyone, with all peoples. We need not obey the government and ask them what we are going to do or how we will do it, this is something that is going to be decided by us. We will also demand respect for our culture, which is what we want to defend, operate under our own practices and customs and defend our natural resources ourselves, the government should not get involved. We, as human beings and as indigenous peoples, also have the capacity to achieve whatever we want to do.[1]

These words from an audio file, which is sailing isolated in the vast sea of the internet, reflect a universal truth for all the peoples of the world: the right to decide in freedom. This thoughtful message launched into cyberspace comes from the heart of the most resolute segment of the Triqui population, which has managed to constitute autonomy in the Municipality of San Juan Cópala, Oaxaca, within the Triqui region.

Throughout history, the Triqui people have been subjected to constant repression, which they have never accepted with passivity or resignation. The Triqui indigenous people have managed to resist Mixtec domination, the Aztec empire and the Spanish empire. They have actively participated in the war of independence of 1810 and, albeit a little late and divided between the sides loyal to Zapata and to Carranza, they were also involved

1 The audio recording, "Triqui Autonomy" (in Spanish, and transcribed by Brenda Porras Rodriguez and Fernando Alan Lopez Bonifacio) can be found at the following link: http://www.genteflow.com/mp3_player.php?m=bjY2YW42R2ZvNkU9&s=sc.

in the movement of the Mexican Revolution. To this day, the Triqui are still striving for emancipation, only now they do so through the struggle for autonomy.

The struggle for Triqui autonomy understood as a revolutionary praxis is a movement of ideas and practices that originate within the indigenous communities. It is a movement that not only is against the bad government, the state and capitalism, but at the same time it is in quest of a new way of life, of a reinvigorated society that will allow them to develop as human beings, without having to suffer any kind of violence, in this case economic, political, cultural and military violence. Indigenous autonomy in Mexico attempts to recover the ability of the peoples to decide in freedom. Autonomy is a real process of social organization that can help reverse the effects of centuries of domination suffered by the indigenous peoples of our America.

In the inaugural ceremony of the Autonomous Municipality of San Juan, a declaration, founded on established national and international rights, was read:

> Declaration[2]
>
> *First.* Starting on the first of January 2007 the autonomous municipality of San Juan Cópala has been constituted, comprising all communities and districts that have broken or are going to break with the subordination to the government and the organizations linked to it.
>
> *Second.* The authorities of the autonomous municipality of San Juan Cópala are the ones elected freely by the communities and districts that comprise the autonomous municipality and which the Council of Elders has vested with power. These authorities may be deposed at any time if they violate the will of the people or are subordinated to government policies.
>
> *Third.* As a result of the above, the Municipal Council elected by the state government since 1993 ceases hereby to be recognized. The same applies to any other authority that is not legitimately elected by the communities and districts.
>
> *Fourth.* The actions of the authorities of the autonomous municipality of San Juan Cópala will be guided by the practices and customs of the

2 In our opinion, the extract of the document quoted here, reflects the most important points since after establishing the legal framework the Triqui go on to announce their decisions. If the reader wishes to read the declaration in full it can be found at http://municipioautonomodesanjuancopala.wordpress.com/declaracion/ or the following link of the Mexican newspaper *La Jornada*: http://www.jornada.unam.mx/2007/02/12/oja118-declaracion.html.

Triqui people, and whenever the latter do not prescribe a form of conduct, by the laws of the Mexican State.

Fifth. The authorities of the autonomous municipality of San Juan Cópala will represent the communities and districts to the outside world, always respecting the will of the citizens and the Triqui culture.

San Juan Cópala, January 20, 2007

In this declaration the Triqui make explicit that they do not want state and government involvement in the most basic and urgent decisions of their people. They make explicit their break with the organizations that exercise governmental control in the area. How have they reached this point? Why have the Triqui decided to take the reins of their own destiny? Examining the history of the domination they have suffered can help explain the maturity of their autonomist emancipation process. However, in order to save ourselves the lengthy historical explanation we will go back only to the most recent and most relevant events of the late twentieth and early twenty-first century that can shed some light on the establishment of the Autonomous Municipality of San Juan Cópala and the origins of Triqui autonomy.

November 10, 1981 is the day of the first public appearance of the organization called Movement of Triqui Unification and Struggle (MULT), an organization that the Triqui created in order to stop the governmental repression that came from chieftains [*caciques*] and gunmen of the Mexican Army or of the PRI.[3] This counterinsurgent offensive was a measure used in the 1970s to control the coffee trade monopoly and prevent an uprising in Oaxaca that could come to support the guerrilla forces of Lucio Cabañas and Genaro Vázquez that were operating in those years in the state of Guerrero. The MULT in alliance with the National Front Against Repression (FNCR) and the Plan of Ayala National Coordinating Committee (CNPA), which at the time were very consistent and coherent organizations, managed to hold back the repression against the Triqui indigenous to a great extent, expelling the army from the area. However, a new event would determine the course of the coexistence between the State and the Triqui.

As 1994 arrives, the indigenous armed uprising of the Zapatista National Liberation Army (EZLN) takes place by surprise in Chiapas. In the wake of this event the Mexican state intervenes again in the Triqui region with a paramilitary organization funded by the Institutional Revolutionary Party (PRI), the

3 Institutional Revolutionary Party (Partido Revolucionario Institucional), the historical state party of the Mexican right.

Unit of Social Welfare for the Triqui Region (UBISORT), an irregular indigenous armed group whose function would be to prevent that the indigenous uprising of the EZLN was replicated by the like-minded Triqui people of the MULT.

Thus began the murders of the moral leaders of MULT and of their families. The UBISORT was committing the murders, but the MULT began to pay them back in their own coin, and thus the resentment began to deepen between these organizations. However this reciprocal aggression left the rival factions leaderless, and this was when the youth of MULT had to replace the old leaders. Here enters Heriberto Pazos, a mestizo who progressively becomes a MULT leader. From that moment on the MULT starts having a rapprochement with the government at state and federal level, a situation that leads the MULT to accept several government requests in exchange for certain concessions and resources.

However, the followers of the PRI had a harder time reorganizing and became engaged in a rather complicated process. The heirs created a new organization, until then unknown in the region: the Union for Social Welfare in the Triqui Region, UBISORT. The project began to take shape when the children of murdered PRI leaders realized that the leading positions their parents had occupied were empty and the movement they had led was fractured, while its rivals, although politically curtailed, had mutated in order to stay alive. (Francisco López Bárcenas, 2008: 211–212)

The conflictive relationship between MULT and UBISORT went on like this, with the murders started undermining social coexistence among the Triqui. Not all members of these organizations were armed and assaulting others, but everyone suffered the effects of the climate of violence that permeated the region. At the same time, the state kept carrying out military incursions into Triqui communities to make sure that nothing else was going on. Among the unarmed Triqui a great deal of discontent was generated due to this situation of violence, especially when the MULT had to resort to internal assassinations to control their own bases. Within the MULT there existed a great deal of dissent.

The movement had developed widely both within and outside the region. It had reached the city of Oaxaca and even extended to Mexico City and the United States. However poverty, violence and lack of education refused to leave the region or at least the communities in which the MULT was influential. This was not just the result of state violence, as the state had also managed to corrupt the leaders of the MULT. They managed to turn MULT into a corporatist and clientelist organization. Most of the Triqui people lived well outside the region. But in the districts and the communities of the region, the Triqui were those who mattered the least.

Within the MULT, when any of the founding members living in the communities challenged the power of Heriberto Pazos, they were found dead after a few days, often with one or more members of their family or close friends. As 2003 arrived, Heriberto Pazos decided to found the Popular Unity Party (PUP), basing this new party on the MULT, but without consulting the rank-and-file members. Thus, the dissent continued to grow, and several of the natural leaders of the communities, who of course were founders of the MULT, decided to hold assemblies, or began to complain directly to Heriberto Pazos. This resulted in Pazos' gunmen killing the dissenters and even more opposition within the MULT.

The shift in the course of the Movement of Triqui Unification and Struggle, the dissociation of the leaders from the rank-and-file members, the corruption of its leaders, the violence used to deal with the disagreements generated by this atmosphere within the organization, led to its division. Those who departed formed another organization called Independent Movement of Triqui Unification and Struggle (MULT-I). There were no celebrations to announce the event, at least not out in the open, as had happened with other state organizations that preceded this change of course. It was rumored that the structure of the organization was so top-down that nothing escaped the will of the leaders, but nothing was known for sure either. (López Bárcenas, 2008: 257)

> The departure of the dissidents from the MULT-PUP was impending. On 20 April 2006, they made public their break with the organization. On that hot day, at a press conference in Mexico City, about fifteen people, most of them of a young age, announced their decision to depart from the organization of which they had been militants for many years, to form a new one called Independent Movement of Triqui Unification and Struggle (MULT-I). The community authorities of Yosoyuxi, Agua Fría and Paraje Pérez were there accompanied by a group of Triqui natural leaders and representatives who had migrated from the region and lived in other parts of the country. Timoteo Alejandro Ramírez, a founder of the MULT and a prominent leader of the dissidents, read a long statement addressed to Delegate Zero of the Zapatista National Liberation Army, the military organization, to social organizations in Mexico and the general public, where they presented the reasons that led them to such a decision.
>
> *"Why did you address such a statement to Delegate Zero* [*Marcos*]*, of the EZLN?"*

> "Because the MULT-PUP was announcing its support to *The Other Campaign* that was headed by him, to pretend that they are fighting for the indigenous peoples, and they even organized a rally in La Mixteca, when *The Other Campaign* was passing by. So we felt it was necessary that he knew about this situation."
>
> The text offered a brief account of the 25 years of activity of the Movement of Triqui Unification and Struggle since its foundation on November 10, 1981. It talked about the causes that led to its creation, its objectives, the struggles undertaken and the popular support it enjoyed from regional and international social organizations such as the Worker-Peasant-Student Coalition of the Isthmus (COCEI), the National Front Against Repression (FNCR) and Amnesty International, which in 1987 produced a report regarding violation of human rights in rural areas of Oaxaca and Chiapas, including the Triqui region of San Juan Cópala. The document also mentioned the initial achievements of the organization and the government's response, as well as the great mobilizations of the 1980s in the state capital and in the Federal District. Another issue analyzed by the statement was the deviation of the organization's political line, the abandonment of its objectives, to the extent of being turned into a state party.
>
> LÓPEZ BÁRCENAS, 2008: 270–271

The problems did not stop, and the MULT-PUP continued its campaign of aggression, now focusing on the MULT-I dissenters and on the UBISORT, whom they attacked mercilessly murdering their leaders. The UBISORT was pretty weak and could not respond to the MULT-PUP on the same level. The members of the MULT-I chose not to respond to the attacks because part of their principles was to end the violence in the region, opting instead for peaceful social and political struggle. In 2006 the MULT-I took a leading position in the Oaxaca uprising of 2006 by joining the Popular Assembly of the Peoples of Oaxaca (APPO).

Within the APPO they enjoyed wide acceptance, to the extent that they participated in its Board of Directors with the finance portfolio, a great responsibility. This, despite not having a strong presence in the popular movement of the state. A contributing factor was the rejection by many organizations of the MULT-PUP, which some of them, such as the Committee for the Defense of the People's Rights (CODEP), had previously confronted, to no avail. This was the reason why by MULT-I working within APPO, sympathy towards them increased and paths of solidarity opened up. Their lucky star was self-luminous (López Bárcenas, Francisco, 2008: 287).

On the other hand, the relationship between the APPO and the MULT-PUP was much more strained. On August10, state media reported that the APPO "literally" had its eyes on the organization of Heriberto Pazos. Citing members of the newly created organization, they indicated that several of the people arrested in violent incidents against the organizations fighting for the deposition of the governor, "have been identified as Beto's people, or, what amounts to the same thing, as members of the MULT." (López Bárcenas, 2008: 288).

With the support and advice of the APPO, the Triqui people of the MULT-I decided to advance in their political struggle, establishing, in 2007, the Autonomous Municipality of San Juan Cópala, an important Triqui ceremonial center, which had lost state recognition as a municipal seat since the 1940s. This achievement was the result of a rapprochement between the dissident base organizations of the MULT-I and the UBISORT, which, sick and tired of the violence, wanted to restore harmony in their communities. After the founding of the Autonomous Municipality, peace was established despite its short life. There was progress regarding productive projects: a community radio, women's participation, and schools. The rest of the Triqui saw that, but the MULT leaders, fearful of losing their political, economic and military power, launched an offensive in collaboration with the state.

> [T]he government also responded, albeit belatedly. The new political geography of the region threatened it with losing its mechanisms of political control, and thus it experimented with new ways of intervention. First, it tried to bring the leaders of the new political movement to its spaces of confrontation and offered to recognize them as a new municipality among the 570 that exist in the state. As the people concerned ignored the proposal, it tried to bribe them, and when this did not work either, it tried to deepen the division among the people by assisting what was left of the UBISORT—which only exists because of government support and adopts a quite belligerent behavior—while continuing its permissive policy regarding financial support of the MULT.
>
> LÓPEZ BÁRCENAS, 2010

The offensive continued with the support of Governor Ulises Ruiz. The MULT-PUP managed to wage a paramilitary siege on the Municipality, cutting off the provision of water, medicine and food, shooting at the inhabitants and raping women. Thus in September 2010 they were able to completely expel the residents of the Autonomous Municipality of San Juan Cópala.

II Timoteo Alejandro, Father of the Triqui Autonomy

It could be argued that indigenous autonomy is the result of a long process of learning of the communities. The Triqui people have reached this level of maturity because the history of violence that permeates the Triqui lifestyle leads to the ultimate conclusion that the end of violence begins by not responding to violence with more violence. It should be pointed out that this is a critical attitude that triggers a revolutionary process from the perspective of social change and transformation, rather than naïve pacifism or a matter of tactics and strategy, as certain members of a bellicose, dogmatic and mindless part of the left have tried to forcibly portray it.

The end of violence, in a context where there is a permanent process of primary accumulation of capital, becomes the soil on which a new society can flourish, that is, it eradicates the old belligerent coexistence to establish new social relations that enable the development of a truly human society, disconnected from interests that are imposed by the predominant capitalist system.

In that sense, Timoteo Alejandro, during his last interview for *Contralinea*, (http://contralinea.info/archivo-revista/) states:

> As I am a leader of this community, this does not mean that I get the money, no way. But we will sign. Work is all we want. We do not want money. I don't care. I can live without money, without anything. What I want is that the people progress, that the people have paved roads. I want a community that is top notch. What we want is the people to be happy, not with money, not with interest, no.
>
> *Is it dangerous to live here?*
>
> It is not dangerous, but for us, who live here, we are aware of the fact that the state government makes it dangerous for us. If it was just our own people, I think there would be no problem. But with the state,[4] there is nothing but problems, because it divides us, it sends money through the budget account,[5] and through money it divides us, because the leaders are people who like money.[6]

4 In this instance, he refers not to the regional state of Oaxaca, but to the state as an economic, political, social and cultural organizational structure.

5 In Mexico, accounts 28 and 33 of the federal budget are destined to local administrative units, with the aim to decentralize the resources of the municipal budget.

6 The full interview can be viewed online in this two-part video:
Pt. 1: http://www.youtube.com/watch?v=_hAK_bQh2Uk,
Pt. 2: http://www.youtube.com/watch?v=MBfi2Vgn1RA.

Timoteo Alejandro was assassinated on 20 May 2010 along with his wife Cleriberta Castro. Timoteo Alejandro was the promoter of Triqui autonomy. He was a natural leader of the Yosoyuxi community in the Triqui region. It should be pointed out that not everyone among the Triqui can be a leader, since the Triqui only regard a leader as a person with many and varied skills. Most importantly that the leaders can speak Spanish, and that they are able to resolve conflicts between the Triqui and keep them united. Natural leaders are also known as moral leaders of the people, because they are the expression, not of the individual mentality, but the will of a community.

Timoteo's murder had as its goal halting the process of autonomy. He was murdered by assassins hired by the MULT-PUP that posed as corn sellers. This happened under the rule and the auspices of Governor Ulises Ruiz, who in 2006 repressed the Popular Assembly of the Peoples of Oaxaca (APPO). Thanks to the votes of the Popular Unity Party (PUP) of the MULT, he managed to be elected. Then, in 2010, the MULT-PUP supported the candidacy of Gabino Cue [of the PRD]. In this context, Rafael Gonzalez, Triqui leader of the Yosoyuxi, offers his opinion about the death of Timoteo:

> *What are the benefits to the community after the change of government?*
>
> It's the same thing, the PRI and the change of government (PRD) is the same. Even the issue of justice has not advanced. [Cue] has not even done that and a lot less in the projects for the communities. Although [the government] proposes them in theory, they never deliver. The government, whoever they are, is not to be trusted.
>
> With the assassination of Alejandro Timoteo, they tried to kill autonomy. Many of our comrades believe that his death is placing the whole project of autonomy that we have been promoting under threat. As a people we do not want to be asked for anything in return. This is what autonomy means. We want to be able to decide how we want to work on our projects. But the people cannot work because of the violence.
>
> http://contralinea.info/archivo-revista/index.php/2013/02/11/triquis-autonomia-indigena-vigente/

In view of all of the above, the question raised is whether the Mexican government has managed to defeat the Triqui autonomy. From our point of view, they have not achieved it, because, first of all, they failed to prevent the emergence of the Autonomous Municipality of San Juan Cópala. Second, they could not erase from the minds of the Triqui people the progress that took place with the consolidation of the autonomy. This is evident in the ensuing struggle for the reestablishment of the Autonomous Municipality of San Juan Cópala, wherein more Triqui comrades were murdered. After multiple defeats, there is now a new ray of hope, as there has recently appeared an article in the journal *Contralínea* titled: "The Triqui people re-launch the Autonomous Municipality." Could this be a new beginning for the Triqui people? We will have to wait and see.

The *Nasa*: Subjects of Dignity

The Cauca/Cali Collective

> This is why we will continue reclaiming the land. This is why we will set it free so we coexist in it and we defend life. This is why the fight for the land is not a problem nor a duty only of the indigenous, but an ancestral mandate of all peoples, of all men and women who defend life.
>
> Indigenous Communities of Cauca Land Reform Commission

On the continent and throughout the world, indigenous peoples are the keepers of the keys to overcoming the humanitarian and environmental crisis that capitalism has plunged the planet into. Autonomy, food sovereignty, respect for others and for nature, the creation of a culture and an economy of their own based on cooperation, solidarity and communal ownership of land, which is the main means of production, are principles and values that should be reclaimed and defended by the peoples who want to break away from capitalism and build a society based on freedom, justice and solidarity.

The struggle of the indigenous movement for territory, for what is ancestral, for what is our own, for our identity, for self-determination of the peoples, for respect and care for nature, is a part of the popular struggles in our nation and in the continent. Their action extends further than local or partial demands, and also envisions a more humane society that opposes and replaces capitalism, regardless of the name one might use (socialism, communism, popular democracy, *buen vivir*). This is a society that has to be built jointly by the populations of the countryside and the city. Regarding this prospect, in 1928 José Carlos Mariátegui was proclaiming: "We certainly do not want socialism in America to be a carbon copy. It must be heroically created. We must bring to life through our own reality, in our own language, the Indo-American socialism."

In Colombia, the indigenous movement of the Cauca has been the one with greater capacity of mobilization over the past ten years, mobilizing tens of thousands of natives in marches and demonstrations in strategic locations, obliging governments to pay attention to their claims regarding breach of agreements related to the restitution of lands and territories, to impunity and reparations, to respect for their autonomy and their forms of social organization, involving various indigenous organizations that are independent of the authorities. This movement continues its effort to liberate Mother Earth, promoting land reappropriations that the Uribe government violently suppressed for eight years, and which the present government keeps on suppressing, leaving behind more dead and wounded. The movement denounced the violations of human rights and of International Humanitarian Law carried out by the government forces and the impunity for the crimes against humanity, made public during the marches to Cali and Bogota and through the information networks.

By "walking the word" widely through highways, streets, public squares and universities of the country, inciting discussion, protest and mobilization regarding the great national problems, the indigenous movement is identified as part of a subject in need of the unity of the popular sectors, especially in the cities, to lay down a proposal for a new society and a new country. Alongside them in this journey are the peasants, the landless, the harvesters of sugar cane, small scale traditional miners, environmentalists, students, workers—men and women who are seeking an alternative to the contempt of the rulers, people who want dignity, autonomy and justice.

1 The Economic and Political Context

The *Nasa* or *Paez* ethnic group inhabits the northern Cauca region and encompasses more than 120,000 people over an area of about 193,000 hectares on the slopes of the central and western mountain ranges. It is a territory, of which they use only a small part for housing and food production, respecting the forests, the water springs and the sacred sites.

It is important to look at the concept of the struggle of these indigenous ethnic groups based on what is happening in the southwest of the country, namely in Cauca and specifically in the north of this region, during the last 22 years. We should consider the historical significance of the foundation of the Regional Indigenous Council of Cauca (CRIC) and the description of Colombia that we find in the Political Constitution of 1991. There we can read of a Pluriethnic and Multicultural Republic; a legal instrument used by the communities to claim ancestral rights; a relevant option also for the black communities and the agro-industrial proletariat, who live together with the indigenous peoples of Cauca, sharing territories and the struggle for land and life. Together, they confront the government and demand that it complies with a great number of agreements and protection laws, (many of which were promulgated in colonial times), and the recognition of their autonomy.

It is true that the Political Constitution of 1991, which was the result of peace agreements with insurgent groups, recognizes national minorities, but this on its own guarantees neither the respect towards indigenous peoples and black communities and their traditions nor their autonomy. Even after it was promulgated, state repression, genocide and plunder of the peoples rose; precisely in the year of proclamation of the new Constitution, drug dealers and the military carried out a massacre of the *Nasa* peoples in the *El Nilo* ranch. As time went by, war in the countryside escalated and this increased the expropriation of indigenous peoples and peasants.

The massacre of *El Nilo* in the Caloto municipality in December 1991 set a precedent in the struggle for reclaiming the land and territory of the *Nasa* community in northern Cauca. This was the greatest bloodshed ever witnessed by the *cabildo* of Huellas and by other families of other *cabildos* that were searching for a plot of land to live on without depending on a landlord, and were aiming to develop their community. Dozens of families were attacked and twenty heroes were murdered for daring to reclaim the 1,100 hectares that the oligarchical state had promised to hand over following agreements that were repeatedly postponed during 15 years.

This crime managed to momentarily stop the efforts to emancipate the Mother Earth but it did not stop the indigenous communities from continuously organizing and mobilizing to gain respect for their autonomy and territory. For 14 years the *Nasa* community engaged in the reclamation of their history, their memory and their culture, in the improvement of their economy and their political influence and, as far as they could, of their social conditions. As they have been doing for years, they kept demanding from the State opportunities for their self-development with essential rights such as education, health, social security, child assistance, technical support and the implementation of a real development plan designed and managed by the community itself. Twenty-one years after the massacre, the genocidal actions continue—the exclusion and the indifference of the State and the lordly society of Cauca—while the *Nasa* population grows, as do their needs.

Cauca has been a territory of social and military conflict since the colonial times. It was there that indigenous and slaves rebelled in the 17th, 18th and 19th century. It was a strategic territory in the fight for independence from Spain, the stage of wars between Centralists and Federalists and of scores of civil wars. In the last 50 years, insurgent organizations—of all tendencies—and state forces (legal and illegal) made the southwest of the country a stage of military operations. Drug dealers, with the production and transformation of coca leaves to cocaine and the production of opium poppies, played an important role in the expansion of the agricultural boundaries and in the violence that shakes this territory and the rest of the country, but most importantly, in the preservation of a semi-feudal economy and society in Cauca.

The problem of violence and plunder is actually not exclusively related to laws and agreements, nor to the political will of the governors. Injustice and violence derive from the very economic and social formation of the nation of Colombia. An aristocratic oligarchy is operating in the lordly society of Cauca—heirs of the *Encomienda* feudal system of trusteeship and the *Mita* system of debt peonage—and preserves the colonial structure of property based on the concentration of land and the servitude of the indigenous and black communities in monoculture production such as sugar cane, oil palm, livestock farming and mining. This has been a painfull process. The elderly indigenous people remember the murders that occurred since the 1940s, with repeated killings that lasted nearly until the '60s of the last century. At that time "the *pajaramenta* (paramilitaries in the service of landowners) would arrive and set the houses on fire and displace the people." This is the way that indigenous people, interviewed in 2012, narrate the events of the period of Violence, which was intensified in Colombia on April 9, 1948 with the death of Jorge Eliecer Gaitan, who had been bravely condemning the atrocities of the oligarchy in the massacres of the early 20th century.

The Cauca department is situated in the southwest of the country between the Central and West cordilleras and the Pacific Ocean. This is a territory with topography of valleys—where we find the most fertile plots of land—and high, snow-capped mountains which contain forests, wastelands and volcanoes. Since the times of the Spanish conquest, landowners have been violently displacing indigenous communities towards the mountains and infertile areas, and have been keeping for themselves the most productive land of the valleys.

> The economy of Cauca is mainly based on agricultural production and livestock breeding, forestry, fishing activity and trade. Agriculture was introduced and developed technically in the north of the region. The main crops cultivated are cane, panela cane, traditional corn, rice, modified corn, banana, fique, cassava, potato, coconut, sorghum, cacao, peanut and African oil palm. In the Pacific region, gold, silver and platinum is extracted. Other non-precious minerals that are extracted are sulfur, asbestos, limestone, talc, gypsum and coal. Manufacturing industry is concentrated in Popayan, Santander de Quilichao, and Puerto Tejada, with food, drink, dairy, paper, packing and wood processing factories, sugar industry and the production of printouts for exportation. The centers of major commercial activity are Popayan, Santander de Quilichao, Patia (El Bordo), Puerto Tejada, Piendamo and Corinto. –Document of Local Government of Cauca

The financial voracity and the mega-mining operations that pillage the natural mineral and energetic resources on behalf of transnational capital have led to the displacement and genocide of the people living on territories that were chosen for these activities, and for the mega-projects of infrastructure that are necessary for the exploration, operation, extraction and transport of these resources towards the metropolises. Furthermore, as part of the economic and social structure, land concentration, despotism and drug trafficking are the agents that historically participate in the dispossession of peasants and indigenous and black communities in Cauca and Colombia.

Nowadays, through neoliberal policies, major transnational mining corporations also aim to take over natural parks and mountains where big quantities of industrial minerals can be found. They want to privatize and exploit holy indigenous places and the sources of precious natural water, as this is where the five most important rivers of the country begin and create what is known as the "hydrographic star." Cauca is a territory of enormous natural and cultural wealth, a place of strategic economic and military significance. More than 60% of its inhabitants are indigenous and black. Approximately 80% of the population lives in poverty; there is lack of decent housing, work, health, education, transportation networks and public services, mainly on the Pacific coast, where peasant, indigenous and black people live. The principal area of agro-industrial and commercial production is located in the northern part of the Cauca region.

II Organization

Despite the consolidation of the capitalist society, indigenous peoples possess their own political and social structures—some of which are ancestral, others were enforced by the Spanish—such as the indigenous reservations on territorial level and the *cabildo* (township) as a form of political organization, which was implemented in order to take advantage of their working force and dispossess them of their material and cultural wealth, especially of their land. After the colonial times, the *Nasa* indigenous groups inverted the significance and utility of these structures and turned them into their own institutions, which allowed them to embark on a unification process to recover their territories, cultures and their political and economic autonomy. They also developed different concepts and methods for doing politics that move away from the Western methods that are prevalent among the left revolutionary organizations, but mainly among politicians, intellectuals and leaders of the Colombian oligarchy. Thus, their organizations are not equivalent to political parties representing class sectors. Their institutions are instruments of community government, such as the indigenous guard, and they have their own judicial system which contributes to the achievement of the goals of their communities.

As a population, the indigenous communities not only maintained some organizations imposed during colonial times, but also created new forms of resistance in the process of the struggle for land, such as the guerrilla movement Quintin Lame, which was active in the '80s of the previous century and later disarmed and dissolved together with other insurgent organizations (the Popular Liberation Party [EPL], the 19th of April Movement [M-19], the Worker's Revolutionary Party [PRT] and a sector of the National Liberation Army [ELN]), as a result of the "Peace Process" which was held with the government of Belisario Betancourt. These organizations along with the Revolutionary Armed Forces of Colombia (FARC) had some influence on the rural and indigenous sectors of Cauca, even though the latter preserved their political and ideological independence. Despite the fact that the religious dominance of the Catholic Church continues, in recent times other creeds which promote docility and conformism have also been proliferating, aiming thus to hinder the struggle for land and autonomy, a role also played by the parties and the political groups of the oligarchy.

There are various organizations that were created during the struggle, such as the Regional Indigenous Council of Cauca (CRIC—1971), the Quintin Lame movement, the Movement for Communitarian Integration (MIC), the Agrarian Leagues established in Corinto, the Association of Indigenous Cabildos of Northern Cauca (ACIN), the National Indigenous Organization of Colombia (ONIC 1985), the Defenders of the Territory. Among them stands out the *Minga* of Social and Communitarian Resistance, which was founded in 2004, initially by indigenous, farmer and popular organizations of Cauca that promoted the march towards Cali named "*Minga* for Life, Justice, Happiness, Autonomy and the Freedom of the People" with a proposal to create resistance and sovereignty mechanisms and strategies—a mobilization in which black communities, students and popular sectors of the city joined, and in which approximately eighty thousand people participated. As a result of these actions the "Indigenous and Popular Mandate" emerged on September 18, 2004, a proposal that led to the creation of the *Congress of the People*, a national organization which gathers more than 200 political and social organizations of all popular rural and urban sectors. It is a framework of popular discussion and unity in which many thematic meetings have taken place about the problems of the poor of the country, trying to legislate through mandates, searching for a duality of powers which could lead to a popular hegemony.

At the same time on a national level the broad *Patriotic March* movement was formed, which promotes popular unity against oligarchy and the current economic model, together with the Congress of the People and the Democratic Alternative Pole in which indigenous communities also participate. They all agree with the indigenous movement concerning the need to negotiate a political solution to the social and armed conflict suffered by the Colombian population for more than 60 years.

On April 30 and May 1–2, 2010 approximately 1,000 indigenous people of different regions of Cauca, as well as from other indigenous territories of the country, together with peasants, students and leaders of other social groups, gathered to hold the first Congress of the Movement of the Landless and of the Grandchildren of Manuel Quintin Lame in Santander de Quilichao (north of Cauca). It is a movement that includes indigenous people, peasants and landless laborers, with the aim of creating a space of reflection regarding social, political and economic matters. Representatives of 67 organizations, as well as founders of the CRIC, attended this congress, an event in which the indigenous leadership's commitment to the statist model was questioned.

During the struggle, many indigenous people questioned the role of their organizations and the real ambitions of their authorities, since in many cases the leaderships (CRIC and ACIN) have turned into instruments of reconciliation and into extensions of oligarchical power. This is the reason some indigenous sectors of north Cauca disobey their authorities, trying to change the submissive practices that promote corruption and the division of communities. Some leaders have reproduced the system of bourgeois values in their communities, flaunting their power with things like cars, houses and luxury, with an unsupportive, contemptuous attitude towards the members of the community that live in poverty, including collaboration with the repressive forces of the state, denouncing the members of the community that criticize their actions and those who refuse to obey their orders or support them.

III Mobilization and Political Activity

The struggle for the liberation of Mother Earth is not only an affair of the indigenous; the popular sectors of the country have always been fighting for land and territory. In the '60s and '70s of the past century farmers and indigenous people, due to the breach of the "Agrarian Reform" that was proposed by the State, managed to reclaim a big quantity of land in the whole country, under the slogan "the land belongs to those who work on it." During this process, alliances were formed between indigenous peoples, peasants and black communities. So far in this century the indigenous peoples of Cauca, amid the armed conflict that generally signifies the elimination of peasantry and the plunder of their lands for more than 60 years, have pursued, as far as possible, the liberation of Mother

Earth. Nevertheless, this struggle has had a high price, as many members on the *Nasa* community have perished in the last two decades.

In 2005 the indigenous people of northern Cauca re-launched the liberation of Mother Earth with the direct action of the community after serious discussions between grassroots groups and the authorities regarding the need to expand their territory and their productive space for the young people and for future generations, as a response to the failure of the state to comply to the agreements that were signed before the massacre of the Nile. Neither the leaders of ACIN nor the leaders of CRIC agreed to these actions, only advocating intervention when the recovery of the *Japio* and *La Emperatriz* estates was already concluded, trying to push the members of the community towards negotiations and obligating them to leave the terrains. This was another defeat of the indigenous movement perpetuated from within, which demobilized and divided the community.

Since the '90s, the mobilizations of the Indigenous Authorities and communities were looking for direct dialog with the State administrators, and managed in 2008—through pressure from the indigenous communities and the national and international support of the people—to have a meeting with the then president Uribe and his government team in La Maria (indigenous territory) to discuss again the breached agreements. Later in Cali, they agreed to meet president Uribe, but the indigenous people left after waiting for him for three hours. To reestablish the dialog, the president had to go up on a pedestrian bridge, where he was booed by the population and he was not allowed to speak. The indigenous people arrived in Cali after a 4-day long march from their territories. They threatened that if the situation was not resolved in the capital of Valle they would march to Bogota. While this was happening, some houses in their indigenous reservations were set on fire and it is speculated that members of the public armed forces participated in this.

This was only one of the most recent struggles. There have been many others:

•

On July 19, 1992, as a prelude to the celebrations of the 200 years of the "Cry of Independence," representatives of different regions and communities of the country met in Bogota in order to hold a "Congress of the People" in parallel to the official events, and with the intention to legislate. Likewise, on July 20 more than 6,000 demonstrators coming from all corners of the country came to the capital to carry out a "March for Independence." This was the first time that the left-wing decided to commemorate a national anniversary separately from the official celebrations. Similar marches took place in the main cities of the country.

•

Along with large mobilizations, the indigenous peoples of northern Cauca also practiced popular democracy: the consultation on the USA-Colombian Free Trade Agreement (TLC), which was called together by the indigenous *cabildos* on March 6, 2008, in the municipalities of Jambalo, Toribio, Silvia, Caldono, Inza and Paez. 51,330 people out of the 68,448 potential voters participated; 98% rejected the TLC and only 691 of the votes were in favor. Despite the fact that this result was indicative of the popular sentiment, the government went on and signed this detrimental agreement. This was an exemplarily democratic event and it was widely promoted through preliminary assemblies. It was a way of rejecting the submissive policies of the governments. Unfortunately the rest of the Colombian population did not react in the same way. Nevertheless that was an indicator of the rising autonomy of the communities of Northern Cauca.

•

On October 12, 2008, the indigenous population occupied the Pan-American highway in Piendamo aiming to reiterate their demands, to protest against the violence, which had been the only response to their demands, and also against the breach of the agreements of 2004 between the *Minga* and the national government, and to denounce the death of Edwin Legarda during his retention by military forces. During conversations in commemoration of the 12th of October, the "Liberation of Mother Earth" took shape, a process that included meetings with the leaders of ACIN in the northeast of Caldono, which would debate on whether to openly call for protest or promote rising of awareness, and evaluate the results of the marches to Santander and Cali. Since these actions did not have a satisfactory response, the members of the communities decided to proceed with occupying the *Japio* and *La Emperatriz* ranches in Caloto.

The indigenous peoples of the whole country mobilized for the same reasons that the Nasa did. In November 2008, more than ten thousand indigenous people gathered in Bogota, as a culmination of a march of the *Zenu*, the *Kamkuano*, the *Wiwa* and the *Wayu*, who started the march in Riohacha on the northern coast; the Bari peoples who traveled the highway connecting Tibu and Cucuta on the northeast of the country. More than 1,200 *Nasa*, *Pijao* and

Embera-Chami traveled on a section of the Pan-American highway, while the *Nasa*, the *Guambiano*, the *Paez*, the *Yanakona* and the *Kokonuco* gathered in La Maria, Piendamo in the southwest. This march represented the interests of 1,350,000 indigenous people of different communities.

•

Due to the intensification of the armed conflict on the territories of northern Cauca, the leaders of CRIC called on April 20, 2011 a "*Minga* of resistance for the autonomy and territorial harmony and for the cessation of war." In accordance with this mandate, they held many meetings with the commanding officers of the official army, requesting them to abandon the territories which were used as war zones. Since these demands were not satisfied, the indigenous people, holding only their command batons, surrounded the soldiers, threw down the trenches and forced them out of this zone just as it had happened on the Berlin hills. Even though the war is still going on and the official media are slandering the indigenous people, presenting them as guerrillas and supporters, today the indigenous population of northern Cauca is politically confronting the State, claiming its autonomy and the respect to its territory, demanding from the armed forces—the army, insurgents, mercenaries and paramilitary mafia—evacuate their territory as a war zone.

In their effort to reclaim land, territory and autonomy, indigenous people of various regions of the country, including Cauca, entered official politics by participating in elections for municipal authorities, local government, regional assemblies and the national congress—organizations which manage the resources accorded by the state to the territorial entities and in the case of the congress, create and approve new laws—gaining positions and seats in their territories under right-wing and left-wing parties as well as the Indigenous Social Alliance (ASI).

These civil servants did not succeed in fulfilling the demands of their communities, which remained in the same condition of poverty and exclusion. The majority of these spokesmen became incorporated in their new political culture and picked up the vices of the representatives of the oligarchy. This created ambiguity regarding their autonomy and the role of the State that oppresses, represses and excludes them, because it is not clear which authority governs these communities.

On the other hand the indigenist conception has prevailed among most of their authorities and leaders, a fact that hindered the establishment of stable alliances with other rural and urban parts of the population. This ethnocentric, sectorial and guild-centric vision exists in all social movements throughout the national territory, even though the indigenous movement has been nationally and internationally gaining respect and admiration the last 15 years.

IV Memory and Practice

In order to be revived as an ethnic group the *Nasa* have followed the footsteps of Quintin Lame, their distinguished leader, who awakened the indigenous peoples of the country to open new paths and create a future of dignity. Thus the *Nasa* or *Paez* together with the *Pijao* were some of the few ethnic groups who have preserved their rebellious spirit against the colonialists and landowners, and today against the European and North-American neo-colonialists. The indigenous leader Manuel Quintin Lame also made his ideas known through his literary work: "He promoted the law no. 89 of 1890 which stated that the land belonged to the indigenous people, and that it was stolen from us." Based on these mandates seven *Cabildos* and an equal number of indigenous reservations were created on February 24, 1971 in Toribio the Regional Indigenous Council of Cauca (CRIC), which appointed the first Executive Committee, but which failed to operate due to the repression of the landowners and the lack of sufficient organization at the time. In September of the same year, the Second Congress of CRIC took place in Tacueyo, where the main points of its political agenda were specified. These political imperatives created the central axis of the movement and picked up the teachings of their leaders, such as La Gaitana, Juan Tama and Manuel Quintin Lame. As a result, the indigenous communities "reinforced our struggles based on the demand to implement law no. 89 of 1890 in the light of the issues raised by the Platform of Struggle of the Regional Indigenous Council of Cauca (CRIC)," which were put forth in the year of its formation:

> Thus, LAND, UNITY, CULTURE and AUTONOMY are the principles that explain and justify the emergence of CRIC, under the following platform of struggle that has as an aim to:
>
> 1) Reclaim the land of indigenous reservations.
> 2) Expand the indigenous reservations.
> 3) Strengthen the indigenous *cabildos*.
> 4) Reject the payment of fees for arable land.
> 5) Promote knowledge of laws and demand their fair implementation.
> 6) Defend history, language and customs.
> 7) Educate indigenous teachers so that they will teach according to the indigenous conditions.

8) Promote community economic organizations.
9) Reinforce and preserve natural resources.
10) Reorganize the *Nasa* family based on the requirements of the life plan.

The indigenous struggle of Cauca paved the way for the rest of the peoples to also promote their vindications and this new potential led to the formation of the National Indigenous Organization of Colombia (ONIC) in 1985, which began to operate based on the following principles:

1) Defense of indigenous autonomy.
2) Defense of indigenous territories, reclaiming of usurped lands and of the collective ownership of indigenous reservations.
3) Control over the natural resources within the indigenous territories.
4) Promotion of the economic and community organizations.
5) Defense of indigenous history, culture and traditions.
6) Bilingual and bicultural education under the control of indigenous authorities.
7) Recovering and promotion of indigenous medicine, demand for health programs in accordance with the social and cultural traits of indigenous communities.
8) Demand the implementation of law no. 89 of 1890 and other regulations favorable to the indigenous peoples.
9) Solidarity with the struggles of all exploited and oppressed peoples.

The process of reclaiming the land begins with the recovery of memory, with the acknowledgment of the condition of servitude (arable land fees) to the landowners, and also with a quest for ideological and political devices that allow for a shift from passivity to assertive action, to self-awareness in collective action and thought, to the vindication of dignity, identity and autonomy. This is a process in which the leading role belongs to women—such as the female indigenous leader Gaitana who fought against the European invaders—and to young people who lead, direct and participate in the struggle.

The comment of a member of the community illustrate the conditions in which they live:

> I was the governor in '47, he used to say, I was the governor but I was in the service of the church and the landowner, he used to say. I was the governor and I was the commander, I was the one taking people out of their

> communities to get them to work for the wealthy, he used to say. And I also collected the alms to give them to the priest, he used to say.
>
> –ANGELA

Repression was constant, to the point that even the books about agrarian reform were to be read in secrecy. "We were secretly meeting in a coffee plantation. It was very dangerous to gather, because if someone came and notified the authorities that we were gathering they would send us to jail." Education was a permanent concern of the *Nasa* peoples. CRIC was publishing a newspaper called *Indigenous Unity*, which was reporting on what was going on in other regions, helping raise awareness on the liberation of Mother Earth—a struggle which in Coconucos was directed against the archbishop of Popayan, who possessed enormous parts of land in the central region.

> Historically the Political Program has stressed the importance of recovering ancestral knowledge and the value of the wisdom of the elders, who are compared to books that the community has at its disposal for permanent consultation. In that respect we have worked towards counteracting the ideological penetration and reinforcing identity with their concepts of autonomy, collectivity and wholesomeness.
>
> –CRIC, *Political Project*

Today the *Nasa* and other peoples of Cauca have various community radios and websites in addition to newspapers, which are tools that allow them to inform, educate, denounce and organize their communities and mobilizations. They have organized forums and workshops on the media; they have proposed the establishment of the Indigenous University; and they are participating in the elaboration of an educational proposal, based on their experience and their demand for a bilingual education in which their history, their world vision and their ancestral language is promoted. All these constitute the foundation in the construction of a proposal of popular unity, which has their participation in the Congress of the People as a starting point.

V Unity and Difference

We ought to keep in mind that the indigenous movement of Colombia is not homogeneous. It consists of more than sixty ethnic groups, most of which have their own languages. It is not situated on only one territory, but rather it is distributed in different areas of the country, and each area has different political stances regarding the role of the State. Different stances exist even within the same indigenous territory and within the same ethnic group. Some of these positions endorse collaboration with the regime, whereas others preserve their rebellious character and their demand for ancestral and current rights. This is true with the *Nasa*, the majority of whom are located in Cauca and Putumayo, and are reclaiming the same territory as other ethnic groups such as the *Guambiano* or *Misak*, the *Inga* and the *Cofan*, who are persecuted and small in numbers, but still remain ready to struggle.

The social composition of the *Nasa* is diverse, among them there are members that develop their economic and social life within their communities; others that behave like peasants holding individual property rights on land and their work tools; and others that are proletarians who do not own land. They work in the plantations of landowners or in the sugar factories. The latter are generally disorganized and isolated from their communities, some of them get involved in social processes, they move in and out of the territory looking for a way to survive as day laborers. Some of them do not lose their attachment to their communities and their fighting spirit and return back home. Others migrate to the cities and settle in the periphery, making a living as workers or small vendors. Very few of them manage to go to university. As time goes by, some members of the community are dispersed, but the core of the community maintains its struggling tradition.

As an ethnic group the *Nasa* have internal political differences and visions which are reflected in the way they accept commitments, in the decision making processes, in the way they carry out political debates and achieve their goals. In this case we can observe the ideological battle between the leadership and the grassroots, which are looking for alternatives in the movement's direction, are learning from each and every experience, and are promoting organization. Even though the indigenous authorities insist on leading the struggles and on being mediators and negotiators in the conflicts that concern them as territorial communities, the large mobilizations of the last years were guided by grassroots groups, often against the decisions of their authorities, who end up playing the role of state representatives, repressing and persecuting their own communities.

In the face of the refusal of the leadership, of certain governors of *cabildos* and of organizations now turned official, such as the CRIC, to join the reclaiming of land, the people made the following thoughts: "What we have gained so far and what we have today has always been created by the families themselves, by the ones that have struggled. It has not been the leaders or the authorities. Let us keep doing the same and we will see along the way." With the participation of the Movement of the Landless and of the Grandchildren of Manuel Quintin Lame, they decided to start their campaign with a ranch next to *La Emperatriz, El Malabrigo*. This is where the movement was launched.

In reclaiming and recovering land, the *Nasa* population of northern Cauca was supported by some governors and ex-governors of *cabildos*, traditional doctors and other senior leaders who had been part of the struggle since the '60s and '70s. Some members of the community suggested that the *cabildos* should buy the lands using the money transferred to them by the State, so that they would then hand them over. But the conditions set by the state hindered this. In addition, the money that arrives for all inhabitants is not enough. Others suggested that the government buys the land and hands it over through the Colombian Institute of Rural Development (INCODER), as it had already done in some cases. But this did not happen either.

In the struggle for land, despite sharing the condition of expropriation by the landowners, of violence and of poverty, the farmer populations got in internal conflict and even confrontation regarding the way of reclaiming and maintaining the community ownership of the land. This occurred between indigenous people, afro-descendants and peasants, with incidences such as the one in the Ranch of San Rafael in the Municipality of Santander de Quilichao, in the Los Naranjos ranch in the municipality of Cajibio bordering the municipality of Totoro, as well as the Filigrana ranch among others. These incidents ended with many people wounded, and caused enmities within these communities. It does not seem reasonable to have social conflict among the oppressed popular sectors that are the victims of landowners and capitalists, that is, to reenact the same violent treatment perpetrated by the State and the bourgeois society.

VI Conclusions

Currently the indigenous resistance is founded on two elements: the struggle for land and territory, and the recovery of their cultures. They confront the state and demand that it complies with numerous agreements and that it recognizes their autonomy. The indigenous movement, like other parts of the population, is still being repressed and the only response of the State is to leave more people dead and wounded every day.

Among the persecution and murder of those who defend their dignity throughout the country, the indigenous people of northern Cauca continue constructing their present and future within their own culture and economy, which shift from the ancestral to the integral development projects, to community enterprises, to cooperativism, to producers' associations—contributing to the construction of a political project of all rural and urban peoples to achieve liberty, social justice, dignity and autonomy for each and every Colombian man and woman. "In 1990–91 we started working on the educational project, the integral project; in Jambalo and Toribio they were already working on the *Nasa* project, the Global project; at that time Huellas created there the integral project.":

- *Nasa* project, Toribio, Tacueyo and San Fransisco, 1980.
- Global project, municipality of Jambalo, 1987. Paez Unity project, municipality of Miranda, 1990.
- Integral project, indigenous reservation of the Huellas, municipality of Galoto, 1990.
- Cxacxawala project, municipality of Corinto, 1991.
- Yu'lucx, municipality of Santander de Quilichao, 1991.
- SatFxine Kiwe project, municipality of Buenos Aires, 2002.

These are programs of community development and new associations of community and solidarity economy to improve their social conditions:

> Today ARISA, in the municipality of Santander, has two cane plantations jointly with members of the community and we have also looked into the people's continuing need regarding production and working processes. ... Let the people themselves produce to feed themselves, their communities, their children and also to trade.

It is contradictory that some indigenous groups sign exploitation or leasing contracts with landowners and agro-industrial enterprises (sugar factories), mining companies or transnational companies, such as *Cartón de Colombia,* which exploit workers and destroy the environment, according to the intentions of the current government with its law of lands restitution. It is also contradictory to fight for the liberation of Mother Earth and at the same time produce for transnational food companies using toxic chemical substances, as many communities have been doing, not only in Cauca, but also in other regions of the country. The food import policies contribute to the transfer of land to foreign ownership and to the expansion of large estates and monocultures, reducing the opportunities for development of the indigenous and rural communities and promoting the loss of food sovereignty. Likewise, just like other sectors of the population, some indigenous communities support and vote for racist, murderous landowners for deputies and for national and regional governors, dividing the indigenous movement, while at the same time asking from the capitalist state to protect them and to respect their territories.

The *Nasa* of northern Cauca are standing at a crossroad, compelled to take decisions of a strategic nature on the present and the future, regarding both political and economic matters. Those with political clarity do not propose their unity isolated from the economic, social and political context of the country. They believe that the struggles for land in the countryside and in the cities should advance together; that urban people contribute to and strengthen the struggle of indigenous peoples, peasants and black communities; that the decisive factors of their struggle for territory, dignity and autonomy lie in economy, education and the unity of families. Food sufficiency—within the concept of food sovereignty—is a goal to be achieved for the development of the community and in order to be able to support the liberation of Mother Earth. They feel the necessity of uniting Western knowledge with ancestral knowledge, to transfer the knowledge of the elders to the young people for creating social leadership and for reclaiming dignity as people and as an ethnic group. In fact these indigenous peoples see themselves as an autonomous social group with multiple political, social and cultural relationships on the national and international level, without losing their essence.

These concerns are issues of discussion and action that only the indigenous people can autonomously define. The indigenous communities are not laboratory rats of political groups, transnational companies, states and national and international NGOs. Their participation with equal rights to the rest of the peoples that compose the nation of Colombia is fundamental for the development of a revolutionary, anti-capitalist, humanist movement, for the construction of our *buen vivir*.

Appendix: Interviews with *Nasa* Activists

Maria Soledad, Indigenous Woman of Nasa Ethnicity, Dedicated Community Leader and Native of Caloto Municipality, Cauca

During my childhood I had a hard time because my parents were persecuted, for example there was a massacre, when the *pajaramenta* [paramilitaries in the service of landowners] was coming to burn down the houses and displace the population. They used to tie people up. Many people fled towards the Naya River to avoid the massacre. The rich had many coffee plantations there. Many people were killed for being indigenous. For example they would come to our houses carrying sacks asking for coffee to organize the festivities and the people who did not want give any were persecuted. So my parents were persecuted and many people went away, but my parents did not go because my mom was a doctor and my dad said that we have to work, we have to rejuvenate; we have to keep on using traditional medicine. So they would not kill us, and this was how we resisted in this region. This is when we first hear this story, that the land is ours...

So when the people who did the community guidance came here, they brought us books, books by Manuel Quintin Lame, saying that the law 89 of 1890 said that the land belonged to the indigenous; that we were robed. It was then that my brother and many more people said look, this is our land, but we keep paying the rich men. This was when we started to think about how to reclaim the land...

This whole process of gathering with the people, informing the people, started back then, and since all the people of this settlement [*vereda*, Colombian administrative division smaller than the municipality] and the nearby settlements, Huellas, Arrayan, were very much united. I was the one who could read and write well, so we created a study group and we started studying the works of Quintin Lame, because the works of Quintin Lame tell a great story of everything that he did. He struggled for this land, he went all over the Cauca region. He did a series of things. So it was like we took up all these ideals of Quintin Lame. The people who did community guidance used to say: from these mandates that were left, the CRIC emerged, back then we were already talking about the Regional Indigenous Council of Cauca with its 7-point program. The first one was to reclaim our land, extend our [indigenous] reserve and create an indigenous authority. It was easy to unite all those people, so then they started to say that we have to struggle...

And a newspaper called *Unidad Indigena* [Indigenous Unity] would come from the CRIC (Regional Council of Cauca). We would also read everything that was going on in other areas, but everything was happening in secret because we could end up in jail. And that's how we started, that's how the whole process started...

It was then that this whole process of struggle for the land started: the men, and anyone else who had the ability, were going to one area or another. They were going towards the central area. They used to say that there was a very tough fight there with the people of Coconuco, because we were fighting directly against the archbishop of Popayan, because the archbishop of Popayan had vast amounts of land in the central area, where the Coconucos are. A great number of people left here to go over there to support the struggle. My husband would come back and say: over there the struggle is directly against the church, and no one knows how it will go. The army was involved in the fight. Women with children were in jail, whole families were in jail, so they were saying that the same thing was going to happen here, but we had to keep up the struggle anyway...

The process of struggle for the land had started more with the men. I would sometimes support them from the kitchen, helping prepare food and coffee. Gradually I learned many things in order to help the leaders, how to prepare food and many other things, and as I told you before. I knew how to read and write well, so it was my task to help others with their studies, read and explain them the meaning. This is how I was linked to this process...

After the massacre the process of reclaiming mother earth was halted, many people were scared, what with 20 comrades murdered in one night, we were very distressed... We didn't expect such a hard blow, and probably this fear remained in people: that if we keep insisting they can kill us, the same thing can happen again...

Grassroots people are willing to keep up the struggle for land, and this was obvious by what they did recently. The people are willing, they want this. The thing is that the *Nasa* people have been in resistance since a long time ago, since the very arrival of the Spaniards. The *Nasa* people are a people that do not give up, but their leaders are now scared. They have all turned law-abiding... and they are the ones who oppose the struggle. The people want to keep up the process, they want to keep up struggling for the land, I don't know, recently there is a lot of dissent within the people in the communities...

Now by signing the FTA [free trade agreement] they aim to take over the whole of our territory, because there is a lot of wealth in our reserve. But this is when I think the people are going to wake up, the owners of colonial reserves, since they are going to be affected because of the wealth that is there. This is where the gold mines are, and the salt mines, and the marble quarries and a whole lot of other things. The government has already made X-ray scans, and they know where the water deposits are. Now with the FTA, the government practically hands it over. Now they don't even have to invade us. The government simply hands it over and that's it. So I think that things are going to get tough in the territories. We already see how everything is militarized, and I don't think that this happens to protect us, but to protect the interests of capitalism. That's what I think. I might be wrong.

José Asunción, *Nasa* Indigenous Leader and Tireless Fighter

I began to get more involved because I was a member of the community council, and I started to like this process, because of the way we had the discussion. We realized that the communities had many different needs such as healthcare, education, housing, public services, so these were the issues that had always attracted my attention. We were delegates of the settlement [*vereda*] and we would participate in these assemblies. Unfortunately on these very days, in 1991, came the massacre of our comrades in Nilo...

After the Nilo massacre we made a pact with the national government, in which they agree to hand us over 15.000 hectares of land, because the Nilo massacre took place in the context of land occupation. So there you go. We had the idea of keeping up the land occupations, but if we went on occupying land they were going to keep on killing us. So we included this in the negotiation, we need such and such. In fact we gave them a list: *Japio, La Emperatriz, La Selvita, La Margarital* [lands]...

This issue of land occupation changed our strategy, or at least that's what the old thinkers said. Basically our strategy was to maintain a relationship with the state, which in the end had no result. We later had to go to the *Maria* to sleep there for 17 days, and then the decree No. 982 comes out, which tries to ratify the issues of land, healthcare, education. There is a lot of protest, a lot of beating, teargas and everything. This demonstrates that these pacts with the national government did not have any effect. After that, we have the issue of occupation of the lands of mother earth here in Huellas. Basically it was organized by just a few people of the Huellas reserve, and then the ACIN and the CRIC got involved. They said they did it to save us, but basically I think that what they tried to do was save their own reputation...

I think that the federal government by killing the people at Nilo dealt us a blow. They achieved what they wanted, which was to scare us. This is the right word. Basically, our leaders had a realization at that time, a leader or an Indian dies here and there are two or five or ten more. I think this had a great effect on the change of strategy that was discussed at the time: We now have legal recognition in the Constitution, so the leaders start talking about rights, and that it is a different thing to have rights. Why try to fight the state when we can enter into dialogue?

But I personally think that the blow of the Nilo massacre was a very important factor in that change, this redirection of the struggle and the end of land occupations...

Basically the shadow of Nilo loomed over some of the leaders more than it did over the grassroots supporters. I am convinced that if the leaders had decided to respond to the Nilo massacre, to keep up the direct action despite the 20 dead, I'm sure the community would have followed down that path.

The Community Police in Guerrero

An Interview with Marciano, an Indigenous Mixtec, on His Work and Experience

I would like to talk a little about a very important struggle that developed in the mountains and the Costa Chica of the state of Guerrero as a utopian movement, a movement that constituted a redemption of democracy, a struggle for security and for justice that the indigenous peoples deserve.

This struggle took place in the mountains of the state of Guerrero, where there emerged the Community Justice and Security System (the Community Police) as an autonomous organization of the indigenous *Mixteca, Tlapaneca* and *mestizo* peoples—three cultures that are integrated within this organization. This struggle has transcended the local level and has reached national and international levels.

The community security and justice project is an important element in the resistance of the peoples of Latin America as rural and indigenous peoples. This project seeks to restore confidence within the indigenous areas, to guarantee safety for the people and to promote social and collective coexistence in the region. It has emerged as a major element within the general project of autonomy of community operation, as a collective project arising from below, promoted by several social leaders and various organizations, because people were experiencing a fourth wave of violence as is the case in present-day Mexico, with conditions of nation-wide insecurity.

The Regional Coordinating Body of Community Police emerged in a climate of violence, rapes, assaults and violations. This was a matter of high priority for indigenous peoples. They were experiencing a security crisis, a crisis of justice.

This project aims to promote a regional development that focuses on the aspirations of the people and respects the principles of education and of an ethical justice system. In the education provided by the state, for example, justice is corrupt. It can be purchased. The Public Ministry [public prosecutor] is operated by people who have a lot of money and it is not accountable. One of the basic elements of the Community Police is respect for people's rights and for justice.

The project of Community Police was born on October 15, 1995 in the indigenous community of Santa Cruz del Rincon, in the Municipality of Malinaltepec, state of Guerrero. There, the first assembly was held and united over thirty peasant indigenous organizations around the issue of insecurity in the region. On October 15, 1995 the organization known as Community Police came into being and was entrusted with guarding, watching over rural roads and patrolling the villages in order to prevent violence.

In the nineties, as well as historically, the population was suffering discrimination, and for this reason they decided to organize and create a security force that would watch over the communities in various municipalities. This police force operates in several municipalities, including the Mentaltola, San Luis Zacatlán, Lázaro Comonfort and Malinaltepec.

The Community Police are playing a very important role in the legal field. The Mexican legal system considers us illegal. However, this project is backed by a document of international law, #169. The Mexican state disregards this project because it considers it outside the law. As a result, since the early days there has been persecution of social leaders. The Community Police has several times been accused of being a guerrilla force and they've tried to repress us by issuing several arrest warrants for social leaders.

Women have played an important role in the Community Police project since the beginning. Women have suffered at lot, including rape. In the community police there are women commissaries, as well as women who are appointed by the community to provide service within the project.

As youth within the Community Police we started a project of intercultural education, a university that aims at training young indigenous intellectuals to be able to guide and advise their own people. As students of the regional university we play an important role in the project, because when an anniversary is celebrated we are there to support. We take care of the logistics for the anniversary. Young people have an important role in the project. We are not excluded. Personally, I have had a lot experience, because as a part of the community police project, a radio station was created to facilitate community communication. Young people were there to promote this project and help disseminate the political aspect of it.

I participated in the radio program for almost a year, and then other young people came in a constant cycle of participation, meaning that there is not just one radio presenter who occupies all airtime. Instead, everyone has an opportunity to participate. In fact, we have several different radio programs on human rights, women's rights, the right to education and the rights of the indigenous peoples. The issue of migration is very important, as are the issues of national security and justice which are dealt with in several programs. One of the important programs that the community developed has been the promotion of peasant community politics, as well as Mexican farming and its products.

One problem of the peasants in Guerrero is that many soft drink companies have entered the territory. Many indigenous people are becoming ill from diabetes from consuming soft drinks. We are not consuming our own products like pineapple, plantain, coffee—what we grow ourselves. It is very important to have good production. However a company comes and takes everything away. What peasants need is to create a regional market where they can sell their produce, to export the farmers' products.

In the eighties, the peasant coffee growers had difficulties in selling their product, because the *caciques* [local headmen] of the region were buying up their entire product in return for a pittance. As a result, several villages and communities were organized to form a very important cooperative in the region, the *Luz de la Montaña*, an autonomous peasant organization, a coffee-growers cooperative that is today playing an important role in boosting the economy of the region.

Another project emerged, the *Unión Regional Campesina* [Regional Peasant Union], by the same coffee growers, with the purpose of promoting the exportation of the peasants' products to other states and countries.

Every two or three months the Community Police holds a regional assembly with the participation of authorities, commissaries, students, teachers and farmers to solve problems that arise within the project. For example, those administering justice within the project are older people who are elected by an assembly as representatives in the Community Police project.

One of the ways in which we work towards economic autonomy is to promote cooperatives, such as coffee growers' cooperatives. Coffee becomes a way to gain a certain amount of economic autonomy through the *Luz de la Montaña* cooperative.

There is also another project that I think is very important, one of community producing its own medicine of good quality. Last year there was a very good production unit of both men and women. It is important for people in the community to be part of the medicine project. They are taught in school to safeguard traditional herbalism, as an alternative to Western medicine. These, along with many more, are projects that are very important to further develop our autonomy.

In Guerrero several organizations are developing within the project of the Community Police. Traditional medicine is promoted, that is, herbal medicine used for treatment, because the indigenous are largely excluded from the health system of the Mexican state. The only option we have left is to organize and promote traditional medicine.

Another very important thing is that the organization runs four or five penitentiaries [cedes: *Centro de Ejecución de Sanciones*], so education is also an important part, because in the southern area there are five penitentiaries that are also within the Community Police project.

Education is a very important issue, on several occasions during the anniversaries of Community Police it was stressed that we need teachers, we need people who can defend the project, we need to create a university, we need to create professionals that can defend us, we do not have trained people in the region, we do not have university graduates, we do not have lawyers. We must create a university within the Community Police project to promote education, create an intercultural, autonomous university of the indigenous peoples of Guerrero, in order to train professionals who are able to defend the people, defend the territory, defend our autonomy, and above all, defend the peoples and communities of the region.

The public university trains professionals, however law graduates defend political parties, accountants defend businessmen, and this is for economic reasons. We need to create a university project that includes the five peoples of Guerrero, that is, *Mixtecos, Tlapanecos, Amuzgo, Nahuas*, and *mestizos*. We need to train professionals who can uphold the Community Police project itself.

CHAPTER 10

Women as Force and Reason of Social Transformations

∴

Feminisms and Liberations in Our America [*Nuestra América*]

Francesca Gargallo

History can only be analyzed from the present; that is obvious. However, when one becomes conscious of this, it overflows into an exercise of political awareness which allows for the adoption of a critical gaze at the social control apparatus which has been in the process of construction and is now catching up with us. To choose feminism as the political theory with which to interpret the place of women in the planning of this control is to define the rebelliousness of women's actions in the face of this entire apparatus.

In Our America, to approach the contribution of feminist theories in the history of emancipating processes, one must take a closer look at autonomous feminism; at class feminism as expressed by the National Coordinator of Rural and Indigenous Women (*Coordinadora Nacional de Mujeres Rurales e Indígenas, CONAMURI*) of Paraguay; at the antiracist feminism of Afro-Latin American women; and at feminisms conceived as practices of women in dialogue for the improvement of the conditions for women from different ethnic groups and original nationalities.

From the beginning of the 20th century, there have been radical acts for female liberation by Argentinean, Uruguayan and Mexican women anarchists, and the demands for women's rights have been tied to struggles for sovereignty and national liberation in Panama, El Salvador and Honduras. However, at that moment as well as in the 70s, there were miscomprehensions and even confrontations between liberal feminists demanding legal, financial and educational equality with men, and women who conceived feminism as an instrument for the construction of emancipating and liberating processes for men and women alike.

At present, due to the pressure put by the women themselves, most American countries have passed laws that guarantee a life free of violence, and punish sexual and gender discrimination. However, at the same time, female immigrants, indigenous women of different ethnic origins as well as women from rural areas and urban outcasts alike, denounce the criminalization of protest, the growing militarization of their countries, the racism encountered by/in education and the impunity enjoyed by the men who violate their rights and their lives. They point out the complicity that exists between states, repression, militarization and organized crime, the legal culture which is taught in universities and applied in police authority headquarters and courts—resulting in all kind of favoritisms towards men—and the unaltered historical practices of female discrimination and invisibility.

In Bolivia, the Feminist Assembly proposes, in the words of Aymara activist Julieta Paredes, "a different form of social organization with no state but, rather, the Community of Communities." In Guatemala, the Association of Indigenous Women of Santa Maria Xalapan, in Xalapa, manifests through the words of *Xinka* thinker Lorena Cabnal (whose grandmother is Mayan) that a process of decolonization that emanates from indigenous women must "get to know the maze of state laws in order to access justice" and, at the same time, "vote for local mechanisms of indigenous justice" so as to break with the hegemonic nation and the individual citizenship of women, both understood as mechanisms of constriction, true straitjackets for the liberation of persons and peoples.

In Our America today, along with the postulates of autonomous urban feminists—from their "mothers" who, in 1993, stood up against the coercion of feminist rebelliousness by the guidelines of financial backers and neoliberal discourse, to the younger collectives of Bogota and Mexico against femicide—exists the powerful resonation of the ideas of certain lesbians of African descent (Ochy Curiel and Yuderkys Espinosa, in particular) and the actions of collectivities of musicians, poets, plastic artists, construction workers, lesbians in communal cohabitation and of those who consider themselves to be autonomous from the academy, the redistributive policies of the state, the "leadership" or "empowerment" of women acting in society, as well as the work of women in Non-Governmental Organizations, weaving and unweaving non-stratified alliances.

As for the communitarian feminists of Bolivia and Guatemala, their process of dialogue and participation in liberation is in tune with the indigenous people's rejection of the domestication of the collective and the integration of the demands themselves into a legal web that would favor the state (any state). It fuels a movement which questions any political discourse that abstracts flesh, experience, sweat and sentiment from the female body, the axis of all actions for the emancipation from the capitalist system which is necessarily misogynous, colonialist and racist. It is, ultimately, a movement that converges in a revolutionary weave which, at present, is not and cannot be led by any party.

I will take a closer look at the assertions of women of diverse origins in order to show that there can be no decolonization without de-patriarchization, as the communitarian feminists of Bolivia claim. Even the more profound process of liberation, which is at the same time antiracist and deeply ecological, ethical and critical of the current forms of education, can only exist when there is a generalized awareness that one half of any people is conformed by women. There is no universality, only interweaving personal stories. There is no modernity, only instances of modernity experienced in particular stories. There are no peoples made up only of men, therefore the right to revert the submission of women is an inherent part of the liberation and transformation of the peoples themselves, not only of their women.

A profound work of de-patriarchization (to use the term coined by the communitarian feminism adopted by Bolivia's plurinational government) can put an end to the discrimination of the essentialized interpretations of what is "one's own culture," allowing constitutive complementarity to become truly of the nation, of its duality, and not only of its men.

Having said that, de-patriarchization is a collective task that implies listening to the discontent of women; that is, it implies a feminist attitude. To the *Nasa* teachers of Cauca (Colombia) who struggle for an education of their own and study a pedagogy of forms in order to acquire knowledge from territoriality, work, art and orality, it is constructive to break with the tradition of the elders who choose to take only the boys of the community on walks through the *Nasa* territory and to play traditional instruments only to them.

Walking and playing music are ways of transmitting knowledge on spatiality and, therefore, on mathematics and geometry; it is an ancestral tradition that the *Nasa* school has incorporated in its teaching and learning system. That is why the women have put an end to the practice of excluding girls from walking through their territory with the elders, recognizing plants, counting and multiplying footsteps and trees, playing the instruments that compose space, cure it and grant it peace.

Wherever women do not have the possibility to participate in *their* culture, the system of patriarchal exclusion results in a mystification of primeval duality and the domination of women, almost always accompanied by exploitation.

At the school "*Compañero* Manuel," built in 2004 by the *Tzeltal* women and men and the internationalists recognized as part of the Zapatista Front of National Liberation in Chiapas, Mexico, the promoters of education and health have conducted a work of "equal opportunities" for women and men which includes the same rights to education, as well as joint participation in economic activities which were once hierarchized and designated to one sex. Jules Falquet has studied the way in which many Mayan Zapatista women who have been educated as faithful keepers of the religious and everyday tradition of their people have rebelled against the present hierarchic vision of sexual duality in their communities, defending their right to participate in the definition of *their* culture in order to attain greater justice between men and women inside the "cultural sanctuary which is constituted by the community, the home and the family." (Falquet, Jules. 2001 "La costumbre cuestionada por sus fieles celadoras: reivindicaciones de las mujeres indígenas zapatistas.")

Certain bilingual *Zapotec*-Spanish teachers from the coast of Oaxaca, Mexico, have recently spread the idea that the more resistance a people have shown against westernization, the more equity between the sexes is experienced inside the community. They assert that the more a people have accepted oppression, the more they have developed violent forms of treating women. This idea is based on a historical interpretation of inequality as a result of colonialism. It belongs to an indigenous feminist current which is quite diffuse, but openly confronts other interpretations: for example those of the Xinka communitarian feminists of Guatemala and the Aymara in Bolivia, who stress the pressing need to unweave the denied—but acting—existence of the "ancestral patriarchate." Indeed, communitarian feminists insist on the urgency of a profound reflection in order to transcend the *situated historical stance* that categorically and exclusively blames the 518 years of colonialism for having caused all the evils of the original people, when women already suffered conditions of ancestral indigenous patriarchate.

The bilingual *Zapotec* teachers make a veiled reference to the effects of colonial domination on the *Nahua* people who, they claim, tried to maintain a privileged relation with colonial rule and, later on, with the independent republican governments through the acceptance of their cultural mandates.

The *Zapotec* women of the coastal area—excellent traders who possess savings and make investments with them, organize "velas" and other festive-religious activities, are catholic, have access to schools and face no cultural obstacles in accessing universities—[1] coincide in this aspect with political militants of the *Nasa* and *Wayuu* women in Colombia, the *Bris Bris* in Costa Rica and the *Ashaninca* of the Peruvian Amazon, who have organized themselves for the recovery and defense of their national territory and cultural rights.

Women from other American native groups doubt this, although some of them might be very skilled in verbal communication. They are women who

---

1 It is difficult to distinguish the economic from the cultural. Many Zapotec women from the Istmo de Tehuantepec area have told me that the limits to access superior education belong to the economic sphere, although on occasions they transcend the issue of having or not the money that is needed to send a daughter to the capital and pay for her studies and are related to the financial responsibilities that a woman can and should assume.

started to participate in the community's politics despite having been told by their fathers that it was not necessary to study, for a woman's destiny is to marry and serve a man-provider and his family, as is the case with certain *Quechua* women from Huancavelica in Peru, *Amuzgas* from Xochistlahuaca, *Zapotecs* from the Mexican Sierra de Juarez and *Q'om* women of Argentina.

The idea that "women and men constitute genders with shared responsibilities since times immemorial, genders that represent the feminine and masculine forces which are present in the totality of life," as *Nasa* leader [*dirigente*] Avelina Pancho asserts, expresses a myth of equity which characterizes a current of indigenous feminism. It is an ideal that has been reconstructed by the women that have taken it upon themselves to claim the collective rights of their peoples and is sustained by an appropriation and reinterpretation of their own cosmogonies. According to this feminist current, there is a tie between the claims of women for a better life and communitarian politics, a common drive which is at times ignored, a giving oneself the right to think from one's own reality and not only defend whatever might have been rescued from the shipwreck of the European invasion.

This feminist current is rescued by indigenous human rights activists, for it allows them to claim a place in the heart of their communities which is not typical of women in the current tradition, but to which they can aspire from a present re-elaboration of the ancient history of their peoples.

Amongst the peoples that resist assimilation, the complementarity of women and men in the field of political struggle, labor and economy, education and culture, is circumscribed in the feminist militancy ("*actuancia*") of few female leaders. For the majority, it is still a desire of women, rather than a reality. It corresponds to a reinvention of indigenous identity elaborated precisely on the basis of the actions of those female leaders. In reality, resistance against westernization does not imply a fair distribution of material resources between the sexes, nor does it lead to an immediate improvement of conditions for women. The resistance of the indigenous people is met with an increase in state violence; paramilitary soldiers use rape as a war tactic; during conflict, families disperse, tearing the weave of solidarity between women; and political leaders [*dirigentes*], women and men alike, consume more alcohol, a habit which greatly triggers domestic violence.[2]

2 All the peoples of America knew of different alcoholic beverages, produced through the fermentation of fruits and cereals; the Zapotecs in Mexico had invented a system of distilling through mud, different from the process that uses the still. However, the use of all alcoholic beverages was regulated and it involved "etiquettes" pertaining to each village. Outside regulated festivities, drunkenness was considered so deplorable that in some places it was

According to Filomena Shaslin, a member of the *Bri Bri* community of Bambu in the municipality of Talamanca, Costa Rica:

> We have always been taught not to talk about what is going on in our lives, to defend the community and say that the men respect us; but the truth is there is violence, starting from the families. We *Bri Bri* feel proud of belonging to our community, we are serene and happy with living as our mothers taught us and we are afraid we might be losing everything. We work in the fields, we learned how to make *tortillas*, how to make bread, how to sell, and now we are learning to have rights. When men deny us the right to go out, to meet with our mothers and their families, to support ourselves that is violence against women. When they beat us and oppress us they prevent us from being free. But, because we also want to defend the rights of the village, we sometimes don't say anything. I tell *Bri Bri* women that what is good for us, even if the elderly say otherwise, is what will allow us to advance with our culture.[3]

Also, amongst the *Mixe* of Oaxaca, the only Mexican people that never surrendered to colonization, the *Wayuu* of Venezuela, the *Nasa*, the *Misak* and many more, "men do not approve of the existence of protection services for women and claim that they cause major problems in the community," says Isadora Cruz, a young Nasa journalist of the Association of Indigenous Councils of Cauca, in a workshop on women and communication organized during the Continental Summit of Indigenous Communication *Abya Yala*.[4]

There are reports on violence against women which support this idea of the feminist current that stresses the need to "go back" to the equivalent

---

punishable by death. What is more, a crime committed under the influence of alcohol was punished twice as severely. The idea that "natives are drunks" is a racist construction of colonial origin, dating back to when the conquerors began to promote alcohol consumption amongst the men in order to break their capacity to resist. Alcohol abuse was accompanied by the tolerance of colonial authorities towards the physical violence of drunken men against women. Today, many indigenous women have realized through their own experiences that alcoholism amongst men causes situations of domestic violence. The banning of alcohol has also made many women drive their families towards conversion to neo-evangelic forms of Christianity.

3 Personal communication during a workshop on the rights of indigenous women imparted by the training center Centro de Capacitación Iriria, Arakorpa Ú and the Universidad Nacional de Costa Rica in Bambu, department of Talamanca, October 8, 2010.

4 The summit took place November 8–12, 2010, at the Maria Piendamo Reserve, Cauca, Colombia.

complementarity or ancestral equality between women and men. For example, certain cases in the Mexican states of Guerrero and Veracruz could support the hypothesis that there is more violence against women in villages that have been more colonized, meaning more discriminated, more Christianized and, therefore, more convinced of the superiority of men over women.

The reports of local governments are not very reliable, for they tend to categorize gender violence according to western parameters, leading to a confirmation of the white cultural prejudice that violence is greater in contexts with less formal education (could this be a remainder of the idea that violence against women is "natural"?).

The insistence of governments that gender violence is something "pertaining" to indigenous people is at present—at a moment when the international vocabulary imposes the denunciation of gender violence with equity and modernism—part of the strategy of a dominant nation-state to discredit the social ethics of indigenous people so as to prove their incapacity for autonomous self-government. However, this violence does exist and it increases with the impunity granted by the judicial system of this same nation-state to the men that commit it.

The impunity with which gender violence is met goes hand-in-hand with the selling of alcohol, racism, the traffic of women for forced prostitution and the insistent reproduction of misogynous prejudices by the authorities. Indeed, certain organizations of *Nahua* women, such as Noche Sihuame Zan Ze Tajome (All women as one) of Chilapa, Guerrero, report a strong incidence of beatings and severe mistreatment of women, to the point of death, amongst the couples of the *Nahua* people of Mexico.

The deaths of women, abortions caused by their husbands' beatings, discrimination, young women who are sold or forced to marry their rapists are a few of the practices that are often encountered in the *Nahua* communities of Ahuacuotzingo, Zitlala and Chilapa, denounces Brigida Chautla Ramos, leader of the indigenous organization *Noche Sihuame Zan Ze Tajome*.

Chautla Ramos, a *Nahua* indigenous woman from Chilapa, founder of the organization *Noche Sihuame Zan Ze Tajome* (All women as one), member of the Coordinating Committee of Indigenous Women of Guerrero (*Coordinadora Guerrerense de Mujeres Indígenas*) and of the Executive Committee of the National Union of Autonomous Regional Peasant Organizations (*Unión Nacional de Organizaciones Regionales Campesinas Autónomas,* UNORCA) regrets that, despite the struggles fought by women in that region for years, they have not yet been recognized as they should.

> [...] in the communities of the municipalities where *Noche Sihuame* operates, there are many cases of women who have been known to abort after being beaten by their husbands and "many of them have been murdered.

The communities with the highest incidence of such cases are Tlalixtlahuaca, Cuauhtenango, Tami of the Chilapa municiaplity, as well as Agua Zarca, in Ahuacuotzingo.

> "There was a deplorable case in Cuauhtenango, of a woman hit many times with an axe by her husband because she did not help him get the wood off the donkey, he struck her so hard he killed her," regrets Chautla Ramos.
>
> She adds: "another case is that of a young woman who got pregnant, her husband left her and the child was born in her house. That is frowned upon, because there cannot be single mothers. This girl was beaten up by her cousin so bad that she died."
>
> She also talked about how, in Agua Zarca, women are forced to marry their rapists: "what people will say is a very big thing there, so women are told they have to marry their rapists so that they won't be looked down upon, that if they don't, no one will ever want them again, that is their culture. Unfortunately, as there are good customs, there are also bad ones."
>
> She explained how most of the cases are not denounced because of fear: "when they are asked if they have been beaten they say they fell; their husbands threaten them, telling them that if they say anything it will be worse for them."[5]
>
> VILLA ARREOLA, 2009

Physical violence against women, girls and homosexuals is greater in communities that have been subjected more to the colonial gender mandates, but this is not the only reason. There are also appropriations of misogynous elements

5 Yamilet Villa Arreola, "Narran casos de muertes de indígenas por golpizas y abusos. Los usos y costumbres en aldeas nahuas, prácticas que generan violencia de género." That same day, in the same newspaper (*La Jornada Guerrero*, March 9, 2009), there were also accusations made by the Amuzga women of Xochistlahuaca and the Tlapanec women of La Montaña about a high incidence of gender violence in their communities. One must not forget that, in Mexico, the 8th of March is the day of the year when all newspapers publish the most terrible news on the victimization of women.

against the female body that correspond to cultural patterns not conducted by churches or states. That is, there are different convergences and insertions of patriarchates in traditional gender relations. An example of this is the adoption, less than a century ago, of the mutilation of the clitoris of little girls at their birth by the Embera-Chami community, near Risaralda, Colombia; they took it up after a brief contact with a displaced people of the Amazon.[6] Performed today by traditional midwives, this "custom" is defended as if it were ancestral, and some of the community's elders claim that clitoris excision helps prevent the rape of Embera women by military and paramilitary groups, because the men of these groups would not enjoy it![7]

However, the idea that patriarchal violence is related to colonial violence is present in the reflections of women belonging to communities which are far

---

6 Certain Colombian anthropologists affirm that the mutilation of the clitoris amongst the Embera-Chami women is a recent practice and that there is no data suggesting the custom has a history of over 70 years. However, it is known that various Amazonian people from Brazil and Peru practiced clitorectomy. Over 20 years ago, perhaps due to the influence of the Summer Linguistic Institute (Instituto Lingüístico de Verano) and of neo-evangelic churches who assured them the clitoris was not a penis and that a woman with a clitoris would not turn into a hermaphrodite, the Peruvian Amazonian groups that practiced clitorectomy in a ceremony conducted before puberty (Yin and Shipido people) ceased to do it. The country's central education had nothing to do with the abandonment of this practice; on the contrary, during the 1990s, the Peruvian state was characterized by the violation of indigenous women through the imposition of a brutal policy of sterilization. Clitorectomy is a practice of gender construction, for it guarantees there will be no similarity between male and female genitals; this dissimilarity provides the basis for the construction of a social disparity between the two sexes, which is accompanied by an imaginary of the destruction of a world that accepts the freedom and sexual pleasure of women.

7 Solany Zapata, regional council member of Risaralda, says in an interview for newspaper *El Tiempo* (http://www.eltiempo.com/media/produccion/EMBERApublish_to_web/) that, as an Embera, she opposed this practice because the rights of women must be respected, and even more the rights of girls. However, in her village this practice is conducted so that women will "not sleep around, leave their husbands or become tomboys." These arguments are related to certain beliefs of the Embera people, namely that when women move during the sexual act they cause natural disasters and that clitorectomy serves to counteract a possible genetic malformation which is known as pseudo-hermaphroditism, in which the clitoris grows to such an extent that it resembles a penis. In an interview for the radio, an indigenous leader from Antioquia said the mutilation was performed in order to protect the community: in the context of conflict when armed groups enter to attack the indigenous communities, they sexually abuse the women; ablation, he claims, serves to prevent militaries and paramilitaries from sexually enjoying their women.

away from each other. Some claim that, before the colony, men would not get drunk and violent; others believe that the complementarity of grandmothers and grandfathers in creation implied that men respected women; others, that women were more powerful before the arrival of the Spaniards; others yet, that men were "better," although women have "always" been behind men; a few believe that, if women share their being with mother earth and their cultures show respect towards its fruits, then men cannot be violent against the representatives of mother earth; and some believe that women who marry men of Spanish descent (*mestizos*) or men who work or live with men of Spanish descent suffer more violence because they have forgotten their true essence. Many more believe that, if their own education and law were taken up and traditional spirituality was practiced, women would stop suffering the ravages of *machismo*. According to Avelina Pancho:

> In the struggle for territory and for the Law of Origin or Higher Law, our communities and territories transform, they change over time. So do our thoughts and actions. Today, women are more equal to men, we have more rights, we have a voice inside the community and we express ourselves in the decisions of the community. We cannot struggle against the men, they are the same people as us. We are together on earth, we are together in struggle. The indigenous people of Colombia form a minority; if the women separate from the rest, we will disappear as a people. Two different parts have always been needed to create life, a woman and a man; it has been like that from the beginning. For the *Nasa* forefathers also, the Neh gods: they shared the knowledge and passed it on to their daughters and sons. By recovering our own education, we can transform and reinforce the relations between women and men so that we can live together each day with trust, solidarity and understanding, inside our territory. And also outside, when we must go out...
>
> When women weave, they help Mother Earth grow, they write our history, that is why we cannot stop working with the men, although we must demand from them that they recognize our participation more.[8]

8 Personal communication during certain conferences on the community's own education and health systems that took place at the headquarters of the Universidad Autónoma Indígena Intercultural—UAIIN—in Popayan, Colombia on the 5th and 6th of November, 2010. In her article "La lucha de las mujeres indígenas en estos 200 años" in *Pensamiento Universitario y Sociedad*, journal of the Universidad del Cauca, num.22, Popayan, October 2010, pp. 6–8), Avelina Pancho insists that, for indigenous women, it is as contradictory to speak of Independence during the festivities for the Bicentenary, as it is to speak of a politics

The idea that the oppression of women is inscribed in colonial history—or, rather, that the complementarity between women and men has become unequal and the order of the community rests on chores that are compulsory, exhausting and morally determining of the submissive character of women—could explain why women have no trouble organizing themselves autonomously when liberated from living with the men of their community for reasons beyond their control[9] but go back to their previous communitarian situation as soon as these conditions disappear.

When alone, they implement forms of relations and financial practices that (a) help them to heal from the violence they have suffered; (b) avoid the intervention of the state or its institutions in the organization of their collective and family life. With men, when they go back to the reconstructed community of their place of origin, they tend to silence the specific forms of violence suffered in the female body and to reduce their capacity to organize themselves autonomously.

A study of affectivity as a meaningful social experience, conducted by Kaqchikel sociologist Emma Delfina Chirix Garcia, tries to explain the construction of subjectivity amongst those women who seek to break free from the tension between acquired gender roles and the social construction of their affection for other women, be they family or friends. According to Chirix García, Mayan women

> have interiorized, acted upon and reproduced a recognizable set of values, conducts, attitudes, expressions and thoughts related to affection, which helps one to comprehend what they think of, how they organize their own thoughts, what idea they express of themselves as women, how they organize the care of their own daughters and sons as well as of the girls and boys of the community, what place they give to themselves. In their world of relations, the woman person does not disappear before the community, before the collective subject; however, her subjectivity is forged in spheres where she is not allowed to grow freely, for "in a relation

---

of women separate from that of men, because "the harsh and unfair experiences we have faced in our struggle as a people" have been the same. And she adds: "We indigenous women have survived so many wars, we are still alive, we have fought and we are still fighting, because it is part of our footprint during these 200 years, we have been maintaining life from the places that life has given us, maintaining the family, the community and the culture."

9 For example, in experiences of refuge within their own national territory (such as Colombia, in the decades of 1990–2000) and in neighboring countries (such as Guatemalan women in Mexico in the 1980s).

> of domination between parents and children, all advice is aimed at the control of the behavior and even the intimate life of people."
>
> CHIRIX GARCÍA, 2003: 54

In families that have a "corporate sense because they value and maintain absolute unity and totality" and whose "practices have developed in a communal context, with great dependence between their members, high precariousness and absence of services, as well as exclusion and discrimination by the rest of society" (ibid. 2003), affectivity cannot be separated from the construction of one's own subjectivity. At the same time, it is linked to the social roles imposed by fathers and mothers in exchange for the affection and care they afford. Thus, the construction of one's own subjectivity is organized from a place where it is impossible to separate affection from the observance of rules, norms, values and principles. That is where the idealization of deception is generalized through the conviction that obedience is an essential prerequisite for women to obtain affection. Thereupon, love is conceived as the prize women receive for their subordination. Though, contradictorily, it is precisely the deception that women experience in their eagerness to be accepted that leads to the emergence of the desire for personal liberation.

One learns to be a Mayan woman from a conception that is idealized, conservative and founded on inequality. In the Mayan conception, men and women are complementary; one cannot develop without the other. They maintain their integrity and specificity to conform eternal unity, but in everyday life one observes that complementarity is not constructed on the basis of equality, for the following reasons: Mayan women do not exercise power in the different social spheres (home and labor space), they do not usually make the most important decisions, they are valued for the domestic chores they perform and are therefore good for marriage but not for study. They are in charge of transmitting culture, taking care of the rest and observing values and moral norms (ibid. 2003).

•

> The dialogue that we are, the beauty pronounced between spirit and heart comes from the word jade with which we can construct our own refuge.
>
> MAYA CU, *Queqchi* poet from the City of Guatemala

The Mayan women of Guatemala have had to learn how to survive, from their complex and subdued weaves of affection, one of the most brutal experiences of genocide, ethnocide and gendercide in recent American history.[10] It is only due to the solidarity of their mothers, their relationships with some of their sisters and to having encountered other women going through the same situation as they are, that they have been able to establish forms of organization and dialogue between women with the support of extra-communitarian networks of urban feminists and women doctors, lawyers and sociologists. This way, they have made reflections that are centered in their own experience and are developed in their own communities, as well as in wider reunions of indigenous women or in healing centers created for this purpose. They venture towards a collective recognition of the methods discovered by each one of them, generating ideas, methods and conceptions of the female being that are explicitly feminist.[11]

They are experiences between women who voice their own reality through first-person narrations, "subjectivizing" people of the female sex insofar as they recognize them as the leading characters of their biographies. These narrations are instruments for the interpretation of female reality as a social one, one that involves the entire group in parity of value with male reality, and they allow for the identification of sexed strategies of good living, including access to a life free of violence.

Of course, not all indigenous women have gone through such a brutal contemporary historical experience as the Guatemalan communities;[12] however,

---

10 "Ethnocide" is a term related to that of genocide, meaning the massive murder of people because they belong to a specific ethnic or cultural group; it is also related to "culturcide" or the attempt to cause the disappearance of a culture that constitutes the identity of a people or nation. The term "gendercide," which refers to the murder of a woman because she belongs to the gender that is oppressed within the men-women relation, was defined by Warren (1985) in *Gendercide: The Implications of Sex Selection*. Today, there is a tendency to speak of "femicide," understood as the massive murder of women or their representation in the scale of violence or abuse against women. To form an idea on the ethnocide and gendercide that the Mayan peoples of Guatemala have survived, one must read the texts written by the Team of Forensic Anthropology of Guatemala [Equipo de Antropología Forense de Guatemala] and the reports of the Committee for Historical Clarification [Comisión de Esclarecimiento Histórico] and of the project for the Recovery of Historical Memory [Recuperación de la Memoria Histórica]; they speak of 699 massacres, with 400 villages devastated and over 200 thousand people murdered and missing.

11 *Tejidos que lleva el alma. Memoria de las mujeres mayas sobrevivientes de violación sexual durante el conflicto armado*, Equipo de Estudios Comunitarios y Acción Psicosocial and the Unión Nacional de Mujeres Guatemaltecas, in the context of the Consorcio Actoras del Cambio (F&G Editores, Guatemala, 2009, p. 450).

12 Or the Peruvian ones. In Peru, during the 1980s and 1990s, the indigenous women and their peoples suffered the terror of the state and the terror of a dogmatic, authoritarian,

no one can dismiss the latent threat of ethnocide if, as a people, men and women do not defend themselves from state racism and its multiple strategies of disappearances-assimilation-cultural annihilation. To ask the women of indigenous communities to adopt a feminism that is not primarily founded on the defense of their people against racism—as a mixed collective—is to fail to recognize the specific history of the women of native peoples and nations. In other words, it is to be unaware of the feminist indigenous identity.

The feminism of the *Lenca* and *Garifuna* women of Honduras, for example, involves other topics than those of the Mayan identity and subjectivity and is related to a different moment in their history: the construction of spaces of social impact, the political recognition of their rights and, since June 28 2009, the resistance against the *coup d'état* and the governments related to it. They claim, together with the women of European descent, that women are like the country and the country is treated by right-wing forces as the body of women. "*Ni golpe de estado ni golpes a las mujeres*" was the slogan chanted in all demonstrations.[13]

In Ecuador, the very strong and creative reconstruction of the *Kichwa* identity on the basis of experiences of self-organization, resistance to the impositions of the urban government and collective education in their own body of knowledge, has been imbued by the participation of women, who organized the first indigenous movements and never stopped seeing themselves in

violent and racist organization, the political-military Maoist organization Sendero Luminoso. The armed forces and the police of Peru had inherited a colonial disdain towards the Andean indigenous communities, they treated local authorities with contempt, displayed open racism against commoners and turned many young women into victims of sexual violence. The members of the Sendero Luminoso hated the Ashanincas and the rest of the Amazonian peoples, subjecting them to humiliations, privation of liberty, hunger and obligatory indoctrination. Quechua-speaking communities suffered massive murders because the military and the police considered them to be "internal enemies" that could ally with the Sendero Luminoso. At the same time, the Sendero Luminoso committed massive murders of commoners who were not considered "loyal," as part of the "popular war" against the state. The Committee for Truth and Reconciliation in Peru (Comisión de la Verdad y Reconciliación del Perú, CVR) estimates that over 70 thousand people died or disappeared during these decades of Dirty War. Jo-Marie Burt, *Violencia y autoritarismo en el Perú: bajo la sombra de Sendero y la dictadura de Fujimori*, Instituto de Estudios Peruanos-Servicios Educativos Rurales, Lima, 2009. According to the Committee for Truth and Reconciliation in Peru, *Yuyanapaq: para recordar*, Lima, 2003, 75 percent of the victims spoke a native language.

13 The literal translation of this slogan is "Neither military coup nor blows to women." However, the Spanish formulation encloses an ingenious play on words, as *Golpe de estado* is the Spanish expression for "military coup," while *golpe* also means "beating."

the mirrors of the rest of the women.[14] According to Monica Chuji Gualinga, *Kichwa* women:

> continue to perform the same role in the family, the home and the community's cultural life, but now they also aspire to play an important role in changing their lives, to contribute in the strengthening of the organizations. There is a certain increase in the number of young women, new *compañeras* that start to assume an organizational role but, I insist, this does not mean they abandon their role in the family. There are more possibilities for women who have no children, who are separated or still single. It is always more difficult for women that have a family, that are married, they do not have a continuous process of participation; they spend some time in a position of leadership, as vice-presidents in some cases or as leaders [*dirigentes*] for human rights or the rights of women, but after that period they disappear because they return once more to the community, to their homes.
>
> [... However,] active participation and the proposals of women do have a bearing on communitarian and organizational decisions. Nevertheless, this level of impact must become even broader. If one makes a general evaluation, it becomes obvious that there is a change amongst men fellow fighters, *compañeros*; many times it is the women they consider and trust more for positions of leadership, rather than the men. They say a woman president in the community is much more effective in asking questions, in relating with the authorities and in dealing with the organization itself and with certain *compañeros* who sometimes become irresponsible. There are women at a regional and national level that have been very active and set an example for grassroots women activists fighting for their rights. They try, by all means, to become more visible and more active in the organizations. But one must ask oneself: how many of them have influence? How many amongst them are much

14 (For a closer look at the history of Ecuatorian feminismo, see Rodas Morales 2002). Vicenta Chuma, Paulina Palacios, and Josefina Lema are some of the Kichwa thinkers that express a specific stance on their condition as women and their condition as political subjects inside their communities. For work that approaches their activities see Suárez (2001). In the municipality of Alausi, the Association of Indigenous Women of Chimborazo "La Minga" has organized radical projects for the preservation of their environment, the conservation of their culture and the financial independence of women who are marginalized by their communities. Monica Chuji Gualinga, an Amazonian Kichwa sociologist, constructs an important relation between the human rights of the original peoples and the rights of women on the basis of social communication.

> more active? How many have the necessary level to debate and discuss with male leaders? I believe that, indeed, there is a positive experience in the few women, quantitatively speaking, that are involved; women are gradually opening up spaces for themselves (*Mujeres Indígenas Hoy* 2010).[15]

In Colombia, Aida Quilcue, a member of the Regional Indigenous Council of Cauca (*Consejo Regional Indígena del Cauca*—CRIC) asserts that the action of women must not ever cut itself off from the spirituality that guides the political acts of their people, for it will lose its force:

> Mother Earth is the original mother. Conceived as a woman, Mother Earth contains the entire Universe. Due to her, women are considered the origin of life and the transmitters of knowledge, the ones who have preserved all the cultural practices and assured the survival of the *Nasa* people.
>
> Amongst the *Nasa*, the *Sat* are systems of women and men. In the survival of the 102 peoples of Colombia, 35 of them almost extinct as there are only one or two members left, the role of women has been essential in the orientation of organizational processes and civil resistance through their own spirituality.
>
> One of the strategies deployed to reduce the indigenous peoples was ideological invasion: using the tool of Catholic religion, priests claimed women should be submitted to men and created machismo as the imposed ideology. This goes against the Law of Origin and all the cultural practices that emerge from it, as well as our own spirituality, which the priests accused as witchcraft when they disqualified women.
>
> Today, we women must reassume our role in spirituality, and therefore in our own health and medicine. We cannot forget that there is an ongoing globalization of disease. That sexually transmitted diseases can be part of a process of extinction of peoples. We must generate mechanisms for health education that respond to sexual relations in the communities, not distribute condoms without reminding young people that the contamination of the earth makes women and men ill.

15 Monica Chuji Gualinga was a member of the constituent assembly in the process of elaboration of the 2008 Constitution of Ecuador, and also general secretary of Communication in the Rafael Correa government at the beginning of his term of office. Today, she is at the head of the Tukuishimi Foundation.

> It is urgent that the life of women be a good one. But how can we do it when there are so many efforts to prevent our law? One example of this are the families of Evangelists who oppose particular law and set their interpretation of the Law of Origin, national law and international laws against communitarian decisions, creating strong imbalances such as accusations between members of the same community. They act side by side with the state when it accuses us, when it says that the indigenous peoples that claim their rights are terrorists.
>
> The liberation of Mother Earth is the foundation of the Law of Origin, thus so is the liberation of women, who are at risk from the violating acts of multinationals.
>
> Today we must assert our identity, where we come from and where we are heading. We must fight against the violation of Mother Earth by mining companies. If the Earth is contaminated, it is not only her that becomes ill; it is also the women and men, the children, the elderly and all living beings. Domestic violence must be understood by the whole community as a serious imbalance in the relationship with Mother Earth, the town council must force the husband that beats his wife to find his own balance once again.
>
> To protect us as women is to protect Mother Earth, to protect life, to guarantee our permanence as millenary people with the orientation of our spiritual authorities and our terrestrial authorities. Today, the salvation of the earth corresponds to us women. We have this great responsibility, we cannot accept being marginalized.[16]

In Bolivia, the participation of Aymara women as wives of miners, coke cultivators and peasants goes hand in hand with the participation of women who are defined from an activity not related to that of a man, such as sellers, or with the reflections of women who have questioned their place in the family because of a lesbian sexual preference, a sexual job, violence suffered by male members of their community or by institutions that violate them along with their communities, sometimes separating them from the community and others by confining them to it.[17]

---

16 These are words I wrote down during her talk at the Universidad Autónoma Indígena Intercultural during the course "Familia Indígena, participación y equidad de género" (The indigenous family, participation and gender equity), on the 15th of November 2010.

17 The work of Mujeres Creando, a Bolivian collective of autonomous feminists who in 2008, after 18 years, was split in two (Mujeres Creando/La Virgen de los Deseos and Comunidad Mujeres Creando Comunidad) because of their disagreement on whether to participate

According to Aymara Julieta Paredes, an autonomous feminist whose work in the indigenous assemblies supports that half of all people are women and bodies are the kind elements of one's own identity and political stance:

> For me, Julieta, to live without this life is now impossible. If I were not what I am—an Aymara lesbian feminist—I would not know what to do or how to begin my days. The very thought of myself as an Aymara woman of the village, quiet and submissive to whatever those around me say, a lesbian having to hide my desire and love for women every day, that would be torture. Feminism gave my life and my thoughts the wings of the condor and the mountaintops, elements from where to look at my time, my people, my history.
>
> If feminism were a word of meaning only for the women of the north, if feminism were an action invented by them, then Women Creating (*Mujeres Creando*), I believe, would not be feminist. We would follow the roots of struggles conducted by the women of our lands which would, surely, also bear a beautiful fruit of conceptualizations and life practices.
>
> The place from which any subject talks, male or female, not only contextualizes the text or discourse. It is also a testimony, the evidence of praxis; that is, of a practice and theory triggered by specific social goals, in this case the struggle of the popular sectors to transform an unfair and unhappy society...
>
> [...] Feminism is not just another theory, it is a theory, a conception, a world vision, a philosophy, a politics that emanates from the women that are most rebellious against the patriarchate.

---

in the government of Evo Morales, a government of indigenous representation which was, however, equally patriarchal. Since 1990, their work informs and analyzes the existing ties between indigenous feminists, lesbians, paupers, prostitutes, women victims of domestic violence and artists who confront the established patriarchal order. In 2009, Mujeres Creando/La Virgen de los Deseos published in *Mujer pública. Revista de discusión feminista* a "Constitución Política Feminista del Estado" (Political Feminist Constitution of the State), asserting that "it was drawn up in a big kitchen while we were pealing potatoes and the children were helping out with the peas. The method of approval was through consensus and speech was organized in a rotating manner. No one was allowed to speak in the name of another woman, and that is why, when their time came, even the dumb women had their say" (45). The intervention of an ideology of communitarian origin (consensus as the unavoidable condition for the creation of a reality) and another of western origin ("The originality of the individual is respected, protected and stimulated by society" (49) maintain that feminism is above the division of cultures and must be freed from states and communities alike.)

> We will look more into this further on, I just want to state this origin so that we will not forget that the material basis of existence from which feminism emanates is we women, thinking of ourselves and feeling ourselves and thinking about others and feeling others, men and women, as well as nature.[18]
>
> PAREDES, 2006: 61–62, 65

Generally speaking, the reflections and collective and personal practices of the indigenous women thinkers are imbued by the experience of violence. It is present in everyday life, and the patriarchal norms of the community combine with racism and external discrimination in such a way, that their implications cover the entire spectrum of fear in the life of women.

Institutional violence is so recurrent that it prevents women from giving priority to the deconstruction of the gendered submission to which they are sometimes condemned by their culture. They rather confront the aggressions they recognize as directed against their community: contempt, incarceration for no good reason, attacks against their religious and spiritual practices, the definition of indigenous autonomy as terrorism. It is only at a secondary level, and because it is linked to the situation of their national group, that they denounce the sarcasm displayed by the prison guards when they visit their imprisoned fathers or husbands, the scorn with which they are treated by the medical staff when admitted to hospital or the discrimination they face in schools and universities.[19]

---

18 Julieta Paredes is currently part of Comunidad Mujeres Creando Comunidad.

19 Although these situations are more intense in countries with dictatorships, such as Honduras, authoritarian governments like Chile, or countries with a strong military presence such as Colombia and Mexico, even in progressive countries with government programs that show respect towards the original peoples, such as Venezuela, the looting of the land by landowners and stockbreeders is tolerated by the forces of order, who consider the inferiority (in the sense of non-modernity) and insensitivity of indigenous peoples to be "natural" and, even more so, the defenselessness of women. The reports of Yupka women on the violations they suffer by the militaries when visiting the men of their communities who are held captives is symptomatic of this. In the province of Zulia, on Saturday the 17th of June 2010, Zenaida Romera, daughter of indigenous leader Sabino Romero Izarra who has been confined in a military fort since October 2009, appeared before the Office of Public Defense to denounce, once again, the maltreatment she had been subjected to by the military guards when visiting her father. According to Zenaida Romera, the rights of all Carib or Yupka women are violated by the authorities of Western Venezuela when, for example, they are forced to undress in order to be allowed to visit their imprisoned relatives. The irregular inspections to which Yupka women are subjected have been denounced by a group of them. "We know that almost no other women

As persons, as members of communities that live in a constant search for their right to be, many indigenous women thinkers maintain that the first instance of violence against women is the fear of disappearing as a collective entity; to that fear they respond through a complex process of asserting their identity, which is never only feminine nor solely national.

> "We construct ourselves from our ethnicity, our class; we can reconstruct ourselves in relation to men and not from the viewpoint of exclusion [...] It is easy to deconstruct submission, but we must not cede ground; for example the agenda of the feminist movement is not our agenda, the subjects we are interested in are the ones we can talk about, the ones we put on the table" affirms Francisca Lopez, of the *Kaqla* group of Mayan women in Guatemala.[20]

At the same time, as persons who are violated not only by the institutions that threaten their community, but also by the men of their own community, insofar as they make up a male collective that abolishes certain rights of their bodies, their sexuality, their labor capacity and their services, indigenous women experience the fear of not being respected in their physical and emotional integrity as something equally violent. *Kich'é* philosopher Gladys Tzul Tzul insists on the educational function of fear:

> [...] it serves as a reminder of who has the power. Mayan women suffer a form of violence that is aimed at their accepting their subordination. It seems irrational and gratuitous but, in fact, it serves to accentuate the relations of power that are exercised by the state on the indigenous communities and by men on women, so that women be constantly reminded of their condition of sexual, financial, physical and emotional inferiority and vulnerability. The state sends its agents to rape them so as to punish the community, and their fathers and husbands blame them for having sexual relations with strangers, violating the pact of fidelity that "customs" demand of all women. The fear of rape in Guatemala is obsessively present in the life of all women of all ages. It reminds us that we do not live in peace.

---

are forced to take all their clothes off when they are visiting," says Lucia Romero, 41, before the Office of Public Defense in Maracaibo, capital of the State of Zulia, and before the Public Prosecutor's Office.

20 In the above-mentioned conference organized by the UAM.

•

> We women must learn to see the wealth we are, the wealth we produce, the value of our art and friendship. We must not believe the external world that undervalues us and condemns us to poverty.
>
> SONIA ENRÍQUEZ, *Kuna* of Panama

The ideas of contemporary indigenous women thinkers in relation to the identity of women, their knowledge and the activities they perform inside the community in order to transform their condition, cannot be reduced to the analysis of the violence they suffer. They also describe sisterhoods of resistance, educational and communication actions and the need to understand why the ties of solidarity between women are severed when a woman claims that a male relative has the right to define a woman's sexuality as good or bad.

Women members of cooperatives and teachers organized for the recognition of their people's right to their own education and art of teaching; defenders of forests and rivers, midwives, women organized to defend the commons and craftswomen recognize the need for collective action, explain their relationship with men and with the cosmos, analyze permanence in history. Above all, they denounce institutional racism in the sphere of health and school education ("So much school makes me stupid" read the t-shirt of a Zapatista girl, in a photo that was widely spread amongst the sympathizers of the movement from Chiapas), as well as the way in which they are treated by women researchers, health personnel and government employees.

Beyond the tendency to present stark portraits of the everyday reality of women, according to a scheme of denunciations which is accepted and controlled by international organisms, the women of the indigenous communities point towards the recognition of women who are guides or thinkers and are able to sum up and unite the knowledge that is generated and transmitted by many. They are women of the community, in it and for it, and not feminists without cultural roots. They assume the corporeality of enunciation and the spirituality of their world vision. As part of a collective of different people, i.e. of a collectivity which considers itself to be a political subject, they also pursue their existence as a separate collective subject, that of the women of the collectivity.

In certain occasions, some indigenous women call these women guides "leaders," according to a terminology which was spread by the UN Permanent Forum on Indigenous Issues and adopted by the native women who fight for their participation in the national and international political sphere, by civil associations and state institutions that receive funds to give "leadership courses" or identify "indigenous leaders." It is a term which is rarely disputed because it does not belong to their linguistic universe. It is only when they reflect upon a term that comes from the dominating language, when they translate and interpret its meaning, that they express their opinion on leadership. They are, as a Kuna woman explained to me, forms of hierarchy, of "someone wanting to decide for everyone. Leaderships do not exist amongst the Kuna, for we do not recognize any authorities that are not constructed collectively. And they last for a long time, for they involve a lot of knowledge and work." The Mapuche women of the areas surrounding Lake Colico, in the south of Chile, are even more explicit: "To speak of leadership is an offense for those who do not recognize hierarchies, as is the case of the Mapuche people."

However, there have been numerous workshops, courses and training programs for "communitarian leaders" or "popular leaders" in Mexico and Peru by almost all state institutions and Non-Governmental Organizations that receive international cooperation funds, as well as by state departments and certain private assistance institutions, churches, educational centers, universities and civil associations in Guatemala, Honduras, Costa Rica and Argentina.

As soon as they identify a woman with a certain social or political talent, they define her as a leader. They speak of the leadership of those who know how to convince, organize, of those who undertake a certain activity to attain a collective good or to gain respect for a certain right. They do it in such a way that certain indigenous women today claim the role of the spokesperson of their community, creating serious conflict when they are not recognized as such by the rest of the women.

In Guatemala, the figure of the 1992 Nobel Prize for Peace, Rigoberta Menchu Tum—a Maya *Kich'é* who gained a lot of visibility after her family was murdered and she began a personal struggle from her exile in Mexico, at the beginning of the 1980s, for the defense of the life and rights of the Mayan people of Guatemala—as well as the figures of the Mayan members of parliament and senators of her political organization have led to a lot of debate about the figure of the indigenous "leader." I seem to perceive, as a backdrop in many discussions that are certainly imbued by elements of envy, but are also substantially fuelled by feelings that emerge from communitarian forms of cohabitation, the existence of a sort of perverse synonymy between "leader" and "corrupt"; in the case of Menchu Tum, this leads to disqualifications, critique and profound resentment, complemented by information on her "personal enrichment," gossip about her character and denunciations regarding her political alliances and financial practices.

The women of the National Committee of Intermediation (*Comisión Nacional de Intermediación, CONAI*) of Chiapas insist on the need to "educate leaders" and in the Civic Council of Popular and Indigenous Organizations of

Honduras (*Consejo Cívico de Organizaciones Populares e Indígenas de Honduras*, COPINH) the word "leader" is used as a synonym for *dirigente*.[21] For many native women linked to organizations that receive international funds, to become a "leader" amounts to obtaining a diploma, for it implies completing a course and starting off a job as organizers of communitarian activities.

Personally, I believe the "fabrication of leaders" is a form of intervention of the hegemonic political culture on different forms of organizations, a form that is often implemented in good faith by feminists who do not question the colonial character of the female model that is proposed/imposed by their conception of individual liberation in emancipated modernity.

Meanwhile, as subjects of the community that have learned to speak with their own voice, the women who guide and the indigenous female thinkers and intellectuals express opinions on reality—diverse as well as particular—that point towards the search for a truth that transcends them but still emanates from them; a truth on the being of life, of themselves and of historical, environmental, financial and cosmic reality.[22] They occasionally point towards the need to re-signify the term "leader," so that it will define women who assume responsibilities, leaderships, authorities and educational roles of a communitarian type towards other women, without demanding public recognition for it.

Judith Bautista Perez, a *Zapotec* sociologist from San Juan Atepec, in the Sierra Norte of Oaxaca, analyzes the world of her everyday actions. She explains that she can participate in her village's community's assemblies, though only because the men think that, because she has a university degree, she has knowledge that could benefit the community; this bears witness to an inequitable distribution of power between the two sexes. However, in the city, at school, she felt she was forced to think about racism and its ties with sexism:

> At the UAM [*Universidad Autónoma Metropolitana*, Mexico City] in 1996 they would pull my plaits and girls hated me just because two middle-class boys approached me and we became friends. At the beginning I felt

21 [Tr. Note, guided by the author's explanation] Spanish words "líder" and "dirigente" are both translated into English as "leader." However, while "líder" has a colonialized and negative connotation describing someone who believes to be superior of the community, a commander or overlord, a "dirigente" has more responsibilities than profit, is at the service of the collectivity and is recognized by her community as such. In this text, the uses of "leader" which correspond to "dirigente" are accompanied by the Spanish term.

22 I doubted whether to use "religious" and finally preferred "cosmic reality" for, although it points towards a metaphysical relation with the absolute and the divine, it does not refer to the ecclesiastic and normative dimension of religions.

> anger, but that brought upon me the role of a victim. Why do they not want me? I felt guilty. Then I perceived all the segregations, the looks that ask you what you are, what you can do and force you to do certain things, segregating you from other tasks. I told myself that it is not true that we indigenous people blend culturally when we become professionals, all we do is look for forms to survive racism. Then my anger became even greater because I understood that assimilation has been constructed from the sphere of academic sociology. I want to recognize, today, the truths from enunciations that pertain to me and are not mediated by constructed voices.[23]

Using almost the same words, Luz Gladys Vila Pihue, a Quechua leader [*dirigente*] from Huancavelica, describes the racism she had to overcome at school in order to later on assert herself as a political *leader*:

> I finished primary school but I wanted to continue studying, and so did my father and mother. But there was no college in my community. So I had to leave. My father did all he could so that I could leave and go study at college. And I studied college in Huancayo, in a city which is relatively close to my community. Well, you get upset a lot; you suffer a lot of racism and discrimination at college. I remember arriving with my two plaits and my skirt… And, furthermore, my Spanish wasn't that good, although my father and mother wouldn't allow me to speak Quechua at home. My father would say "no, what we have suffered is enough, we don't want you to suffer." My father has been in the army, he has done military service, which was then an obligation in Peru. In the army he suffered a lot of racism, discrimination and humiliation because of speaking Quechua. And the same had happened to my mother who had been to Huancayo and also here, to Lima, as a domestic worker. So, there was something inside of them telling them "no, Quechua is bad and my daughter will suffer because she speaks it and I don't want her to…" And as my father and my mother had learned Spanish, even by force and poorly, they would only speak to us in Spanish at home. But my mother had many children and she could not take care of me, as I was the elder, so she was forced to hand me over to my grandmother. So I was raised by my grandmother who was totally monolingual.
>
> Of course, she only spoke Quechua, and they would laugh at me at my school. So, ever since I can remember, I have always been Quechua,

23 In a personal interview conducted on the 12th of August 2010 in Mexico City.

completely Quechua. And when I would visit my house, my father's and mother's house, they would have me insulted. They would say "call her a *Quechuista*, tell your sister she is a *Quechuista*." And my younger brothers and sisters would all go "Quechista, Quechista." But they too, although it was forbidden to speak Quechua at home, learned the language, because outside the house everyone spoke Quechua. Their friends, the neighbors, the cousins, we all spoke Quechua. So that is why, when I went to Huancayo to study they would say "you Indian half-breed, you smell of llama." Once, I remember, a friend even poured a lot of cologne on me, telling me I smelt of llama and maybe that way the smell would go away. So I did suffer a lot of aggression, many times, from the children. I learned how to defend myself with force. I knew I couldn't answer back that way, but sometimes my defense was to provoke them with physical aggression. And of course I would win. I have had lots of fights with girls that would make me angry, and with a boy too, I got into a fistfight. And I would win. I would win because they had no strength. And it was a kind of revenge, that's how I saw it. I knew how far to stretch things... And I would also say "I have to keep my grades up, I don't care about how these kids treat me but I must have good grades."

So I would tell myself they couldn't beat me. And I had the best grades. It was something coincidental, we fought for the first place with another boy who was also provincial, like me. But he had a different way of surviving in that environment, a way of putting up with it without saying anything. On the other hand, I would say "I can't just keep my mouth shut." But after that, little by little, I also made very good friends, not with everyone, of course. Sometimes I would feel that the children that came from wealthier families were the ones who treated us the worst, especially the insults. They were insults that hurt your soul; they would even insult you for how you dressed. And, sometimes, if you made a mistake with the o, the u, the e, the i, they would call you "motosa." Motosa is a pejorative word for those who confuse Spanish with another language. They would say "you speak as if you have your mouth full, you can't separate words" and things like that. They would always say things about how I dressed; they would call me "huachafa." That means you don't know how to combine colors, you don't know what's in fashion and what not, that you'll put on anything, break the patterns of color combinations or fashion or whatever... That's what I understand. I have never actually looked into what it means exactly. But they are clearly insults. So when the classes would end I wouldn't wait for the next day to go to my community. I'd always go back to my community.

> But in that whole period when I started to study in the city my identity changed a lot. Until that moment, in my community, I would always say "I am Gladys; I come from a peasant community." When I left the community, I adored it, I loved it, I loved my family, but there are so many things they try to put in your head that I started to believe that belonging to a community was wrong. In order to avoid suffering, one starts changing one's own way of being. I started to change the way I dressed, yes, of course, I can't get it right until today, maybe in the issue of clothes I have not had a very successful assimilation. I began to assimilate the language faster and to speak less Quechua, or, if I did speak it, it would be in very private places, not very public ones.[24]

The way a woman who has suffered racism assimilates the dominant culture finds its counterpart in how western feminism places indigenous women in the sphere of the "victims that must be saved" This inscription/adscription is part of a cultural construction of domination which, according to Judith Bautista, allows the racist system to ignore that "poverty implies the invisibility of domestic workers, the impossibility of women belonging to indigenous peoples to obtain a well-paid job, apart from the fact that, if they see fear in you, you become the object of violence and abuse." The academic sphere, in its effort to construct and transmit the ideology of this system, does not listen to those who try to explain the doubts created by their interpretation of indigenous women: "the role of the academy is to legitimize a discourse which is read only from one side."

At the same time, the women that conceive their reality as women in dialogue with other women in the inside-out of their community—sharing with the men the exploitation, racism, institutional violence, the negation of the value of their knowledge and arts, the theft of their lands, water and mobility, but at the same time suffering the violence of the father or husband who comes home angry and needs to take his frustration out on them—and in the inside-out of a racist society, challenge a complex social order.

To study, they are forced to migrate to cities where racism is a common feature, suffering, because of that, the social rejection of the society they arrive to and the loss of the affectivity of the family they leave. Thus, they think of strategies to liberate themselves from tasks that are structurally differentiated by sexes to the point of enslaving them (in Mesoamerican and Amazonia cultures, the preparation of food constitutes an exclusively female environment; the preparation of *tortillas* with cooked maize is a task that takes up four hours each day, while the cooking of *casave* or the preparation of manioc break takes

24 During an interview she granted me in Lima on the 15th of January 2011.

up a whole day, guaranteeing the reclusion of women in the domestic environment) as well as from the violence exercised upon their bodies, their sexualities and decisions.

To sum it up: At present, the most disruptive feminist thoughts are surely those emanating from the different conceptions of what it is to be a woman in indigenous communities. They confront the western idea of the individual as the only subject of rights and political participation and, at the same time, they point towards a relationship with men which is based on metaphysical assumptions different from the western ones. They are feminist ideas which are sometimes radical, such as those pertaining to communitarian feminism, and others akin to communitarian institutionalism, inspiring different female spiritualities and participating in the struggle for the earth and the recognition of the historical rights of their peoples, constructed during the colonialist modernity of America. They make fundamental contributions to the materialist relation between the earth, the body, law and history and express clearly anti-colonialist positions. These positions, in turn, translate into anti-capitalist stances in agriculture and demands for the right to their own education, which constructs different gender systems not necessarily corresponding to the hegemonic gender system of European origin.

At the same time, we witness today the manifestation of a feminism of women who participate in the "indignation" caused by the neoliberal system that prays on nature and has led millions of young women and men, in dialogue with people of all ages, to strongly disagree with the unequal distribution of wealth in the world and amongst social classes. The feminists of the movement of the "indignant" are materialists who reject the bourgeois idea of the state and the existence of a sector of intermediaries between the people and social and financial organization; these "representatives" of the nation who, in Modernity, have been considered as those in charge of giving state norms to the nation or the people.

The Role of Women in the Struggle for Autonomy in Mexico

Raquel Vázquez

I Zapatista Women and the Issue of Autonomy

Within any organization, the use and significance of words is tremendously important, especially those that can give new life to a proposal that might seem a simple matter. On the issue of autonomy —What is it? What is it for? Why? And for whom?— Zapatista women have made their voices heard inside their own organization. Every revolution is a struggle against a system of oppression, but how do we work from within to transform the deep inequality that exists in the political and personal relationships between women and men? Zapatista women have made their contribution from a place all their own: "The Zapatista Women's Revolutionary Law." This document reflects their advances in a political discussion on the unequal relationship between Zapatista women and their male comrades.

To what extent is it a priority to establish our demands as women regarding what we want to build outside of the Indigenous context, but at the same time intimately linked to it? How can we do this? Insofar as we make the issue visible, we are recognizing and contributing to the construction of women as revolutionary subjects, an unfinished task that involves both sexes.

The concept of autonomy has transcended the realm of community, with the *self* being the acknowledged autonomous subject, yet a part of a *whole*, a *collective*. In this sense, decision-making, the heightening of consciousness, is important for women who recognize themselves as autonomous subjects, *being* in a collective group, but also concerned with personal self-determination.

In an interview granted to journalists Matilde Pérez U. and Laura Castellanos in 1994, 26-year-old Infantry Major Ana María (who was responsible for the taking of the city of San Cristóbal) talks about the participation of women in the historical phenomenon known as the EZLN (the Zapatista Army of National Liberation):

> I'm an insurgent. I've dedicated all of my life and time to the cause. It's a long, long story. From the time I was eight years old I participated in peaceful struggles, in marches, in rallies. I come from a family of fighters who has always organized to gain a dignified life, but we've never achieved it through those means... I was 14 when I joined the struggle. At first, there

> were only two of us women among eight or ten people who began the movement more than ten years ago... When I had left home and learned that an armed organization existed, I came to a decision. I said to myself, "I'm going to take up arms, too!" One of my brothers was already with them... The majority of our family had no idea... There, my brother and I learned our first letters and how to speak Spanish. Later they trained us in combat tactics and gave us political skills so we could talk to the people and explain our cause. We asked for land and the government didn't give it to us, so we began the land takeovers. The response was repression.

In the same interview Comandante Ramona spoke about the political work developed in the communities:

> The women came to understand that their participation is important in order to change this bad situation, so they've joined in, although not all of them directly in the armed struggle. There's no other way to find justice. *That's what women are interested in.*

Over time, the clear ability to persevere that the EZLN has demonstrated and continues to demonstrate, even under a constant war of extermination, is based on the participation of women in many important ways. In all the work geared towards organizing peoples and communities, Zapatista women have acted as community leaders, health and education promoters, committee heads, members of autonomous councils, captains, insurgents, and militia members, just to mention a few of their everyday tasks in this historic movement. In it, imposed gender roles have been broken, and another kind of education has been created, based on the perspective and contributions of women in all the communities. It is important to stress that the process initiated is in permanent construction, as not all of the demands of the women have been completely resolved. Like other in-depth processes, it takes time and is based on the awareness of a need for political, human, philosophical and re-educational change, in other words, work that is our responsibility as women. A broader consciousness, albeit a collective one, is not enough; what is required is our engagement in praxis in all spheres and dimensions of our humanity. In order make themselves known politically in the world, Zapatista women first needed to reach agreements with their male comrades in life and struggle, agreements that didn't place them at a disadvantage or keep them in an inferior situation. They needed to work *together* to build the political and personal project to which they continue to aspire and in which there remains much for *us* to do.

II The EZLN and the New Autonomous Process

It is interesting to analyze the evolution of the term "autonomy" in Mexico 18 years after that key date, January 1, 1994, taking as our reference point the movement that placed the issue of autonomy on the national (grassroots) political agenda.

From the start, the EZLN initiated a dialogue with the civil society. In her book entitled *20 and 10 The Fire and the Word* Gloria Muñoz retraces the historical and political steps of the Zapatista Army month by month, year by year, beginning in 1994. She writes that "on January 20 (1994) they addressed themselves for the first time to the indigenous organizations of the county, in a communiqué which, ten years later, continues to define the relationship with the national indigenous movement." In it, the EZLN began the dialogue as an invitation for each organization to struggle in its own way (not demanding that they join in the armed struggle, but with respect for the variety of organizational forms), thereby initiating an important *new* process that not only includes accompaniment and solidarity, but also recognition of the *other* and the *others* in struggle, albeit in different geographical locations, united by three general demands: freedom, democracy and justice.

Besides providing a historical review that informs us of the timing of events, the chronology helps us *understand* both the process that has gone on in the movement and the relationship built with the civil society, whether organized or not. The *new* autonomous process has been the product of a dialogue between the EZLN and the civil society, an interchange based on encounters, dialogues, consultations, and conventions, a process that is most concretely defined in the San Andrés Larrainzar Accords.

The following brief chronology highlights the new process of autonomy that began in 1994:

1. After the emergence of the EZLN, a conversation with the civil society (through a series of communiqués) led to the declaration of a cease fire that was observed in good faith by the EZLN and followed by the San Cristobal Dialogue (February 20, 1994).
2. The Second Declaration of the Lacandón Jungle (June 10, 1994) included a call to the National Democratic Convention, the EZLN's first direct encounter with representatives of a wide variety of political struggles in the country and also with people not organized but interested in the process.
3. On December 19, 1994, the EZLN "launched a new political offensive, breaking the military cordon enclosing them and appearing in 30 municipalities in the state, which were declared autonomous and rebellious. Thus began the long process for the recognition of their autonomy..." (Excerpt from the book *20 and 10 The Fire and the Word.*)

4. The Third Declaration of the Lacandón Jungle (January 1, 1995) proposed as its main goal, a struggle "by all means and at all levels for the establishment of a government in transition."
5. The EZLN and the federal government signed the Joint Declaration of San Miguel and Protocol on the Grounds for Dialogue, naming the town of San Andrés Sacam'chén de los Pobres as the official seat of the dialogue.
6. On August 27, 1995, the National Consultation for Peace and Democracy was held throughout the country after an intensive publicity effort both nationally and internationally; people who expressed their opinion on the future of the EZLN said it should become a political force.
7. During the sixth round of negotiations (San Andrés Dialogues, September of 1995), six work tables were set up: Table 1: Indigenous Rights and Culture; Table 2: Democracy and Justice; Table 3: Well-being and Development; Table 4: Conciliation in Chiapas; Table 5: Women's Rights in Chiapas; Table 6: Truce.
8. The Fourth Declaration of the Lacandón Jungle (January 1, 1996) called for the formation of the Zapatista National Liberation Front (FZLN) as a new political force "that does not aspire to take power. A political force that is not a political party..."
9. The National Special Forum on Indigenous Rights and Culture was inaugurated on January 4, 1996. As a result of their dialogue and work, participants agreed to call for the formation of the National Indigenous Congress (CNI), which to date, engages in work that is fundamental for social struggles in Latin America.
10. On March 8, 1996, the women of the Zapatista Support Bases took over San Cristobal de las Casas: "... Zapatista women struggle for their own rights as women. They also confront the sexist culture that Zapatista men perpetuate in many ways. Zapatista women are not free simply because they are Zapatistas. They still have many reasons to struggle and much to win..." (EZLN speech, March 8, 1996).

It is emblematic that it was Ramona, the first woman insurgent commander, who broke the military cordon, and that she did it precisely to attend the inauguration of the National Indigenous Congress. What is the *new place* from which indigenous peoples, communities, and nations will construct themselves in relationship to *others*? Perhaps the words of the speech she made that day hold a glimmer of the response: "Never again a Mexico without us" (CNI Inaugural Address, Comandanta Ramona, October 12, 1996).

Through negotiations and work table discussions with the participation of different indigenous peoples and nations along with their advisors, those present arrived at the spirit of the San Andrés Accords (with which the government refuses to comply even now). A precedent was set that continues to be the basis for working on the *agenda from below*, the struggle for the autonomy of the peoples. In his book *Other Geographies. Experiences of indigenous autonomies in Mexico*, Luis Hernández Navarro writes:

> The demand for autonomy has become the hard core of the program of the indigenous movement in Mexico. The Zapatista insurrection didn't invent the indigenous struggle or the demand for autonomy, but it gave them both an impressive stimulus. The encounter between an armed Zapatista movement and a peaceful indigenous movement had the immediate consequence of opening the doors to in-depth political discussion about autonomy.

If there's anything that has characterized the EZLN, it's an engagement in constant political praxis, which doesn't save any movement or organization from committing errors, given that all practice is experimentation and a trial run of what might function with regards to particular proposals. The outcome is unpredictable because there are no recipes in revolutionary movements, but instead profoundly human and ethical philosophical practices that have to do with a specific task.

III Autonomy in Permanent Transformation

At the present time, the autonomy exhibited in concrete practices by peoples and communities reveals a way of thinking that is independent of the State, a product of the awakening of consciousness and a struggle for the emancipation of the liberation movements of a people. It implies a loss of credibility for the institutions, the State, the political parties, and "oficialdom."

The struggle for autonomy that initially appeared to be a priority for indigenous peoples has now been taken up by some social movements on the left that pose the need to create alternative structures to those of the state, and especially to create something different from the government rationale imposed by the capitalist system and neoliberalism.

For some peoples and communities, this means governing themselves according to their collective needs and normative systems. Within the concept of autonomy there are subtle differences regarding the meaning of being autonomous for each political subject. While for some, autonomy is constructed on a given territory, for others, it involves the appropriation or recovery of different kinds of spaces: cultural, educational, informational, or those necessary for attaining security and justice, etc.

The construction of autonomous projects in the city is not the same as it is in the countryside or in indigenous communities; it has specific demands and distinct expressions. We are speaking, for example, of alternative or autonomous news media, self-run cultural centers, independent health projects, production cooperatives, or educational projects, depending on the needs of the group or collective that initiates the project and the process that it implies.

This kind of appropriation or gestation of an autonomous project reveals an independent process. The meaning of autonomy goes beyond a theoretical concept; it is conferred through a concrete practice by those who use it as an instrument for socially building something alternative to what is official or institutional.

The *new autonomy* implies a series of social, political and organizational practices that lead a people, collective or organization to the resolution of problems and demands having to do with social well-being and the administration of justice, which the government has demonstrated in practice that it is incompetent to resolve because its interests have nothing whatsoever to do with the well-being of the people under its rule. Scorn, omission and deception have marked the posture of the State with regards to the pressing problems it faces.

Autonomous practices are derived from a previous process of organization and development that leads it to adopt collective or community decision-making as part of its practice. How do collectives develop their autonomous practices? What does autonomy mean to people who are organized? In the majority of cases, numerous young people, neighbors, and highly marginal groups, starting out from small cells, have found it necessary to propose the resolution of demands through different organizational processes. In the repetitive question of how to confront capitalism, many groups have found in *autonomous processes* an answer that may not get to the bottom of the problem of destroying capitalism, but does respond to the construction of new structures that provide guidelines for making deep changes in society. They generally understand that social well-being is a priority common good that doesn't necessarily have to do exclusively with the economy and only does so to the extent that others can also enjoy it. There is no such thing as a partial search for justice that can only be handled through the State as property, which in any case, in the construction of a new society could be a collective good in which *all* could participate.

IV The Women of Cherán as Revolutionaries

On April 15, 2011, Cherán, a town on the Purépecha Plateu in the state of Michoacán, organized itself to confront organized crime groups, which in addition to having devastated 80% of its forests, had kidnapped and killed community members who had been involved for approximately four years in an ongoing labor of denunciation that had intensified with the large-scale looting and plunder of their natural resources.

Many articles have been written on the process that the townspeople experienced since they decided to take on the defense of their community: barricades, checkpoints, campfires and community patrols are images that were seen around the world in the first few days. Yet there's one tremendously important moment that is mentioned in passing but that has not really been subjected to deep analysis despite being decisive and fundamental: The women were the ones who started the rebellion against an unjust system that scorned the entire community and turned a blind eye to the denunciations of crimes.

History would have been different if the women of Cherán had not *decided* to organize themselves to put an end to what was happening in the community, if they hadn't taken the initiative and assumed responsibility for the situation. What would have happened? How much more time would have gone by before a rebellion occurred? These questions will never be answered because history changed when they decided it would take a different course in their community as they got organized with other women.

The women of Cherán have dared to break with the logic of fear, a logic that had been imposed on them through a system of government, a fear that had palpably permeated the society, manifesting itself in suffering, apathy, and impotence. The reaction to what happens to the *other* inside a community or as part of it, is definitively tied to what happens to *all*. The Cherán women have found an answer through getting organized with other women; they have found their answer in *others*.

In the face of so many different national and worldwide problems, what is it that places us in a situation of equality and what is it that makes us different in relationship to *others*? It seems to me that we are equal to the extent that we all generally live and suffer the havoc wreaked by a voracious capitalism that pillages all that we have, even what is most essential to us; we are different when it comes to specific local conditions or different segments of the society that we belong to, or to different issues in the social struggles that affect us. None of this, however, should fragment us into different battle fronts that often seem irreconcilable.

It would appear that some processes begin with an imprecise turn of events. Politicization seems slow, but after 17 or 20 years, bears fruit. The process of autonomy in Cherán has not been gratuitous; it is the product of at least 17 years of work (counting only from the time the community joined the CNI), work, in any case, that began long before the Rebellion of 2011.

The spontaneity that sparks a movement reflects deep anger and the sense that "enough is enough." It is a luminous moment that is both decisive and historic, and not only for the people in question; for the rest of us it is a living example of struggle. The question is how this spontaneity relates to subsequent political structures, to organization, to what comes next.

What's happening now in Cherán, after the women acted as forerunners of a significant autonomous movement in their community? The challenge for them is to keep those spaces of participation alive that they took over the day they decided to put an end to organized crime, an action that also fundamentally changed their relationship with their male comrades, with the other gender. On May 24–27, 2012, the National Meeting of Anti-capitalist Autonomous Resistance was held in Cherán, attended by representatives of around 500 national organizations as well as some from other countries. One of the goals was to debate and exchange experiences with other organizations on how different groups in resistance have confronted more than one form of capitalism, given that praxis has to do with the political context in each region, and the priorities are different. The gathering was *big*, not in the numerical sense, but rather because Cherán K'eri was taken as a current point of reference for sharing different aspects of the organization of other struggles. The experiences and dialogue undoubtedly enriched us all, but I couldn't help feeling a certain void upon observing that the women of Cherán were not present at most of the work tables. As precursors of this important movement, their direct participation, without mediators, would have allowed us to hear, in their own words, the way in which relationships within the community are being constructed as of the rebellion. The issue of autonomy and how women are constructing it doesn't end when they assume a different position in the change of roles imposed on us by our upbringing; it is definitely the commencement of a different stage in which ongoing work is required. To the extent that we can achieve a change in the way we relate to different social structures, minimal or even smaller, we can gradually extend this change to other structures: of thought, politics, gender, experience or coexistence. In the final activity, a general forum that grounded the issues of the different work tables, we were finally able to hear the voice of the women of Cherán, a voice that in my opinion, was lacking during the four days of the gathering.

The struggle of the people of Cherán K'eri is essentially a struggle for life, where once again, as in all wars, the community is marked by the stigma of institutional violence (as it is in many towns, cities and nations), not of low-intensity warfare, but openly declared war.

V Possible Democracy in an Authentic Left

If some kind of democracy is to exist, this will only be possible among equals, among those at the bottom of society, among political organizations on the left, and this will only be possible to the extent that we are able to direct our gaze towards the *other*. Democracy could also include the search for constructing something new with those who are different, with those who are marginalized, as we are: with the indigenous movement, with women, with sexual dissidents, with domestic workers, with workers in the city or the countryside who aren't reported in statistics and aren't part of a visible spectrum, with men and women workers who have been robbed of their rights and the fruits of their labor down through history. Democracy will only be possible among organizations on the left. It can't be a product of agreements between institutional power and those of us at the grass roots. A necessary democracy could lead us to reach agreements and these could lay out a way to build other collective imaginaries; it would definitely not lead to the sole, exclusive question of an agenda or to prioritizing the demands of one sector over another, or to the search for a leadership that would direct the collectivity that we can potentially become.

The political agenda of women in the countryside, whether indigenous or non-indigenous, is not the same as that of women in the city who also struggle for their emancipation and the rights of all. Questions, for example, have been raised to rural women about issues like abortion. The key question is the low level of education that prevents an awareness of a necessary change in the situation and position of both women and men in the family, the community, and the society. In other words, the family must cease to be an oppressive institution and instead begin to establish fair relationships in which all its members can be recognized with respect and can have a place of their own, without hierarchies. Gender differences exist; it's a fact. We have the possibility as women to decide whether or not we want to have children, a partner, or if we even want a family. But these differences shouldn't place us in a position of inequality or disadvantage as women. Violence and gender constructions are not particular to any specific culture, or they shouldn't be. It's just a pretext to say that poverty and ignorance convert people into potential perpetrators of violence or to say that indigenous men are sexist just because they are indigenous and that their culture is backward. Domestic and gender violence occur in all socioeconomic classes. In any case, the construction of gender is an issue profoundly related to education, and to a certain extent, to the culture that is passed down from one generation to another. The family as such, acquires its own dynamism in the society, where the "head of the family" is not always a man, but rather, in a large percentage of homes, a woman. At present, families are also formed by homosexual couples with or without children; the traditional structure is changing and will continue to change with the passage of time. Only through a heightened consciousness and new practices can the family cease to be what it has been up until now: an institution that oppresses its members and, instead of being educating them, deforms them as human beings.

In order for the situation of women to change in the revolutionary political terrain, it must also change in the particular, and in the way relationships are formed with the other —woman with man, woman with woman, and men and women with sexual dissidents and those with sex-gender differences, who at all times are some of the people oppressed and excluded in an exclusive vision of the world imposed by capitalism.

Appendix 1: Women in the Montaña Region of Guerrero: The Other Arm of Community Justice[25]

(*Las mujeres en La Montaña de Guerrero: el otro brazo de la justicia comunitaria*)

It all started when we heard of Commander Ramona, Commander Esther and the Zapatista women.

Guerrero, Mexico. The Zapatista experience specifically that of women, reached the ears of the women of the regions of Montaña and Costa Chica in the state of Guerrero. They found out that just as in their communities there was the Community Police, a coordinating body comprising of authorities -regional coordinators, regional commanders and police officers who guard their territories, in Chiapas there are grassroots communities, the "Councils of Good Government" and a rebel army, the Zapatista National Liberation Army (EZLN). Unlike the EZLN, the CRAC-PC is not an insurgent organization; it was created and supported by the people, according to their normative systems, where officials and other members are elected in assemblies.

The women of Guerrero listened carefully to the experience of the Zapatista women, who after discussion and deliberation created the Revolutionary Law of the Zapatista Women. A woman called Commander Ramona and another called Commander Esther, were the ones who spread the word of their comrades and, what is more, they were commanders! They occupied important positions in the military ranks, and their words were heard and respected, as it was not Ramona and Esther that were speaking, but all the Zapatista women, and so men, their companions, paid attention to them and respected them. One of the women of Guerrero stood up and asked the others: "And us? When are we creating our own law of the women?"

Women in the Community Police

It has been almost 16 years of community justice in the regions of Montaña and Costa Chica in the state of Guerrero, and its achievements have gone beyond those of any state legal institution anywhere in the country. Here, the Regional Coordinating Body of Community Authorities—Community Police

25 Originally this article appeared in *Desinformémonos,* Mexico. Article written by *Colectivo Contruyendo Resistencias.*

(CRAC-PC) stands as an example of struggle, resistance, continuity and coherence, but it has also been, and still is, subjected to harassment and unfounded accusations. In addition to being marginalized, the communities have to face increasingly more voracious attempts at plundering. Its territory is coveted by of one of the meanest monsters of capitalism: mining companies.

It is in this context that this justice system has developed and grown, this is where the *me'phaa, ñuu savi, mestizo* and *afromestizo* peoples live and commune with nature and with their gods. This is where men realize that they cannot struggle, resist or move forward without the fortitude, participation and aid of their women companions, who in turn are convinced that the process of justice will guarantee them a place equally important to that of men in the assemblies, in decision-making processes and in political positions in their communities as well as in the CRAC-PC.

"It is important that women have a voice and vote, since we also have the right to hold important positions and we should not just stay in the kitchen," affirms Adelaida Cayetano Herrera, of the Chilixtlahuaca community.

It would be impossible to consolidate this process of community justice without the active participation of women, and furthermore there exists the foundation for this significant step, since there is already an institution of law enforcement in place that can ensure compliance to the principles established in the Charter of the Rights of Women.

Every Evening a Parade of Traditional Embroidered Dresses

From 2008 to early 2010 there were long and heated discussions. Women were starting their duties early. From four or five in the morning they were grinding corn, lighting the stove, kneading in the *metate* [mortar], cooking *quelite* herbs, making tortilla, brewing coffee and preparing breakfast for their husbands, who at around six o'clock were going to work in the fields. The rest of day they were keeping busy with caring for the children and the domestic animals and, again, grinding corn, kneading, baking beans and waiting until the husband is home to eat. In those days, once everything at home was in order, they were letting their families know they would be at the commissary [municipal government building]. This started happening every day, some men were watching their meetings from afar, a few of them were getting involved and others were staying out. The women, at all times, were inviting them to participate.

Some husbands and authorities expressed their disagreement and, with discouraging words, opposed the onset of something that continues to grow today. However, there were those who defended this initiative, among them the councils of elders of many communities, the wise men, the fathers of each and every one of the members of the communities, who became an important source of support. The women were supporting and encouraging each other and they were explaining to the men that they did not want to be in charge, as many were saying, but to walk together, and that they did not want to be the same, since they were not born the same and each one has a different body, and being a man or a woman means to do different things. "But both," they said, "have thoughts and ideas, one is not better than the other, but rather both together are better able to serve their family, the community and the CRAC-PC."

So, a few days a week, in some seasons more often, for about two and a half years in the communities of Zitlaltepec, San Marcos, Santa Cruz Cafetal, Llano de las Flores, Llano de las Flores I, Nuu Savi Kani, and Chilixtlahuaca of the municipality of Metlatónoc and Llano Perdido of the municipality of Cochoapa el Grande, in the region of Montaña, state of Guerrero, every evening there was in the communities a parade of beautiful colorful traditional dresses adorned with figures of flowers and animals that gathered at the municipal government buildings, at the school's only classroom, at the small medical center full of expired medicine, or at the house of one of them whose husband was away for years as an agricultural laborer in the fields of Sinaloa or perhaps in the United States.

It was in those spaces where the issues concerning the indigenous peoples, the education of children and the situation of women were discussed. It was in those spaces where they decided to form committees of women that would be responsible for the organization of the talks and discussions.

First Meeting of the Women of the Region of Montaña. Presentation of the Charter of the Rights of Women

In 2010, in the community of Zitlaltepec, Metlatónoc, Guerrero, the First Meeting of Indigenous Women of the Region of Montaña took place. There, men and women, boys and girls of the communities of Zitlaltepec, San Marcos, Santa Cruz Cafetal, Llano de las Flores, Llano de las Flores I, Nuhu Savi Kani, Chilixtlahuaca and Llano Perdido held an assembly to approve the Charter of the Rights of Women.

This was the first political event where women of the region of Montaña presented before the community authorities of the Zitlaltepec municipal seat the result of their organizational work that had gone on for nearly three years. A work consisting of extensive discussions in each one of their communities about the reality of indigenous peoples and specifically their situation as women, organized around five topics, in which they proposed solutions to their problems. That is how the issues of revaluation and recognition of the work of women, violence against women, the freedom to decide on their life and their body, ensuring education for women and ensuring political participation in community affairs came to occupy an important place in their daily lives.

Each community wrote a draft for a Charter of the Rights of Women and all drafts were presented at the meeting of Zitlaltepec, in order to jointly come up with a single charter that would take into account each and every one of the points of each community. It was a long and disputatious meeting, where representatives of committees and community authorities agreed on the final principles of the Charter and the way in which they would formally present it to the authorities of the CRAC-PC. A decision was make the presentation of the Charter a part of International Women's Day celebrations.

Back in their own communities, committees reported what happened at the meeting and set about collecting signatures in support of the letter, in order for it "to become law in our communities."

Weeks before the event, the women sent invitations to all the communities the constitute the municipal seat, recorded a series of spots that were broadcast on community radio "The voice of the Region of Montaña" and began preparations for not only a momentous political event for the organization and for the communities, but also a triumph of women and of the whole population.

The day before the event, intense mobilization began in the municipal seat. The women prepared food for the attendees and saw their event through with the support of the community authorities.

"We think that this charter will help strengthen our project of community and whoever violates these rights will be punished by the community authorities. We know that only if men and women start working together our communities and our process of community justice will be strengthened. If we respect the rights of women, are own rights as native peoples will also be respected" said Paula Gálvez, member of the Zitlaltepec community, who along with Guillermo Vázquez Cayetano, then Regional Coordinator, chaired the event where the Charter was approved.

Voices of the Women of the Montaña Region

We women organize to defend our rights, but some men disagree, believing that the Charter is there to provoke fights between husband and wife. We would like to make clear that this is not true; the Charter of the Rights of

Women is put forward so men will respect and recognize our rights. We would like to tell the other women's committees that they are not alone, because now we are all together and the Zuitlaltepec committee is with you.

Cándida Vázquez Penafort, president of the women's committee of Zitlaltepec. In December 2009, we held some workshops in the community of San Marcos, municipality of Metlatónoc and we discussed what the rights of women are. There, we agreed that there should be no violence towards children and women or between members of the community. That hitting or raping a woman is considered violence. We think that this discussion helped men realize what they are doing and that it is bad to mistreat women. We, the members of the community of San Marcos think that it is important that people recognize these rights in all communities. This new law will protect all women whenever something bad happens. And for this reason, we present the collected signatures of men and women who agree that this law should be enforced throughout the territory of the Community Police. We also request to the Community Police that from this moment on this charter becomes law in our communities.

Leticia Ortiz Comonfort, member of the women's committee of San Marcos. Now we are going to make sure that when a husband has a mistress proof should be provided and that men are obliged to support their families. From now on the daughters are not going to be sold off; instead, they will be able to marry whomever they want, so they can live well with their husbands. Women's decisions on whether to surrender their bodies will be respected, and they will not be forced by their husbands. Men who do not comply with these principles are going to be reeducated and the Community Police will monitor compliance with this law.

These are the things included in the Charter of the Rights of Women, and in this community we agree, we think the Charter is fine. From now on there is a new law and that is important, because things will change so that there is no violence against women.

Rufina Reyes Ramírez, president of the committee of Santa Cruz Cafetal. In this charter, we request that we be allowed to go out as we please, and this is not in order to abandon men, but rather because we are entitled to it and this helps us live better. We also request the prohibition of selling off women as brides, since when we are sold off we suffer a lot, because men claim that we belong to them and they have the right to abuse and bully us, however we now know that we are all born free. We also insist that it is important that husbands support us with the house chores when we are pregnant, in order for us to have a better life and health.

We demand that the husbands do not spend money on alcohol because this way they do harm to themselves, as well as to their children, wife and community.

We would like to say that we are very pleased that there is Community Police and Community Justice in the mountains to also defend the rights of us women.

Lourdes Vázquez Evaristo, member of the women's committee of Llano de las Flores. Women are important in the community because we prepare food, we grind corn, we wash, we care for the children, we sweep, we clean the house. Men do not do all these tasks, they need the women. So, the whole community of Llano de las Flores I, agrees with the Rights of Women laid out in the Charter and collects signatures to request the Community Police to ensure that the community respects women.

We are handing in these signatures and we request that this charter becomes part of the Regulation of the Regional Coordinating Body of Community Authorities, CRAC and that from now on the Community Police monitors compliance to the principles of the Charter.

Julia Julian Galvez, member of the women's committee of Llano de las Flores. In our community, we believe that the Charter is important for promoting respect for the Rights of Women. The provisions of the Charter are good, e.g. that boys and girls should have equal opportunities to study and work so they are able to progress in life. Because women have the same rights as men and we believe that we can also act as Commanders and Commissaries. It is important that the Charter be submitted to the authorities of the Regional Coordinating Body of Community Authorities—Community Police, so justice prevails.

The men and women of the community of Nuhu Savi Kani agree with the letter. This is why we submit these signatures of people who demand that the Charter becomes law, that from now on it is enforced in our community, and that it also becomes law in all communities belonging to the Regional Coordinating Body of Community Authorities—Community Police.

Tomasa Martinez Moreno, member of the women's committee of Nuu Savi Kani. Just as women respect men, we want men to respect women. If this charter is included in the Internal Regulation of the Community Police, it will gain validity and it will help promote the protection of women. We also want to tell men that the Charter of the Rights of Women only promotes equality between men and women; it is not an attempt at switching roles. Instead, it is necessary so men and women help each other.

It is important that we women have a voice and vote, since we also have the right to hold important positions and we should not just stay in the kitchen. We want the people to continue supporting and respecting the Community Police, so we do not have the same things that happened before happening again; this is why I am submitting the signatures collected in my community.

We thank all those present, because this charter benefits our children and we will continue promoting it.

Adelaide Cayetano Herrera, member of the Chilixtlahuaca community. We think this charter is good because people are not going to fight anymore and women will be respected. We agree that women should not be sold off, because they are not things or animals, and that when a woman has a boyfriend and the man loves her, he must respect her and not force her to do things or threaten her.

We therefore believe that the Charter will help improve the community, so we submit these signatures requesting that the Charter of the Rights of Women becomes part of the Internal Regulation of the Community Police and be turned into law in our community from this moment on.

Florentina Esteban Aguilar, member of the community of Llano Perdido. Each committee submitted the signatures of its respective community to the community authorities, and then the Charter was put to the vote and approved by the general assembly. All hands were raised, of both men and women, of people of all ages, so, without even counting the votes, the woman moderating the panel screamed into the microphone "We have won!" This triumph was not the triumph of women; it was the triumph of the peoples of the region of Montaña and of the CRAC-PC.

One Year Later

One year has gone by since the submission of the Charter of the Rights of Women to the community authorities of Zitlaltepec, Guerrero, and its subsequent approval. Throughout this year, the women have been persistent in their efforts and they have kept up the work within their communities. Some committees have changed, they have become larger, positions of responsibility were passed along to other members and new members have been appointed.

The organization of the women in the region of Montaña has also had an impact on other regions, and the CRAC knows it is important that in each and every community the participation of women is guaranteed and accepted by all members, who in turn are convinced that it is impossible to struggle without the other half of the sky, without the other half of the world, without the other half of resistance, of the struggle itself: women.

•

Charter of the Rights of Women in the mountains of Guerrero

To ensure that throughout the territory of the community women live in dignity and free from violence, that the value of their work is recognized, that their freedom to decide on their life and their body is respected, to guarantee respect for their rights to health and education, political participation and a full life as acting subjects and promoters of the development and future of their people, we agree:

1. To respect the women's right to decent and well paid work.
2. To equally recognize the right of women and men to inherit the family assets.
3. To prohibit all forms of violence, be it bashing, insult or general abuse against women and their families.
4. To prohibit any person from forcing a woman to have sexual relations against her will, even if it is her own husband.
5. To oblige men to financially support their families.
6. That when a husband is jealous of his wife and accuses her of having an affair with another man, he is obliged to provide proof. Likewise, when a woman is jealous of her husband and accuses him of the same offence, she is obliged to provide proof.
7. That all women are entitled to be looked after and helped by their husbands during pregnancy and/or disease so their welfare is ensured.
8. To recognize the freedom of women to decide on matters concerning their lives and their bodies.
9. To ban the sale of women.
10. To recognize the right of women to go out of the house, and to go wherever they want whenever they want to.
11. To ensure that women and men, girls and boys, have equal rights and equal opportunities to study at all levels of education.

12. To establish that fathers are obliged to cover any expenses incurred for the education of their children.
13. To promote and respect the organization of women and their participation in community affairs.
14. To guarantee the participation of women in the Assemblies, respecting their right to have a voice and vote.
15. To guarantee the women's right to be elected and to act as coordinators, commissaries, commanders or in any other position of responsibility, and their right to be respected during the exercise of this office.

To ensure compliance with and full enforcement of the 15 points of the Charter of the Rights of Women, the eight communities that put it forward mandate the Community Police appointed by our people and the Regional Coordinating Body of Community Authorities to submit anyone perpetrating and failing to respect the indicated 15 points to a process of re-education.

This charters brings together the proposals of eight communities in which the Workshops on Women's Rights have been conducted and the Assemblies of deliberation and discussion on the issue of Women's Rights have been held: Zitlaltepec, San Marcos, Santa Cruz Cafetal, Llano de las Flores, Llano de las Flores I, Nuhu Savi Kani, Chilixtlahuaca and Llano Perdido, all of which participate in the Regional Coordinating Body of Community Authorities—Community Police (CRAC-PC) and are part of the municipal seat of Zitlaltepec in the municipality of Metlatónoc, state of Guerrero.

DESINFORMÉMONOS, http://desinformemonos.org.mx/2011/10/el-otro-brazo-de-la-justicia-comunitaria-organizacion-de-mujeres-en-la-montana-de-guerrero/

Appendix 2: Political Statement of the *Xinka* Communitarian Feminist Women: There is No Decolonialization without Depatriarchalization!

Association of Indigenous Women of Santa María Jalapa Xalapán [Guatemala]—
AMISMAXAJ

Members of the Sector of Mesoamerican Women in Resistance, of the Communitarian Feminism Assemblies and of the Global Women's March

We, the communitarian feminist *Xinka* women, mountain dwellers, with fighting spirit, living and coexisting in the Xalapán mountain, we make a statement today on October 12, on the day of commemoration of the Indigenous Resistance and Dignity Day, to proclaim before the indigenous and western peoples of the world:

- That we, the indigenous women, continue to suffer in our body-territory the effects of the ancestral as well as the Western patriarchy, which is reconstituted and expressed in different forms of oppression against us in our homes and communities.
- That the historical expropriation of our bodies is still underway, when we cannot make our own free and autonomous decisions regarding our bodies and our sexuality.
- When we indigenous women are assigned the role of safeguarding and reproducing the culture with all of its ethnic fundamentalisms.
- When we are assigned, within the indigenous or territorial organizations, tasks that reaffirm our domestic role.
- When our thoughts, feelings and actions are not valued, because they question the indigenous and Western patriarchal system.
- That because of our political stance as communitarian feminists, we have suffered and we continue to suffer oppression in the mountains from some comrades of the indigenous movement and from the current Indigenous Government.

For all of the above, we declare ourselves:

- In permanent resistance and struggle against all forms of indigenous and Western patriarchal oppression exercised against our first body-territory.
- In permanent resistance and struggle against all forms of patriarchal capitalist oppression that threaten us with plunder through metal mining in our mountains and our territories, and against all new forms of transnational plunder.

- Against all forms of colonialism that attack women in the intimate, private or public sphere, and this is why we engage in action that, from an individual or collective standpoint, promotes the decolonization of our bodies and of our territories.
- In constant struggle to bring about the depatriarchalization of our body-territory and land-territory, without which the decolonization of our peoples is unattainable.

Communitarian feminist *Xinka* women...
Reclaiming and defending our body/land territory!
Depatriarchalizing our body/land territory!
Decolonizing our body/land territory!
Because without depatriarchalization, there is no decolonization!

Altepet, October 12, 2011

CHAPTER 11

Youth, Popular Education, Teachers

∵

The TIPNIS March: New Horizons for Popular Education

*Benito Fernandez**

> I believe we should be asked how we want our development to be according to our worldview, rather than have an alien culture imposed on us. Everyone is different and we cannot all be skewered in the same *pacumutu* [Bolivian skewered meat dish].
>
> BERTHA BEJARANO, indigenous leader of the Ninth March

The TIPNIS (*Territorio Indígena y Parque Nacional Isiboro Sécure*: Isiboro Sécure National Park and Indigenous Territory) is a strip of land located in the Department of Beni, bordering the Department of Cochabamba, in Eastern Bolivia. It is inhabited mainly by communities belonging to the ethnic groups *Yurakaré, Shiman* and *Mojeño-Trinitario*. In 1996 it was declared Native Community Land [*TCO: Tierra Comunitaria de Origen*], a form of land ownership recognized by the 1994 Constitution, where peasants and the Indigenous develop systems of communal economic, social and cultural organization. With the passage of time, peasant settlers have penetrated the area and established the *Polígono 7* [Polygon 7], where the land was divided into lots by families of Andean origin that have the cultivation of the coca leaf as their main source of income.

The Government's decision to build a highway that would go through the heart of the TIPNIS was opposed by these populations, because it violated their right to be consulted and to decide on their territory in accordance with the Political Constitution of the Plurinational State of Bolivia, the Convention No. 169 of the ILO and the United Nations Declaration on the Rights of Indigenous Peoples.

This will to assert their rights and defend biodiversity and the environment in one of Bolivia's protected areas with most natural wealth culminated in the organization of the Eighth and the Ninth March of indigenous families, leaders and authorities of the TIPNIS area from their hometowns towards the city of La Paz, the seat of the central government, after long journeys and great hardship.

---

* University Teacher and Popular Educator.

Ignoring these demands as well as the very Constitution in force in Bolivia, the National Government, through Law 222, has implemented a "prior consultation" with no legal validity,[1] designed to provide the highway project with the desired legitimacy. This consultation, as well as the entry of government officials in the TIPNIS area, is being resisted by the indigenous peoples of TIPNIS who, apart from the constitutional backing, have the solidarity and support of a large majority of the Bolivian population.

The indigenous peoples of eastern Bolivia have staged numerous marches, which set the struggle for life, dignity and territory as their objectives. Among their demands was that Bolivia attained a new Constitution, a demand that was satisfied a few years later (2009) during the government of Evo Morales.

1 The Eighth Indigenous March

The marches for TIPNIS, led by the *Shiman, Yurakaré* and *Mojeño -Trinitario* Indigenous communities, began with the Eighth March (August-October 2011) that was aimed at the defense of the collective right of the peoples that inhabit the TIPNIS to consultation regarding their own territory. This campaign was launched when it was learned, through various channels, that the Bolivian government had made agreements with the Brazilian government and had signed contracts with the Brazilian construction company OAS, with loans from the Brazilian Development Bank (BNDES) for the construction of 303 km of highway between Villa Turani (Cochabamba) and San Ignacio de Moxos (Beni), which would go right through the heart of the TIPNIS.

These agreements were made behind the back of the park's indigenous inhabitants and in violation of the Political Constitution of the Plurinational State of Bolivia, which recognizes the right of indigenous peoples to self-determination and to prior consultation.

The Eighth March was a collective decision that was made at a meeting of representatives and authorities of the TIPNIS communities that took place in the first days of August 2011 in the community of San Pablo del Rio Isiboro. The march traveled hundreds of kilometers, reaching the city of La Paz on October 19, where they were enthusiastically received by the local population. Men, women, children and even elderly people managed to cross the mountainous territory and, above all, overcome the numerous obstacles that the government and its allies—*cocaleros* [coca growers] and settlers– put up to the marchers.

1 Decision no. 300 of the Plurinational Constitutional Court establishes the agreement of the affected indigenous population as a precondition for the legality of the "consultation." The condition has obviously not been met.

Indeed, from the very first moment the MAS government tried to stop the march resorting to persuasion and the dirty war of the media. When the march obtained massive support from the Bolivian people, the government resorted to the repressive apparatus, particularly in the town of Chaparina, the scene of a violent intervention on September 25 in Puente San Lorenzo. The operation was recorded by oral, written and televised media, and was particularly violent, even towards women and children. Indigenous organizations made appeals to international forums, and plead that to this day the government has made no serious effort to identify and punish the real culprits of the repressive operation. The courage of the marchers and the solidarity of the Bolivian people that was expressed from all over the country, allowed the march to regroup and finally accomplish its goal of arriving at the seat of government.

In this context of popular pressure, coupled with allegations of corruption in contracts with the OAS and with the consistency and force of the arguments of the indigenous peoples, the Bolivian Plurinational Assembly was obliged to enact the Law no. 180, which prohibits the construction of the highway and declares the "inviolability" of the TIPNIS.

Another significant consequence was that the continual harassment of the indigenous during the march by groups of farmers and *cocaleros* affiliated [in the original *adictos*: addicted] to the ruling party, resulted in the breakup of the Popular Block that backed the rise of Evo Morales to the presidency. As Pedro Nuni, indigenous member of the Plurinational Assembly, affirmed:

> We the indigenous delegates will assume a position of independence as indigenous members of parliament with our own voice, because we do not want to belong to MAS anymore. From now on the indigenous benches will respect the State Constitution and the rights of the peoples as legitimate children of Mother Earth (…) We have not come to overthrow Evo, we want to create an agenda that allows Bolivian people not be subjected to a party that wants to dominate and create a dictatorship.[2]

However the government never conceded defeat and, using their "social movements" as a spearhead, organized a "countermarch" that demanded the construction of the highway. In response to this mobilization, Evo Morales undermines the legitimacy of Law no. 180, and instead promotes a new law of

2 "El conflicto del Territorio Indígena Parque Nacional Isiboro Sécure (TIPNIS) y sus consecuencias para el Estado Plurinacional de Bolivia" ("The conflict of the Isiboro Sécure National Park and Indigenous Territory [TIPNIS] and its implications for the Plurinational State of Bolivia"), en "La victoria indígena del TIPNIS" ("The indigenous victory of TIPNIS "), La Paz 2012, pp.41–42.

"prior consultation," Law n. 222, which seeks to legitimize the construction of the highway that would cross the TIPNIS by changing the rules of the indigenous democracy. An expensive media campaign to discredit the main leaders, accompanied by promises and "gifts" to those who accept the new law on consultation have been the most commonly used strategies to get the insurgents of TIPNIS out of the way.

II The Ninth March

The indigenous communities of the TIPNIS realize the ploy and decide to launch the Ninth March. The Ninth March was organized and led by the Sécure Subcentral and the Tipnis Subcentral, which represent the indigenous communities of TIPNIS. This march was jointly supported by the Confederation of Indigenous Peoples of Eastern Bolivia (CIDOB) and the National Council of *Ayllus* and *Markas* of Qullasuyo (CONAMAQ). These organizations bring together the greatest part of the indigenous peoples of the Amazon region and the highlands of Bolivia.

The Indigenous March set as objectives: "The defense of life and dignity, of the indigenous territories, of natural resources and biodiversity, of the environment and protected areas as well as the compliance with the Constitution and respect for democracy."

The Ninth March began with about 300 marchers comprised of families from the Yurakaré, Mojeño-Trinitario and Shiman ethnic groups. They left the city of Trinidad, capital of Beni, on April 27 in order to reach La Paz, Bolivia's seat of government, to assert their main demands:

> Compliance to Law n.180 enacted by the Plurinational Assembly in October 2011, which prohibits the construction of the Villa Tunari-San Ignacio de Mojos highway, which would split the TIPNIS territory in two.
>
> Repeal of prospective Law n.222 that the government and its allies are promoting under the title of "prior consultation," withdrawal of the naval and military forces and of government officials responsible for handing out "gifts" (outboard engines, mobile phones, tools…) in exchange for support for the proposed consultation.
>
> Compliance to the Political Constitution of the Plurinational State of Bolivia and to the commitments of the Government regarding the National Park and the Integrated Management Natural Area of the Park.

As with the Eighth March, the Ninth March had to face natural obstacles, difficult weather conditions, the "fences" put up by villages loyal to Evo Morales, as well as a new and more sophisticated dirty war of disinformation, contrary to the statements of those in power that claimed to "guarantee the free expression and right to protest of the population."

The Government, according to Gonzalo Colque, director of *Fundación Tierra*, has violated the most fundamental principles of any consultation process, such as acting in good faith and providing accurate information. The constant calls for dialogue of the appointed Ombudsman and the United Nations' representative were all but ignored.

The Ninth March arrived at the city of La Paz on June 27, after having walked 600 kilometers in 60 days. The population of La Paz, as well as intellectuals and human rights activists,[3] once more took the streets, where the marchers were received with cheers and offered food. Despite the harsh La Paz winter, the marchers camped near the Vice Presidency of the Government, unable to enter Plaza Murillo and have a much-desired meeting with president Evo Morales.

III The TIPNIS Challenges the Established Power

The TIPNIS conflict at first appeared insignificant for national dynamics due to its remoteness from major population centers and the public administration. The TIPNIS area is sparsely populated and has no perceivable contribution to national development and the GDP. How did a conflict of these characteristics manage to have the government continuously in check and stay on the political agenda for more than two years, gaining the support of the greatest part of the population and of leading personalities and artists?[4]

The answer is becoming clearer: the TIPNIS gained this position because it dared question and subvert the model of development and the project of government of the MAS party, which has nowadays become a conservative project.

Indeed, the TIPNIS Indigenous March is shattering many of the myths that fueled the political project of the MAS as a ruling party. The myth of

3 "The institutions and organizations working on issues of development, human rights, indigenous peoples' rights, women's rights and environmental rights, firmly demand the initiation of dialogue and the search for a solution that guarantees full respect for the Political Constitution of the State and the rights of indigenous peoples that participate in the Ninth March, as well as for their organizational structures "(Press release of organizations and institutions regarding the Ninth March in defense of TIPNIS, La Paz July 6, 2012).

4 A popular action against the untimely and deceitful consultation has been promoted, among others, by singer Luis Rico, political scientist Roger Cortes, intellectual José Antonio Quiroga, attorney Waldo Albarracin, former member of the constituent assembly Loyola Guzman and journalist Remberto Cardenas.

the rights of Mother Earth (*Pachamama*),[5] the myth of "governing by obeying the people," the myth of the Plurinational State, the myth of the "democratic cultural revolution," the myth of community education, intra- and intercultural...

All these myths have given to MAS and its leader Evo Morales great advantages in the international political scene, thanks to a constant mass media makeup campaign. The TIPNIS conflict has questioned the indigenous image of Evo Morales, and revealed him to be a *cocalero* leader that is closer to unionism and nationalism, ideologies that are now comfortably coexisting with the capitalist and extractivist model of development.

The TIPNIS does not only protest and question, but it also proposes new paths of transformation. Against the government's attempts at promoting division between inhabitants of the countryside and the city and between the indigenous of the east and the highlands and *cocaleros* and settlers, there is emerging a new political subject, which promotes proposals for integration and unity in diversity, which builds bridges of support and solidarity between the indigenous of east and west. This new political subject calls to join the fight for a true participatory democracy, for a model of development that respects the rights of nature and the individual and collective rights of all Bolivians, which is to say that it first and foremost guarantees the right to life. In other words, the TIPNIS shows great ethical, political and educational potential, which makes it an important example for popular educators.

IV The TIPNIS as an Educational Event

I would now like to examine the TIPNIS event as a true "*locus pedagogicus*," a privileged space from where we can understand the educational and learning processes related to the construction of Popular Power and of the Popular Emancipation Project, which constitutes the horizon of popular education.

Popular educators have always emphasized the people's struggle for their basic rights (food, clothing, housing, etc.) and their strategic rights (power to decide) as important places and moments for learning. This emphasis does not

5 The MAS government has brought Evo Morales to the Rio +20 Summit to campaign for the approval of the "Law of Mother Earth." It is strange and cynical that the indigenous peoples of the TIPNIS, who precisely champion this cause, are vilified by the government of Evo Morales because of their opposition to an imposed highway that would lead "development" to the indigenous communities.

exclude other, more institutional, forms and places, but rather it highlights these events' great potential for raising awareness and for organization of the oppressed classes, and therefore their potential for transformation.

This has happened in the Chaco War, when those in the trenches were making analyses of the national situation and speculating about the changes that would come after the revolution of 1952 and the Agrarian Reform. All dictatorships, apart from bloody and repressive events, have been moments of increasing awareness, organization and transformation for the popular classes that were struggling for a new order of justice and equality.

We do not have to go far. The Cochabamba Water War (January-April 2000) and the Black September in La Paz and El Alto (October 2003), were recent events against the dictatorship of capital that sparked changes in our political and social life, changes that benefited those who hold power today.

So we should not speak of a "process of change" in singular, as if it were something new in our history, but of "processes of change" which have been emerging and getting articulated and which form part of the heritage of the -as yet incomplete- emancipation of the Bolivian people.

Likewise, with the current government of the MAS and Evo Morales and we are witnessing similar events such as the resistance to the *Gasolinazo* (Christmas 2010) and now the march of indigenous peoples of TIPNIS. As an educational event, the TIPNIS is a breeding ground for subjects, methodologies and learning experiences, which constitute a living heritage of popular education.

V The People Teach the People

The TIPNIS experience poses a pressing question: Who are "the people," the subject of the transformation? Are they the Indigenous? Are they the *cocaleros*? Is it the social movements? Is it the government that claims to represent and "obey" the people?

A lesson learned through the TIPNIS is that the people have to be a subject, not an object, and that this subject has a Liberation Project as its horizon, – liberation for everyone, for men, women, children, the elderly, workers, entrepreneurs, the middle class and the high class. It is the people that build popular hegemony, not understood as a "dictatorship of those who hold state power," but as a capacity to steer all social agents towards a society where the individual and collective rights have full validity. This is expressed in the slogan that people were constantly chanting in the numerous marches throughout Bolivia: "We are all TIPNIS. Another development is possible."

Therefore, the principal trait of people as agents of transformation is that they are the subjects of change. Paulo Freire (1993) has expressed this very clearly when he claimed that the "vanguards," the "political elites" who claim to represent and enlighten the people but are actually undermining the initiative of the people and expropriating their words, symbols and dreams, are not true promoters of change.[6]

> Argument, discussion of ideas and debate, protest and criticism are essential and indispensable mechanisms for the left to attract the attention of those who govern and often do not obey. The monolithic and uncritical acceptance of the 'line' that comes from above is a sad artifact of the Latin American, as well as the international, left. Participatory democracy does not involve attempting to silence the people, but on the contrary, encouraging the exchange of opinions, the variety of proposals, and the different points of view.
>
> CUEVAS, 2011

> Now that things, at this critical circumstance, are letting their true nature show, we realize that decolonization is something much more than a discourse, and the government does not have the slightest idea of what it means to decolonize the state. Therefore, if they claim to be the vanguard of this process, they have to snatch that place from the real vanguard. This is why the government interferes with the indigenous march in defense of the TIPNIS. This is an appropriation. They can only be the vanguard by establishing themselves as the vanguard. The people did not vote them in so they could make decisions despite their will, but so they obey the decisions of the people. They do not have a first-hand

---

6 "The authoritarian left turns out to be more elitist than the right. Indeed the latter fears that the popular classes may become critical of the situation of injustice and organize for change, while the authoritarian left discourages the critical activity of the people, and dismisses it as idealistic, populist and even spontaneist, thereby admitting its distrust in the ability of the people to understand causality. Therefore, the left places its stakes on ideological propaganda, and on the effect of political slogans. By doing so, it affirms its capacity for knowledge and promotes *its* truth as the *only truth* (...). This truth, produced far away from the people's experience and independently of it, should go down to the body of the "uneducated" working classes in order to "save" them. Thus, the popular classes need not be called to dialogue, being as they are incompetent by nature. They just have to open up and obediently follow the orders for which they are technically and scientifically competent" (Freire 1993).

> experience of the process, yet they claim to govern it from a position of "enlightened" infallibility.
>
> BAUSTISTA, 2012: 211–212

This is something that those who have participated in the TIPNIS march have not ceased to point out. The allegations most frequently made are: "we have been deceived," "we have been used as a ladder to get into power," "we have been manipulated," The revolutionary people is not an artificially constructed subject that exists a priori, but rather, it is a subject that affirms its existence through a process of constructing this popular project and through its own ability to exercise hegemony.

Returning to the questions posed at the start of this discussion: Using the TIPNIS as a starting point, can we identify who is "the people" that constitutes the subject to this processes of change? Who is "the people" that undertakes the struggle for transformation, for the defense of individual and collective rights, for the protection of nature, for the prospect of a country where all people, all individuals, all cultures are guaranteed inclusion and recognition?

The answer seems clearer now. It is the Indigenous people of the TIPNIS and those in solidarity to their struggle. It is all those who show their material and intellectual solidarity with this cause and are willing to support this struggle from their own identities and workplaces. In short, it is the oppressed, for whom there is no justice and no protection of their rights.

Certainly, there have been times when the *cocaleros*' organizations, the farmers and the settlers (now oddly called "intercultural") that support the MAS government and are represented by it were "political subjects of change." However in the face of the TIPNIS proposals they have shown themselves to be conservative, not revolutionary. They have defended their sectarian interests without taking into account the interests of the oppressed, such as the indigenous peoples of the East and the highlands. A people that oppresses another cannot be considered revolutionary or the main agent of a change process. As recently deceased Giulio Girardi used to say, either self-determination of Indigenous peoples is based on solidarity or it is non-existent (2003, 59).

Therefore speeches, laws and propaganda are not enough. Being the people means to engage in action for change, to respect the laws that the people have made for themselves, to respect the other along the spectrum of diversity of gender, culture, trade, even ideas.

The political subject is at the same time constituted as an educational subject, i.e. a subject that teaches other sections of the population and their allies about the project of transformation. But at the same time, it also learns from these people, embodying the true sense of the Zapatista motto: "governing by obeying the people" and "fighting not to seize power but to change it..."

VI How the People Teach the People

There are various ways that the people can teach the people. The thoughts of leaders and intellectuals, courses, workshops, conferences, articles and debates in the media... are all important ways to raise awareness and ensure commitment in the construction of a political subject and an emancipatory popular project.

We would now like to acknowledge the strengths of the particular methodology developed by the TIPNIS marchers, which has made so much impact, has gained the support of the people of Bolivia, and has even thrown many individuals identified with the political project of the MAS into crisis.

We could say that the "TIPNIS march and mobilization" was a kind of "methodological axis" around which has emerged and developed a set of educational methods and devices, the impact of which we can detect in the massive mobilizations and debates that have taken place throughout Bolivia, as well as abroad, for the defense of the Park and for a new model of development.

The *demands for enforcement* of individual and collective rights, as well as those of Mother Earth, have been one important method. These demands for enforcement are at the heart of the new Political Constitution of the Plurinational State, which stands above any endeavor that seeks to accrue power on the fringes of it or above it.

These demands for enforcement are complemented by a *quest for consistency between theory and practice,* between principles and actions, between words and reality. The fundamental contradiction that afflicts the current ruling party is that since the very beginning of its term in government it has been abusing language and spreading propaganda at the expense of practicing governance, and it has been violating any laws that have presented it with obstacles to the concentration of power. *The TIPNIS is a prime example of this contradiction.*

The use of *dialogue* is another method that the TIPNIS marchers have advocated and employed. Since the very first moment, they demanded to talk with president Evo Morales, who never accepted their invitation. We have to examine carefully the numerous attempts at "dialogue" proposed by the government of Evo Morales, which, as we all know, failed. Was there a genuine will to dialogue on the part of the government's representatives?

Everything seems to indicate that the ministers were not there to "dialogue," but to try to persuade the marchers and impose an unconstitutional decision that was already taken: the TIPNIS highway will be constructed with or without your consent, as there are already signed contracts and commitments made behind the backs of the inhabitants of the Isidoro Sécure Park. President Evo Morales, who never misses an opportunity to visit the *cocaleros* of Cochabamba or to participate in international events, has no time for "dialogue" with the marchers. In any case, they are the ones who should come to La Paz to talk to the president. Is this a novel version of "governing by obeying the people?"

It is evident that in order to have the possibility of genuine dialogue, i.e. the will to solve a problem or conflict as the one that emerged in the TIPNIS, certain conditions should be met. The first condition is the *observance of the laws*, if they are fair and the result of national and international agreements. The laws should not be negotiated but adhered to, and dialogue can only be engaged on that basis. Did the government committees have knowledge of these laws and the will to respect them? What has been obvious during the conversations and conflict dynamics is that there was no intention of observing these laws on the part of the government representatives. The marchers, however, have constantly resorted to what is stipulated by the Political Constitution of the Plurinational State of Bolivia and by international regulations.

Another important condition is *respect for others*, for their views on the issue. Did the government representatives respect the marchers by resorting to insults, unsubstantiated claims, allusion to "dark forces at work" [*mano negra*] that were never revealed, and the convenient claim that the marchers are instruments of the right and of imperialism? The marchers, however, have exercised their legitimate right to express their views to the authorities and it is for that reason that they demanded the presence of the president.

Respect for the other is violated when there is *resort to violence*. The systematic use of verbal violence and propaganda against the marchers was topped off in the Eighth March with the sad events of September 25, when there were acts of physical and psychological violence dictated and directed by senior government officials, with the complicity of our "settler brothers (?)" [*hermanos colonizadores*] (in their present "intercultural" guise).

Was there violence by the marchers towards Chancellor Choquehuanca, who paid them a visit to get them to desist from their demands? Were fully equipped police officers carrying powerful weapons "viciously attacked by the arrows" of the indigenous? It was the women who forced Choquehuanca to respect their right to free passage in order to stock up on water and food for their children. Who was the one who exercised violence there? For how long was the minister "kidnapped," since he was able to return peacefully to La Paz after admonishing the marchers, rather than engaging in "dialogue" with them? The people teach the people using the *force of argument* and not the argument of force (Girardi 2003, 53).

Moreover, here is another important nuance: the people learn and teach not only with the argument but also with the heart and the insistence on nonviolence: "The process of change is not built with kicks and punches, but with the heart" (Celso Padilla, TIPNIS leader). The TIPNIS marches have been moments of great emotion and solidarity, becoming the source of inspiration for posters, songs, dance, poetry and numerous books.

VII What has the TIPNIS Taught us?

As an important educational event, the TIPNIS march has generated a lot of learning experiences through an unwritten "curriculum" built in the heat of the struggle for the defense of the fundamental human rights of Mother Earth. The TIPNIS march, as a methodological axis of the learning processes, has meant a break with the logic of power that was being imposed on the population by different routes and was generating fear, on the one hand, and conformity on the other. It has opened up new possibilities and generated hope for those who strive for a more democratic and equitable society. Let us now consider some of these learning experiences.

VIII Another Process of Change is Possible

Bolivia's history has been marked by moments of social and political conflict, products of the contradictions arising from the conflict of interests and of the peoples' unshakable will to emancipation. This means that there have always been processes of change, and that their outcome has been conditioned by the balance of forces and by the direction of these processes within specific contexts. The struggles for the independence of Bolivia (1825), the Revolution of '52, the overthrow of the military dictatorship (1982), the El Alto uprising and Sanchez de Losada's flight from the country (2003), to mention the most remarkable, have been caused by -and in turn have sparked- processes of change.

However, these "processes of change" have been determined by their contexts and by the political actors who have steered them towards an emancipatory direction. There is no doubt that the "democratic cultural revolution" has constituted such a process of change, through the leadership of Evo Morales and the Movement Towards Socialism (*MAS: Movimiento Al Socialismo*).

However, as history teaches us, many of these processes of change can deviate from the principles that gave rise to them and become "impediments" to change.

It is common to hear those who once supported the "democratic cultural revolution," such as members of the progressive middle classes, social movement leaders and left-wing intellectuals, claim that the process of change launched by the MAS has deviated from its initial course. They also suggest that the TIPNIS march has laid bare for all to see the government's blatant violations of human rights, both individual and collective, as well as the "political justification" that those in power have provided for these violations.

The "government of change" does not govern by listening to the Bolivian people and that is a serious political mistake, because a developmentalist and mercantilist project such as the TIPNIS highway is not only threatening a protected area, it is also dividing the social groups that have historically fought side by side and it is beginning to undermine the foundations of a process of change that is the product of long years of struggle (Contreras Baspineiro 2012).[7]

IX Another Development is Possible

People have finally understood that the discourses on Mother Earth, *Pachamama*, community development and environmental protection that the government brags about in national and international events, have given way to the logic of "state capitalism," in alliance with international (IIRSA -Initiative for the Integration of Regional Infrastructure- megaprojects for Bolivia, financed by the BNDES -National Bank of Economic and Social Development of Brazil) (Soto Santiesteban 2011) and Bolivian capital: bankers and the agro-industrial oligarchy. They go as far as telling us that the development of our country depends on the "*gasolinazo*" [gasoline price gouging], on mega projects such as the TIPNIS highway, and on setting the interests of coca growers and settlers against those of the indigenous of the East and the highlands.[8]

The TIPNIS march has exposed and "deconstructed" all these discourses, revealing the underlying developmentalist schemes that are based on obscure

7 Additionally, scholar Luis Tapia (2012) views the plans of the MAS Government and the coca growers to "modernize the TIPNIS" as a feature of an "internal colonialism" that aims at conquering the indigenous territories to allow the expansion of extractivist capitalism (265).

8 Manifesto of the group of dissident intellectuals of MAS: "Por la recuperación del proceso de cambio para el pueblo y con el pueblo" ("Reclaiming the process of change for the people and with the people"), La Paz June 2011.

agreements and negotiations and are disastrous for the natural environment. With the TIPNIS march, a great part of the population has "gained awareness" of the importance of the defense of this, as well as other, natural and ecological reserves in Bolivia for our quality of life, for "living well" [*vivir bien*]. We have also realized that modernity and technology can coexist with the conservation of nature, based on a truly alternative vision of development.[9]

The Peoples' Summit for Social and Environmental Justice that took place in parallel to the Conference on Sustainable Development Rio +20 (June 2012), underlines[10] the defense of human rights, nature and the commons, as an alternative for our ailing planet against the "green economy" promoted by capitalism. The TIPNIS is undoubtedly an exemplary experience of struggle for a new model of development, based on "living well" and on respect for the rights of Mother Earth.

X Another Communication is Possible

Freedom of speech and press is essential in order to strengthen democracy and to dismantle the apparatus of propaganda that promotes the concentration of power. This is what we have learned by going to the scene of events, by faithfully recording images of what happened, by listening to the indigenous population, to their experiences, their proposals and their denunciation of the acts of persecution and repression, by giving visibility, through the independent press, television and radio, to their suffering during the exhausting walks and to the frequent threats and insults from government officials.

What is striking in the TIPNIS events are the frequent changes of discourse of the government officials, and the use of the propaganda apparatus to discredit the opponent or bewilder the population with half-truths.[11] Often the

9 "There remains the challenge of building another kind of development, truly postneoliberal and post 'statecapitalist,' founded on our plural reality, which will steer public policies towards a new pattern of generation and distribution of postextractivist wealth, based on the principles of productive transformation, creation of dignified labor, social justice and environmental conservation " (Wanderley 2012).

10 "The defense of the commons is dependent on the safeguarding of the rights of humans and nature as well as on solidarity and respect for the worldviews and beliefs of different peoples, such as the defense of "Living Well" (*Buen Vivir*) as a manner of living in harmony with nature, which presupposes the transition to an equitable society constructed jointly with the workers and the people."

11 "Moreover, we disapprove of the attempts at manipulating the Bolivian population through biased information that is designed to discredit and criminalize this mobilization

government attempts to give legitimacy to this type of communication as a means to deal with the right-wing press, which only seeks destabilization.

We believe that manipulative and false communication is what instigates the conservative counter-popular press. Therefore, the TIPNIS shows that another communication is possible. Another communication is possible because the indigenous peoples and many of the individuals that support them have finally "shed their fear" and started to speak in front of the cameras and write in newspapers. "We are not afraid of this government," was an oft-repeated motto in marches, blockades, night watches, hunger strikes in support of those involved and leading the TIPNIS march. The real "TIPNIS voices," not infiltrated or distorted by governments, are becoming louder and louder despite attempts to silence them.

> Democracy, unlike dictatorship, means transparency in the exercise of power; within this framework, a government must employ a kind of political communication that can transform dissent into consensus and promote diversity, plurality and deliberation as the basis of a quest for collective solutions to shared problems, particularly in situations of crisis. To that end, we need public media rather than propaganda machines who make use of language games to counter the truth with lies and to crush those who think differently through libel and insult.
>
> GOMEZ, 2012: 18

This kind of machine was put to operation again during the Ninth March, disseminating messages that violate the dignity of individuals and criminalize the march and its supporters. The ghosts of imperialism, the oligarchy and the destabilizing right reappear (the latter being a ghost because its capacity of mobilization in Bolivia today is minimal). The attack on critical NGOs that are not aligned with the government is intensified (García Linera 2011).[12]

Information manipulation also spreads internationally through a well-oiled media network, which leaves no room for dissenting voices on the current political processes in Bolivia. This explains why the voice of the indigenous of TIPNIS, the clamor of the marchers and the majority support of the population is hardly noticed. What does the progressive left have to gain by hiding these facts?

---

and link it to undemocratic interests. The greatest threat to democracy is creating a precedent of authoritarian relations and, above all, not listening to the voices of the people" (Press release of organizations and institutions on the Ninth March in defense of the TIPNIS, La Paz July 6, 2012.)

12 See also García Linera 2012.

XI Another Leadership is Possible

The long TIPNIS march has allowed us to clearly distinguish two kinds of leaders within the social movements, those concerned with the accumulation of power and personal benefits, utilizing the mechanisms of corruption and clientelism, flattering the President and supporting him unconditionally, and those who are guided by solidarity, are concerned with the welfare of all, are incorruptible, and use as their main weapon the veracity and rightfulness of their arguments.

Bertha Bejarano, President of the Confederation of the *Moxeño* Peoples of Beni, leader of the Ninth March who walked the 600 kilometers with six of her children and her sister Delia, said upon arrival in La Paz:

> We are not against development. If the President says development means they will bring us schools and health centers [*postas sanitarias*], it is the obligation of the state to look after the communities. He does not have the right to deceive our brothers, saying that 'as soon as they have the highway' they are going to have a school. It is their duty to attend to our basic needs.[13]

In the TIPNIS conflict we managed to get a glimpse of how a leader that identifies with his/her people and is attentive to everyone's needs should be, for us and for the people. It is ultimately akin to being a "popular educator." According to Giulio Girardi's description (2003, 103) the popular educator:

- Is a person that identifies with the oppressed as acting subjects, both on an ethical/political and on an intellectual level.
- Is a person motivated in his/her actions by a strong belief in the ethical/political and the intellectual potential of the poor, in their ability to become new men and women.
- Will be considered professionally successful not if he/she manages to accumulate more money or more power, but if he/she manages to serve the people more effectively.
- The popular educator does not lead the pursuits of the people but rather he/she helps them take center stage, thus he/she is considered a "midwife" of the people.
- Is able to explore new paths and take up struggles for justice without the certainty of victory.

13 Article in *Página Siete*, La Paz July 8, 2012.

- Aims to help develop a new model of power, based on the prominence of the people, i.e. those excluded both yesterday and today, through a non-violent strategy for the construction of alternative power.

XII The Plurinational State and Interculturality, Pending Challenges

Ironically, it is the former Minister of Autonomies [*Ministro de Autonomías*] and now Minister of the Interior [*Ministro de Gobierno*], Carlos Romero, who headed the government commission responsible for the "dialogue" with the indigenous in order to get them to give up their demands and conform to the MAS' developmentalist vision.

One lesson learned from the TIPNIS march for has been precisely the divisive nature of the government's plan, which incited conflicts of *cocaleros* and settlers against the indigenous of the East and the highlands, and bribed the leaders of these organizations with promises and gifts in exchange for their dissent.

The current government of the Plurinational State has shown disregard for the constitutional rights that guarantee the representation of all indigenous peoples in the Plurinational Assembly. This is the reason why one of the demands of the Ninth March has been "the inclusion of one representative from each aboriginal nation or tribe in the Legislative Assembly, subject to election by each nation's own rules and procedures." Moreover, is it not ironic that the settlers and *cocaleros* who form the social base of the MAS government define themselves as "intercultural communities?"

Interculturality is characterized precisely by the recognition of others, by taking into account their viewpoints, by appraisal of their culture, by respect for others, by the "dialogue between the culturally different." Is this the interculturality that inspires the plans of the government and its allies?

The TIPNIS march gives us hints for the construction of a Plurinational State: it must be a state where all cultures, all Bolivians have a place: unitary thought [*pensamiento único*], unitary power, must give way to interculturality and the construction of power structures that value and promote diversity.

XIII Ethics-driven Politics

A political project of government, especially one based on popular power, should not use repressive methods or violate fundamental rights. These rights, thoroughly recognized in the new Political Constitution of the Plurinational State, are not "negotiable" and they cannot be violated. They just have to be adhered to.

To this set of rights, we must add the ones recorded in Convention 169 of the ILO and the Declaration of the Rights of Indigenous Peoples put forward by the United Nations and signed by the government of Bolivia. These rights are disregarded and violated when the government, through a persistent media campaign still underway, resorts to the ghosts of imperialism, the right-wing, '*gonism*' [referring to the neoliberal policies of Sanchez de Lozada], or blatantly racist and sexist arguments to discredit the march.[14] These rights are disregarded and violated when indigenous and peasants are bribed with gifts and promises in order to accept the government's plans, reminiscent of the practices of America's first invaders, who lured the indigenous with mirrors and bric-a-brac in exchange for access to their wealth. These rights are disregarded and violated when public protest, guaranteed by the Constitution, is criminalized.

These rights are disregarded and violated when the indigenous peoples are systematically confronted and divided. This is the case with the two most representative organizations of indigenous peoples, the CIDOB and the CONAMAQ, who have supported the TIPNIS marches, and within the TIPNIS communities themselves, where communities are set against each other.

These rights are disregarded and violated when the TIPNIS marchers, among them children and women, are brutally repressed, their leaders imprisoned, while the real culprits are acting with total impunity as they are protected by the Bolivian justice.

These rights are disregarded when women, children and the rest of the marchers are denied access to water and food. The marchers' stay in the city of La Paz during the Ninth March was particularly arduous, due to the harsh winter conditions. The government refused to provide shelter and support for the "brothers" who defend Mother Earth, and denied them a hearing with the President that they demanded as Bolivians and as indigenous. They were even repressed with tear gas and water jets when they tried to protest in Plaza Murillo, where the Presidential Palace and the Plurinational Assembly are located.[15]

A project of popular government is respectful of human rights, and places ethics and values along or even above politics. This is put to practice through democratic methods, conflict negotiation, unlimited respect for freedoms, both individual and collective, freedom of speech and thought, the construction of hegemony based not on imposition and authoritarianism but on dialogue, the substitutions of a culture of corporatism with the culture of solidarity, thereby

14 "The indigenous peoples are incapable of having their own ideas and making their own decisions," "The young Chaparé men should try to get YurakarésTrinitarian women to fall in love with them, so they can convince them not to oppose the construction of the highway."

15 *Página Siete*, Friday July 6, 2012.

demonstrating that the popular project of government is superior to other projects and interests, such as the ones sponsored by the right and neoliberalism.

A project of government that is authoritarian and violates individual and collective rights is what instigates the right and imperialism to continue conspiring and intervening in the lives of our peoples.

And since ethics should go hand-in-hand with politics, we must applaud those intellectuals and government officials who, in the wake of the TIPNIS events, have resigned from their positions as agents of a political project that represses the indigenous and violates the rights of humans and of nature. Because ultimately what the indigenous of the TIPNIS are fighting for is their right to live, and the life of any human being must be respected.

On Urban Resistance and Processes of Formation of Subjects for Emancipatory Action: An Examination of the Cultural Breakthrough Brought about by the Medellin Youth Network,* 1991–2011

*Edison Villa Holguín***

Medellin Youth Network emerged as a community organization that offered support to youth work in lower-class districts and neighborhoods in the city of Medellin in the 1990s. Along the way, it got transformed into a collective experience which, based on flexibility in its methods and a reliance on a wide spectrum of nuances to formulate a multitude of perspectives that aimed to understand, interpret and transform the social context, reached to overcome adversities and to negotiate moments for diverse and radical interventions. It was concerned with the construction of emancipatory projects for nascent societies that required a different kind of relational code of ethics and aesthetics, which in the case of the "Network" were gradually constructed as forms of resistance against the structures of domination that condition human relationships.

> Along this path of transformation we began to identify the way in which violence becomes incarnated in us and is reproduced in our actions, we began to reflect on injustice and the way militarism and patriarchy perpetuate this kind of social structure.

This process was constructed through the efforts of the youth community activists of the neighborhoods of Aburrá Valley, attending to their interests and needs. Its participants were young people who decided to create autonomous proposals, challenging the dynamics of socioeconomic domination and the cultural prejudices of the patriarchal society of Antioquia. Its political action was oriented towards the need for critical expression within a militarist and alienating social order such as that of Colombia, shaping a political project of social sensitivity that, setting out from its work in partnership with autonomous youth collectives, was consolidated through actions of awareness-raising and mobilization in the surroundings of the city of Medellin.

---

* The indented texts were excerpted from the testimonies of many different activists who spoke about their organizational experiences within the Medellin Youth Network.

** Popular educator. Nodo de Formación Popular. Medellin. Activist of the Youth Network.

> Our story began on the streets. We started by decorating them in many colors amid a unilateral declaration of death in our neighborhoods, in the same neighborhoods where we had put into practice our organizational community action, and which were now beginning to be flooded with death and anguish. Our desire to "exorcise" them led to the creation of the Youth Networks as a collective action in defense of life. Two years elapsed among parades, campaigns and direct actions of disobedience and insubordination.

1 Community Youth Organization, 1991–2001

As a process of organizational action based on youth and community, the Youth Network has carried through for two decades in the communes [*comunas*, municipal administrative division] of Medellin, where it emerged, in an urban context plunged in a deep social and political crisis of de-legitimation of the state and decline of its governance.

> In 1997 I got to know this organization and I began to approach their ideas of resistance, their methods of resistance and non-violence as a form of popular struggle. The collaborative games motivated us to carry out personal, social, political and philosophical reflections on the necessity to find ways to overcome violence. The loss of institutional legitimacy, a result of the crisis of the hegemonic patterns of collective identification, was decisive in the 1990s for the birth of the civilian-based [civilista] approach in community organizations and the expression [expresionismo] of youth oriented towards alternatives of transformation.

Over the course of 20 years, besides being a stage of analysis, discussion and disobedient action, the cumulative experience of the Youth Network nurtured both the organization of youth on a national level and the local urban mobilization, in a number of ways: through the contribution of elements of political education and organizational work methodologies; through the proposal of processes from a grassroots point of view; and through its support for social processes of resistance to the naturalization of economic and cultural oppression in the life projects of the communities and specifically of the children, youth and women.

> We use our potential as social subjects, breaking with the adult-centric institutional arrangements that loomed over our forms of organization

> and action, to generate new forms of unconventional and less focal forms of organization, progressively interjecting the perspective of neighborhood, culture, the communal and the collective as a way out of our own organizational crises.[16]
>
> MALKREYENTE, 2011

In Medellin, between the 1970s and the 1990s, the violence of mafia formations allowed the emergence of new bourgeois practices that originated from the economic dynamics brought about by a large entrepreneurial sector of Antioquia. This sector decided to recapitalize the plantation-based economy and the business spirit of the area, this time, not only based on the corruption of the administrative apparatus, which is where historically it has thrived, but also based on the "purchasing power" resulting from the accumulation of drug money.

The phenomenon of drug developmentalism gave an impulse to the city's and the country's economy, and the supposed "social and economic mobility" it generated, is still being paid back at a high price: The lives of more than half of the young people of five generations. Approximately 60 percent of the families living in the city have had a victim among their members in this genocide of youth, in the eternal mafia spring of Medellin.

> I remember like it was yesterday: curfews, raids, disappearances, executions, massacres and the war that the police declared on us just because we were young and we were sitting on the sidewalk, in parks or staircases of our neighborhoods and our streets. I remember my cousins, my friends, my neighbors and my comrades murdered in these assaults for control and social order that they wanted to impose at any cost.
>
> Ibid.

Under these circumstances, the government tried to regulate the coexistence in the Aburrá Valley by handing over the control of the city's periphery to the military, directly affecting mobility, the imaginary and the experiences in the neighborhoods. As a consequence of this process of militarization we are still suffering today the strengthening of the "values" of subjugation, coercion and violence as a means of conflict resolution by public and private, legal and illegal, justice.

> Back at that time, the people's organizations and the youth practices in the neighborhoods, along with those of us who were participating in

---

16 *Malkreyente* is the semestral newsletter on the actions of the Youth Network.

> organizing the community, felt incapable of firmly proposing alternatives of transformation for our communities due to our fear of the armed groups and the state apparatus. But fear did not break us apart; we maintained a marginal resistance and we countered the official stigma of "No Future" by promoting a parallel development, an experience that sometime later gave rise to the proposal of objection and anti-militarism.

The traditional two-party system, historically nurtured by the actions of the communes and the clientelism of the local administrative authorities, goes into a crisis due, on the one hand, to its inability to gain legitimacy when faced with the needs of the communities and, on the other hand, its lack of spontaneity and creativity in solving the real problems of the population.

> This was a time of great learning, great protests in the streets, protests that led us to think that an autonomous community movement was possible. However, this was cut short by the credibility of the institutions and the refusal to have an anti-capitalist community movement in the city.

Thus in 1991, the ground was prepared for a milestone in community leadership brought about by the aspiration to participate in a stage of popular construction and in collective processes of transformation oriented towards autonomy, civil disobedience and counterculture—to advance, through social struggle, towards an inspirational utopia.

A multitude of organizational forms became part of such a challenging endeavor, among them youth groups, art groups and parish groups of neighborhoods such as Villatina, Castilla, Aranjuez, Santander and Manrique. These were later articulated in regional processes such as the ones in the eastern central district, north-eastern district and north-western district and other organizational expressions of the youth that emerged in the city, including "La Candelaria" youth movement, the "Association of groups of Santo Domingo," the youth and cultural work of "Bello," as well as a multitude of activists and organizations that were opposed to the militarization and the violence that prevailed in our social context. Among them were organizational undertakings such as "Barrio Comparsa," the "Committee for Life and Democracy," and other endeavors that—from a community organizing standpoint—began to converge in a process called Youth Networks.

> A joint creative process of a group that was, in itself, a break in the cycle of war and oppression. But the best part was the daily experience of complicity with other people, of manifest solidarity, of laughter, of joking and

> teasing and experiencing love in all its splendor. It was an opportunity to understand and realize that the deceit and trickery that this capitalist, patriarchal and militaristic society used on us was going to cease being our daily bread. We wouldn't be in a constant search, like automata. On the contrary, these would become the elements that we wanted to eliminate and remove from our lives. At the sametime, we remained aware that the struggle was not all roses; quite the opposite. It was a constant effort to avoid being permeated by this other reality, and to become conscious of the strategy of the right-wing, of the ruling class of this world, to isolate our dreams and desires of building different forms of social interaction.

In this journey, the political subjects and social actors who envisioned and participated in the initial process of the Youth Network arrived with experiences of different currents and organizational trends such as ecumenical movements, university student movements, neighborhood art groups and the community and civil development planners who originated in the NGOs that supported youth organizations.

> The Youth Networks were embraced as a convergence of the pluralistic experiences of the particular development of various anti-hegemonic Latin American movements, which, through grassroots popular education, attempted to deal with the problems of their community.
>
> Ibid.

The first configuration of the Network consisted of instances of leadership originating in the youth networks of the districts, young people from lower class neighborhoods where the Network had been influential, such as the eastern central and the north-western. Most of these people had organizational experience though their participation in youth and community groups. On this basis, a non-representational and non-delegatory approach to collectivity was progressively established, which allowed for continued joint creation.

This plurality was favorable to discussions and educational processes. Even for many university students, the Youth Network becomes the real space of political education and criticism, considering the empirical and academic experiences that informed each current's contribution to the formation of a critical subjectivity in the sphere of popular youth leadership. This was due to the fact that political education within the university, along with the student organizations, experienced an institutional decline into functionalism, plunging them into the technocratic pragmatism in which educational processes regressed in the nineties, and from which they have not recovered.

The organized groups and individuals who have chosen to participate in this experience, have done so with the aim of consolidating a space of articulation for youth networks, appropriating organizational forms and codes and sharing a sense of community, mutual help and solidarity on the basis of one's own experience.

> A critical stance against the abuse of power, a belief that a situation of injustice can be transformed through action and that action is motivated by reflection, and a reflection stimulated by unveiling the ways in which violence, especially structural violence, undermines and threatens our right to live with dignity as a people [informs us].

The Network thus envisioned the formation of a political subjectivity that would acknowledge the presence and plurality of the young people, and would try to commit society to an understanding of the youth as social subjects, valid interlocutors, bearers of knowledge, of values, of aesthetic principles, of sensibilities, of practices, of enquiries, of proposals and interests in permanent construction and configuration.

> I must admit that I always felt listened to [in the Youth Network]. I admired, and I still do, the decision making process and the value of dissent in the quest for consensus, because, when I tried to reenact these modes of relation in different contexts, I would crash against the wall of authoritarianism and abuse of power. However, I managed to recognize this and take a position on the matter, and this was the moment when I turned into an insubordinate woman, a free woman.

The people who do organizational work within the Youth Network insist in their ideas of emancipation as a permanent state of transformation, aiming to do things better and to engage, on the basis of a common strategy, "new participants, thus enabling competent social and political action that can facilitate critical and technical elements in the society they seek to transform." (Youth Network educational process, 2005.) As a Network of autonomous collectives since its inception, and in spite of difficulties and rifts, some consensus was reached in order to operate jointly. Each group had its own school of thought, maintained its autonomy concerning methodology and resource management. At the sametime, there was an effort to organize joint actions. Throughout this period there has been in depth analysis on issues such as: the [conscientious] objection process and anti-militarism, non-violent popular defense, art in resistance, the enforcement of rights, popular education and feminism.

> In relation to local work, we initiated the formation of groups that had as a goal promoting a neighborhood or district identity, overcoming the territoriality and the invisible boundaries imposed by the armed conflict. We would arrive with joy, with recreational and cultural activities that engaged the whole community. These activities were called "Cultural Occupations" with exhibitions of art from the local area. Particularly, I remember the one we called "my neighborhood has no borders." In fact, these were important spaces of rendering visible, of transforming, of reclaiming youth, and of linking more young people to this process. On the district level, at that time the Youth Network was present through district promoter groups—eespecially in the north-eastern district, north-western district and eastern central district. Meetings between groups of the three areas were convened, which made possible to really go beyond the neighborhood, recognize ourselves as a city, as peers in the process of construction and as friends.

Within the youth network, the focus on the grassroots has been understood as the creation of people's power that emanates from the subjects that participate in the groups of the neighborhoods where the support work takes place. In the early years, this was done by the implementation of community projects through the use of guides and booklets that enabled us to detect the needs and opportunities of the communities, with the intention of countering the influence of traditional politics in the sphere of action of the youth.

> Our action was in the streets, in occupying the public space of the neighborhood, so that the community, the young people, got to know our proposal. We developed many actions and processes, we began by processes of group reinforcement, articulation with community organizations in the district, reinforcement of the district's networks, inter-district meetings. We made assessments in order to explore the interests and expectations of the young people of the city. We organized cultural activities accompanied by sessions of learning and reflection such as social gatherings, canelazo [hot alcoholic beverage with cinnamon] nights, banquets, meetings at dawn, film forums, academic meetings where the main topic for many years was "Youth Rights." These were included in our organization's annual report: "Do we have rights?" and "The current state of affairs concerning the rights of young people in the city of Medellin," developed in 2001–2002.

Over the course of more than a decade, organizational youth work was carried forward by workshop groups and district promoter groups, and also incubators [*semilleros*], groups of local youths, who initially would meet one day per week, going through all workshops and thus getting ready for a more intense training process that was focused on making an impact on political issues. We saw the gradual emergence of a subject that had the ability to lead projects and proposals of community and neighborhood development. It was believed that in order to express and defend oneself, it was necessary to master a set of technical and methodological tools that would enable the development, implementation and evaluation of community proposals.

> This political bid is starting to take to the streets based on the principles of non-violence and anti-militarism, conscientious objection and insubordination, which resulted in non-violent direct action, antimilitarist concerts and the denouncement of the forced recruitment carried out by the legal and illegal military structures that have occupied the neighborhood.

Around the beginning of the new millennium, the emphasis of the process shifted towards resistance to the homogenization promoted by the single thought of a globalized and neoliberal world. With this as a starting point, the Network initiates an internal discussion concerning the utopia of a cultural and economic autonomy, which has its origin in a debate on counter-cultural action and the consolidation of a libertarian, emancipatory, iconoclastic project.

> At that time I was surprised by the information provided by the conscientious objectors, since for the first time I heard about military spending and the fact that a bullet costs the same amount of money as a lunch. I felt outrage at seeing so much poverty that could be alleviated if it wasn't for the interests of those who hold political and economic power. So together with some of my friends we took part in some direct actions. We kept trying to have our way by boycotting events like the military parade of July 20, or the parade of the Flower Festival [feria de las flores].

The assembly meetings were the places of political education where the bid of the young people for youth was more forcefully manifested: The project of education and collective reinforcement involved counter-arguments, consensual decision-making, learning to respect dissent, examination of internal issues affecting the processes, subjective interpretation of the context, analysis and planning in perspective. It was in these spaces where agreements were reached and the decision to work together as a Network was reaffirmed.

> Although music and youth expression were not independent of the market, they did not always depend on it. There were "underground" groups and processes that were upheld as a parallel project that generated countercultural environments. In backstreet artistic expressions of the neighborhood, the subversive element has always been present—a condition fomented by the bands and university students of the time.

The Youth Network made an impact in the city not only by technically and organizationally advancing the support of youth by the youth itself, but above all, by political appropriation: self-determination, based on defining their own discourse and constructing their own way of thinking.

> Despite keeping the inherited institutional organizational structure in place in order to be able to manage the resources afforded by the European cooperation, we learned how to get around formalities and institutional rituals so we do not get accustomed to them. We understood that our objective was elsewhere. This was manifest in our direct actions and cultural occupations through playful and artistic practices in various spaces such as military posts, parks, neighborhoods, and militarized public spaces [that we felt] were antagonistic to alternative and countercultural youth proposals.

The Network, with its practice of non-cooperation, raised its voice in the organizational events in which it was involved, aiming to create a rift in the ideas of adaptation to the system and to express its dissatisfaction, in order to make clear that the democracy, equality, freedom and social consensus that the hegemonic powers are proclaiming through their mass media have never existed.

> Currently the process is created and re-created through the dialectic of subjectivity and collectivity, maintaining certain elements and strategies of its legacy, such as participation from below, cooperation work in support of experiential educational processes and reflection through play, physical and artistic expression with groups of children and young people, meeting spaces, debate and expressions of an emancipated subjectivity, which outline alternative paths of social construction, through feminism and anti-militarism.

11 The Organizational Consolidation Process

During the process of organizational consolidation, the Youth Network decided to establish as one of its political objectives enabling the organized young generation of the New Millennium to develop a different mentality towards political participation. This required taking small steady steps, acknowledging the setbacks occasioned by the lack of a long-term perspective regarding the projects of societal transformation and addressing the absence of political education in the majority of the members active within the organization.

> The intent was to establish a permanent space for the education of young men and women as critical subjects, to contribute to the creation and strengthening of youth groups and to help produce active social and political subjects. We also developed the "carnivalesque" ["comparsa"] educational process, which sought the re-appropriation of the city through reclaiming the public stage. It was an attempt at initiating processes of social recognition by reinforcing identity relationships between young people and strengthening youth practices. Our intention was that young people reassert themselves as subjects capable of taking a stand and defending their rights.
>
> Youth Network educational process, 2005. Systemization process

These educational events helped to gradually make evident that the rules of the game and the participation mechanisms imposed by systems of power were neither the method nor the ultimate objective of the Network. Although in certain circumstances the human rights discourse was used as a tool, there always existed the awareness that within the rhetoric of public policy the desired transformation could not be achieved, nor could there be any substantial change in terms of improving the living conditions of communities, since the laws are made within the framework of domination.

> We concentrated our efforts on the assembly. It was our bid for horizontality and collective political orientation: the assembly as the ultimate guidance and decision-making body, offering to groups a first collective space and a stage of power. All this political creativity went hand in hand with the question of how to organize ourselves in a way that enables us to meet our goal that corresponds to the kind of society we envisioned and we desired to construct. What kind of structure should we adopt according to principles of horizontality? Who has to make the decisions? How? What is the function of international cooperation? How can we avoid falling into a trap concerning the cooperation that could affect our actions, topics and programs? We debated about self-management or international financing, our administrative structure, and the ongoing issue of not becoming institutionalized in practice or in structure, of thinking of ourselves as a social process, as a movement. All this was a

> process of action, error and learning, because we knew what we didn't want, and this allowed us to shed some light on what was our desired objective. But at times it was difficult to follow the path towards that goal. We initiated many processes and modes of operation that over time proved to be inadequate, but we kept starting over up until we arrived at the current state of the network. Because this is the outcome of a prolonged period of creation and action, we cannot forget what we have already experienced, since the path we are following constantly reminds us of where we come from, who we are and where we are going.

Very few organizations managed to achieve equilibrium and maintain their practices, intentions and points of reference regarding political activity, while at the same time preventing the international cooperation or local budgetary concerns from making them lose their organizational autonomy. Various initiatives follow a mixed model, drawing resources from institutional sources, a practice which ends up fragmenting and isolating them, making them lose perspective of the movement.

> That was one of the many questions we collectively posed within the Youth Network: To what extent can our dreams of building a new society be reflected in state policies? I don't think this was a very elaborate question back in those days, but it was an indication that we did not want all this, all the false promises. We saw many of those who were walking along the same path with us taking other directions, in which emancipation and freedom seemed things of the past. So these very considerations divided the group, because the coordinator was member of a political party. There were, however, many more reasons. Only two of us were left, two women that felt strongly and passionately about all we were experiencing: the cultural occupations, the gatherings, the banquets, the meetings at dawn—on the whole a possibility of youth action and organization that could be experienced and enjoyed.

This kind of political autonomy involved a high price for organizations that embraced it. Having limited resources, or none at all, affected their capacity to have a real impact, which translated into sparse and localized incidence of their actions in the space of the neighborhoods. Operating within a network alleviated somewhat this condition and made possible, in organized communities, to put various issues of a generational interest in the social agendas, such as conscientious objection, anti-militarism and civil disobedience.

> It was at that moment when the disobedience to war emerged. We started to practice a method whereby we would talk about ourselves, the hegemonic values we embodied, but also the ones we wanted to experience. Up until the moon came out we would play cooperative games, we would sit there talking about the need for another kind of ethics concerning humanity and life. Thus we began to develop a conscience of why we shouldn't participate in the war. This consideration created the need for political action, which we carried out in any downtown park or military post, expressing our outrage at the fact that poor young people like us participated in the war.

Linking such organizational processes within a network proved seductive. Soon they became an organizational point of reference in the city, a critical emancipatory process which proposed a path different to the dominant within society. The challenge then was to keep up and to go on fostering these experiments. Even many instances of social leadership and many organizational processes that were not part of the Network itself were positively affected by this experience, and some of them made it part of their mission within the city. Projects such as the Network of community organizations, the "Youth sector of ASAPAZ," various collectives of anti-militarist music and youth expression developed.

> At that time our main concern was not to perpetuate that cycle of pain, violence, death and resignation to which we young people were destined, but rather to assert ourselves as people with ideas, life proposals and joy.

This organizational strength is soon translated into the opportunity to gain great legitimacy particularly among the young, who are driven by the desire to break the silence and proclaim their right to be left alone, to live in peace in their own lifestyle and their alternative world project.

> The process was accompanied by cinema, by films like Tango Feroz, Rodrigo D No Futuro, and Antonia, and theatrical plays by specific writers, such as Angelitos Empantanados by Andres Caicedo. These became the reflection of a rebellion and of the need to begin to express our refusal, but also our will to construct something different. [This was] even more so when the 'clean-up' groups were more active: the paramilitaries, people from the same neighborhood, who were on the payroll of people who offered them colored mirrors so that they would monitor us, exert control over our homes and vaccinate us.

In planning the future as a youth organization through strategies of "non-violent popular struggle," an orientation towards joint action with respect to social mobilization with the Network of community organizations was gradually consolidated. Based on this joint action, the Youth Network carried out a profound analysis of the structural causes of political and social conflict in Colombia, thus offering support to numerous campaigns that aimed to highlight the social issues that threatened dignity and social justice, which are fundamental conditions for people's lives.

> This conjuncture came about at the same time that, through reflection, we came to understand the structural causes of war—a war about which we understood very little, despite having experienced it first hand, and having mourned many friends and family members. Gradually our reflections were becoming more mature, clearer, this is why we felt that our actions should be directed not only against recruitment, but also towards making visible how the conflict was exacerbated, who were the participants, and how we could construct an alternative discourse and practice that would allow us to lead lives that challenged the hegemonic model.

III Processes of Reclaiming the Social Practices of Young People

Within the particular circumstances of the organizational experiences of young people, the divisions of class, gender and age group emerged as central motivations for mobilization around the demands of dignity and social justice. Mobilization around the issues of social class was prevalent in the organizational processes of university students, who had taken up the fight against the obstacles that prevent the access of the children of the working classes to secular, free and quality education. This struggle was just one in a multitude of transformational processes that aimed towards a fairer society.

> It was imperative to learn how to defend ourselves, to prevent our project from ending up like many projects of our left-wing comrades who do not preach taking up the arms. They believe in this path... obviously recognize the many contradictions that non-violence presented, contradictions reflected in the common questions: If I get violated what do I do with the perpetrator?
>
> [We saw ourselves as] a group that had the ability to define and jointly conceive a collective project—[in opposition to] what this system of

> dominant values did to humans—and obviously a group composed of human beings who believe that if we could experience other ways of interrelating based on freedom, we could have a small victory against this hegemonic and capitalist logic.

In discussions, meetings and organizational assemblies, there emerged the voices of the differentiated rights of the youth, which reinforced a diverse articulation in terms of district groups. They distanced themselves from the ideology and indoctrinating political militancy of the university at the time, where the position of the young people was not taken into consideration. In this climate of tension, the Youth Network sought to participate, through anti-militarist activism in spaces of confluence of social mobilizations, thus succeeding to go beyond the traditional role that has been assigned to young people—that of being passive recipients and cannon fodder in the armed conflict.

> I still remember the night that three of us, members of the "United Youth" group, walked to Maracaná stadium, where there was a meeting of the Youth Network, to which we had been invited a few days before. In that meeting we would talk about "cultural occupation," as we used to call it back. We used to occupy a park or a street, in order to demonstrate that the young people did not want to live among the dead. That particular cultural occupation was going to be bigger, since many young people from the northwest were going to participate. It was called "Life in the north-west is lively." All groups were committed to do a wall painting right in the area that appeared to have no life at all: in the "universal" cemetery.

The Network took up the issue of conscientious objection, "which moves from the scope of the national to the local, and ceases to be a movement in itself in order to contribute to the movement as an organizational option." (*Systemization process*, Youth Network educational process, 2005.) By addressing the issue of conscientious objection, we decided to counter the idea of progress that underlies the right-wing discourse, by posing the question: what kind of participation and what for? Thus [we were] undermining consumerism and militarism as forces of socialization in and out of the schools, forces which claimed the bodies of the young people in order to objectify them or adapt them to the status quo.

Through a process developed by and for the youth, the Network takes up the challenge of dealing with the adverse social context, a result of the urban social unrest, by going against the traditional perceptions of youth and the conservative vision that predicates control over the bodies of young people and women as the principle on which social order is established. Among the many predicaments of social coexistence, we observe the pathological stigmatization of young people, young people who refuse to be homogenized or to fulfill the norms of conservative society, [where they] are treated with suspicion, and their insubordination is equated with delinquency or maladjustment.

This stigmatization reached a height in Medellin in the eighties, as a result of the utilization of the youth by mob capitalism in its disputes and in its structure of production and marketing of drugs, as well as a result of other aspects of the urban conflict. This alarmist perspective culminated in a normative interventionism as the objective of the welfare-ist [*asistencialistas*] control policies that have since been imposed on young people. This generated a conception of the young people as a high risk social component in need of a process of conversion into conservative citizens.

> Throughout the nineties, the city was offering many action plans and programs aimed at youth, a youth stigmatized by violence, and where many classified these youth as perpetrators and not as victims of this cruel war that was looming every day over the city. Most of us grew up like this. We lived every day of our lives within this war, and to some extent it became part of our lives. There was a lot of "Institutional offers" that promoted youth groups, youth clubs, trying to involve us in educational, playful, recreational and cultural activities.

This governmental intervention in the control of juvenile behavior materialized in terms of a civilian catechism organized since the beginning of the nineties, when the principles of public youth policies had as a backdrop the ideological arguments that bore the biologist and psychologistic biases of patriarchal society, which tried to deal with the problems of the "youth" based on stigmatizing, discriminating, policing, authoritarian and repressive approaches.

> It was in fashion to discuss a Law of Youth—about youth public policies, creating an expectation that it was possible to influence the domain of the state. I must admit that I fell for this discourse myself, which is why I took part in the CMJ (Municipal Youth Council). I saw it at the time as a real space of participation and influence that could generate interesting proposals for the benefit of the youth of the city. It took me longer to realize that this was not the correct way, and that what it really was doing was to legitimate and reinforce a state apparatus that captured, deceived and obliterated the young people according to its own interests. Eventually we

> came to this realization, and the lesson that was learned helped strengthen our individual and collective transformation processes. My youth group in the north-western district, called ECOVIDA, also fell into this vicious circle. This group was the actualization of a vision of friendship that sought to create alternatives for young people in our neighborhood. Its objective was to nurture and preserve the environment. It was a youth club in which we also enjoyed certain comforts provided by the state. We learned a lot, we got to know new methods of operating and new realities, and finally, we challenged this idea and we realized that this was not the path of transformation. From all this there remain experiences, acquired knowledge and some fond memories—but also the conviction that the state apparatus is not a viable option for the young or for society itself.

In fact, institutional arrangements, such as the Law of Minors or the Handbook of Coexistence in School, are essentially detrimental to the free development of one's personality and autonomy as a critical subjectivity in conditions of diversity. Likewise, it is suppressive of the proposition and aesthetic expression of the young subject's thought, which seeks a humanist and integral progress for society.

In the course of two decades, the Youth Network has been calling into question the plans to transform the youth through an institutional project, because such policies do not resort to intergenerational dialog or to a standpoint that is constructed by the free thinking of the real acting subjects of the youth experiences. Neither are they oriented towards a political approach of social emancipation.

> Most of these institutions had a Christian discourse of charity and an outlook of the young as in constant need of help and support. Some institutions developed activities in order to co-opt the youth initiatives; others yet proposed specific actions without a long-term plan other than the 'activity for its own sake,' and a very few dared to create spaces that would truly allow us to develop as empowered subjects of rights. Thus, many young people became accustomed to this type of institutional-state support, and they refrained from getting involved in actual processes of collective creation and transformation.

The grounds on which they are based notwithstanding, the theories that describe youth as an organic period of life, reducing it to merely a biologically deficient stage in human life, are inadequate, generalizing and degrading. They disempower the subjectivity of the young people who, through their social practice, seek to transform human relationships by promoting alternative ways of being and acting in the world.

The majority of the local academics have played a decisive role in these processes of institutionalization by reducing "youth" to merely an object of study. They were found lacking in the delicate task of understanding youth beyond the organic, as integral processes of social expression and as specific modes of being and of addressing the complexity of the micro-politics of social relations.

Thus, youth became the domain of "youthologists," whereby external analysts became legitimated to invoke "youth," obviously with no understanding of the complexity of the expression of young subjects.

Consequently there is a perpetuation of welfare-ist tendencies and discourses of "protection" that conceive young people as a sector of the population that is "deficient, lacking, vulnerable and at elevated social risk." Thus, the practices of the young people are converted into treatises on social control, against the backdrop of the Judeo-Christian ideology of a double standard that denies the development of subjectivity, consciousness and an emancipatory outlook. Instead, it is replaced with the imperative of functional adaptation to an alienating arrangement of production and reproduction of an increasingly debased type of society: schooling, consumerism and adult-centric perceptions of life.

IV Youth and Urban Mobilization

Art as a form of resistance and expression of alternative proposals has been one of the strengths of the Youth Network since its inception. It has been appreciated as a means of social mobilization that, rooted in counterculture, can help raise awareness towards social transformation. The aesthetic expression of the youth has been the counter-informational medium that has made possible the transmission of different messages. Artistic cultural expression was taken up as an instrument of power of the people, bolstering the appropriation of its own reality by the community, unfettered by the biases and the agendas imposed by the hegemonic media.

The artistic cultural expression, an experience originating in the eighties, was the first to break through. Dance, *chirimia* hornpipe music and various underground bands that had developed in the city begin to claim their place and pave the way for expressions of mobilization that would later reappear in a more political guise and focused on specific issues such as armed conflict, participation, youth identity—all within the turmoil of the social crisis of the time, which had youth as its focal point.

This proved an important aspect in the mobilization of urban youth because the artistic format permitted advancing protest and activism through musical and visual expression and the artistic installation of confluences in the streets under different emblems: trying to reassert the collective diversities that are in dialogue, seeking to give voice to the underdog and make the voice of change from below heard. [This meant] seeing the world through the eyes of other subjectivities in order to understand their perspective, discussing and partaking in change themselves from the standpoint of their unique aesthetic principles and their social, cultural and political sensitivity.

Over the last four decades in the Western world, the art of music in particular has been one of the means of transmission of messages of change and rebellion, as well as fashion and frivolity. [However, this meant] facing a dilemma: several youth processes in various areas that engaged in visual and musical expression as an end in itself, were coopted by the entertainment industry, which historically has been utilizing and exploiting the expression of the youth. The lack of a clear code of conduct regarding commercialization made these musical projects go astray in terms of their commitment to the political processes that were gaining ground in the world of youth, away from the institutions.

Economic pragmatism ends up conditioning the relationship between youth expression and the market. Consumerist cooptation becomes another adversary of youth struggles. Numerous political expressions of the young people have been stereotyped because they were appealing and creative. And from that springs the association of young people's protest with fashion, frivolity and superficiality, and its close link with globalized commerce.

The current generation has experienced this process of alienation from its own expression, which treats young people as avid consumers of models and patterns emanating from North America. In the commercial domain, governed by the value that their tastes and styles have in the marketplace, the young people are turned into objects in the world of the commodity. Organizations that emerge in these population groups and share their aesthetic preferences, end up converted into consumer communities. This way, social phenomena like youth clubs, festivals and concerts emerge, guided by the appetite for stereotypes that prevail in the West, influenced by the mass media and advertising.

A mass culture of these characteristics and the economic focus on entertainment did the same with the massification of marijuana, which was used on the outside of a cultural project based on ritual, creativity and mysticism. It was utilized as a psychoactive substance that numbs and alienates consciousness, with no transcendent purpose for the user, but with great gains for those who produce and distribute it commercially. This condition necessarily led the political organizations of the youth to think of new ways to mobilize and motivate the bodies, because the objective was not only self-expression, but building and communicating the message of transformation by other means.

Besides the consumerist appropriation of youth expression and protest, we saw the rise of the cooptation of popular mobilizations and the institutionalization of the aspirations of the youth through the intervention of various local governments in the 1990s in the city of Medellin. Scheming politicians bought out youth participation and turned it into an electoral clientele that adapted public policy according to their interests, based on the oversupply of approaches of "citizens' adaptation" that allowed political control over the mobilization efforts of young people and the expression of their discomfort.

> Another avenue that we thought was opening up was that of public policy, whereby many of the boys from the youth groups believed that somehow they would strike it big as well. So we participated in all celebrations or receptions organized by candidates; or [the politicians] would hand us candy or gifts from the companies that were close to the youth group. But deep down, we were looking for something else. We soon got tired of populating meetings, believing in the promises of any slime bag that offered us colored mirrors. This made us move away from such cliental-ist institutions that represented a vertical, absolute power.

After rejecting the dialogue with the institutions, the Youth Network started to take shape, shaking off its passivity and its dependence on the NGOs that were carrying out the management. We witnessed the formation of a new generation of subjectivities, [youth] who were determined to be an alternative force not subordinate to the system, and oriented towards building a comprehensive youth social movement that would represent its own interests and needs.

> This fresh start had two lines of activity: youth empowerment and conscientious objection. The debates revolved around the issue of how to exert influence, from our subjective standpoint, towards social transformation. We knew that our actions were still nascent and marginal. It was obvious that we were dancing to the tune of our rivals in terms of our economic, cultural and political practices.

V The Youth Network and Its Contribution to the Process of Formation of Political Subjectivities

When I look back at myself and my trajectory with the Youth Network, I feel that I am narrating the story of my life. I reaffirm that I still feel part of it and that it's impossible not to feel part of it, as it has shaped my life

> in the same way as someone who teaches me to write, speak and understand the world around me. Although my path has now taken me to other directions, my pursuits remain the same, that is, freedom, disobedience, emancipation and hope.

The process of defining our project was consolidated through reflections and voices on conscientious objection, anti-militarism and feminism—on the basis of expressions, symbols and images that represented the complex web of diversity, different styles and organizational methods. These transcended the vacillating political effervescence of each one of the temporalities of the project of the Youth Network, based on the pursuits and the political imperatives of the moment. Thus, there was no accumulated experience that transferred from generation to generation. Rather, each age group made an effort to contribute to the different political intentions of the project.

This organizational path of this process led [the Youth Network] to adopt a humanist project, influenced by anti-militarist anarchism, ultimately drawing from feminism, and the approach of popular power. It went beyond trade unionism and the parties that sought to "humanize" capitalism, as if it were even possible to keep society frozen in time, in a kind of conformism. [This pathway] widened the generation gap between the classical and historical subjects, and the new subjectivities identified as declassed, ethnic-ized, gendered, and ecological. It signified a generational break with the customary models of protest and revolution.

Expressing its dissent against Western culture and its systems of domination incarnated in the church, the state and the market—amid the vicissitudes of war politics, the predicament of the great influence of capitalist consumerism and the laws of value—(and the need to build a present "not a future" as has been the classic proposal for youth), the Youth Network reaffirmed the ability of young people to take into their own hands—in a collective, autonomous, conscious, and reflective manner—the control of their destiny as youth, based on strengthening the networks and links for the participation, and the reclamation of youth as a social and political subject.

> We saw the gradual emergence of "critical subjects with social awareness and sensitivity" that could "transform the militaristic, adult-centered, authoritarian, sexist, unjust culture." We are talking about the development of an approach based on alternative education that seeks to promote a pedagogy of resistance.

If the strong point of the social context we seek to transform is its focus on the economic aspects, it is imperative that the people who elaborate the alternative proposals possess critical knowledge that enables them to carry out analyses in order to understand, challenge and intervene in the reality, transmitting this knowledge back to their communities.

The Youth Network resorted to popular education as a strategy for building knowledge and self-awareness based on the recognition of reality and of the conditions of oppression and colonization, [the need for] the development of horizontal organizational structures and collective action, with the intent to promote self-awareness and mutual appreciation. [The Network was] seeking, through its practices and methods of interrelation, to bring about freedom, social justice and the transformation of the value system of the Catholic hierarchies, the patriarchal paradigm that is predominant among the Colombian population.

> Thus, among the many strategies we elaborated, we started to think about a School of Popular Education, a totally autonomous project where we would decide how we were educated, by whom and most importantly, for what objectives. We felt the need to be able to discuss with other political formations what were the Latin American peculiarities in political practice and action. We identified the necessity of a rigorous interpretation and understanding of the system of capitalist domination, and we began to appreciate the importance of popular communication and artistic resistance as organizational political practices. Although these proposals already existed, we were aware that our political action, based on art and communication, was not there to entertain or to embellish our methods, Rather it was a way to bring to the foreground the issues of rebellion, resistance and the construction of a processes of dialogue, where we could collectively put up for discussion the issue of community, of humanity.

The development of a critical consciousness that could promote and carry out life changes towards self-emancipation takes place within every being and within every complex process of emancipation experienced by the collectives (awareness—criticism—transformative action). There are behavioral changes elicited by individuals, autonomously and collectively making the decisions concerning their own life projects. This [transpires], not in order to have only the superficial appearance of rebelliousness, but [rather] a graphical discursive externalization of one's own experience of transformation. To lead a life of revolutionizing the present moment, of battling internal oppression, against one's own hegemonic and conservative discourses and practices, seeking a day-to-day application of alternative cultural practices that grant freedom and sovereignty to individuals and communities, [is the authentic reality].

> Gradually this process has led us to what we are today, a project that has made a great advance in defining what we do not want, that is well aware of our contradictions as men and women who have been dominated in different manners. Hence today we cannot speak of equality in the way we learned it in the liberal school. Rather we can speak with clarity of our of class, race and gender oppressions.
>
> That is why every time we make a change, we do so with the firm conviction that we reaffirm our commitment to our rebellious, anti-militarist, humanitarian and libertarian project, which we have been carrying forward for the last 20 years. We have made changes looking for the best way to organize, to balance knowledge, to understand the world around us, and most importantly, to understand, criticize and repudiate the country in which we were fated to live in.

The Youth Network is upholding a subjective and collective praxis of liberation from the Western project, defining resistance as the transformation of the dominant human and social relations and their methods of production that treat people as data and objects rather than as subjects.

The praxis of its activists transforms the Youth Network into a formative process of critical subjectivity in permanent construction, which aims to constitute social and political subjects, offering them a space in which to dream, to enquire, to emancipate themselves, to become empowered, to transgress, and carry out actions that pave the way towards a desirable diverse society.

VI Towards Grassroots Organization

In the course of organizing the grassroots non-violent struggle, an encompassing proposal of political-pedagogical education was elaborated, which was based on a comprehensive view of the educational trajectory and the history of the subject, where the immediate social context is comprehensively acknowledged as a concrete experience of reproduction and transformation of practices and customs, creating the conditions for gaining awareness and making decisions geared towards collective transformation.

Along the path of mobilization it has traversed, the Youth Network learned that the proposal of an emancipatory project goes beyond following along the line of dominant thought, by becoming a forum for debate and proposal regarding society, based on a humanist praxis of non-violent popular defense that does not consider capitalism an inevitable fate.

As a grassroots organization, the Youth Network aims to construct different political nuances in contemporary society that could overcome the dynamics of domination in the sphere of social and human relations, and could go beyond the Western anthropocentric and patriarchal paradigm that perpetuates the global historical forms of oppression by means of which the world has been governed and controlled for the benefit of a few. This, despite the fact that these practices have been asphyxiating the "*Pachamama*," that the people of many nations are starving to death, and that the material alienation inflicted by single thought puts an end to the construction of a happy and diverse existence.

VII Processes of Emancipation of Young Women

> This historic moment generated great expectations, especially regarding leisure. Disobedience was blooming. We were no longer afraid of the night, we could dance, stay out until late. We women began to disobey at home, since for our mothers, and especially mine, it was a sin to be out in the street until late, with all that this implies about a woman, and what's more, with all the groups of 'social clean-up' that were still roaming our territories.

There was a need to examine more carefully how capitalism operates in the domain of culture and social relations. This led the women of the Network to analyze the oldest system of oppression, which was ignored by the materialist analyses of history: patriarchy. This was defined as oppression against women, expressed in sexism, exploitation and the symbolic subordination to everything masculine.

> Many of us started to wonder how to experience different relationships among us based on solidarity; how to initiate a reflection on our condition as women; how to show our rejection of the war. Back then we did this out of solidarity, because we didn't want our friends to be recruited, and implicitly because of our need to have a destiny different than being a mother. Thus the group "Itzas" was created.

[For some,] it was possible to walk along a libertarian path without denouncing the present conditions, without proposing alternatives grounded on feminism, which, as a political theory, had revealed through analysis and conceptual elaboration, the subordination of women within the patriarchal system of domination, enforced through capitalist ideology and the hierarchical system of Christianity.

> Hope persists today, although the social context of those years has not changed much. On the contrary it seems exacerbated. However we are more convinced today about what is the object of our struggle, or which are the most important spheres of conflict: patriarchy as a system of cultural domination and capitalism as a system of economic domination. We know that we must continue the dialogue concerning our own contradictions, because the oppression keeps being reproduced in our bodies. But we also know that the decisive confrontation is with the social structure, which is where this model obliges us to be under constant control and in conditions of humiliation. This process has allowed us to get to know ourselves and assert ourselves as a group that has made possible an informed dialogue geared towards an emancipatory project, where I have the sensation that the utopia is taking shape, as my body and my words are interwoven with feminist practice and socialist values, free of relations of domination. We embark on this line of enquiry from the standpoint of an emancipatory practice such as popular education that allows us to advance a critical analysis, but also a revolutionary practice.
>
> This analysis also enables us to unveil all the oppressions imposed as an all-encompassing life project by hegemonic ideologies, based on the moral subordination of women's bodies and the use of their invisible labor in the tasks of reproduction and housework. It proposes a new ethics, under which human relationships are devoid of subjection, subordination and oppression of the feminine by the masculine.

The analysis, the activism and the elaboration of a social model based on a critique of customs of upbringing, create different role models, different desires and different conflicts that originate not only in sociopolitical class and mode of production, but also in gender, identity, age and diversity. Therefore, from the standpoint of the critical female subjectivity that is shaped within the Network, it is becoming increasingly necessary to radicalize the libertarian project and expand its sphere of action, reasserting the role of young women as protagonists of the sexual revolution, who can make decisions about their bodies, can make use of the public space and have fun by themselves (without a male partner who would "take them out" and accompany them), can choose their partner by themselves and decide whether they want to be mothers or not and when.

> Hence, this woman who looks in the mirror can spend a long time contemplating the past, realizing however, that it has been a long road. Now I can declare openly that I do not want to have a determined fate; I do not want to be silenced or endure the most abhorrent oppression on my

> body. Rather, I want to collectively advance towards emancipation. Many troubles and many friends have been left behind. I can understand that, as I hope that they can understand what is the revolutionary project we want to advance as men and women who seek to experience freedom, disobedience and a sense of community.

Besides the organizational work within the youth processes themselves, action should be taken geared towards the transformation of family structures and the educational institutions, in order to promote different relationships between mothers and sons and daughters on the one hand, and students and teachers on the other. These two institutions are currently spaces of reproduction of the patriarchal imaginary and of reaffirmation of traditional male supremacy and conservative policies.

VIII Towards a Youth Network that Promotes Change through Awareness of Subjectivity and Collectivity

The multiple forms experienced within the Youth Network remain as an organizational memory and as a point of reference regarding grassroots activism in the city of Medellin and in Latin American mobilization processes. The present text seeks to examine the specifics of that history, defined not as a succession of events, but as a web of accumulated experiences that stimulated the transformation of the subjectivities and collectives who have envisioned, facilitated, participated and cooperated with it. This has enabled it to remain a force of mobilization and resistance for two decades, within the adverse circumstances of a state institutionalism that coopts and ideologically utilizes all projects of autonomy initiated by a range of urban territorial forces in this country.

In this context, the Youth Network has no choice but to keep unfolding its educational processes, so that its activists are able to make decisions concerning their own lives, enquiring about the meaning of individuality and collectivity. It is something that each individual has to consider and decide about, in order to be part of this experiential process, and to put into practice in the day-to-day existence values such as solidarity, cooperation, teamwork, trust and positive conflict management.

As a result, the process itself has sought to maintain consistency between means and ends, since what really matters in this historical construct is the political relationship between subjects in every interaction, aiming to exclude, to the greatest extent possible, the exercise of domination in the relationship between knowledge and power.

The accumulation of reflection-action of this experience is the result of an internalization of learning in the complex road to emancipation. The historical memory of an organizational journey such as the Youth Network will reveal that its emerging and emancipatory development, as we know it today, has been accomplished and consolidated by effectively dealing with contextual tensions such as social struggles, the criticism of institutional functionalism and the specific needs and organizational capacities of grassroots processes.

The Battle for Oaxaca: Repression and Revolutionary Resistance

*Eugene Gogol**

Oaxaca is a land of revolutionary upsurge, repression and resistance. At the present moment, (the end of December, 2006), repression with a *mano dura* (hard hand) is the order of the day as *Oaxaquenos*, who have been active in the upsurge, are picked up on the streets, beaten by local or state police as a warning to spread fear in the community, and then released. Others remain imprisoned weeks after being swept up by the federal prevention police, who viciously broke up a protest march in late November. Ulises Ruiz, the fraudulently elected, corrupt governor and the undoubted author and manipulator of the present repression, still remains in power.

Nevertheless, on the day I began this essay, December 22, thousands took to the streets in Oaxaca, as the Popular Assembly of the Peoples of Oaxaca, (*Assamblea Popular de los Pueblos de Oaxaca*), APPO, organized a march with a large contingent of teachers, as well as activists recently released from imprisonment and family members of those still detained, participating in resistance to the state and federal police occupation of the city. This same day, supporters in some 37 countries held demonstrations on a Day of World Mobilization for Oaxaca, originally called by the *Ejercito Zapatista de Liberacion Nacional* (EZLN). The date is also the 9th anniversary of the massacre (*la matanza*) of 45 Indigenous in the community of Acteal, Chiapas, an obscene horror, which goes unpunished to this day, including the intellectual authors of this crime, who remain uncharged.

This continuous repression must not obscure what has occurred from May/June through November, and continues in open and underground ways—the emergence of a Oaxaca in revolt, first responding to Ruiz's crude attempt to crush the teachers' strike, and then blossoming and developing in a multitude of ways, encompassing the dimensions of Indigenous, of women, of youth—all joining the labor dimension of the striking teachers. Indeed, one often finds Indigenous, teacher, woman, within a single person. Further, in at least one of the mega-marches in Oaxaca City, the number of demonstrators far exceeded the population of the entire city as tens of thousands came from hundreds of municipalities in the state of Oaxaca, claiming the struggle as their struggle. It

---

* My participation in an Emergency Human Rights Delegation in Oaxaca in the third week in December 2006 served as the catalyst for this essay.

was truly the population to a woman, man and child taking matters into their own hands.

How can we comprehend this new moment of emancipatory struggle in Mexico with its multiplicity of creative forms? Some have spoken of the Oaxaca Commune, finding historical echoes in the 1871 Paris Commune, where the population seized the city and began to create a "non-state state" including attempts to reorganize work and move toward freely associated labor. Marx would note that the greatness of the Commune was "its own working existence," which encompassed, not a reform of the state, but smashing the old state-machinery and replacing it with the Commune. Oaxaca has not at the present moment reached such a stage. While some may have such a vision, others have argued that only a reform of the state machinery is needed.

Another commentator writes of moving "toward dual power" in Oaxaca, intimating the Soviets of Russia 1917. Is APPO a 21st Century form of the soviet, embodying within, not the industrial proletariat, but the multitude, here encompassing many different subjects of social change?

Before we label the events historically, or for that matter globally, we need to probe the Oaxaca uprising in and of itself. Among its important dimensions:

(1) the creation of APPO, rooted in an Indigenous tradition, which, as we will see, became the most crucial forum to organize action and express ideas from below; (2) the multi-faceted participation of women: from a group of APPO women who took matters into their own hands and seized a radio and television station, thus finding and speaking with their own voices, to many women building barricades in the streets together with the men to defend their new voice and halt the "death squad" caravans that sought to intimidate, injury, and at times shoot the population who were protesting and doing so in a peaceful manner without arms; (3) the youth, particularly from the university, who fought to defend and extend the gains of the struggle, including the important act of seizing the university radio station when the teachers' *Radio Plantón* was destroyed; (4) the neighborhood activists, who, particularly in poor areas, defended their streets, building barricades in the evening to stop the caravans, and pouring out to participate in the mega-marches that stretched from the summer into the fall; (5) the teachers, tens of thousands strong, who had catalyzed the rebellion with their initial strike and occupation of the central plaza, and continued to remain at the heart of the occupation of Oaxaca City, until, through lack of pay and faction fighting within their hierarchal union structure, finally felt forced to return to work; (6) the teachers, *campasinos* and others from outside Oaxaca City who created their own *assemblas* where they lived, and traveled to the capital to join

the protests; (7) And always, always, the Indigenous dimension, the heart and soul of Oaxaca.

Let us begin at the beginning, with a brief survey of the immediate social-economic-political background, then trace the unfolding of the revolutionary upsurge with concentration on the organizational form of APPO, the role of women, and the participation from *Oaxaquenos* living outside the capital—all occurring in face of, indeed catalyzed by, direct governmental, or government-sponsored, repression. Perhaps then, we can return to situating the specificity of Oaxaca within a historical and global context, including its contributions and limitations for the present moment.

(For the following I am indebted to the many presentations and testimonios, which I was privileged to hear while in the State of Oaxaca.)

I The Background

The origins of the crisis lie far deeper than Governor Ruiz's attempt to break a teachers' occupation of the central plaza of Oaxaca on June 14, 2006. In a political sense, they can be traced to the seven decades-long domination of the *Partido Revolucionario Institucional*, PRI, in Oaxaca. While the mid-1930s era of Lázaro Cárdenas was a limited, progressive consolidation of the Mexican Revolution, that heritage was transformed in the decades that followed into a single-party authoritarian, repressive governmental state apparatus, nowhere more suffocating than in Oaxaca.

The limited "opening" in Mexican politics in the 1990s and 2000s was repressed in Oaxaca, where the PRI continued its single-party rule. A particular egregious manifestation of this was the fraudulent election of Ruiz as governor in 2004, and his subsequent corrupt and increasingly repressive rule. If there is one slogan that has united the masses of Oaxaca it has been *Afurera Ruiz!* (Out with Ruiz!).

The origins of the rebellion encompass not only the political, but the economic-social. Oaxaca's population of three and a half million is more than two-thirds Indigenous, with 16 different groups, 15 languages and many additional dialectics spoken. For decades a social exclusion has been practiced, resulting in deep poverty. Statistics indicate that some three-quarters of the population live in poverty or extreme poverty. The majority of the poor don't even earn the poverty minimum wage of $6 a day. The crisis is greatest in the *campo*, the countryside, where, for much of the population, it has become impossible to earn a living. There is little government investment to assist the rural population. The North American Free Trade Agreement, which has permitted U.S. government-subsidized farmers to flood the marked with cheaper agricultural products, has cut the ground out from Mexican farmers being able to making a living in southern Mexico, particularly from corn production.

Economic devastation in the country-side has contributed substantially to large-scale migration. Some have gone to the city, in Oaxaca and other parts of Mexico. Others, hundreds of thousands, have been forced to survive by leaving to find work in the United States. This vast social dislocation has meant that in some communities in Oaxaca upwards of 50% of the population has left. Those migrants are both men and women, with women making up an estimated 45% of the migrants.

Some 85% of Oaxacan land is communal in one form or another. Only 15% is private property. The Indigenous communities have fought to preserve their land and their ways of organizing their communities, through rules and traditions called "*usos y costumbres*." Oaxaca is the one state in Mexico where the government has been compelled to recognize "*usos y costumbres*" in hundreds of communities. These autonomous organizing centers around fiestas, communal work, certain governmental and religious services. Even this limited self-rule, often decided in community *asambleas*, has been subject to continual government pressure and fragmentation, played out in the economic whirlpool of neo-liberalism, and the change in the Constitution implemented by Salinas to open up the collective lands of the *ejido* to division and individual sale. It was the historical form of the *asamblea* that would be infused with a content of rebellion and resistance when Ruiz chose to try and break the teachers' strike and occupation.

II The Unfolding of the Oaxaca Rebellion

A *The Teachers' Strike and Occupation of the Central Plaza*

On May 22, after a week of unproductive negotiations with the state government, tens of thousands of teachers, other educational workers, family members and supporters marched to the central plaza in Oaxaca to set up an occupation and express their demands which included a salary increase and educational improvements. This was by no means the first time the teachers had taken such an action. For more than 20 years their fight for wages and improved educational conditions had resulted in the occupation of the central plaza for a few days as a way of compelling the state government to negotiate a settlement. But this year, events would unfold in a different manner.

The Oaxacan teachers are organized under Section 22 of the CNTE (*Coordinadora National de Trabajadores de Educacion*). Some 70,000 strong, the Oaxaca CNTE has a militant, fighting history. On May 22, after a week of fruitless negotiation, the teachers and their supporters occupied the central square and dozens of surrounding blocks. Rather than a settlement in a few days, the teachers' found themselves in a battle with the Ruiz regime. Over the next three weeks the confrontation grew. Faced with a government-influenced near monopoly over the means of communication, the Oaxacan teachers broadcast information to the community through their *Radio Plantón*. Support for the teachers grew dramatically as the occupation continued, with two "mega-marches" of June 2 and June 7 drawing supporters of 75,000 plus and 120,000. The call was no longer only for a settlement of the teachers' demands, but for the removal of Ruiz from the governor's office.

In the pre-dawn hours of June 14, Ruiz gave his response, sending state police to attack the sleeping teachers, many of who were encamped with their families. Facing physical force, including large amounts of tear gas, the teachers were driven from the central plaza, their encampment broken up, *Radio Plantón* destroyed. But the teachers refused to yield, battled back, and after several hours, took over the center of the city.

The government's unprovoked attack, designed to terrorize and break the teachers, proved to be a major turning point in the battle of Oaxaca. Not only did the teachers in a courageous and determined manner hold their own, but an outraged citizenry throughout the state of Oaxaca came to the aid of the teachers and saw the battle as their own. Two days after the attack a third mega-march was held. The more than 300,000 who poured out included members from Indigenous communities from the coast to the *sierras*. In support of the teachers workers from other government unions, Indigenous groups and *campesinos* participated. Traditional Indigenous authorities joined with political organizations, students, human rights activists. The following day the movement created a revolutionary form to catalyze its struggle—the Popular Assembly of the Peoples of Oaxaca, APPO (*Asamblea Popular de los Pueblos de Oaxaca*).

B *APPO—The Indigenous Asamblea Infused with New Content*

APPO is the synthesis of many movement organizations. Hundreds of organizations would eventually come together "in all colors and flavors" to become part of APPO. The central demand was the removal of Ruiz. As the movement developed, this came to mean not only his person, but all the representatives of the political authoritarian system which had been in power for some seven decades. APPO was anti-systemic. At the same time there was the beginning of the construction of popular power.

How to communicate with Oaxaca's multitude was central to this construction. With *Radio Plantón* smashed, students at Benito Juarez Autonomous University of Oaxaca took over the university radio station. It became one of APPO's principle ways of reaching the cities masses, informing them of news of the movement, of marches and other protest activities, as well as warning of state police threats. Communication as governmental manipulation and propagation of falsehoods from above was replaced with a communication *desde abajo*, from below. As we will see shortly, this was particularly true in the action of a group of APPO women, who seized and ran a national television and radio station, a crucial high point in the development of the movement.

Because the state government greatly feared this revolutionary communication from below, they organized their police force and their "private" underground forces to carry out assaults on the movement-controlled communications. This included "death squad" car caravans roaming the streets of Oaxaca at night. For protection, members organized their own security forces and used communications media to defend the rebellion. Appeals went out over the air to guard the radio station(s) and resist government attacks. One form of resistance was the building of barricades to protect the occupation of the center of the city, the radio stations and transmission towers in the movement's hands, and in general to prevent secret night attacks by the government-sponsored forces. Sometimes these were fortified permanent-type barricades, including using commandeered buses. Others were temporary barricades to stop the movement of caravans in the evening. These were constructed anew each night. When a call went out to construct such barricades, it was answered immediately with the construction of several hundred the first night, a thousand the second and hundreds more the third night.

The barricades also meant a new form of communication within neighborhoods. Neighbors went out at night to construct and occupy the barricades. They began speaking with one another in a way they had not done before—discussing questions of radical reform, how to transform the state, and beyond reform: What did it mean to not only transform institutions but take to the streets?

APPO's form of representation was simple and direct, born from Indigenous practices. Decisions were taken in *asambleas* in which all participated. While there are spokespersons, the organization was horizontal, not with a hierarchy of leaders. Activists speak of APPO not only as an immediate form of organization, but as a spirit of rebellion and communalism that has grown over many, many years.

The formation and practice of APPO brought forth the creative activity of many social subjects. Two of the most important were the women in APPO and the mobilizations outside Oaxaca City—of Indigenous communities, *campesinos* and teachers.

C Women in APPO—Finding Their Own Voices

August 2 marked an important leap in the movement. It was on that day when a group of APPO women seized the state television and radio stations whose signal covered the state. They had gone to the station with a simple request—to have 15 minutes a day in which to present the movement's point of view. But when they were refused, the women responded by taking over the entire station. A new stage in the struggle had arrived. Now working women, Indigenous women, who never had had a chance to tell their stories in public, to present their ideas, were able to speak, to find their own voices and be heard in a way they had never been heard before.

The television station was in the hands of the movement for three weeks: "What a vision of hope sprang from the screen those three weeks! Ordinary people in everyday clothes spoke of the reality of their lives as they understood them, of what neo-liberalism meant to them, of *El Plan Puebla Panamá*, of their loss of land to developers and international paper companies, of ramshackle rural mountain schools without toilets, of communities without safe water or sanitary drainage." (George Salzman, Oaxaca resident.)

The women were everywhere, in front of everything. Not alone the radio and television, but in the numerous mega-marches as well as *La marcha de las caserolas* (the march of women beating their pots and pans with wooden spoons). They were building the barricades and defending them. They brought food to those operating the radio stations. Women in APPO formed *Cordinadora de Mujeres de Oaxaca* (COMO) and held their own general meeting at the end of August.

D Outside Oaxaca City

If Oaxaca City was the storm center of the upsurge, the countryside was by no means passive. During the months of the uprising, many communities in Oaxaca took the initiative to form their own local APPOs. They traveled to Oaxaca City to participate in the mega-marches. These communities had also felt the repressive hand of the state government for decades. The Emergency Human Rights Delegation traveled to the community of Tlaxiaco, several hours outside Oaxaca City to hear presentations on the conditions in the countryside and *testimonios* from teachers and *campesinos* who had participated in the movement and felt the government's heavy hand. What was clear from the presentations by a local human rights organization, *Nu-Ji-Kaandi*, were the difficult conditions faced by Indigenous communities. Particularly powerful was the presentation by an Indigenous woman human rights worker on the continual violence against women.

We hear stories of the self-organization of the community as teachers organized to have their own *asamblea* to voice their concerns and to support the activities occurring in Oaxaca City. Many traveled to Oaxaca City to participate in the marches. When a group of teachers organized a contingent of several hundred to travel to the city and participate in the mega-march of October 30, they were directly confronted by the Federal Protective Police—the troops sent in by President Fox's government to try and crush the movement. Traveling in several buses, the contingent faced a blockaded highway manned by hundreds of the federal police. The police pulled people off the buses, roughly interrogated and detained those who they thought were the leaders and prevented the members of the Tlaxiaco community from traveling further to join the protest march.

During the *testimonios* a discussion/debate occurred which perhaps reflects some of the battle of ideas occurring in the movement today. A *campesino* activist, in telling of his experiences in the protest bus caravan that was stopped by the federal police, argued for the need to directly confront the repressive state authorities. A teacher quickly responded that the only way the movement could success was through a peaceful route. The unresolved question is what happens when the peaceful protest is continually met with repression?

E *The Authoritarian State in Oaxaca*

Our concentration on the creativity of the movement in not meant to minimize the repression which *Oaxaqueños* face day in and day out, and which has been expressed with particular viciousness, brutality and outright murder in the battle for Oaxaca over the last seven months. At least 17 people have been murdered directly during, and because of, their participation in the movement. Hundreds have been arrested and many of those remain as political prisoners. The emergency human rights delegation heard numerous testimonies to this effect. One student who had been arrested, beaten, made to pose falsely with arms while the police took pictures, forced to write a "confession" of a crime he did not commit, was imprisoned for several weeks. After testifying before us in the morning, he was later in the day again kidnapped by police with two other activists, beaten and then released!

We heard testimony from a woman teacher who was participating with her husband in one of the protest marches. Suddenly shots rang out and her husband fell mortally wounded.

Another woman, a mother of three, was just leaving work, not participating in the protests but simple in the area when the police on a rampage rounded her up: "I couldn't see, I was trying to find my son... They [the federal police] grabbed me, shoved me against the pavement, handcuffed my hands behind my neck and hurled me onto a pile of other women. They kicked and beat us if we moved and kept us that way for almost two hours." She, together more about 140 others, were taken by helicopter to a prison in Nayarit, hundreds of miles away. The charge? "Sedition." At the end of her testimony she said that after this experience she now wanted to join the protest movement.

F *The Battle of Ideas; Questions for the Movement*

What is the meaning of the battle for Oaxaca?

(1) It is clear that the vast majority of *Oaxaqueños* call for the immediate removal of Ulises Ruiz as governor. The wholesale repudiation of the PRI in the July 2 federal elections spoke strongly to this. Furthermore, removal of Ruiz has come to mean more than the mere change from one governing face to another. After all, the federal government may find it convenient for its own purposes to oust Ruiz. The call demands as well a removal of the federal and state police occupation of Oaxaca, a dismantling of the repression nature of the state apparatus, and reform of the state government in Oaxaca. But how deep that reform will go, whether the battle for Oaxaca will reach to challenge the very nature of the state, remains an unanswered question. However, should it be an unexplored question?

The question of the state of course, is inseparable from the social-economic composition of the society. This would mean a probing of the nature of capitalism, particularly in underdeveloped lands, and even more concretely in poverty-stricken regions such as Oaxaca within those lands. The Zapatistas, in their 6th Declaration from the *Selva Lacandona* and in the *La Otra Campaña*, have called for a movement that is anti-capitalist and from the Left. What does it mean to be anti-capitalist today? Is anti-imperialism sufficient, or do we have to reach deeper? Do we see capitalism as more than mere property forms—private vs. state or nationalized forms—and centered instead on the extraction of value and surplus value in the labor process? To be anti-capitalist in full comprehension is to recognize the necessity to destroy value-producing, commodity production, and begin to implement freely associated labor. Communal, collective labor of Indigenous groups, as in Oaxacan communities, will have much to contribute here if we recognize that that this cannot "co-exist" with value production. Rather, it is only the destruction of the capitalist mode of production that will allow a freely associative mode to arise on its ashes. If instead we remain in the reform of or remaking of existing institutions, won't we be trapped in a "self-limiting revolution" that does not reach the fullness of a new human society? Let us beware of our own "mind-forged manacles."

(2) What the battle of Oaxaca has brought to the fore is the creativity of mass self-activity as an emergence of diverse social subjects. Indigenous, worker, women, youth and other human dimensions, not as fixed essences, but as self-developing individuals and groups, as, paraphrasing Hegel, individuality which lets nothing interfere with its quest for universality. What Oaxaca demonstrates, as so many other creative movements have borne witness to historically and globally, is that masses are not alone muscle, but Reason of social transformation. Their actions, ideas, questions are not limited to moments of revolutionary practice, but a form of revolutionary theory. This is one of the lessons from the movement. Oaxaca has much to teach here. It is a lesson we need to study over and over as each new revolutionary moment from below arises.

(3) As crucial as is the emergence and recognition of the creativity of new social subjects of revolutionary transformation, is it in itself sufficient? Some have argued that such social subjects within non-hierarchical forms of organization are sufficient to allow for uprooting social transformation. That is, that the active organizational participation by a multiplicity of revolutionary subjects can of itself bring forth new beginnings.

Here, *form of organization*, in this case the popular assembly of APPO, but other forms as well—the autonomous communities and *juntas del buen gobierno* in Chiapas, or historically such magnificent mass organizational forms as the Commune of Paris, the Soviets of Russia, the workers' council of Hungary 1956—have become transformed from a crucial particular to a universal. However the only absolute universal is the creation, the absolute becoming, of a new society. We cannot substitute a particular, as revolutionary as it may be, including a particular form of organization, for the universal reaching toward and entering a new society. The particular is a necessary concretization of such a reaching, but it is not in itself the totality of the reaching. For that we need not alone the practice of reaching toward a new society, but the mind, the philosophic vision that is part of the journey.

An emancipatory philosophic vision worked out concretely—thus a concrete universal—can arm us against the imposition of false ideological solutions. Such a philosophic view is what is needed to fully work out the meaning of Oaxaca's revolutionary upsurge. Being rooted in emancipatory philosophic thought is central to the present moment. The double rhythm of revolutionary transformation, the negation of the old society and the creation of the new, is not alone the action of practice. It is as well the act of cognition, of the emancipatory Idea, and it is precisely the unity of the two, of practice and of theory/philosophy, which opens the door fully to a new society.

December 29, 2006

Appendix 1: *Yo Soy #132*

(Excerpts from *Yo Soy #132, voces del movimiento.* Ediciones Bola de Cristal, Mexico)

1 The Beginning

On May 11, 2012, the first lines of a new chapter in the history of the student movement in Mexico were written. The place: the Ibero-American University. The context: The visit of Enrique Peña Nieto, then candidate of the Institutional Revolutionary Party (PRI) ... and ex-governor of Mexico State, who was repudiated by students holding up placards labeling him as a killer, a clear reference to the repression he ordered against the people of San Salvador Atenco in May of 2006.

Peña Nieto's response to student accusations incensed his audience. "That was an action I personally ordered for the purpose of restoring order and peace based on the legitimate right of the State to rely on military and police forces..." The irate crowd in the packed auditorium booed him, shouted their opposition, and chased him... to the university bathroom, where he hid out. That moment, his flight, the celebration in the Ibero, the subsequent belittling of the students by the PRI campaign team, media manipulation, the video appearance of 131 students with credentials in hand, the use of the social networks, and the incipient construction of a movement are all recounted here by a chorus of voices that arose in a place where outspoken dissent was least expected. The new movement would be called "I Am 132."

A *First Steps*

Javier: After May 11, the word began to get around almost surreptitiously, especially in the Ibero [the University]... and a small group was formed that began to move the information in the social networks, particularly in Facebook and Twitter. Without knowing where they were going or how they were going to get there, people began to get organized.

David: The rally [at the Estela de Luz] was a way to support the comrades at the Ibero, but also to launch a movement that could oppose the powers that be and the way information is twisted by the political parties.

Vladimir: I first joined the movement at the Estela de Luz rally. I got there just as they were reading their document in which they made two important points: The movement's plurality, which was an effort to break with the paradigmatic division between public and private universities, and its non-party identity. I later found out that the writer Paco Ignacio Taibo had tried make a speech in support of the Party of the Democratic Revolution (PRD) and that everyone shouted him down... People then decided to march to Televisa [a major commercial TV station]... We wanted to identify one of the main factors responsible for the country's social and political problems and settled on the direct relationship between Enrique Peña Nieto and Televisa. Nothing was planned, but the almost automatic move to go to Televisa was contagious. It was a place where we could focus all the feelings of nonconformity and indignation.

II Assemblies, a Challenge for the Organization

A *The First Discussion*

Mariana: Everybody who went to the Inter-university assembly at Las Islas in University City had an agenda, and all the different issues were jotted down. There were two that we knew were especially important: the movement's political position and its organization. An agreement was reached that people speaking in the assembly would be those who more or less had a mandate from their local assemblies. Everyone else could participate in discussion tables according to their interests. An effort was made to cover as many issues as possible. One particularly important discussion table dealt with history and another focused on environmental issues. The main problem was how decisions would be made because almost six thousand people were there, organized into 15 discussion tables... The level of consciousness was amazing. That day at Las Islas I was in the group discussing movement organization, and it was surprising to hear the agreements that were reached in the different groups. We came up with a common agenda with a lot of content and an impressive level of social criticism... It was a collective catharsis... When the assembly as a whole began to shout "Justice! Justice!" after each speaker finished, it was really exciting. It was in incredible sensation of a cry that brought us together even with all our differences.

Javier: Right then we said that the movement would not only be in the streets, but that it would also come up with political responses and would be broad-based. And for the first time, we saw a way to go beyond the strictly electoral situation, a way not to die on July 2 [date of the presidential election].

At that meeting we made a proposal to transform the country. We began to decide who we were speaking to. Our document was not only addressed to Peña Nieto, but to the entire political class. We were speaking to everyone.

III An Organizational Structure?

Mariana: It was established that the base of the movement would be the assemblies of autonomous schools... and that each one would be free to act and adopt political positions. By-n-large, this structure is what has made Soy #132 operative. There was a big discussion over whether or not the movement was anti-Peña. In our Las Islas meeting, a consensus was reached on our political position. The most important thing was not our opposition to a particular person, but to his imposition, to anti-democratic practices and to State violence and repression, which are now represented by Enrique Peña Nieto, but could be the case with any other politician and is true of practically the whole political class. There was also a healthy debate on anti-neoliberalism that was really interesting. The basis was social inequality and poverty and the way it hurts all of us. We noted the way each person defended a position and finally decided to define ourselves as anti-neoliberal.

IV Only a Student Movement?

Nestor: A decision was made to include the demands of other struggles because in the discussions that began to take place in the schools, the conclusion was reached that we couldn't be strictly a student movement. We would have to include more people. There were many segments of the society that wanted to join in and that have been with us in our mobilizations. The point was not to struggle as organized students, but instead as an organized people.

Mariana: There's one overall characteristic of the movement: it takes in everything. For example, instead of choosing between Facebook and the streets, or between public and private school, we opted for both. This characteristic is unsettling for many traditional leftists and for many of us, as well. Is it a student movement or isn't it? Yes, it is a student movement, and at the same time it includes all the struggles that we deem relevant. We've been heavily criticized for going for everything, yet I think this diversity is what makes us unique. The movement came out of a context marked by exclusion, and I think this is an almost natural way of making a utopia real.

A *Important Allies in Mexico and the World*

Javier: The support we have or haven't received also shows the limitations of the movement. We haven't been able to unite the most important sectors in the country. The workers haven't come out in our favor; neither has the *campesino* movement or the indigenous movement. We haven't established channels for dialogue.

B *The Cultural and Artistic Movement Joins 132*

Mariana: When the contingents filed into the Zocalo, everyone was silent. If you looked around, you'd see thousands of people in silence. Many were crying. That silence was so solemn. ... But then you heard that noble cry: I am 132! That day the program of struggle was read aloud. People from all the different schools were on the platform and you could identify each one... One of the great contributions of the movement was that it released us from a depressing solitude and gave us what had been denied to us as young people: community. The strong message that day was that we are neither an electoral nor an elector movement. Even though we emerged in that situation, we're not tied to it. We took on a program of struggle... It said that we want to go beyond the electoral context, and the message was more for us as a movement.

V Beyond 132

Mariana: Then there was the meeting in Huexca, Tlaxcala... where there's a struggle against megaprojects and the destruction of autonomy, of people deciding for themselves what happens in their territory. In many of the discussions the intention was expressed to join forces... but not to accept ties of links to a political party because we're not struggling for the candidacy of López Obrador [presidential candidate].

David: In our assembly we've also talked about the importance of going out into the streets to win over more people from other segments of the society besides the students. We're students, but we're not going to be able to go it alone. We've begun to look for ties with other actors... I think the meetings that have been held are good, but not as a way to bind us together. We should understand that they have their own dynamics, their different organizations, their struggles, their goals. But we share spaces and there we can generate joint actions. We have some rough times ahead, not because we're a movement of opposition, but because of the economic policies that are in store for us. The very day after Enrique Peña Nieto was declared the winner, they came out with an economic package that they're going to implement. They say people are asking for labor reforms, energy reforms, and who knows what else. That's when you realize how tough things are going to be. Their plans are going to generate a lot of friction that will compel people to march in the streets. Why not do it in an organized way so as to avoid Atenco-style repression on a national level? That's what we're trying to do, get people moving.

VI Counter-State of the Union Message

Ivonne: We saw the need to write a counter-State of the Union Message because President Felipe Calderón wasn't going to say anything about what's really happening in the country. That's why we're here. To say that it's all a lie; that there've been more than 65 thousand deaths, countless feminicides, repression in Atenco; to say that they've left us in dire poverty, that they've sold the territory of Mexico to the transnational corporations and haven't left us anything of value; to say that they've raised the sales tax and the price of the basic necessities. The only thing we young people have gotten from Calderón is exploitation. He promises us jobs but with a ridiculous salary. We don't even have the privilege of education. So what are our options? Joining the armed forces? Working for the government? Becoming street vendors? Even though Mexico is a country that produces petroleum, gasoline prices are hiked every month. It's outrageous. And most people just sit and do nothing when we should all be out here supporting each other and joining together to help make a revolution happen, but not necessarily an armed one; revolution means change.

Lucio: We came here to inform the country that what happened during the past year was the militarization of the territory, curtailment of workers' rights, a higher percent of the population that fell into dire poverty, a hike in the prices of basic necessities, and the opening of the market to foreign interests with very little support for national industries. There are now less job opportunities for the youth. Those of us who want to study and work are offered very little except really low salaries. There are no opportunities for us in this country.

VII We're All Beans

Sandra: The movement changed my life. I spent many years studying in a state of frustration because I come from a family that has given me a lot, a well-off family. I never knew what suffering was. I didn't have to decide between studying and working, and I didn't begin to question these things until I was working on my degree. What was my place? Why was I able to be at the Ibero when others couldn't be there? I didn't matter to anyone here... I felt like I was just a bean in a big pot of rice... After getting to know each other in the Tzotzil communities in Chiapas where some of us had gone with the Jesuits, a group of friends from the Ibero and I tried to bring about an awakening in the university. It had been incredible to find other beans in the big pot of rice made up of all the different departments of the Ibero. That was a relief, but it wasn't enough, because we were just a few beans in the huge pot of rice that was our social circle. My life changed on May 11, when I looked at my classmates and realized that instead of being grains of rice, we were beans. And it wasn't just the Ibero. Our anger spread to other young people in Mexico City, in other states in Mexico, and in other countries. I see that 132 exists in London, Buenos Aires, and China, and I don't think it's just my life that has changed, but life in the country as a whole. My own life underwent a big change because I was lucky enough to be involved in what was going on. I'm going to remember that summer as the most incredible moment, a moment when my dream came true of seeing the youth of Mexico awaken and make demands. Of seeing that everybody's priority was democracy and justice, values that we thought only existed in textbooks. Of seeing how we marched, hand in hand, young people from both public and private universities, breaking stereotypes. How could this not change my life? How could it not change all of our lives? There's no doubt that this experience will leave its mark on me for my whole life.

VIII Politics and Political Parties

Aldo: The political system in Mexico is divorced from Mexican society and from the country in general. The politicians live in a bubble. I don't know what country they see, but the real country, the one where we live day in and day out is totally different... The political system in Mexico is not all-inclusive. The actors are always the same, and they don't represent most people in the country.

Virginia: They've tried to use the term "political" as something apart, as if it were an illness, something alien to us. Many people even think the 132 Movement is apolitical because we are not associated with any party. We're always involved in politics. We just have to understand what kind of politics... With regards to the political parties, I don't have faith in any of them. Not a single one. Not even those that a lot of people in some organizations support. There are other forms of organization to which we can aspire as a society.

IX What Kind of Politics Do We Want?

Virginia: I believe in making decisions and reaching agreements on a horizontal basis. I believe in communality, in autonomy, and in local processes that many people are attracted to. We can reach agreements and do the will of the majority in local situations.

Oscar: I believe in self-determination, both on an individual and a collective level. I think one of our great challenges is to find a point of equilibrium between the two. How? I don't know. Don't ask me because I'm going to start crying if you do. But it's one of the great challenges. We need to rethink the concept of collectivity.

Vladimir: We've been brought up in this filth and slime that the political parties have produced, but the problem is structural. If someone asks me what I believe in with regards to politics, I begin with a negation. I don't believe in this system, but I think the main problem is that it's impossible to conceive of politics in an isolated or abstract way. I believe in giving a political-economic response in a more social sense. Politics should be totally tied to our cultural processes and our culture as a people, including the original peoples. I believe in the kind of politics where people constantly participate in making decisions, the kind of politics that is not only limited to the sphere of power, but instead includes other elements, such as economic development. It's very important for people who participate in politics to also have the ability and the means to decide on the country's economic direction. People control the economy and also control politics; yet there's a lack of social vision because, as of now, this has only been constructed by a reduced group of people who decide what course the country will take and also impose their candidates.

X Democracy

Vladimir: We can't speak of democracy in the abstract. We have to ground it in a concrete historical moment and in relationship to specific powers. Democracy includes an entire series of social processes. In the case of Mexico, the specific form this takes is a party system of representative democracy undergirding processes of inequality, plunder and exploitation that fit perfectly well in this system. To me, democracy is now a form of government that allows for the participation of a single group in making decisions. I would like to see a change in democracy coincide with a transformation in an equitable division of wealth, so that the people can have access to a democracy that is not strictly representative, but instead participatory.

Julio: It's offensive to say that Mexico is a democratic country. They tell you right off that your moment of democracy comes down to the seconds it takes you to put a mark on a piece of paper and throw it in a box. Worse still, how can you ask for free voter participation when millions of people in the country don't even have enough to eat, when their schools are of a really low level (if they even have schools), and when they have to go to work at an early age. The question is: Why could we as members of 132 take part in a process to democratize the country? Because we had education. Because we're from one of the cities where there's food to eat. Because we're not working people. For me, democracy means having economic democracy, democracy in education and health benefits, etc, so that we all have the same opportunities.

Virginia: Since the beginning of 132, democracy became a challenge; it became something to construct. We know perfectly well what democracy is *not*; we know what they taught us democracy was and has not been put into practice.

XI *Yo Soy #132* Emerges in an Electoral Context

Juan Carlos: Many politicians thought that we young people were not conscious of what was going on in the country, but there came a time when we got fed up with the way they so blatantly imposed a candidate like Peña Nieto on us. There was a lot of indignation about them saying that truckloads of us had been brought into the Ibero for political purposes and widespread discontent over the radicalization of the right. They thought young people were asleep, but it was just that we hadn't yet found a place to focus the discontent that existed among us.

Max: We came out of a period where the Zapatista movement existed and where the youth had mobilized during the UNAM student strike. All of this left its mark on us. Not even ten years had gone by in which young people were isolated or apathetic. The period from the year 2000 up until now has also been a time of youth mobilizations all over the planet: in Spain, Chile, United States, Colombia. This kind of collective mobilization permeates us and gives us the notion that we're capable of transforming things and saying, "That's not the way it is." Felipe Calderón is one of the main people responsible for the war on drugs and calling the armed forces out into the streets. So we see that all these struggles have emerged in the context of a crisis of legitimacy. When transitions occur, even though they may be a farce, things can change. The electoral situation is a period that is broader than just the vote; you can take sides in order to respond wherever you are or whoever you are. In a way, it was positive for 132 to say that we're a non-party movement, but not an apolitical movement. On the contrary, we stand for another way of engaging in politics. This has happened in a situation where it seemed like young people have no future.

Maria: The movement served more as an escape valve in the face of a political system that, as we know, is rotten to the core, a mere mock drill, in which certain rules are obeyed that only suit a few people. That's where they're insulting our intelligence. We want them to know that we're here. It seemed like young people were asleep, and it upsets them a lot because they're realizing that we're able to make proposals and that we have the intelligence and strength to pull the country out of a deep crisis.

XII The Awakening Didn't End on July 1

David: We weren't able to stop the imposition, but we're achieving a level of politicization and political participation that's tremendously important. It may not have been our main goal, but it's happening, so the movement is making advances. There's an important part of 132 that didn't have ties with other groups, people that weren't organized before and that are now inspiring other organizations. They're beginning to get to know groups and participate with them. That's something really basic, because if the 132 movement isn't able to consolidate itself as a single entity, it will at least create other nuclei, working groups that will play a key role in supporting other movements.

XIII Our Fears

Max: The 132 generation was presented as the lost generation––an apathetic, individualistic child of neoliberalism. We showed that this portrayal wasn't true, but we may have entered what the Zapatistas call "the long night"; we may have entered into a spirit of deception, dejection, discouragement that stagnates us, in view of the fact that we still have very few democratic freedoms and that even those are being reduced as we find ourselves in a totally authoritarian state. One challenge that we organizations have in 132 is to strengthen ourselves and not allow the people we've gotten into the streets to now go back home, indignant but disappointed, admitting that the country is in terrible shape but that there's nothing we can do. Thus everybody tends to their own business and we begin a long dark age that lasts for 10 or 20 years. There are no recipes for doing things; they're gradually constructed.

Samadhi: In the long run, I fear depression and disillusionment, because this is an enormous investment of energy, energy that comes from the spirit and from ethical principles, but this investment isn't organized. We're acting out of necessity and a desire to win something better for everyone, not just for the students. There's something that many people don't fully consider, and that's the question of direct repression on our bodies, lives, families and loved ones. I was in Atenco. I escaped, but they tortured many people I care about. I've lived this emotional devastation in flesh and blood, and I'm still somewhat shaken by it. It's not easy. It cost me a year of depression, deep depression, not wanting to live, only to cry. I remember sitting down on the sidewalk outside Almoloyita and feeling totally devastated. I asked myself how people have managed to be in a social struggle for years, withstanding disappearances, torture, kidnappings. How have they managed to deal with the State taking people's humanity away and turning them into an animal to be thrown into the trash with no rights whatsoever? This is something really personal that I experienced. I think what's worthwhile, what sustains us through all this, is that our principles show us the value of life. We're alive. We're here. Let's make life worth living. I think what sustains me are ethical principles.

Julian: I think one of the main fears is the possibility of defeat... In our personal lives, the fear is that the time comes when the fear of being afraid wins out. Fears are going to be there. As activists here in Ciudad Juárez, at certain key moments, we've learned how to control them, not to conquer them, but to understand where they come from and to explain this. They emerge because we're experiencing this policy of repression and we aren't able to understand where the repression comes from, where the aggression comes from. I think we're taking a step forward when we look at the face of this regime of terror; thus we begin to control our fear. Movements have life depending on the current situation, and we're focusing on what Peña Nieto represents. This is going to continue, whether or not he or another candidate is in power. In the strategy of security, repression and militarization now being developed, if we are able to orient a really abstract anti-neoliberal demand and sensitize the people, we'll have a demand that can help us stay organized in the streets. Maybe not with the same force as when the movement first began, but with sufficient political capital to maintain a line of continuity so that when something else happens, we'll be able to emerge with great force.

Bruno: We've been able to prick many consciences so that a lot of people now relate to this and are aware of what's happening in the country. One of my fears would be, recalling the movie *Matrix*, when the boy wakes up and is given the choice between two pills, one that would awaken him for good, and the other would prompt him to decide to go to sleep and return to the world he was immersed in, where everything was all right, although not really. That's what I'd be afraid of. That many people whose awareness we've been able to raise, people we've helped to see another part of the world, would take that pill and go back to sleep. That Mexican society and humanity as a whole would decide to take the soma of a happy world and live that other reality. My other fear would be that in that panorama, all the possibilities of struggle would be cut off for me, all the spaces where I could express my dissent. And I'd be trapped in a straightjacket, inserted in capitalist modernity while being conscious that things are all wrong. In spite of that fear, what moves me is that I believe humanity has come to a stage in which it no longer believes in that eternal return conceived of by the Greeks, overthrowing a tyrant who would be replaced by another. I think humanity has the possibility to go beyond this, to make ourselves more human, to make ourselves freer.

XIV El *Yo Soy #132* and the Media

Mario: 132 accused the media, in its association with political and economic interests, of making a huge exaggeration that was obvious to any communications consumer with a critical eye. Not only did the media give a biased view of reality, but they totally falsified what happened and tried to construct a different reality based on what they had communicated. Enrique Peña Nieto's visit to the Ibero-American University and the lies told by some news media about what happened there, made it necessary for the young people involved to say: No, what really happened has nothing to do with what's being reported. 132's highly relevant media proposals are a starting point for beginning to work and transform the situation. But we can't expect that movement to have an answer for everything, because we'd be holding a single collective responsible for everything, including the appraisals that all of us would need to make in order to work with them.

Claudia: The demand of democratizing the media is one that has also been made by the Zapatista movement… What they said explicitly was that if the media don't want to take us into account, what we have to do is turn the tables on them and appropriate them, take them over, make them ours. I think that's in keeping with what's happening in 132, and what happened in 1999 in Seattle, in the last meeting of the millennium of the World Trade Organization (WTO), when *Indymedia* (independent Media Center) was formed. As a result, people with access to mobile technologies like cell phones, cameras and home video cameras, were able to generate alternative information centers that were independent of the big television networks. In Seattle, people were able to disrupt the OMC meetings, and *Indymedia* played a tremendously important role in that, with worldwide resonance. The whole movement that has direct ties to the Zapatista movement and the struggle to democratize the media, which has been a pillar in the creation of independent and alternative media, is in some way connected to 132. What's now happening in the social networks is that that same spirit is maintained, where people say: Let's make our own media, our own networks.

Magaly: Our demand of democratizing the media is really important because we've realized that television has prepared the society to accept repression like the massacre of students in 1968, the military operation against the APPO (Popular Assembly of the Peoples of Oaxaca) and the attacks on the Mexican Electrical Workers Union (SME). That's the way dissident voices are silenced... One big danger for the future of democracy in Mexico is what's known as the "telecracy." A true democracy cannot exist when the society is misinformed through media manipulation. And this is a big problem because most people don't have access to internet or to the social networks, which have a huge potential for liberating people. Democratization, not only of internet media, must also take place in television and radio.

Tania: The 132 movement's impact has a lot to do with the centrality of this demand, which has brought many young people together. All the social movements have raised the issue of communication as a demand because they've been lynched in the media, but it's usually a secondary demand. 132 has made this demand its own because its a generation that has had experience in the social networks and is accustomed to freely expressing itself. The point of the first mobilization was to denounce Peña Nieto. By manipulating the coverage of the May 11th event in the Ibero, the media itself gave rise to this demand. This has to be taken far beyond the social networks because the conditions in the country don't exist for exercising the right to express ourselves. Moreover, it's not only a matter of proposing a way to democratize the media, but also of generating another way of communicating within the movement itself. There are important experiences from Oaxaca, where the tradition of indigenous communities has been directly integrated with the use of new communications technologies.

Vladimir: Many of us didn't go to the first mobilizations because we were at our computers, watching what happened in real time. Then we heard the news media say the students were hired thugs, that they were from the PRD, and we thought that was outrageous. Our indignation prompted by media portrayals began to spread and to be exacerbated by the outrage that had already built up inside us, and we realized what was going on. That's why one of our slogans has been "Wake up, Mexico." After all Peña Nieto had done, there was no way he could be president. We realized that we had access to all the information necessary to have an overview, but the majority of the population did not. Furthermore, many people who use the social networks don't use them to gain information. This was the tip of the iceberg, and we began to see the details: Approximately 95 percent of all radio-electronic space belongs to two television chains, which have captured an audience of more than 70 percent of the people, and the possibility of constructing reality for the country. We see that the same thing happened in 1968, in 1971, in 1988, and that every time there was a problem, the media had the possibility of changing reality. I really like what Malcolm X said: "If you're not careful, the newspapers will have you hating the people who are being oppressed, and loving the people who are doing the oppressing."

Appendix 2: Chilean Student Protests

Camila Vallejo

(Excerpts from *Podemos cambiar el mundo* [We Can Change the World], Ocean Sur, 2012)

I Speech of Acceptance of the Presidency of the University of Chile Student Federation

My name is Camila Antonia Amaranta Vallejo Dowling and I would like, first of all, to say that it is with great pride, but also with a sense of challenge, that I accept the leadership of the largest Student Federation in Chile. It is a great responsibility to uphold 104 years of history, 104 years of adventures and misadventures, 104 years of struggle within the student movement. And it is an honor and a great challenge because I come from places that do not receive any awards, places of which very little is said because very little is known, places that sometimes even end up forgotten.

I completed my secondary studies at a small school whose name means "land full of flowers." A strange paradox, since in the schoolyard one can smell the soil rather than the flowers, and its wooden classrooms gather the dust of generations of non-excelling students who will never occupy the important positions of power in our country.

My academic course, one of the smallest of this university, is hardly present in the collective conscience. It is lost in the corridors of the Faculty of Architecture and Urbanism and confused with other disciplines. Another paradox: geography in this university has practically no time or space.

Nonetheless, it is alarming to realize that this does not happen only in geography, but also in the Public Administration course, an academic course that ought to be essential for strengthening the public sector. It is an eight-to-six academic course, since after six p.m. there is no university for them. The same occurs with Education, and we suddenly realize that it is more than just a few academic courses. It is a whole area of knowledge which has fallen into academic neglect as a result of the imposition of the logic of the market over the last thirty years.

And to the fact that I come from a small and forgotten place, you can add my young age. At twenty-two years of age I will be the second woman president of the Student Federation of Chile (FECh) in over a hundred years of history. The current university rector will have the privilege of being the second in the history of the University that is accompanied by a woman as a president of our Student Federation.

Well maybe it is now my turn to hold the office of President, but I must say that I would never have achieved all this alone, and that my effort is but a small contribution among that of many others. All together we are bringing forth this collective project called *Estudiantes de Izquierda* (Left-wing Students), which is already heading for its third consecutive term in command of our Federation.

If I may tell you a little about *Estudiantes de Izquierda,* I must say that as a political collective we are present in many areas of our university, that within our ranks there is great diversity, that we realize that the left must be built through participation and democracy, and that this election, where we have received almost 400 votes more than in the previous one, proves that as a movement we are organically linked with the bases of the students of our university.

As *Estudiantes de Izquierda* we feel an ethical responsibility to exercise politics, because the administration of power by the same people who have always held it, prompts us to meddle in their affairs, because these affairs are also our affairs, and we cannot allow the privileged few to determine the measures and directions that our country should follow and to always adapt them to their narrow interests.

We believe that the key to success for the student movement is to situate the Federation in a leading position nationally, promoting social networking with city dwellers, workers, social and trade union organizations, young people who are outside the university or unemployed. In other words, we propose to place our attention on all the social problems that surround the university today, with which we are closely involved and committed.

We must break with this conception of university that establishes individualism, competition and pursuit of personal success as a behavioral model for students, above ideas and concepts such as solidarity, community, and cooperation. We are opposed to the belief that the university is just a place to get good grades and that one should leave its classrooms as soon as possible in order to earn money in the labor market. We have our eyes open enough to realize that there is a whole world out there to conquer, that this world requires our dedication, our effort and our sacrifice.

For all of us that have opened our eyes to the social inequalities looming in every corner of our city, it is impossible to just close the door and pretend that we have seen or heard nothing. We will not give up our commitment to social transformation, because we deem necessary, today more than ever, a profound discussion regarding the country we want to build and, with this as a starting point, regarding what kind of university we want to place at the center of this process. We do not believe in the university as a neutral space within society. The university is an active agent in the construction of society and in the development of the country that we as citizens are furthering every day. It is our responsibility to propel a process of organization within the university that allows us to transform it in order to transform society.

Our concept of university is that of an open, participatory and democratic space, inhabited by a university community that is active and open to dialogue; a community that is actively involved in the design and management of the abode of its studies. Our vision is of a university that is situated not among the first in the competitive rankings of university marketing—nowadays a widely discussed issue—but rather in the first place, in its contribution to the social development of the country; in the promotion of equity regarding the social composition of its students; in the development of science and technology in the service of Chile and its people. We believe in a university permanently committed to solving the problems that our people are facing, active in finding solutions and contributing to society through knowledge.

However, the reality is nowadays far from the concepts outlined above. Today the university is increasingly a project without a clear direction apart from the imperatives of the market. A price has been put to higher education, and our universities are evaluated using criteria of industrial production, as if they were mere companies within our nation's productive framework—a special kind of company with a more agreeable production process, but a company nevertheless.

A pivotal role in this state of things was played by the systematic financing that the public university experienced at the time when neoliberal policies were implemented. Self-financing, established as a doctrine, was a blow that hit the very essence of the university's operating mode to date, subjecting the university to a logic that was alien to it. Public universities were forced to compete in unfavorable conditions in what was called "the new higher education market." A price was set to them, so they had to sell themselves off to attract more resources to be able to go on with their educational mission. They lost their brightness and warmth, they lost their transformative essence, and they were dumped in a corner, unable to recognize themselves.

What we are talking about here is a strategic shift in the development of the university, which has been impossible to hold back until now. There have been important sectors of the university that have fallen fast out of favor and into neglect due to their low profitability. Public universities became closed in on themselves; they developed an institutional chauvinism, where each one was concerned solely with its own survival, losing the holistic vision which our old system of public higher education had.

This process, brought about during the dictatorship, continued its course with the governments of the *Concertación*, which carried out no major changes, but rather went about administering the inherited model and even expanding it in certain respects. However, the years went by and control of the government was turned over to those who long ago had ruled with civilian suits behind the soldiers' uniforms.

In our view, this poses a grave danger for public universities today. We believe that this government of businessmen seeks to put the finishing touch to the complete privatization of higher education, and conclude the work that they started behind the scenes in the eighties. The appointment to our university board of Harald Beyer and Alvaro Saih, two great defenders of the market model and the current national budget regarding higher education, are indicative of that. These are measures imposed as a part of a large-scale privatization agenda and therefore, the year 2011 will be strategic in their implementation.

This will be a major battle that we have to fight next year. To meet this challenge we must mobilize a movement that goes beyond university students. We need academics, workers, university officials, altogether in the streets demanding that the state upholds its universities, that the state upholds public higher education in our country.

However, the problem cannot be reduced to demanding that the state accords to our universities what it owes them. We must also engage in self-criticism and ask ourselves what it is that we provide to our own people as a university. We need a new mode of conduct of the state towards public higher education in our country and, at the same time, we need a new commitment of public universities with the people of Chile, The university has to be of all Chileans and not only of a few.

No one is indifferent to the fact that within our university fundamental inequalities are perpetuated, which have as a result, for example, that the richest 20% of the population is more than 50% of the enrollment. In any society that claims to be fair and democratic this fundamental inequality is unacceptable.

Will we continue to educate only the socioeconomic elites, or will we implement a system that permits all young people with talent and skills, regardless of their background and ability to pay, to stay in the university? Will we continue to allow only those disciplines that are profitable in the market to develop and reach levels of excellence, or will we ensure that all areas of knowledge are treated fairly so that they may contribute to creating the society we desire, not only in economic terms, but also in cultural, intellectual and civic terms, in terms of values, that is, relating to integral human beings?

As much as they want us to believe otherwise, for us the university cannot be a business, and even less can education be a commodity. The fight will be tough, but it is the future of the university that is at stake and we are not going to sit with our arms crossed.

I cannot conclude my speech without first referring to a fact that is for me of great importance, something I alluded to above, but would now like to expand a little more on: I am referring to my condition of being a woman. As a woman I can see and experience first-hand the forms of oppression of which we are victims in the present sexist configuration of society. In Chile we consider ourselves a developed country and we are filled with pride about our recent entry into the OECD. However, behind the curtain of economic progress and the optimism regarding the "Latin American jaguar" lays a history of oppression and sexism that lives on to this day. Women today continue to suffer all kinds of discrimination when looking for work, regarding health coverage, regarding wage scales, even regarding participation in politics.

Just yesterday I was reading some ideas that I would like to mention now, as I find them enlightening regarding this issue, I quote:

> In regard to women, when they are looking for work, apart from qualifications they are required to have a good presence, and it is not enough that they are kind and generous, but they must also be funny, friendly and flirty, but not too much. They are required to be presentable but when they are considered to have crossed the line by a step, they are dismissed as vain. They are commended for being mothers and they are excluded for having children. Women are under suspicion when they are young because they destabilize the herd and they are rejected as the years go by because they are not competitive. They are banished when they are ugly and also when they are beautiful. The former are considered repulsive, the latter provocative. When they are neither, they are branded as mediocre.

These are the conditions in which women are found right now, these are the conditions which my presidency will also seek to transform. Thank you very much.

•••

II What is It That Has Already Changed in Chile?

Regardless of the outcome of the ongoing mobilizations, we need to be aware that over the past four months Chile has experienced profound social change.

The present conflict has gone far beyond a problem regarding education, since it has shaken and questioned structural elements of Chilean society.

The demonstrations have given visibility to an issue that many parts of society have been declaring since the transition to democracy: that the contract imposed on us to regulate social relations leaves civil society practically powerless. If Chile was a truly democratic country it would not have been necessary to mobilize for more than four months to satisfy student demands that enjoy the support of more than 75% of the population.

The political class as a whole is called into question. The parliament, formed through the binominal electoral system, offers no guarantees of holding debate representative of the national sentiment. The executive has lost all legitimacy, with a president that has such low rates of approval that in any other country it would mean an early resignation of the government. Businessmen watch in despair as their avenues of enrichment are put into question by the mobilization of people demanding their rights. Meanwhile, the people awaken and mobilize in unity, gaining awareness that their rights are not negotiable.

We are experiencing an awakening of the Chilean society. Anesthetized for over twenty years, unwilling to assert our demands under the threat of compromising the democratic stability achieved, we have lost our orientation regarding our national development. Bereft of any significant political debate other than the meaningless discourse of "overcoming underdevelopment," today we must take on the task of founding Chile anew.

It is our duty, as the active parts of Chilean society, to launch a debate and offer proposals on how we can fight the horrific inequalities that are increasing every day; how we can provide decent education and health to society as a whole; what we can do so that everyone benefits from the great wealth that our country possesses in natural resources.

It would be irresponsible on our behalf to delegate these decisions to those groups that promote social immobility. We can only trust those who invite us to jointly initiate a participatory project of social transformation. History tells us that if we do not have the people as a whole participating in setting up a project of national development, it is likely that this will end up benefiting the traditionally privileged groups, which will defend their sources of wealth and power through all violent means available to them.

If Chile is now different, it is because our mobilizations promoted a cultural shift in Chilean society, because we want to take part in building the future of our society. Citizens' assemblies are budding everywhere, the topics of conversation over the table have changed, the media that used smear tactics against our mobilizations have been discredited and have been replaced by the social networks as sources of accurate and timely information.

Chile is experiencing a great change initiated as a result of our mobilization.

Appendix 3: The Books of the Zapatista Little School

Zapatistas from the Indigenous Communities in Resistance

In August, 2013, the Zapatista Indigenous communities in Chiapas invited activists from Mexico and throughout the world to come to their communities to learn "La Libertad según l@s Zapatistas." The response was overwhelming, with some 1,500 attending and hundreds of others turned away because of space limitations. The school was like no other: The activists lived for a short period with Zapatista families in dozens of communities in the five autonomous regions, the caracoles, experiencing the autonomy that the indigenous communities had been developing over the last decade and more.

The "texts" that the students studied—working with the families they lived with in the morning and reading the four books in the afternoons—Gobierno autónomo I; Gobierno autónomo II; Participación de las mujeres en el gobierno autónomo; Resistencia autónoma. [Autonomous Government I and II, Women's Participation in Autonomous Government, Autonomous Resistance]

The creation of the books was an important step in developing autonomy. Each of the five regions—La Realidad (Madre de los Caracoles Mar de nuestros sueños), Oventik (Resistencia y rebeldía por la humanidad), La Garrucha (Resistencia hacia un nuevo amanecer), Morelia (Torbellino de nuestras palabras), and Roberto Barrios (Que habla para todos)—had meetings in which the Indigenous spoke of their experience of constructing autonomy. These experiences were recorded, transcribed and presented in book form. The books were not written by intellectuals, though perhaps they assisted in compiling the thoughts of the Indigenous community members in book form. It was a living practice in breaking down the division between mental and manual labor carried out in the communities, in the Caracoles. This breaking down of the division between thinking and doing, I see as part of a movement from practice that is itself a form of theory. Below are excerpts from the four books. The complete texts in Spanish can be found at:

http://seminariodefeminismonuestroamericano.blogspot.mx/2013/09/participacion-de-las-mujeres-en-el.html

In English:

http://dorsetchiapassolidarity.wordpress.com/zapatista-freedom-school/

Each paragraph beginning with italics indicates a new speaker:

•

Prior to 1994, when we were in hiding, some of us, of the comrades that had been working together, were already participating in collective work, but at that time no one thought that this was autonomy. Afterwards, when we were in operation, the villages and municipalities began discussing about ways to support this group of comrades, since they were constantly occupied in these tasks. The villages started to get organized and they decided to provide a contribution of 10 pesos each, 10 pesos per volunteer in the area, so they would provide a payment of 30 pesos a day to each of those comrades while they are holding this position. We concluded that getting used to working in that manner was not sustainable, so we the people were informed, and every village, every region, every municipality considered different ways of supporting the volunteers. Some decided to offer support in one way, others in some other way, but it was not with money anymore. Since then, there has been no more monetary remuneration, that's how we realized that money is not the way to breed the work of autonomy or the work of self-government.

In the operation of self-government, in the tasks of a local or municipal authority or of the Council of Good Government, responsibility is undertaken through awareness. In self-government we operate through awareness, without any interest to earn a salary, because the participation of each and every one of us is needed for the good operation of self-government. Serving the people is done because of the awareness that we all possess, not because of money, not because we want to earn an income. It is about serving our people, regardless of whether we receive compensation we carry on the work of constructing autonomy.

When we take up the work, not everyone has that ability to understand what our role really is. We often start working without knowing what our role is, so these are the reasons why we manage the government collectively, why we do all the work collectively. First, because we know that responsibility belongs to everyone, it is shared. Second, because we are also aware that within a group of people that undertake responsibility as an autonomous authority, not all have the same abilities. There are comrades who have more experience at work and others who do not. What we do is that we share the experience; people who have more knowledge of the work share it with the others.

In the region where we work there are different ways of being, different ways of dressing, different colors, different beliefs, different ways of speaking, and it is a right of all comrades to be respected at work, regardless of who they are. All that matters is the willingness and ability to work. The way people are doesn't matter.

Comrades who hold a position of authority have the right to be heard if they have a proposal, or, in the case that they have made a mistake at work, they also have the right to be heard by the people. Each and every one of us has the right to hold public office at any level, regardless of our color, our creed or our formal qualifications, this right is shared by everyone.

We believe that one of the obligations of an autonomous government is to tend to anyone coming to the office for any issue. Regardless of whether a solution is offered, the people have to be heard. Whoever it is, Zapatista or not, is given attention, as long as they are not government agents sent by the government. If they are, they are not admitted. But if they are not, they are given attention regardless of what social organization they belong to.

In the course of our work, we are always trying to make sure that we comply with the seven principles of "mandar obedeciendo" (govern by obeying):1. To serve rather than self-serve. 2. To represent rather than supplant. 3. To construct rather than destroy. 4. To obey rather than command. 5. To propose rather than impose. 6. To convince rather than defeat. 7. To work from below rather than seek to rise.

After the uprising we had in 1994, we considered how we could move ahead to create our autonomous authorities in each municipality. This is why we have all gathered here to talk and share our experiences of how we began to operate our autonomous government. Why am I explaining this? It is because I think that this is when we started to advance towards where we are now. We had many meetings and we reached many agreements, not just one. We realized that this is hard work. It is not easy to do. Why? Because we do not have a guidebook; we don't have a book to consult, to follow. We were just working together with our people according to their needs.

As a[n Autonomous Municipal] Council this is our task and our commitment: to only represent the people, because everything has to be of the people We have to serve rather than self-serve. Everything belongs to the people. We are here in front of you thanks to the grassroots supporters [*bases de apoyo*]. If it wasn't for the people, if it wasn't for the grassroots supporters, we would never have gotten here. They have their say and because of them we are here today.

We have to find out how we have to govern, but learning this is really hard because, as some comrades already mentioned, there are no instructions. There is nowhere to get guidance, there is no text to guide us. We have to remember how our antecedents served. When they served they were appointed not by the authorities but by the people, and they served the people. There was no salary; corruption and mismanagement started when the salary was established.

It is true that there are not enough women [in government], we must promote and encourage them, and I think it's our job to keep encouraging women so there are more women in the work positions, so there is equality, because that's how it should be.

As authorities of all levels we have the right to govern, to propose, to watch over the people and to resolve problems. As authorities of all levels we have the right to be respected by the people. We have the right to demand that the people comply with the agreements they themselves have set up.

We as women also have the right or duty to work together with our people and with our fellow women, to encourage them, because they too have the right to work. We as women organize; we have our rights, our duties. We don't only have to stay at home. I have always enjoyed working with all authorities of the communities in my area, because there we learn, we lose the fear, we stop hesitating.

But before all this, in the villages we were discussing about how to certify the studies of children and young people that attended the autonomous schools. We were talking about school certificates, report cards. Finally we came to the conclusion that this was not necessary. The important thing for us was that our children learned to read and write, to do sums and many things more, to learn how to carry out and manage all the work that is necessary for our people. We concluded that a report card or a school certificate was not necessary. The same for an assessment, an exam, which would present a number of questions to the students and if they managed to answer them and pass they would be considered good students. We also concluded that this wasn't right. The right way was to demonstrate it in practice, at work, in the performance of public office. We thought that this would be the best assessment of whether this young person is really learning.

Regarding the issue of justice, in the first period of the Council of Good Government many cases were examined, many disputes. The problem was that, as the comrades knew that the Council of Good Government was one more institution of the [Autonomous Municipal] Council, they all wanted to go to the Council of Good Government to resolve various issues. Sometimes they did not even pay attention to the municipal authorities or the [Autonomous Municipal] Council and they went straight to the Council of Good Government. This happened because we had not determined which things were in the competence of the Council of Good Government and which things were not.

In the area of health, there have been two editions of a book to train health promoters. It started with just one edition. The first edition was distributed in our area only. The second edition was also distributed in the other caracoles. That was because we realized the need for health coordinators to have the material to train the new health promoters. There was nothing at that time. They would use pamphlets or sheets full of information, so that is why we thought about printing this book. The resources for the book came from a project; the edition was supported through the solidarity of comrades who helped us to edit the book. But the words, everything that's in the book, are words of coordinators and health workers, including ourselves as the Council of Good Government. We all realized that this would help the work of the health promoters.

The "Guadalupana" clinic, located at the central *caracol*, is a central clinic, which started being built in 1991–1992. Why was this clinic built? Because at that time, this community was completely isolated. They didn't even have electricity or a road such as the one they have now. There was no way of transporting patients to the city. There were no clinics or health centers run by the government or the federal state. For that reason the people themselves had to organize and think about how to build a health center or a clinic. Thus in 1991–1992, construction began.

Recently, about a year ago, a need arose. We decided to get all authorities together, especially the Council of Good Government that has control of this area. We are going to get together so that our comrades from the Council of Good Government have an idea of how they will govern and what people are doing in this area.

It is the only way we could think of, although it is not the only one available. Back at the moment it was all we could do, have meetings where we share experiences in each area of activity: health, education, agro-ecology, several areas were missing and they were absent from these meetings.

We called the text we produced "document of real education," and this document remained as the starting point of the autonomous education, in which we set out the objective of our education, which connects the four areas of knowledge—mathematics, life and environment, language, history- with the 11 demands. Because, as we know, we have 13 demands. Since they were not all fulfilled, two demands are still pending, we made an agreement.

The other kind of justice that the Council of Good Government and the Autonomous Councils are promoting is that, for example, if there is a theft of an animal or whatever, we investigate and when we catch the person who stole the animal what we do is that we return the stolen animal to its owner and the person who has stolen it apologizes to the animal's owner. The next time, if he does it again, he will be punished. This is a different kind of justice that is promoted by the Council of Good Government.

The role of the autonomous government and of the Council of Good Government is to monitor that all the tasks are advanced with the resources that are sent to the municipalities; to see that all work is done and that there is a little bit of profit. Because it is no use if the resources arrive and they are just spent and there is nothing left. If we cannot see what the money was spent on, it is not useful. We can not make good use of the money. What we want to do is to take advantage of all the work we are doing.

In our area, we women did not participate. Our fellow women that came before did not have this idea that we as women can participate. We had the belief that we women are only useful for staying at home, caring for children, preparing food. Perhaps these ideas come from the very same ignorance that exists in capitalism. But we as women also felt the fear of not being able to do things outside our homes, and we didn't have approval from the men. We didn't have the freedom to participate, to speak, as if it was thought that men were better than us. So, it is thanks to our organization, the EZLN that has taken us along this new path. We women are participating right now. Our organization made it possible for us as women to awaken, to open our eyes and see where we were standing; to realize that it was bad to feel that we were unable to do the work; to recognize that we as women are able to do it. This resulted in ourselves as women beginning to hold public office. We are aware that in no other political or religious organization has there been this kind of progress as the one we've had here in our organization.

As time went by, within the work that we have been doing, we kept facing obstacles that were making it hard for us to remain involved in the struggle. In some villages there didn't—and maybe still doesn't—exist the moral support necessary for many of us women who are now starting to participate and hold an office. This gets worse if we are feeling unable to carry out the tasks when it is our turn to do it. Another difficulty is perhaps the fear of making mistakes in the tasks that we have to carry out, or the fear that men will mock our participation, even though we all have to start from below. Having a great number of children is another reason why we as women do not dedicate enough time to our share of the tasks in the Zapatista struggle. This difficulty is made greater when the man in the family doesn't assume the responsibility for looking after and feeding the children when the woman leaves the house and goes to carry out the tasks.

There is a village where the new authorities were appointed, the outgoing group finished its three-year term. In the new group there are several women and one of them cannot read and write, but she will come to participate when it is her turn. She says she is not afraid to do it because she is learning a lot and because she is supported by her children, who can read, and by her husband. They gave her a prompt where they are recording what she is going to say, because she is also experiencing this in the village. This is how we are progressing in the village. We are also realizing that we are not disheartened because we are lifting each other up.

To overcome the difficulties we have done several things. For example regarding the number of children women are having, among the 47 key points of prevention in healthcare we have one about family planning. We have explained to our comrades that this does not mean they will not have children, but that the couples will be able to plan how many children they can care for. Both women and men [need to care for the children], so that the woman can carry out her share of the tasks and the man can stay at home and look after the children. The men have also understood that we as women have that right and the space to participate. There are men who stay at home to care for their children and give the woman the opportunity to go out and carry out the task.

When private property came about, women were relegated, they went down to a lower level and what we call 'patriarchy' was imposed, with the privation of women's rights, with the dispossession of the earth, it was with the advent of private property that men began to rule. We know that with this arrival of private property three great evils arose. The exploitation of all men and women, but especially of women. As women we are also exploited by the neoliberal system. We also know that along with this came the oppression of men towards women for being women. Moreover, as women we currently suffer discrimination for being indigenous. So we have these three great evils, there are more but this is the subject of another discussion.

We are talking about a revolutionary struggle, and a revolutionary struggle is not fought only by men or only by women. It is everyone's task. It is a task of the people, and among the people there are boys and girls, men and women, young men and women, adult men and women, elderly men and women. We all have a place in this struggle and that's why we should all participate in this analysis and in carrying out the tasks that we have pending.

Proposed extension to the Revolutionary Law of Women: 1.—Women have the right to be respected within the family and within the Community. 12.—Women have the right to defend themselves when being attacked or physically assaulted by family members or by outsiders, and they have the right to punish the offenders according to the rules and regulations of the organization. 14.—Women have the right to demand that the bad habits that affect their physical and emotional health are changed. Discriminating against women, mocking or abusing them shall be punishable. 19.—Women have the right to possess, to inherit and to work the land. 26.—Women have the right to organize in the cultural sphere, for example regarding poetry, singing, theater, dance, festivities, etc. 28.—Widows, single mothers and single women have the right to be respected, considered and recognized as a family and supported by the community when they need it.

In 1994 it was revealed that our women's law was in place, this was a great thing. It was great to have participated in it. Since then, there have been demonstrations where we have seen the women participating. For example in the National Consultation women took part. I also showed up at that time. I was 14 and I did not know how to participate or how to talk. But I did it as well as I could. The women demonstrated that they could fight. The government realized that the women also refused to give up, that they kept on fighting. Now we want our autonomy to work, we have our rights as women. Now we are going to be constructive, to carry out the work. It is our obligation to move ahead.

Those of us that are present here, we know who made that revolutionary law. It was someone who fought for that, someone who defended us. Who was the one who fought for us women? It was Comandanta Ramona. It was she who made that effort for us. She didn't know how to read or write or speak Spanish. And why are we as women not taking up that effort? That comrade, who already made that effort, is an example; and it is her example we need to follow in order to do more work, to demonstrate what we know in our organization. We also have the example of our comrades, men and women commanders, who went out to the Color of the Earth March. It was Comandanta Esther who spoke in that place where only people who have university studies and wear a suit and tie are allowed to enter. She went in, she spoke and she said, "Here I am, I am an indigenous woman and a Zapatista." That's a step forward, an example to follow, in the struggle of our women.

Many things happen but how can we make a change if men cannot yet bake *tortas,* if they don't know yet how to serve their corn, if they don't know yet how to wash their clothes? How can we change those ideas? How can we improve? I have always declared in my area that education has to take place inside the home. We have to teach the boys to wash their clothes. The boys have to learn to serve their food and wash their plate. The boys must learn to work in the kitchen and the girls must learn to work in the field.

What we are trying to achieve is equal rights between men and women, but there is still a long way to go. There are still many things to do before the men understand that the best education takes place inside the home. We, men and women, are the teachers in our home, if we manage to teach our children, to give them a different education, things are going to change, but if we don't manage to be good teachers, things will remain the same.

This is also part of our job as women, because it is necessary to also offer help to our fellow women. Herbal medicine has had very good results. I don't know much about the medicine of the pharmacies but herbal medicine is very helpful and it's cheaper. We know that the government has raised the prices of pharmacy medicines a lot. On the contrary, what we do is cheaper and more wholesome. It heals faster. We women, the poor, we have recognized the need to do this because we have no money to go to the doctors.

We did an extensive analysis of when this Women's Revolutionary Law was written. We gave it a good deal of thought. We analyzed what it is we are fighting for. It was then that we understood what our name, Zapatista National Liberation Army, really means. We started to think that maybe this was the reason why it was written that "women, regardless of race, creed, color, political affiliation, have the right to participate in the revolutionary struggle." We realized that this phrase is addressed to the women of the different organizations that are also fighting against this capitalist society that dominates us here in our Mexican land. This is how we interpreted this phrase. I think it speaks mainly of the Mexican people.

Some fellow women have taken up responsibilities and they hold positions in women's committees, autonomous councils, health and education committees, etc. However, they need to be supported, and they need to achieve organizing the rest of the women in the villages. They need to receive political training so there is equality between men and women at work. We should reinforce, promote and reorganize collective work of men and women in the communities to achieve equitable participation in all work areas and at different levels of government. These are the difficulties and obstacles that our women comrades in the Northern Zone have identified.

One of the reasons why we see the necessity to organize collective and community work is because in every village there are various workers: there are health promoters, education promoters, men and women administrative officers, men and women commissaries, local officials, various figures of authority. So we have to come up with a way as a village to be able to at least cover their travel expenses. Maybe we cannot offer a lot of support, because there are many workers. But at least we can cover their travel expenses so they can carry out their work within the organization. As a village we have to make that effort to organize according to what the people agree on.

All these work positions are not meant for distributing the few resources that we are receiving, but for creating a small village or regional fund in order to be able to support each other as comrades, to support those of us who carry out various tasks within the organization. The work we're doing, from family level to regional level, is not supported by any solidarity funds. Comrades themselves get organized and try to secure funding, even if it is a small amount, and get these tasks under way, making sure they keep advanceing. It is an effort to set up an economy within our struggle. Those tasks are always carried out by comrades.

It's kind of what we do in our area. It is the way we have been organizing ourselves from below in our families, in our villages, regions, municipalities and our wider area. All this collective and community work is not for us to turn a profit. We have to start from the family in order to be able to properly sustain our family. The collective and community work in each stage has a particular objective in each level of government. This is how we are trying to organize, to build resistance in the economic field in our area.

How do we resist the evils of government ideology in our *caracol*? Our main weapon is autonomous education. In our *caracol* [education] promoters are taught real stories related to our people, so they can transmit them to the boys and girls, thus getting them acquainted with our demands. We also began organizing political lectures for our youth so they remain alert and they don't fall so easily for government ideology. The local people in each village also give lectures on the thirteen demands.

Concerning ideological resistance, we organize children's meetings, where they present their poetry, their dance acts, so that children are getting a grasp of what our struggle is about and so that they realize that we, the comrades, are the ones who have to build our education. We have been working on all this a little, but we keep on promoting this work in our area.

In our area we began by reclaiming our culture through the wisdom of our ancestors, our grandfathers and grandmothers, in what we called the three areas. Bonesetters [*hueseros*] and herb healers were trained there. We also have a group of midwives. We have these women so we don't have to go to government hospitals or village clinics anymore. Thus we are reinforcing our autonomy, our demand for healthcare.

We are building political resistance to the education programs of the government. Nowadays in our area, there are new public schools, and all children attending these schools are required to wear a uniform so they look better. But we don't agree with that. Wearing a better uniform does not mean that they learn more. This is not what matters in education. What matters is the quality of education provided by the teacher or the education promoter.

We maintain in our communities and our villages a way to resist in the social sphere. For example, we help each other when someone passes away. We maintain this custom of helping with whatever is needed, such as digging the grave and carrying the deceased at the funeral. Another form of resistance is that life in the villages is organized for example in the communal land work [*ejidal*], in opening roads, building bridges and making hammocks. We still have those tasks that are the tasks of the whole community.

Resistance does not mean that we are not going to work. Resistance means that we have to work, because it is made and built by the people. That is, resistance is our house, our roof, our tent where we will take shelter as a people and as families, as comrades who are going to work together. Resistance means that for us the bad government is our enemy. We cannot ask the bad government to give us anything even if they offer us, even if they tell us, even if they try to buy us off. We cannot afford to accept because we are not struggling for their charity, for a piece of sheet metal, for a bag of cement, a bag of nails. We are not struggling for that. What we will do is resist all projects proposed by the bad government. The bad government has a different kind of politics. They try to buy our comrades off, they try to buy us off or offer money in exchange for surrendering our weapons. But we have never surrendered them and we will never do so.

The bad government could not destroy our autonomy. Why was that? Because we knew that autonomy lies in our hearts. When we raise our awareness, when our awareness is not fickle, then we can move ahead working collectively together, men, women, children, the elderly, all working together.

Through our experiences of resistance as grassroots supporters [*bases de apoyo*] we have exercised our autonomy without having the need to be in contact with the bad government. We train promoters in different areas of work, such as general healthcare. The advance in general healthcare in our area is a result of having appointed health promoters in the villages who receive training to help develop the true health of our people.

We have sexual health promoters in the area, both in the villages and in the municipalities. The women sexual health promoters work in shifts in the area's clinic to achieve a decrease in maternal and infant mortality. These health promoters have managed to detect some diseases in comrades as well as outsiders that receive medical attention in the area.

The bad government wants to convince us to give up the struggle, but if we always keep in mind that our only hope lies in resistance, and if we hope to enjoy the outcome of our efforts, even if the government sends us thousands of pesos or constructs buildings, we will not give up our struggle because it is a matter of consciousness.

Within our autonomy we have great respect for our positions of authority, regardless of whether they are held by minors, young people or elderly people. We respect them equally because they hold positions of authority. This power was not bought off, as is often the case in political parties. Sometimes they buy votes, they use intimidation. They give away food, beer or spirits to get their candidates elected. Our case is nothing like this. Here, it is the people; it is our comrades who choose their authorities. If any people holding a position of authority do not do their work well in their three years of office, they will have to receive criticism from the grassroots supporters, from the authorities.

We are going to address this issue through education. Why are we talking so much about education? Because education is very important to us, through education we can have both theory and practice with the students. But we didn't always have our autonomous education. We first had to go through a process of convincing ourselves, because many of us who now are comrades, before 1994 we were affiliated to PRI. Some of us were Zapatistas beforehand and many of us became Zapatistas in 1994. But at that time we still retained some ideas from when we were with PRI. When the need arose to teach our children and the official teachers left, we said that it was not a big deal and we started to think how we can make our own education. That was when the criticism started.

We are now seeing the result of our education. It was not in vain that we endured hunger and lived on plain toast in order to create our own education, because the toast gives us strength and wisdom. When we started with our own education, collectivism proved very useful. We learned along our comrades in every village, in every municipality. We confronted the fucking soldiers who were in our area, who came to harass us. There, our women comrades learned to defend themselves: with clubs and stones or with shouts and insults, they drove the soldiers away. Women got organized like this. I witnessed it and I can tell you that back then, the women found the strength to confront the soldiers. They demonstrated that they have what it takes.

The resistance began when the Spanish came to conquer our people. They wanted to impose on us a different way of life. They wanted to destroy our own governments so that they could rule and govern. They wanted to take away all our grandparent's land so they could appropriate all and control the population; so they would only work as laborers. They wanted to change our ideas, to make us believe that they are the wise, that they are the virtuous; they are most advanced in language, imposing their education, their religion. They wanted to convince us that to live happily and in abundance there must be inequality, so that a few could live in luxury without worrying about those who have nothing.

But resistance does not only mean not to receive the support of the bad government or not to pay property tax and electricity bills. Resistance is to create everything that helps us keep our villages alive. That's why resistance is a weapon of struggle to confront the capitalist system that dominates us.

How do we resist the attack on our culture? We are building our own media, such as the radio station and the community video. In our education, we are promoting the use, writing and reading of our language. The knowledge and the wisdom of our grandparents are being taught to children in the autonomous schools through tales, legends, beliefs and stories. We maintain our ways of celebrating religious and secular holidays. We keep on promoting and safeguarding our native seeds and our eating habits based on products that exist in our communities, because they are healthy and organic. We conserve and keep on promoting our ways of taking care of mother earth, of respecting the earth and all that is in our environment. We are promoting ways of coexistence, comradeship, brotherhood and the services that we should provide for the good of our people.

•••

Compañero Zapatista *Galeano*

José Luis López Solís, Galeano, teacher in the Zapatista Little School, was brutally assassinated during an attack in La Realidad, a Zapatista community/Caracol on May 2, 2014. The assassination was directed at: (1) Galeano, as activist and teacher; (2) at the entire Zapatista community of La Realidad, with more than a dozen wounded; (3) at the whole of Zapatismo—their fight for autonomy, their struggle for a different form of life, a new world. La Realidad is the heart of the emancipatory vision of the Zapatistas. After teaching in the first Zapatista Little School, August 2013, Galeano was interviewed on his view of the experience of the Little School. Below we publish his evaluation.

Galeano: We are a team of teachers participating at various levels in The Little School for Freedom according to the Zapatistas, like in the video conferences. We are all affiliated to the "Mother of the *Caracols*, Sea of our Dreams" *caracol*, located in the Frontier Jungle region. I come from the village of Nueva Victoria, in the municipality of San Pedro de Michoacán.

For me, I see *La Escuelita* [the little school] as a very important initiative, because it is a means for us to communicate with people from the city, so that we can share our experiences, our great achievements during these 19, almost 20 years of autonomy. So I say it's a means, a means for us to be able to share the progress we've made in building autonomy with people from outside, and a place where they have been able to come into our territories, to stay with indigenous families, to share and to learn. And at the same time, the visitors come to understand how the Zapatistas have their own ways, our own forms of organizing, our own means of self-sufficiency, and how we do not have to rely on the bad system of government, but rather we build our own system.

Now they have seen it with their own eyes and have come to understand the sacrifice we are making in order to attain all that we have achieved. While staying with families in the communities, the visitors have seen how much has been sacrificed, how much this family has endured in order to harvest, in order to provide for the whole family and to sustain us all in our resistance to the bad government. The visitors have seen how much effort it takes to survive and how the bad government makes us pay with this misery.

Now with their own ears and eyes they have seen the things that we have always said. Maybe they had heard our speeches or read our communiques before, but perhaps they did not really believe what we were trying to say. They knew that the Zapatistas were in the mountains, that's what they always say, but they never thought of us Zapatistas as flesh and blood, that we are human beings like them, and that this is what we do: we are in the communities and we are organizing.

So *La Escuelita* for me is a means for us to communicate with other people from the city, from our country and the world. It is like a bridge to communicate.

La Escuelita is one more of our accomplishments that we have achieved through our resistance, through our struggle. We can consider this one more of our accomplishments because during these 500 years of being robbed and exploited by the bad system, the bad government never allowed us this kind of space; the bad government never gave us this kind of freedom that we have now to meet and work with people from other parts of our country.

I value *La Escuelita* because here in our struggle, there are many young people who were born after the uprising, as well as those born in the city who had not been born in 1994, and they had only heard about the Zapatistas in the media, in the newspapers or on the radio, but they never really knew what the struggle was all about. So I think *La Escuelita* has been a great achievement, because of course the bad government would never have given it to us. No other organization has accomplished what we have done here in organizing *La Escuelita*.

Not only are people from the city and from other countries being educated through *La Escuelita*, but we are also educating ourselves, the youth are being prepared to continue the work of governing ourselves. Through opening up the space of *La Escuelita*, the youth are being guided and orientated towards learning how we govern ourselves, how it is that the people should lead. For me, I value the school as a very important thing. We ourselves learn many things, and people coming from outside learn from us.

The other really great achievement we see here is that the government is no longer in control; here the people are in charge. The people decide for themselves how things are to going to be, and that is what others need to understand. As we have already pointed out, the people from outside who come to attend *La Escuelita* may have heard that in Zapatista territory the people are in charge and the government obeys, but now they have come to see with their own eyes just how the people here govern from their villages, municipalities and at a district level. That's the best thing of all, how people from outside have come to understand the Zapatistas process of self-government.

What is our assessment of the students?

I have a great respect for those *compañero/as* and students who have come to attend *La Escuelita*. You can see the great spirit here, you can see the importance of the initiative for them; they are very interested in what they have come to learn about. So many compañero/as, intellectuals, school teachers, artists, urban dwellers, collectives, student and university groups, have come here and have told us that they have never experienced anything like what they have experienced in *La Escuelita*. They seem very pleased.

Furthermore, I respect them because they make a commitment. They say that they will pass on what they have learned here with their *compañero/as* who for whatever reason were unable to attend; that they will share what we have taught them, what they saw, what they learned. So for this reason, I respect the students who came from outside, because I saw that they were very excited by the experience.

While some students were somewhat confused or unsure about what they were meant to be doing in *La Escuelita*, or they were asking questions that reached beyond what *La Escuelita* was about, I can say for sure that there were no bad intentions, just that they were feeling disoriented or unsure of themselves, and so they went beyond the boundary we had established. I am sure that they did not mean any harm but it was simply that their concentration was not on *La Escuelita*.

But the students who came to this *caracol* were very content and greatly appreciated all they had learned. For this, I applaud them because apart from people who came who had the means to do so, there were others who had to take time out from work, or students who had to save up their money to come learn in our school. I appreciate that they made this effort to get here because they had a desire to learn and were interested in what we are doing.

On a rather more general level, we could see that the students came to learn from us, and for me, that was something that I respected a lot. Aside from the questions they asked, it became clear from their comments and what they said, that they too are exploited, that they too suffer in a similar manner to us, the indigenous. The most important thing is that they themselves said we share a common enemy, which is neoliberalism, and only united can we defeat it.

PART 4

Battle of Ideas and Practices; Conclusions

CHAPTER 12

Horizontal-ism, State-ism, Marxism and the Indigenous Dimension—Raul Zibechi, Álvaro García Linera, Hugo Blanco

I Raul Zibechi, Chronicler of Latin America in Social Rebellion

> The only certainty is that only a broad and multifaceted ensemble of uprisings, rebellions, and insurrections, on the global as well as local scale, can allow us to discover paths, necessarily new ones, to turn the crisis into a process of superseding capitalism. We'll have to rethink the rest, for, in times of systemic confusion, new forms of action must be created.
>
> RAUL ZIBECHI, "Our everyday crisis," *La Jornada* (2009)

The work of Raul Zibechi as chronicler of Latin America's social movements has been an invaluable contribution to understanding the power and creativity of the movements from below, and the threats to those movements from without and within. He has documented their successes and weaknesses, observing and analyzing the rise of the new Left governments, including critiquing the threat from "progressive" State-ism, while at the same time exposing the harsh realities of present-day neo-liberalism, the threat from the old oligarchies, and the increasing militarization of the Americas via the United States' Plan Colombia and Plan Puebla-Panama.

While much of Zibechi's work is found in journalistic form, here I will concentrate on his writings in two books. *Dispersing Power—Social Movements as Anti-State Forces* [*Dispersar el poder—Los movimientos sociales como poderes antiestatales*] focuses on the movement in Bolivia between 2000 and 2005; while *Territories in Resistance—A Cartography of Latin American Social Movement* [*Territorios en resistencia: cartografía política de las periferias urbanas latinoamericanas,* published also as *Autonomías y emancipaciones—América Latina en movimiento*] traces a number of liberatory movements in Latin America.

A *Societies in Movement: Creativity from Practice*

Dispersing Power—Social Movements as Anti-State Forces is a description and analysis of the social movement(s)—particularly the Community as Social Machine—that contributed to the emancipatory transformation of Bolivia in the first decade of the 21st century: "Community does not merely exist, it is made. It is not an institution, not even an organization, but a way to make links between people." (Zibechi, 2012a: 14).

The community Zibechi singles out is El Alto, the primarily Aymara Indigenous city above La Paz. It is this community that challenged the power of the Bolivian state. Zibechi views El Alto's creativity as community *in movement* rather than simply movement organizations within the community, which could become fixed and static rather than in movement. The old organizational forms of social protest from the 1960s and '70s, such as unions, were created in parallel to the oppressor organization of the state that they opposed. As such, these old organizations replicated some hierarchical organizational forms they were fighting. In contrast, Zibechi sees the Aymara self-organization in insurrection, 2000–2005, inseparable from the everyday community life.

Spontaneity is not posed in opposition to thinking action in Zibechi's view. Rather, "spontaneity, in the deep voluntary sense, based on lessons learned previously... a general intellect at work or, in other words, a collective common sense constructed in the heat of action" (Zibechi, 2012a: 62–63).

In *Territories in Resistance: A Cartography of Latin American Social Movement* Zibechi expands his commentary to take in various movements in Latin America: the Zapatistas in Mexico, the landless workers movement in Brazil, recuperated factories in Argentina, the Mapuche in Chile, the urban peripheries, among others—"Latin America in Movement." The focus is on the movement from below, the movement and creativity from practice.

In *Territories*, a crucial dimension of the movement from practice is made more explicit, what I would term after Dunayevskaya, "a movement from practice that is itself a form of theory." One sees this most specifically in a chapter titled "Collective De-alienation." Here, Zibechi questions the old concept of theory as the preserve of specialists of the state, the political parties and academics: "the space for emancipatory practices is not to be found there" (Zibechi: 2012b: 52). Furthermore, "we can only understand the meaning of social practice *in* and *with* that—from within" (52). He elaborates on this methodology, this way of finding meaning (theory):

> New ways of thinking emerge from this other world [the movement from emancipatory practice]. Up to now, the production of theory was undertaken by agencies of the state, the academy, and political parties. Now the movement itself produces theories that are embodied in non-capitalist social relations. This, in my view, is an epistemic turn and represents a difficult challenge for us in the movement. The emergence of new

> subjects constituted in the social margins, the so-called excluded, turns upside down the knowledge and practice of the specialists.

As against the specialists seeing these subjects (Indians, peasants or the poor) as "obstacles," we are witnessing a time "when these 'obstacles' become subjects, and begin to change the course of history and produce forms of knowledge that call into question the monopoly of the specialists..." (53)[1]

B *Is a Concept of 'Anti-Systemic,' of 'Dispersal of Power,' Sufficient? The Needed Movement from Theory*

Together with his powerful descriptions and acute observations of social movements, societies-in-movement, Zibechi gives an important, creative reading of Marx's relation to the social movements of his day. In the Introduction to *Dispersing Power* he quotes from Marx's writing on the Paris Commune: "The workers have no ready-made utopias to introduce *par decret du peuple.* They have no ideals to realize, but to set free the elements of the new society with which old collapsing bourgeois society itself is pregnant." Zibechi sees "to set free" ["*dar suelta*"] as crucial to Marx's concept of social transformations occurring "naturally," growing from within the old society, "a result of their own internal dynamics" (3–4).

Spontaneity, Zibechi notes, even if Marx did not directly use the word, was at the heart of this concept of social transformation. Other categories from Marx—"self-activity" of the workers, and "self-organization,"—are singled out

1 At the same time that we read Zibechi's breakthrough commentaries on subjects and the development of theory, we need to call attention to two puzzling short statements found in these books:

1. Zibechi's Foucault-centered view that "this struggle between two poles [movements/communities vs. state/political parties] is not one of an exteriority relationship but rather that the party/state logic lives in the bosom of the community, and the movement; it permeates them, not as something that comes from the outside but rather something the exists in an immanent relationship..." (2012a, 89–90).
2. In the Epilog to the English language edition of *Territories in Resistance* (2012b), which is a 2012 interview, Zibechi continues in this same vain: "[C]apital continues to seep into our minds and our hearts with an attraction so compelling that it is destroying not just our humanity but also the planet itself. One overcomes this situation not by destroying capitalism, because capitalism is within us, but by developing a love for life, something that cannot be created artificially" (334).

These two claims sit very uneasily within the rich body of description and analysis that Zibechi gives of societies in movement, one which argues a fundamentally opposite view of revolutionary subjectivity than any Foucault-ian one.

as well. Crucially, he points out that for Marx, the need for *revolution* was central to social transformation, a concept "that has been buried by the Marxists" (*Dispersing Power*: 2). At the same time, Zibechi argues that the revolutionary act for Marx was "just a short step in a long process of creating that other world" (*Dispersing Power*: 2).

Seeing today's social struggles in Latin America as resonating with what Marx had discovered in relation to the Paris Commune and other social struggles in the 19th Century, and which many of today's post-Marx Marxists have lost touch with, Zibechi writes of the "internal dynamic of social struggles" in Latin America weaving "new" social relations, ones that lay the basis for "a new world," "a different world from the hegemonic," the "'old' social relation—essentially statist relations." He then gives a devastating critique of the 20th century Left: "Twentieth century history is full of births of worlds that embody 'old' social relations. This tumultuous reality has brought disastrous consequences in general, revolutions that have not given birth to new worlds, though revolutionaries have tried to build them with the state apparatus" (*Dispersing Power*: 4).

There is much to appreciate and learn from in Zibechi's description and critique of Latin American social struggles, and in his reading of Marx's relationship to the liberatory movements of his day. Marx and today's Latin America social struggles can speak to each other. And yet, there is crucial dimension of Marx that Zibechi does not take up. Marx based himself on the liberatory struggles of his day, *while at the same time continually developed new theoretical points of departure.* As revolutionary intellectual, he became, as Dunayevskaya expressed it, "*philosopher* of permanent revolution." If, as Zibechi correctly asserts, "new forms of action must be created" today, then do we not have to create new theoretical points of departure at the same time? He would agree as we saw in the previous section: "the movement itself produces theories." At the same time, a movement from practice that is a form of theory is not the sole form of theory. We cannot shift the full responsibility for the creation of a philosophy of revolution in permanence for our day onto the shoulders of the masses in movement. Revolutionary thinker-activists have a responsibility as well. They need to work out theory, but *not* in an elitist, hierarchical manner that Zibechi correctly critiques. Whether this is or is not what Zibechi meant when he noted theory produced by the social movements represents "a difficult challenge for us in the movement," this is *a crucial task* within the revolutionary movement. Thinker-activists do not of course create theory *ab novo*. Theory must be rooted in the movement from practice, but it must as well be grounded in the fullness of dialectical philosophy. We need the connecting threads to Marx's philosophy, to his creation of the dialectic in his day. This form of theory reaches toward the movement from practice, practice seen as revolutionary reason. At the same time, such development of revolutionary theory reaches toward/is rooted in the historically developed philosophy of emancipation that is the dialectic in Marx and in Hegel.

However, Zibechi appears to misread part of Marx's dialectical thought. He contrasts Indian rebellious thought to the dialectic: "Ultimately, how could we go beyond the dialectic... Marx has said that the new world exists within the old and could think of non-exclusory terms, which is to say non-dialectically..." (*Territories:* 321) Why would such a way of thinking be "non-dialectical"? Only if one narrowly views dialectic as consisting solely of binary opposites, and having no room for other categories, would one think that Marx had suddenly moved beyond dialectical thinking. In truth, Marx was the deepest of dialectical thinkers precisely because he was constantly developing the dialectic in response to all the "new passions and new forces" arising in his day.

Zibechi questions the role of the revolutionary intellectual, which is all well and good given the deeply problematic history of many so-called revolutionary intellectuals in the 20th century. However, he seems to go further and question the *need* for revolutionary intellectuals. Zibechi does so even though he himself makes some important contributions in this regard.

> I do not believe in the intellectual role as defined by Lenin or Gramsci: the intellectual who takes theory from outside and inserts it into the movement or the organic intellectual who is with the movement. I believe that movements form their own intellectuals, good or bad, but they do it, and that is very valuable. What I can do is contribute to their disappearance...
>
> TERRITORIES: 331

Zibechi seems to be arguing that what is needed is the power and creativity of social movements—what I am here calling the movement from practice that is a form of theory—period. The other dimension of this powerful dialectic—the movement from theory to practice that has its roots in a philosophy of liberation—remains absent. Zibechi's own theory projects that the movement from below contains the totality, and any other contribution is external to the dialectic of freedom.

•

I would argue that Zibechi's theory has two fault lines in need of further examination/critique. First, with all his sensitivity and focus on the creativity of the masses, his concept is burdened by this Foucaudian caveat—"that the party/

state logic lives in the bosom of the community, and the movement; it permeates them, not as something that comes from the outside but rather something that exists in an immanent relationship…"

Second, the role of theory, philosophy, and revolutionary intellectual is read in too narrow a manner. Zibechi is right to reject elitist theory, and vanguardist intellectuals wishing to impose theory in an external manner. However, he fails to fully come to grips with the role of a revolutionary intellectual who is not elitist. Yes, we need to strive to breakdown the division between theory and practice, between thinking and doing. But the process of doing so does not mean the abolition of revolutionary philosophy, the dialectic, but its realization in life, in practice. For this, dialectic, both in thought and in practice, is crucial for revolutionary transformation.

11 The Statist Marxism of Álvaro García Linera[2]

As we have seen in Chapter 7, powerful social movements in the first decade of the 21st century have transformed parts of Bolivian society. The social mobilization from the Water War to the Gas War, from Indigenous protest in the countryside to rebellion in the Indigenous city of El Alto—succeeded in bringing down the neo-liberal government of Sánchez de Lozada and then Carlos Mesa. The election of Evo Morales, backed by an overwhelming majority of the Indigenous population, opened the door to the possibility of alternative development. However, as we have also seen, it has led to a developmental-ist strategy, with many characteristics of state-capitalism. Here, we want to examine the ideological underpinnings that have reduced the concept of socialism to state intervention and control. To do this, we want to will take up some of the ideas and actions of Álvaro García Linera, the intellectual most closely associated with the ideological underpinnings of the Bolivia state post the election of Morales.

García Linera was an important observer of the process of Bolivia's social transformation in the first half decade of this century. In writing of the social

2 García Linera, Vice President of Bolivia, was a founding member of the Indigenous Marxist guerrilla organization EGTK (Tupac Katari Guerrilla Army). He spent five years in prison after being captured in the early 1990s. After being released, he joined the Sociology Department at Universidad Mayor de San Simon (UMSS) in La Paz. He was a member of the radical Bolivian collective *La Commune*, and has authored a number of books analyzing Bolivia's social composition. He became Evo Morales' running mate in 2005, and subsequently Vice-President.

movements in El Alto (*Sociología de las movimientos sociales en Bolivia*, 2004) he recognized that in El Alto "organizational networks, solidarities, and initiatives [were] developed in an autonomous manner above and, in some cases, outside the authority of the neighborhood council." As for rural workers in the countryside, García Linera saw CSUTCB (*La Confederación Sindical Única de Trabajadores Campesinos de Bolivia*) as a social movement that "not only mobilizes part of society, but generates a distinct society, a new set of social relations with non-capitalist forms of working, and modes of organization, meaning, representation, and political authority that are completely different from that of the dominant society."

Despite this recognition that the social transformation which allowed for the election of Morales was autonomous, outside not only of political parties, but even much of the established neighborhood organizations and councils, García Linera argues that building a new society in Bolivia proceeds not on this de-centralized, creative basis from below, but through the *state*: "[E]very struggle goes through the state; even the struggle against the state passes through the state." (Intervention in seminar *Pensamiento y movimientos sociales* Niteroi, Oct. 25, 2005) This is not just the thoughts of a radical sociologist-Marxist. This ideological construct has become the practice of state power of Bolivia, with García Linera as Vice President. If our sociologist-Marxist-intellectual could recognize the power of the social movements from below in overthrowing the rulers of Bolivia, 2005–2006, why does he not seek to base the Bolivia post-2005 on this same creativity in building a new society? He presents his theoretical-practical reasons:

> It is not realistic to think that in a country where only 10 percent of the working class has a clear consciousness of itself as a class, we can build socialism, because socialism cannot be built without a proletariat. It will take decades of hard work to build the class consciousness necessary for this transition. Therefore we must construct a strong state that assumes a leading role in the economy and mobilizes its resources to strengthen community organizations and communal forms of production.
>
> GARCÍA LINERA, interview by Linda Farthing, August 3, 2009

In another interview he expressed it even more succinctly: "We want a capitalism with a big state presence." It is this ideology and practice of a statist-"Marxism" that we have already witnessed as a bitter reality through much of the 20th century. (See, among other works, Dunayevskaya's writings on Russia and China as state-capitalist societies.) Surely the illusion that state-capitalism is a transition to socialism rather than the ultimate logic of capitalism should have been destroyed by now. How have we arrived once again at such a statist concept of Marxism?

I would suggest there are two interrelated fault lines in García Linera's concept of Marxism, though by no means is he the only one to hold such a position. First, perhaps due in part to the difficulties of technological underdevelopment in Bolivia as in much of the world, he holds a developmental-ist, an economic-determinist, concept of the pathway to socialism or authentic communism. Second, he projects a view bordering close to "the backwardness of the masses," in terms of who is the creative source, the "organizing principle" the motor for building a new society: masses in motion or the "progressive" state, the political party, the "leadership."

With regard to the first point, García Linera analyzes Bolivia society as being composed of four civilizations: modern industrial, domestic (informal) economy, the communal, and the Amazonia. Whether or not one wishes to accept this view, what is key for García Linera is that a multi-cultural *state* will be the principle conduit for constructing the future. As Raul Zibechi has noted,

> García Linera proposed in his book *Estado multinacional* the founding and developing of a multi-cultural state "to include sectors marginalized up to now—the indigenous, respecting their forms of community organization." To end the ethnic discrimination that has been the hallmark of Bolivian society for centuries García Linera argued for language and cultural practices to be inclusive in the public administration, including ministerial positions occupied by the Indigenous. While ending ethnic discrimination is crucial and the need immediately, the means the García Linera has proposed—a multi-national, multi-cultural state *in combination with* "Andean-Amazonian capitalism" "capitalism with a big state presence"—seems problematic.[3]

For the Bolivian Vice-President, the only pathway for the transition to a non-exploitative society lies through capitalism with a large state presence. He seems to view non-capitalist economic forms existing in Bolivia as obstacles to such a transition. But as Zibechi succinctly points out, Marx in his interchange with Vera Zazulich on the possibility that Russian non-capitalist forms in the countryside (the *mir* or *obshina*) saw non-capitalist economic forms as a crucial strand for Russia to avoid all the vicissitudes of capitalist development.

3 Zibechi's *Dispersing Power* (2012) contains a section "Toward a Multicultural State?." This section includes an important analysis/critique of his concept of a multi-cultural state (113–117) which I have utilized in my analysis here.

No doubt, García Linera would point out that capitalism has developed much more fully, its tentacles reaching everywhere in the more than a century since Marx explored this question in Russia. But he has missed a crucial point: Marx's focused on the *human* forces as the only ones that can overcome, can transform, oppressive, exploitative economic relations.

This is at the heart of García Linera's second fault in his concept of Marxism for today: the subordinate role of the social movement from below to a "progressive" state. Despite the rich Bolivian experience of the movement from below, 2000–2005, it is not that mass movement, in Zibechi's terms "society in movement" that can become the organizer, the founders of the new. For García Linera, "It will take decades of hard work to build the class consciousness necessary for this transition." Rather, it is the multi-cultural *state* that will be the conduit for constructing the future.

It is not that García Linera dismisses the movement from below. As we saw, he recognized its importance 2000–2005. However, his way of seeking to solve Bolivia's half a millennium of colonialist-capitalist imposed underdevelopment does not base itself on that movement from below, but on the state—to be sure, a multi-cultural progressive state—to act in the interests of the movement from below. It is the new multi-national state-apparatus that can articulate the "four civilizations."

But have we not already had as full century of experiences of "what happens after the revolution?" with the state and not masses in motion as determinate, not *leading to a transition of a new human society, but* the consolidation of oppression, *a new form of capitalism?*

All of this in not a theoretical question in Bolivia, but the here and now of the practical. We can see this and the fault lines of García Linera's Marxism in his book on the TIPNIS—*Geopolitics of the Amazon: Patrimonial-Hacendado Power and Capitalist Accumulation—after taking power.*

With *Geopolitics of the Amazon: Patrimonial-Hacendado Power and Capitalist Accumulation*, our Bolivian Marxist-sociologist-historian-economist has evidently decided to give us all a lesson in history-economics-Marxism in the context of Bolivia with a little Lenin thrown in for flavor. Not being an expert on the exact number of kilometers of road/path paved and unpaved has already been built and used in the TIPNIS region, I will have to accept the Bolivian Vice President's figures, though others may have corrections. Nor am I interested in disputing his history of extractivism and development in the Amazon region of Bolivia. But one need not accept his questionable concept that extractivism in all societies from pre-capitalist, to capitalist to so-called post capitalist is the same. With today's technology, extraction is on a level never seen before. Some development and extraction of natural resources is no doubt necessary. But to act as if there is no way to transform extraction in a thoroughgoing manner, *when not exchange value, but use value predominates,* is wrong. There is another manner of development, even within a capitalist world in the short term, if one works from a different premise then "developmental-ism." This is not to ignore material realities. Rather we need to put material realities in the context an emancipatory vision of human development. This García Linera fails to do.

Two points in *Geopolitics of the Amazon* show his methodology/mentality: First, he has presented an essay for developmentalism in Bolivia. Not private developmental-ism, but state-sponsored developmental-ism: a state that is now supposed to represent the best interests of the Bolivian nation, particularly its Indigenous majority. Figure after figure, statistic after statistic in García Linera's discourse shows this drive for developmental-ism. What kind of developmentalism? A state-capitalist developmentalism. A state that, he argues, has the best interests of the nation, not private interests, at heart. Our teacher of this so-called Marxism assures us that there is no other choice. Communism is an illusion unless it is a world system, so forget about it. Meanwhile, there is development for development's sake for the Bolivian people. How close we are to Marx's remarks on capitalism production for productions sake, accumulate and accumulate! Perhaps the Vice President might want to re-look at Marx's writings on Russia, his drafts of the letter to Vera Zazulish, where he wrote of a different manner of development being possible in technologically underdeveloped Russia: the *mir* or *obschina* as a means for generating a non-capitalist way of development.

Does García Linera perhaps not believe that such a way of thinking might have relevance to Bolivia, *not* as his "Andian-Amazonial capitalism," but as truly a different pathway? Marx's point was trying to find an alternative to capitalism. Can Bolivia do it alone? Of course not. But if Bolivia and others do not dare to try, then how can we have the new points of departure for moving forward, for destroying capitalism root and branch? If Bolivia dares, will not others perhaps follow as well? No one can answer with certainty. But if Bolivia and others do not dare, then what are we left with? Well for the Vice President of Bolivia it is very clear—state-capitalist development. Haven't we already had enough of that in the 20th century with Russia's 5-year state plans in Stalin's time? Where exactly did that lead? Or Mao's China (which our author evidently admires) with his Great Leap Forward of 1957–59, and his Great Proletarian Cultural Revolution of 1966–76? Have we not already had enough of these kind of experiments in developmental-ism; this kind of catching up with the West? Is *this* the lesson that Bolivia needs today?

The second point that is clear from García Linera's discourse is what is *missing* in his book. There is no discussion of the life and labor, the desires and wishes, the activities of the Amazonian Indigenous population in Bolivia. When they are mentioned at all, it is a mere qualitative account of their presence. There is no *human* view of the Amazonian region. Marx wrote of his view of what would be necessary for an alternative to capitalist development: "A thoroughgoing naturalism of humanism" (*1844 Manuscripts*). If the needed development in Bolivia and elsewhere is not created as a humanism for the here and now of Bolivia, of Latin America, indeed globally, if it is not constructed in such a manner, then what is it worth? Statist Marxism is not based on Marx's Marxism in any way. It is a state form of capitalism, not the construction of a new human society. State-ist "socialism" has a logic of its own: a mode for enslavement to the logic of capital, production for production's sake, a developmental-ism that is the only true logic of capitalism. No matter what is in the hearts of those intellectuals who propound this State-ism, such ideas have real, living consequences for the Bolivian masses.

III Hugo Blanco—Peruvian Revolutionary: From Trotskyism and the Peasantry to the Indigenous Movement for Land and Mother Earth

> [T]here is no contradiction between my indigenous struggle and dialectical materialism.
>
> HUGO BLANCO

Hugo Blanco, a Marxist revolutionary out of the tradition of Trotskyism, was a leader of a movement of peasants who self-organized in the valley of *La Convención* and *Lares* at the end of the 1950s and into the 1960s, demanding land and agricultural reform as against feudalistic share-cropping. When attacked by the military, this movement organized in self-defense. Blanco was captured in 1962 and sentenced to life in prison. He served eight years before being released. He wrote of this experience in the context of Trotskyism in *Land or death: The peasant struggle in Peru.*

Forced into exile and at times able to return and participate in social struggle in his country, Blanco made a transition from orthodox Trotskyism to activism and writing on the Indigenous movement in Peru—the struggle for territory and the environment: "Indigenous peoples have been fighting for eco-socialism for 500 years." He is editor of *Lucha Indigena*, a Peruvian journal.

Blanco's history as Marxist and in Indigenous struggles allows us to explore the relation of Marxism and the Indigenous movement in Latin America—a conflictive, contradictory story. He comes, of course, from the land of José Carlos Mariátegui, that most creative Latin American Marxist, who in the 1920s forged a unity of the struggle for socialism in Peru with the Indigenous dimension: "In Peru—the working class—is four-fifths Indian. Our socialism would not be Peruvian—it would not even be socialism—if it did not first consolidate itself with the indigenous demands."[4]

Mariátegui's view, his re-creation of Marxism for a Latin American reality, did not go uncontested. "Orthodox" Marxism, that is the dogmatic concepts of Stalinism, were just being foisted on the Latin American revolutionary movement. Mariátegui was in opposition, but died in 1930, and his views were quickly dismissed. Only under the impact of the emergence of Indigenous struggles in the latter part of the 20th century, and now the 21st, has his concept of the centrality of the Indian question within the context of a struggle for socialism come to the fore. For the vast majority of the twentieth century a closed, rigid concept of Marxism was the dominant strand in vogue. On the one hand, these Latin American Communist Parties were quite reformist in nature, viewing the need for a bourgeois "revolution" in the "feudal" oligarchy before any talk of socialism could be undertaken. Their practice was essentially class-collaborationist with bourgeois parties/governments against a Latin American oligarchy. (The Cuban Revolution dealt a decisive blow to such concepts.) On the other hand, the legacy of "statist" Marxist (a contradiction in terms in relation of *Marx's* Marxism) in power remains to this day as a bastard child contending for power. (See my chapters in part II on Venezuela and on Bolivia.)

Unfortunately, Trotskyism, though in opposition to these Stalinist concepts and practices, historically proved itself to be no viable alternative. In Latin America, we saw this most clearly in the one country where Trotskyism had important influence among Bolivian workers. The *Pulacayo Thesis,* based in part on Trotsky's Theory of Permanent Revolution, was written in 1946 by Bolivian Trotskyists for a congress of the powerful Miners Federation.

However Trotskyism in Bolivia failed to come to grips with the Indigenous dimension. The 1952 Bolivian Revolution, with its crucial worker-peasant alliance that Bolivian Trotskyism helped to develop, brought forth a role for the mining proletariat, but failed to take in the reality that both the peasantry and the working class in Bolivia were overwhelmingly Indigenous. The Indigenous dimension was pushed aside, subsumed in thinking about reconstructing Bolivia. Instead, all were citizens of Bolivia. Trotskyism, was part of

4 See Chapter 4, "José Carlos Mariátegui: Striving to Re-Create Marxism for Peru's Latin America *Tierre*—A Brief Overview" in Gogol 2002. See also Gogol 1994.

this revolutionary process, a process that failed to concretely elicit the thoughts and actions of the Indigenous dimension.

It is against this background of Communism's and Trotskyism's contradictory presence in Latin America's revolutionary history that we can turn to Hugo Blanco at the present moment. Blanco is a revolutionary, who has an important history in the Marxist movement in Peru, and who is making serious contributions in the Indigenous movement today. The fact that he has his feet both in the Marxist movement and the Indigenous movement in Peru could serve as a place to renew the dialogue, the possibilities on interchange between the Indigenous movement and Marxism. Blanco is certain aware of this, as he notes: "There isn't any contradiction between my indigenous struggle and dialectical materialism."

At the same time the question is complex. Given the long history of distorted Marxism projected by "Marxists" in the 20th century, the question is: "What kind of Marxism," "What concept of dialectical materialism" in Latin America today? When it comes to those who have claimed to be following Mariátegui, Blanco grasps the difficulty:

> In Peru all the left self-defines itself as Mariáteguist, but it seems that none of these Mariáteguists have read *The Seven Interpretive Essays of the Peruvian Reality*, Mariátegui's fundamental work, in which two of his essays are dedicated to the indigenous issue: 'The Indian Problem' and 'The Problem of Land.' And they completely ignore the indigenous problem, that's why, together with some comrades, we have started to publish the newspaper *Lucha Indigena*.

If anything, the problem is even more complex when it comes to Marx, that is, Marx's Marxism. This is not just a question of betrayers, counter-revolutionaries such as Stalin and Stalinism. It is as well as a problem of revolutionaries, including Trotsky and Trotskyism post-Trotsky.[5] Blanco notes,

> For Marx there were no bibles, reality is worth more than a thousand books, all of this is why I'm a Marxist... I don't like to define myself as Marxist, because it isn't a religion. But I have a lot to be grateful for to Marx, because he taught me dialectical materialism. And by being

5 For Dunayevskaya's analysis of Trotsky see, in particular, "Trotsky as Theoretician" in *Philosophy and Revolution* (1973) and "Trotsky's Theory of Permanent Revolution" in *Rosa Luxemburg, Women's Liberation, and Marx's Philosophy of Revolution*. See also my *Towards a Dialectic of Philosophy and Organization* (1982).

> dialectical I know that the American reality is different to Europe. That's why I try to interpret American reality as an American. Therefore, for me, there isn't any contradiction between my indigenous struggle and dialectical materialism.
>
> BLANCO, 2008

Reality may be worth many books, but without a theoretical standpoint, a philosophical vision, one cannot discern the full significance of reality. This has been the problem of a fragmented, partial Marxism post-Marx. The expression dialectical material can be a beginning, but it is hardly the totality of Marx's philosophic new continent of thought. It is here where a revolutionary such as Hugh Blanco *can make a crucial contribution*. His indigenousness to revolutionary struggle in Peru, his important relationship with the here and now of the Indigenous struggles in his country, can open the door for a genuine discussion of Marxism of Marx and its relation to today's Indigenous struggles. One point for discussion would be Marx's own interest in the Indigenous question as seen in his *Ethnological Notebooks* of his final years where he comments upon the Indigenous dimension that he takes up in his reading notes on Lewis Henry *Morgan's Ancient Society* on the Iroquois on North America. Another can be a reading of Marx's interest in the peasantry as a subject of social revolution, seen particular in his writing on the Russian *mir* or *obsina* in his draft of letters to Vera Zazulich.

Another place where Blanco's commentaries are of interest is on the question of taking power vs. building power:

> I do not agree with *Sendero Luminoso*—and neither with those who believe in taking power by elections. Whether by arms or by elections, both are struggling to take power. In this sense, I am a Zapatista. I do not believe in struggling to *take* power, but to *build* it... The villages in the Sierra that are standing up to the mining companies are *building* power. The *indigenas* in the *Selva* who are now controlling their own territory are *building* power.
>
> BLANCO, 2009

Certainly this has much in concert with Marx's concept and little with post-Marx vanguardism. At the same time, the challenge of explicitly uniting Marx's Marxism—not a recipe but as methodology and emancipatory vision—with the practice and thought of Indigenous movements in Latin America demands a continual exploration of the fullness of Marx's ideas in relation to the present moment. We will return to this question in our final chapter.

Appendix 1: The Organization and Building of Mass Power: Horizontalism and Verticalism, Utopia and Project

Rubén Dri

On May 20 and 21 of 2001, the third mass eruption in the recent history of Argentina took place, which signaled the end of one historical period and the beginning of another. People poured onto the streets demonstrating a power not controlled by anyone's leadership, nor by preexisting slogans. The middle class was there, becoming a vacant lower class. There were workers, low-paid teachers, shop keepers-turned-self-employed-workers, destitute intellectuals, youth who see no future for their lives. All of the social elements, together with all their contradictions, were present.

They weren't merely present, but rather *made themselves* present: through the screaming, jumping, chanting, singing, insulting. It was a transcendent moment in the history of a country that produces the rare miracle of the uniting of the emotional and rational; the mass impulse that is self-realizing in its actions, when *eros* and *logos* come together à la Plato's maxim.

In these sublime, ecstatic, burning, impassioned moments, everything seems possible. The floodgates open and all barriers disappear. Suddenly the universe opens up. There is a "storming of the heavens" and an all-revolutionary Utopia. The dawn of a new spirit begins to sketch its figure.

I Utopia and Project

All mass insurrections are the founding instances of Utopia. That is to say, of the immeasurable longings, wishes, and desires that enliven and inspire the social Subject. So it was with Thomas Münzer and the peasant insurrection, as well as the French Revolution, the May Revolution, May 1968 in France, the October 1945 mass uprising that freed Perón, the *Cordobazo*, and many others.

It is in these exceptional historic moments, in which the broad layers of the mass movements say, "Enough is enough! It's our turn!" In this moment, the mobilized, sensitized, agitated masses "feel their wings grow" as Plato says. All impediments to movement, to running, jumping, flying are dropped like a ballast. A space opens, and all of a sudden nothing seems able to impede their triumph.

This is the step in Hegel's *Phenomenology*, the leap from independence to freedom. The bondsman in his new beginning fearfully recoils when faced with the death that awaits him in his struggle for freedom and he submits to the master. This anguished fear liberates him from the objectivity in which he found himself trapped. He experiments in the deepest way in the negativity of his Subject-being.

A new dawn now looms, one in which all that once held the slave steady disappears in the liquification [melting] of all that is solid and tangible. The return to reality happens through his creative labor, which is at one and the same time creation of a different world and *self-creation*. His reality as a subjective-objective totality is founded anew after being destroyed by his distress and anguish. It is a reality where the Subject is in control, where the Subject sees itself in the world it has created.

From a subjugated and miserable servant forced to work for the master comes a Subject that has gained its independence. From independence to freedom there is but one step. Once a servant, the Subject draws its own, new horizon of freedom with newly-opened eyes. With one leap, the Subject attempts to set itself into this freedom.

Utopia bursts in like a wind that destroys all in its path, in a moment in which nothing can detain it. It is free now to express all it wants—which is everything—and to put it into practice. It wants all, and *that all* is now within reach. There is no difference between Utopia and projection, between fantasy and reality.

The floodgates open, and like a river newly thawed in a rushing torrent down a mountainside it carries itself over whatever obstacle is in its path. Akin to a collective orgasm, the Subjects feel themselves transported to higher regions. Social utopias usually find expression against a backdrop of misery and oppression. The classic example is Thomas More's *Utopia*, whose formulation was a response to "the sheep" which are "placid creatures, which used to require so little food [that] have now developed a raging appetite, and turned into man-eaters. Fields, houses, towns, everything goes down their throats." Marx's "Primitive Accumulation" showed how it required the expulsion of the peasants for the "transformation of arable land into sheep-walks" to produce the wool that was necessary for nascent manufacturing.

The formulation of Utopia is the protest against misery and the declaration of its supersession, Marx would say. Though the utopia that arises against this negative reality isn't always formulated clearly, it nonetheless never ceases to occur, because it is the negation and the supersession of that negative reality.

The negative reality against which such a clear expression of Utopia was formulated occurred during the December 19–20, 2001 uprising [in Argentina]. It is, at first glance, expressed with great clarity. It is expressed in "*¡Que se vayan todos!*" ("All of them must go!"). In contrast, a positive element was also expressed in the proclamation by the direct and full form in which power was taken by the demonstrators, without representatives. Everyone simply represented themselves.

It's necessary to elucidate what exactly was meant by the chant "All of them must go!" There is an interpretation that one could call the "literal" interpretation that meant that the actual individuals of the "political class" that had brought us this disaster should be thrown out of their posts, to give way to new, uncontaminated individuals.

Right off, the momentum of the movement caused people to form neighborhood assemblies, soon transformed into "popular assemblies." These were the driving force behind all of the mobilization that demanded that the stepping-down of the Supreme Court, the Senate and all its deputies; in a word, they demanded the resignation of any and every politician and functionary that was still in office.

But as time passed, the fire was quelled. Instead of fleeing, the politicians returned. Or, better said, they never left in the first place. What happened? Was it all an illusion of self-deception? Can the mass Subject, when it rises up in the manner that it did, make such a grave error?

What happened to the Subject with its cry of "*¡Que se vayan todos!*" is the same thing that happens to the Hegelian subject that made a leap from independence to freedom. This subject proclaims itself clear of all obstacles, a citizen of the world, immune to whichever contradiction presents itself. It is prideful and stoic freedom; whether on a throne or in chains, be it Marcus Aurelius or Epictetus the freed slave.

When the subject is set to put to practice this proclaimed freedom, (this *impavidum ferient ruinae*) the ruins knock him down. The Subject had experienced the depths of freedom, and it wasn't enough to declare it, dream of it, imagine it, or think about it. Their proclaimed freedom was tangled in the contradictions of the real world and the Subject, instead of overcoming those contradictions, turned into a Skeptic. The Subject did not discover how to overcome the contradiction between imagination and reality, between utopia and project.

In order to discover a useful answer to this problem, we should pay attention to the difference between utopia and project: two moments of the Subject that in its cry of "*¡Que se vayan todos!*" appear mixed, superimposed, and unmediated, with Utopia as the dominant term.

Utopia is the moment when the Subject is most open. Being so, the Subject is open to a limitless and unimpeded totality. The Subject is motivated by an unstoppable impulse to surpass all exiting limits. It is *conatus*, as Spinoza would say, that which always goes beyond. This is not merely an illusion. It is an essential moment of the *Reason of the Subject*. To be Subject is always to be more than Subject; it is to go beyond.

The utopic moment is that moment that has moved individual and collective Subjects since the origins of humanity. It is the driving force of all the new moments in culture, science, literature, philosophy, economics, politics, and society. The Subject is always more than itself; it is always beyond. "You could not discover the limits of soul, even if you traveled by every path in order to do so; such is the depth of its meaning" (Heraclitus).

There are exceptional moments in which this opening where Utopia exists and is shown to be urging its own realization. It is when the individual Subject has a waking dream, when he finds himself moved to act by a burning passion. It is when the collective Subject bursts into an irrepressible action, shouting at the top of its lungs what it wants to be, what it will be, and what it is to discover in its realization.

All of this happens in a single instant, or better said, in a *kairos* [right or opportune moment]. It is a qualitative moment, charged with meaning, pregnant with the future. It demands immediate realization, without delays or hesitations. Utopia is to be realized fully and immediately. It accepts no delays or exceptions, which is what never ceases to be the origin of the confusions that can bring about disillusion.

Both of these moments appear in the great thinkers, sometimes in a confused way. This is the case with Plato and his celebrated *Republic*. It is very common to interpret that work as a Utopia. But Plato didn't undertake the elaboration of a Utopia, but rather as a project to solve the crises of the *polis* in the fourth century B.C. The problem is that his project ended up as a Utopia, something that he himself ended up sensing after repeatedly trying to make it real.

Convinced that he had effectively created a Utopia, though without explicitly saying so, he proposes changes, first in the "Politics" section but more fundamentally in the "Laws." This work can be considered as the project that Plato elaborated in the space opened up by the Utopia of the *Republic*.

Neither did Aristotle escape this confusion. Effectively in his first project on the *polis*, Books VII and VIII of the "Politics" were, in reality, a Utopia. He only later realized this. He formulates a new project for the *polis* that comes in Book IV. With good reason he does not destroy his previous project that now appears as it really is, that is, as a Utopia. It opens a space in which he formulates his project for Book IV.

Another writer who mixes the two moments of Utopia and project is Rousseau. To overcome the distortions that are posed by what he terms "civil society," which is really nothing other than capitalist society, he proposes the celebrated "social contract." According to the social contract, everyone is completely alienated from everyone else, leave everything behind, where they more or less die, only later to be resuscitated as the "general will" and the "collective 'I.'"

When one asks how to apply the "social contract" to Poland and Corsica, Rousseau proposes formulating the respective projects in the realm that was opened by the social contract, and which remained valid in their cases. Like other Utopias, it centers on the grand values and ideals that should make effective the project it engenders.

Utopia cannot come about immediately, nor completely, because that would signify the end of the Subject who essentially constitutes the utopic space. Utopia is wide open and demands, pushes forward a realization of itself. If that is to be, another moment is required, and that moment is that of the project.

II Between Scylla and Charybdis

As Homer tells it, when Odysseus and his companions leave the island of Circe they strike a course that passes between two monstrous obstacles, Scylla and Charybdis. The first monster comes at them from above.

No man though he had twenty hands and twenty feet could get a foothold on it and climb it, for it runs sheer up, as smooth as though it had been polished. In the middle of it there is a large cavern, looking West and turned towards Erebus; you must take your ship this way, but the cave is so high up that not even the stoutest archer could send an arrow into it. Inside it Scylla sits and yelps with a voice that you might take to be that of a young hound, but in truth she is a dreadful monster and no one-not even a god-could face her without being terror-struck. She has twelve misshapen feet, and six necks of the most prodigious length; and at the end of each neck she has a frightful head with three rows of teeth in each, all set very close together, so that they would crunch any one to death in a moment (Homer).

You will find the other rocks lie lower, but they are so close together that there is not more than a bowshot between them. [A large fig tree in full leaf grows upon it], and under it lies the sucking whirlpool of Charybdis. Three times in the day does she vomit forth her waters, and three times she sucks them down again; see that you be not there when she is sucking, for if you are, Neptune himself could not save you (Homer).

Odysseus is the subject that goes through the phases of his own realization. He leaves Ithaca, from his mother's breast, from nature or the "universal abstract," as Hegel would put it, to travel far and wide in his journey of realization. It is the individual Subject and the collective Subject, Odysseus and the *polis*. From contradiction to contradiction, obstacle upon obstacle, the Subject in its adventures is actuating, creating, traveling on the road of liberation back to Ithaca.

Odysseus always leaves Ithaca, and always returns. He returns, not simply himself but as his Other-being. He has become this Other through his crossing, overcoming limits and obstacles, storms and monsters. Through moments of euphoria and also extreme sadness, through unhappy and vile consciousnesses, from death to resurrection.

One of the obstacles to be overcome is the one that I've already mentioned, the passing of Scylla and Charybdis, the two monsters then menace from above and below. Scylla, the monster from the heights, lures Odysseus by barking like a puppy. Upon getting a little closer the barks are like the horrible howling of hounds and there appears the evil monster ready to devour her prey.

There is no more appropriate example to use to warn of the danger of bureaucratization that threatens all organizations. Any group of individuals, whoever they are, that seek to a transformative subjectivity, to realize subjectivity and to be effective in their actions, need to organize themselves. This step of organization is absolutely necessary; the result of not organizing is impotence. Whether the organization is that of a family, a club, a union, a school, a church, or a group of friends. Otherwise, being merely "the multitude," they are doomed to the aforementioned impotence.

So far, so good. The problem arises just when an organization is coming into its own, it creates an atmosphere contrary to one that engenders the creation of the Subject. In place of forward movement, there is a countermovement. Organizations tend to become rigid, deadening creativity. In other words, bureaucratization threatens to devour the Subject and turned it into Object.

It is necessary, then, to flee from bureaucratization. But often the escape from Scylla can drive you right into the arms of Charybdis. Charybdis is found below, sucking and vomiting the "dark waters," poisonous and lethal to those who fall in. This is horizontalism, pure multiplicity, individuals dispersed and atomized.

Vertical bureaucracy and inarticulate horizontalism; both will spell the end of the Subject. He either becomes frozen in the rigid structure of bureaucracy, or disappears in an anthill of atomized individuals. Where, then, is the way out of this conundrum? Even better, is there an out? Circe proposes to Odysseus: ... you must hug the Scylla side and drive ship by as fast as you can, for you had better lose six men than your whole crew (Homer).

Holding close to Charybdis means disappearing in the dark, poisonous waters; to be below, without organization, milling about in the multitude, traveling from once place to another, in permanent "assembly-ism" or activism. It means disappearing as a Subject and being sucked in by the dark waters of impotence. The product of this, then, is what Hegel described in the Germany of his time with its different associations:

Such associations are like a heap of round stones which combine to form a pyramid. But since they are completely round and must remain so without interlocking, as soon as the pyramid begins to approach the end for which it was constructed, they roll apart, or at least offer no resistance [to such movement] (Hegel).

Better, then, to hold closer to Scylla, but making the passage as quickly as possible. This is to say, that it is preferable to organize and run the risk of bureaucratization. To do otherwise is to meet a sure death in the dark waters of disorganization. Skirting these dangers demands organizational criticism of all phenomena that might lead to bureaucratization within the organization.

If a group isn't organized, everyone belongs. It is impossible to construct a Subject, to construct power, if one is steeped in disorganization. Charybdis sucks up everything. To organize always means the loss of something, but the danger can be skirted if the proper steps are taken against bureaucratization. The contradiction can be overcome. By this path, and no other, will you reach Ithaca.

III Horizontalism, Organization, Collective Will, and Leadership

To be a Subject is to make it so, to "subjectify" one's self. To subjectify one's self is to potential-ize one's self, to apply one's self. This goes for any subject, as much for individual as for a group, social class, or nation. This is precisely Marx's point on social class, where the movement is from "class in opposition to" or class in-itself, to class for-itself. This Marxian for-itself is like the Hegelian in-itself-for-itself. In fact, many times Hegel leaves out his third step to highlight the fact that the essential factor is the becoming, self-affirmation, the self-creation, the self-bringing-forth, that is expressed in the for-itself.

The Subject requires organization and leadership. The Subject is, firstly, an organized physical body. All of the life energies and vital impulses that move the Subject are impossible without this bodily organization. More, the Subject needs an organized idea of what he is to be to make himself, what to put into action to be able to self-actualize. In other words he needs to organize his life project with all the other diverse undertakings that this general project requires.

For the Subject to set out, he requires an organization of the tendencies that will serve to overcome the contradiction between horizontalism and verticalism, democracy and leadership. A certain leadership should be exerted by free will. Without this leadership, subjectivity isn't possible whether in the individual or the collective. For centuries the analogy between the human body and society has served to justify all types of domination. It is functionalism, plain as day, where everybody part has its place and function, and all is commanded by the brain.

But there is another thing to consider about this analogy. The subject is a self-becoming entity that assumes various forms or configurations, in all of which it is all; that is to say all that is of the senses, the perception, self-consciousness, feelings, desires, projects, and Utopia, all is the Subject. The self-projecting of the Subject is the moment of the free will. The leadership role of this free will isn't the type of leadership that is imposed on others, but rather is the condensed kernel of the consensus the Subject has arrived at.

The organization, obviously, functions best when all its moments are in tune with each other. That is to say, when all participate. If free will acts without the senses, it impoverishes the organism. The ascetic decides by force of will to sacrifice the sensual, all feelings, and imagination. This is how the organism dissects itself.

The result is the unhappy conscience or schizophrenic. The Subject does nothing more than jump from one extreme to the other, from emotions to intellect and back to emotions. From *eros* to *logos* and back. In a dialectical loop, the Subject is swamped down in its own contradictions and can't find a way out.

The functioning of a living organism requires all parts to work together. With free will, feelings and emotions find themselves "overtaken." It is the totality of the organism that moves. All parts have been horizontally integrated, and act in an organized fashion, with the leadership from free will. If free will errs in its judgment, the punishment is meted out by way of the body's discomfort.

People don't just exist: they are self-made, self-constructed, self-created. To self-construct the subjectivity of a group of people is to construct a collective will. This isn't simply a mere "will" but the supersession of the collective's potentials. It is a magnificent and enlightening will. It is a will that, to be such, necessarily begs to be expressed by a leader or leaders. They are the measure of the true expression of the collective will.

Here is where we again see the contradiction between horizontalism and organization. Leadership carries an inherent impulse toward domination, full power, and self-perpetuation. This is inevitable. This contradiction can only be overcome if it is clear to all that power truly lies in the base of the group, of the people. The organization has to exercise the will to truly make this part count.

IV The Beautiful Soul and Full Horizontalism

Here, the problem that presents itself is the problem of power, a thorny topic if ever there was one. Max Weber, with his customary wryness and profundity, put it like this: "Whoever intends to engage in politics at all... [is] becoming involved with the diabolical powers that lurk in all force" (Weber). He later defines political action as "a slow drilling through hard boards with both passion and a sense of proportion," adding that "what is possible could never have been achieved if one had not constantly reached for the impossible in the world."

What Weber deems a pact with "diabolical powers" is, in reality, the dialectic of the struggle to the death of recognition on a political level. This dialectic is diabolic when it is thought of with the "Beautiful Soul" in mind. In fact, it is point of view Max Weber—who is no "Beautiful Soul" himself—that declares, "The great virtuosi of the unworldly love of humanity and goodness, whether they come from Nazareth or from Assisi or from the royal palaces of India, did not work with the political means of force."

The Beautiful Soul is the "moral genius," the highest realization of the moral conscience that "knows the inner voice of its immediate knowledge to be a voice divine" and itself holds "divine creative power" (Hegel) that finds expression in the community.

The Beautiful Soul isn't solitary, but rather of a community. In this way, the best of the Subject nests itself in the most remote parts of the Beautiful Soul. What does it lack? It lacks force to externalize itself, the power to make itself a thing, and endure existence (Hegel).

It lacks the bravery to leave itself, to confront the world, its contradictions, its power. It is precisely here where authors like John Holloway tie-in with the Beautiful Soul. During a revolution, or when taking or constructing power, one lands into a vicious circle of power. The struggle is lost once power itself seeps into the struggle, once the logic of power becomes the logic of the revolutionary process, once the negative of refusal is converted into the positive of power-building (Holloway 20002).

The proposal, as a consequence, is the fleeing of power: anti-power. Anti-power is imbued with the most sublime qualities, it "develops forms of self-determination" and is found in the "dignity of everyday existence" and developed in "love relations, friendship, camaraderie, community, cooperation" and culminates in the beautiful affirmation that "dignity (anti-power) exists wherever human beings reside" (Holloway 2002).

Anti-power, like all things "anti-," is a creation of power itself, or is the response of one kind of power to another. Fichte understood this perfectly. To whatever thesis, or statement, or power, there is counter posed a counter-thesis, counter-statement, or counter-power. We never leave the realm of power. The Beautiful Soul flees from power. As a consequence it will suffer the cruelest of endings, which is to be crushed by power.

But power isn't a devilish circle as Foucault urges and Holloway confirms. It's a circle, but not necessarily one that meets itself to form an endless circle. Rather, it is unwinds like a spiral in its overcoming. It only continues in a diabolical endless circle if the logic of domination wins out. But if the bondsman sets out on a path in his struggle to the death for recognition, inequality gives way to levels of equality. Never perfect, never fully formed, but always on the way to greater realization of the Subject.

The Beautiful Soul is like Utopia. It is in a way, itself Utopia. It is the utopic moment of all Subjects. It is what the Subject seeks to be, breathe, desire, aspires. When the Subject falters, it becomes frustrated. To be self-realizing it must wrest power from alienation, confront all obstacles, struggle, move forward.

Horizontalism as well is a utopic moment. It is the "social contract" of Rousseau, the *Republic* of Plato, the ideal *polis* of Aristotle. This moment need not disappear. It should always be present, demanding development of projects that seek to implement the ideas put forward by Utopia.

Utopia and project, horizontalism and verticalism, direct democracy and representation, are moments in the dialectic of totality that is the Subject, whether individual or collective. Utopia without the project is the self-consumed Beautiful Soul, smoke that vanishes into thin air. Project without Utopia is a closing-off, the death of the Subject. Utopia demands its own realization by way of the project and the project demands the contents of Utopia.

Utopia is the impossible. The project is the possible. Wanting the impossible, strongly needing it, is how the possible is realized. Only with grand Utopias can magnificent projects be realized. By wanting a just society, one of brotherhood, we can bring to existence a new society, one in which the inhuman inequalities and oppression that characterize our society today disappear.

Buenos Aires, March 3, 2003

Appendix 2: The "Top-Down" State and the "Bottom-Up" State

Guillermo Almeyra

In several Latin American countries, such as Bolivia, Ecuador or Venezuela, we are currently witnessing efforts to enforce equal rights for indigenous peoples, as well as democracy in the totality of social relations, which form the foundation of the state. At the same time, there is a debate about the construction of forms of governance that best fit the needs of the different social groups that sometimes unite, sometimes simply coexist, or some other times enter processes of differentiation and conflict with each other within the political space of the nation.

In this struggle to escape from the backwardness and poverty that have been exacerbated by the global crisis of capitalism, many different revolutions come together and intermingle: the decolonizing one of the indigenous peoples, the democratic one in favor of national unity, and the anti-capitalist one in its seminal stage. As it turns out, not all revolutionaries pursue social and economic transformation, that is, the construction of non-capitalist relations all the way to the end. As a result, both in the government and in popular organizations everyone talks of revolution, but each one ascribes a different meaning to this concept.

Owing to their relationship with international finance capital and their integration into the global capitalist market, these countries, the same as the other Latin American countries, are characterized by capitalist relations of production and a client state. What is contested in each of these countries is the extent to which neoliberal policies are applied and, therefore, the politics, mode of operation, and sustenance of local capitalist governments. At the same time, the autonomous political activity of the parts of the population that are most oppressed by capital and less integrated into the capitalist lifestyles of consumption, (a state of affairs that governments and the establishment present as something natural), leads them to draw on traditions and remnants of past forms of community organization, apply them to the present struggles, and use them as the basis of new collectivist social relations that are at odds with capitalism.

This gives rise to forms of authority that run parallel to the authority of the capitalist state and its government (e.g., community or labor union police forces, non-official laws and legal institutions). This network of local real powers is gradually making its way into the national constitution, thus becoming established as the nascent expression of a transitional non-capitalist state, created from below and legitimized and legalized through the struggles against the centralized state, which is intertwined with the domestic and foreign capital.

The central state, of course, attempts to defend itself by resorting to violence and cooptation of social leaders in order to unify the country under its rule, since it has no intention of eliminating the capitalist system, but rather of reforming it, of creating an "Andean" or vernacular variant of capitalism. The state insists only on formal equality before the law (for example between an owner of a big mine and a member of an indigenous community) rather than on the development of autonomy and widespread social self-management that could create the conditions for a "voluntary federation of free communes," which, as Marx suggested, might mark the transition to socialism and the dissolution of the state to make way for a new social organization in which, to quote Saint Simon, "the government of people would be replaced by the administration of things."

On the one hand, the revolutionaries of the modernization of the state, like García Linera, Bolivia's vice president, want to reinforce the unitary, centralist aspect of the state in the Constitution and convert the state into an efficient apparatus for the capitalist development of the country, ending corruption, regionalism and caste privileges. This centralist stance leads them to detest autonomies. On the other hand, autonomy and self-management revolutionaries want to strengthen the nascent bottom-up state that is still under construction and promote the collective decision-making processes of the assemblies of indigenous peoples and communities of all kinds, which are protected by the current Bolivian constitution, but are violated by the modernization-revolutionaries when this suits their interests, with resort to violence rather than consensus.

If there was a consultation of those whose territory, life and culture is directly affected by the technical or economic options proposed, (e.g. on whether to build a highway through a virgin forest or circumvent it and opt for other areas that do not reject the project) not only the political consensus supporting the government would be reinforced, but also citizenship, critical thinking and democracy would be promoted.

Jacobinism, *caudillismo* (warlordism), verticalism, the use of the state apparatus to impose policies designed behind the back of the real subjects of social change, are all phenomena that weaken the very state they are trying to modernize and strengthen. The driving force of change in Venezuela is not Chavez's government, but the organization, raising of consciousness and capacity for initiative of those who support Chavez, and on which his government rests. A "citizens' revolution" in Ecuador without the left, the indigenous and leftist environmentalism would depend only on the questionable discipline of the armed forces.

Of course, the network of autonomies and self-managements should yet be constructed and reinforced in order to become a state, rather than a "state from below." Moreover, we have to improve the existing distorted and inadequate state and employ it for navigating the world market, as well as for mending social injustices in the national field. However, if we opt for social change we must build consensus, autonomy, self-organization, self-management, democracy.

(*This article appeared originally in* La Jornada, *Mexico*)

CHAPTER 13

The Zapatistas and the Dialectic*

> *The Time of the No, the Time of the Yes. ...* We defined the "*no*," we still haven't fully delineated the "*yes*." ... "could it be another way?" This question could be the one that sparks rebellion and its broader acceptance. And this could be because there is a "*no*" that has birthed it: *it doesn't have to be this way. ...* We have gotten to this point because our realities, histories, and rebellions have brought us to this "*it doesn't have to be this way*." This and also because, intuitively or by design, we have answered "yes" to the question, "could it be another way?" We still need to respond to the questions we encounter after that "yes." What is that other way, that other world, that other society that we imagine, that we want, that we need? What do we have to do? With whom? If we don't know the answers to those questions we have to look for them. And if we have them, we have to make them known among ourselves.
>
> SUBCOMANDANTE MARCOS, "Them and Us Part V—'The Sixth'," January 2013

On December 21, 2012, in the Mayan calendar the end of an era and the beginning of a new one, 45,000 Indigenous Zapatistas (*Tzeltales, Tzotziles, Tojolobales, Choles, Zoques*, and *Mames*) occupied the streets of five cities in Chiapas in a disciplined, silent outpouring. "*Did you listen?*" read the Zapatistas Communication. "It is the sound of your world crumbling. It is the sound of our world resurging. The day that was day, was night. And night shall be the day that will be day. Democracy! Liberty! Justice!" read the Zapatista communique.

This March in Silence was followed by a series of additional Zapatista communications over the next several weeks, "Them and Us," from Subcomandante Insurgente Marcos and others in the name of the Clandestine Indigenous

---

* In writing on the Zapatistas and the dialectic there is no intent to "fit" the Zapatista struggle into some kind of ready-made dialectic. This would be both a mechanical reductionism of the Zapatistas and a misreading of the revolutionary nature of the dialectic. The Zapatistas do not fit into anything. They are a most original self-creation. In turn, as we examined earlier, the dialectic is not a static structure to be filled with content, but an emancipatory practice/view unfolding anew at each historic moment. Rather, what we wish to explore is the possible resonance, concordance between the dialectic, as historically developed first in Hegel and then in Marx, and the mode of activity and thought that the Zapatistas are in the process of living today—what I would term an ongoing, living dialectic.

Revolutionary Committee—General Command of the Zapatista National Liberation Army (EZLN), in which they described "the (un)reasonable ones" above (Them) and "the Pains of Those Below" (Us). In one document Marcos created the category: *"The Time of the No, the Time of the Yes."* The "No" referred to their decades-long struggle against the bad government, the old political parties, the economic system that has despoiled Mexico's land and subjugated its peoples. "No" as an act of resistance and rebellion.

The "Yes" was first a question, "Could there be another way?" born out of the "No": *"It doesn't have to be this way."* Other questions followed: "What is that other way, that other world, that other society that we imagine, that we want, that we need?" And, "With whom" will we construct it? Marcos continued: "If we don't know the answers to those questions we have to look for them. And if we have them, we have to make them known among ourselves."

These Zapatista questions, this concept of *"The Time of the No, the Time of the Yes,"* together with their concrete practice, their struggle to build autonomy, what they refer to as "Freedom according to the Zapatistas," I see resonating with the *dialectic* in Hegel and in Marx. As we explored in Part I, it was this philosophic expression, dialectic, that gave word to the emancipatory struggles of women and men throughout history: The dialectic that G.W.F. Hegel forged under the impact of the great French Revolution was a revolution in thought that Karl Marx, in turn, transformed into a philosophy of revolution—*revolution in permanence.*

The question, of course, is not whether the Zapatistas discerned liberatory threads between their ideas and actions and those of Hegel and of Marx. The Zapatistas surely create dialectic in their own time and place with their own practice and thought. *The dialectic is in life and not alone in books.*

And yet, in exploring, at one and the same time, the living *praxis* of the Zapatistas, the dialectic in Hegel's major philosophic writings, and in Marx's dialectical thought and practice, can we find common threads that can assist us in reaching toward an emancipatory future? Can we find in the outpouring of documents that were written following the March in Silence of December 21, 2012 categories of theory/practice that reach toward moments of the dialectic in Hegel and in Marx? In turn, does the dialectic of Hegel and of Marx find new life, re-creation, in the action and thought of the Indigenous masses in rebellion in Chiapas in the last two plus decades? Is there a two-way road in the biography of the Idea of Freedom as worked out historically and as it is created anew today? Does the labor, practical and theoretical, of the Zapatistas, precisely because they are in a new moment of time and place—or as the Zapatistas express it, of "calendar and geography"—enrich dialectical thought for our day, and move us toward a freedom-based future?

I want to begin by looking at certain ideas of the Zapatistas that are rich moments of theoretical expression found not only in their political analyses, but as well, in their stories, and in all cases, emanating from their experience, their practice.

I "The Time of the No and the Time of the Yes"

As we noted above, the time of the no refers to being against the bad government, the old political parties, etc., while the time of the yes asks how we build the new. Further, the document noted that the Yes comes out of the No—it doesn't have to be this way. Dialectical thought as we saw in Chapter 2 is centered on negation, on a No. Emerging out of that negation is a second negation, a negation of the negation that contains the positive, a yes, the positive emerging out of the negative. When "translated" in Marxian terms of revolution, we can speak of a revolution having a dual rhythm—the destruction of the old (negation or first negation) and the construction of the new (negation of the negation, the positive within the negative, or second negation). It is crucial to not separate first and second negation, of not putting into separate stages the destruction of the old and the construction of the new, but making them an integrated whole. When this double rhythm of revolution is fractured, one ends up with revolutions that are incomplete and transformed into opposite.

The Zapatista time of the no and time of the yes breaks with the tendency of many revolutionary movements to focus only on what they are against and fail to work out what they are for. The Zapatistas, in positing the need for the positive in the negative, the emergence of ideas, explorations—the time of the Yes emerging out of the time of the No—are constructing anew a radical dialectic that reaches toward an emancipatory future.

II The Zapatista Concept of Time

In one of the communications, Insurgente Moisés, an Indigenous Tzeltal and rector of the Zapatista Little School, discussed how the Zapatista sees time:

> The time has come, and its moment too. There are times that all human beings experience, good or bad; one is born, comes into the world, dies, and is gone. Those are times. But there is another time, in which one can decide in what direction to walk, a time when the time arrives to look at time. That is, when one can understand life, how life should be, here in

this world, and that no one can be the owner of that which makes up the world.

We were born indigenous and we are indigenous. We know that we came into the world and that we will leave this world. That is the law. We began to walk through life and we realized that we as indigenous people were not doing so well, we saw what happened to our great great great grandfathers and grandmothers, that is, in 1521, in 1810, and in 1910, that we were always used, that we gave our lives so that others could take power, that once in power they forgot about us again and went back to disrespecting, robbing, repressing, and exploiting us.

And we encountered a third time. The third time is where we are now, for a while now we've been walking, running, learning, working, falling, and getting back up. This is important because one has to record, to fill a tape that can be reproduced later with more lives from other times. Yes, we have been left a full bag of tapes, even though some of us aren't here anymore. So others continue on and the process moves forward like that, and what is yet to come is yet to come, until we get to the end and we begin that other work of construction, where another world begins to be born, where they cannot screw us over again and where we are not forgotten as original peoples, we will not allow that again. Now we have learned. We want to live well, in equality, in the city and the countryside, where the people of the city and the people of the countryside rule and the government obeys, and if it doesn't, it gets kicked out, and another is instituted.

ENLACE ZAPATISTA, 2013

Moisés is writing of several dimensions of time:

1. "[O]ne is born, comes into the world, dies, and is gone. Those are times." A straight-forward linear time.
2. "But there is another time, in which one can decide in what direction to walk, a time when the time arrives to look at time. That is, when one can understand life, how life should be, here in this world, and that no one can be the owner of that which makes up the world." Here is the time when *Ya Basta* is shouted and a collective decision made to change life.
3. "The third time is where we are now... walking, running, learning, working, falling, and getting back up" This is a time which remembers others, "the tapes," memories of their struggles, and as well, a time that reaches for the future: "[W]e begin that other work of construction, where another world

begins to be born, where they cannot screw us over again and where we are not forgotten as original peoples, we will not allow that again."

I see these various expressions of time in concert with Marx's view of time. He had worked out the real measure of capitalist time, with the category "socially necessary labor time," wherein the extraction of value and surplus value takes place: a worker's concrete labor is transmuted into abstract labor, the heart of alienated labor. In bourgeois society "Time is everything. *Man is nothing*; he is, at the most, *time's carcass*."

At the same time Marx posed time free from capitalism's shackles: "But *time is in fact* the active existence of the human being. It is not only the measure of human life; it is the space for its development." Laboring outside the capitalist integument "acquires a quite different, a free character, it becomes real social labor." And further, beyond this necessary realm lies "*disposable time*," where "the realm of freedom really begins."

For both Moisés and Marx there is an active *human* subject to transform time into free human existence. With Moisés, it is the living resistance and struggle of the Indigenous who transform time. With Marx, the proletariat was singled out as the living force to abolish capitalist labor time and open the realm of disposable time.

III The Rewinds: Our Dead, the Living, Biographies, Diversity, Stories, Our History, and Other Subjects

In three documents called "Rewinds," written in November and December 2012, Subcomandante Marcos undertook a "retrospective/perspective," on how the Zapatistas see their history, the present moment, and walking toward the future—their view of the path of rebellion, resistance, and struggle for freedom. Here, there will be no attempt to summarize these rich, complex essays. (They can be read in full at http://enlacezapatista.ezln.org.mx/) Rather, I want to single out certain developments that I see speaking to the question of the Zapatistas and the dialectic.

A *Rewind 1—When the Dead Silently Speak Out*

In one part of this document Marcos writes of a nun known as Chapis, who "was with us," working tirelessly for the *collective* Zapatista cause. It was story of an *individual* who had made her decision to participate in the Indigenous struggle with the Zapatistas in Chiapas. His relating of this little history became a discussion of the relation of the individual and the collective: "The struggle [for freedom] is collective, but the decision to struggle is individual, personal, intimate, as is the decision to go on or to give up."

Marcos examined this dialectic of individual-collective not alone in what has been occurring in Zapatista territory, but also as a wider view:

> [W]hat makes the old wheel of history move are collectives and not individuals. Historiography thrives on individualities but history learns from a people. Am I saying that we don't have to write/study history? No, but what I am saying is that it is best done in the only way that it can be done, that is to say, organized with others. Because… when rebellion is individual it is pretty. But when it is collective and organized it is terrible and marvelous. The former is the material of biographies; the latter is what makes history.
>
> ENLACE ZAPATISTA, 2013–2014

He sees this rebellion in all of humanity: "[R]ebellion… does not belong exclusively to the neozapatistas. It belongs to humanity. And that is something that must be celebrated. Everywhere, everyday and all the time. Because rebellion is also a celebration."

At the same time that rebellion is universal to humanity, it is specifically, concretely Zapatista at this moment, with rebels from many geographies recognizing and seeking association with it:

> The bridges that have been built from all corners of the plant Earth to these lands and skies are neither few nor weak. Sometimes with gazes, sometimes with words, always with our struggle, we have crossed them to embrace that other who resists and struggles. Maybe that's what it means, not anything else, to be '*compañeros*,' to cross bridges.
>
> ENLACE ZAPATISTA, 2013–2014

Marcos expresses ideas that both look back and forward—a "retrospective-perspective":

> It is these men, women and others [like the nun Chapis] who always, alive or dead, place themselves before Power, not as victims, but to challenge it with the multiple flag of below and to the left. They are our *compañeras compañeros y compañeroas*… although in the majority of cases neither they nor we know it… yet.

This "… yet" portends freedom struggles to come. Marcos ended *Rewind 1* with the following:

To those who carried a backpack and history on their backs in the night.
To those who took lightning and thunder in their hands.
To those who put on their boots without having a future.
To those who covered their face and their name.
To those who died without expecting anything in return.
So that others, everyone, in a morning that is yet to come, would
be able to see the day as we must,
that is to say, head-on, on our feet, and with the gaze and the heart upright.
For them, there are neither biographies nor museums,
For them our memory and rebellion,
For them, our cry:
liberty! Liberty! LIBERTY!

B *Rewind 2—On Death and Other Alibis*

Marcos continued his discussion of the relation of the living and the dead in Rewind 2, noting that at times the living think they have a "copyright" on the lives of the dead, writing biographies and histories, often with the purpose of obscuring rather than revealing actuality. His critique is merciless: "[U]seless cult of historiography from above... [is] nothing other than an infantile way to domesticate history from below." In sharp contrast, Marcos puts forth the Zapatista view: "What is important is the path [of rebellion, resistance, struggle, freedom] not the one who walks it."

He elaborates on this view with rhetorical questions which against touch on the relation of the individual and the collective: "Does the decision to struggle made by [various Zapatistas *compañeros* who have died] matter because someone gave it a name, a calendar and a geography? Or because that decision was collective and there are those who continue to carry it out?"

And he poses more questions: "[D]o we ask ourselves 'did we take a step along the path?" and "will someone keep walking it?" "What I mean to say is, does it matter who we are? Or does it matter what we do?" The "answers" Marcos gives become new points of departure for thinking about and acting in freedom struggles (Enlace Zapatista, 2013–2014)

> I feel that the accounting I have to give to our dead is in regard to what has been done, what still has to be done and what we are doing to complete or fulfill what first motivated this struggle. ... the conditions of injustice, of slavery (which is the real name for the lack of freedom) and of authoritarianism.

•

> It was not the eagerness to 'survive' but a sense of duty that put us here, for better or for worse. It was the necessity to do something in the face of millennial injustice; the indignation that we felt was the most forceful characteristic of 'humanity.'

•

> [Justice] means putting an end to the repetition of injustice, so that it cannot simple change the name, the face, the flag, ideological alibi, or political, racial or gendered justification.

•

> We [honor our dead] by struggling, every day, every hour. And on and on until we meet the ground, first at eye level, and then above us, covering us with the step of a *compañero.*

•

> [F]or those masked men and women here the struggle that matters to them isn't the one that has been won or lost. It's the struggle that lies ahead, and for that calendars and geographies must be prepared. There are no definitive battles for either victors of vanquished. The struggle continues and those that today bask in their victory will see their world crumble.

•

> Statues and authoritarianism have to be taken down from below, so as to assure that the base upon which they stood disappears and thus to assure that a new face doesn't simply replace the one that was there before.

Marcos' discussion in Rewinds 1 and 2 are powerful indictments of histories and biographies written by those above, as well as those by intellectuals who feel themselves to be progressive, but who write in isolation from the collective movement for freedom that emerges and has its creative power from below (*desde abajo*). It is that collective movement from below that Marcos argues is the key to transforming social change.

I would argue that Marcos *is* writing history and biography, but in a completely different, revolutionary manner. The Marxist-Humanist philosopher Dunayevskaya, who wrote of history as masses in motion, and "biographies" of Marx as philosopher of revolution-in-permanence, had a provocative expression on biography—"The only biography worth writing is the biography of an Idea." And that Idea was freedom! Marcos is writing a Zapatista "history," "biographies" of those fallen Zapatistas, or those who were with the Zapatistas, precisely as the biography of the Idea of freedom in the Southwest of Mexico, in a state called Chiapas.

C *Rewind 3—EZLN Communication Written for Their 30th Anniversary*

Rewind Three's (Enlace Zapatista, 2013–2014) focus is first on a story that Marcos said was related to him by Durito (the beetle that Marcos has communicated with often) about another unusual being—a "cat-dog" or dog-cat. Second, Marcos will tell how the Zapatistas see their own history.

In Rewind 2 Marcos had written "[I]s [it] better to tell a story... or write a biography... or put up a monument [?] Of those three things, I am firmly convinced that the only the first is worthwhile."

In Rewind 3 he begins with a story, that of "cat-dog." No words can substitute for Marcos,' and I will not attempt to do so, only singling out two or three concepts in Marcos' telling of the cat-dog story. The conversation is between Durito and "cat-dog." One crucial concept is that of *difference*, especially "fear of difference." The cat-dog explains that he is neither cat nor dog, but cat-dog. Durito, the beetle, and cat-dog converse on this concept of difference and the fanaticism that insists on either/or, refusing to recognize difference, and thus be open to alternative ways of being, doing and thinking:

> *"But, how does one avoid ending up in one of the sinister rooms of that grim house of mirrors that is fanaticism?* [*asks the beetle Durito*]. *How does one resist the pressure and the blackmail to join in and embrace religious or lay fanaticism... the oldest kind, yes, but not the only current one?*
>
> *"It's simple," said the cat-dog laconically, "don't join. Build many houses, each their own. Abandon the fear of difference. Because there is something that is the same as or worse than a religious fanatic, and that is an anti-religious fanatic, or secular fanaticism. And I say that it could be worse because the latter uses reason as an alibi. And, of course, it has its equivalents: homophobia and sexism, phobia of heterosexuality and hembrismo* [*the assumed moral superiority of women*]. *And you can add to this the long etcetera of the history of humanity. The fanatics of race, color, creed, gender, politics, sport, etc., are, in the end, fanatics of themselves. They all share*

> *the same fear of difference. And they pigeonhole the entire world in the closed box of exclusive options: "if you aren't this, than you must be its opposite...*
>
> *"Avoid the trap which holds that freedom is the power to choose between the two imposed options. All categorical options are a trap. There are not only two paths, just as there are not just two colors, two sexes, or two beliefs. The answer is neither here nor there. It is better to make a new path that goes where one wants to go...*
>
> *"And let no one neither judge nor condemn that which they do not understand, because difference is a sign that all is not lost, that we still have a lot to see and to hear, that there are still other worlds to discover..."*

Following the cat-dog story Marcos turns to explain "the way in which the Zapatistas see and are seen in their own history." For the Zapatistas it is a *living history*: "It's necessary to clarify that for us, our history is not just who we have been, what has happened to us, and what we have done. It is also and above all, what we want to be and do."

Later he notes, "[O]ur way of explaining our history seems like an image of continuous and repetitive movement, with some variations that give that sense of mobile immobility: always attacked and persecuted, always resisting; always being annihilated, always reappearing." This is history-in-the-making, a reaching for the future.

In discussing how the Zapatistas see their history, Marcos speaks of a kaleidoscope to put forth the succession of changing images and actions he wishes to describe and critique. First is an old film clip (1894) *"Annie Oakley"* showing the cowgirl shooting a coin flipped into the air, bringing "civilization." Every one admires her shooting as well as the government employee flipping the coin. But, Marcos notes, the coin being shot at over and over is us, the Indigenous.

Next is a film clip from 1895 called *"The Arrival of a Train."* The train signified "progress," the modern. Marcos explains, "We were the ones who stayed on the platform while the train of progress came and went." He then notes that someone from the outside will perhaps comment, "We have here another example of why the indigenous are how they are—because they don't want to progress." But Marcos responds, "The pertinent question is not why we don't board the train, but why you all don't get off of it." In contrast to those from the outside, the so-called civilized, are

> those who come to be with us, to look at us looking at ourselves, to listen to us, to learn from us in the little school, discover that in each still shot [in the Zapatistas' own film] we Zapatistas have aggregated an image that

> is not perceptible at first glance. It is as if the apparent movement of the images hides the particular that each still shot contains. That which is not seen in the daily comings and goings is the history that we are. And no smartphone captures those images. Only with a very big heart can they be detected.

In ending Rewind 3, Marcos summarizes as follows:

> This is our history. Because when we Zapatistas draw a key below and to the left in each still shot in our movie, we are thinking not about what door to open, but about what house with what door we need to create so that this key will have a purpose and a destiny. And if the soundtrack of this movie has the rhythm of polka-ballad-corrido-ranchera-cumbia-rock-ska-metal-reggae-trova-punk-hip-hop-rap-and-whatever else is added, it's not because we don't have musical taste. It's because this house will have all colors and all sounds. And there will be therefore new gazes and new ears that will understand our efforts... even if we are only silence and shadow in those future worlds. Ergo: we have imagination; they only have plans with terminal options. That's why their world is crumbling. That's why ours is resurging, just like that little light that, although small, is not less when embraced by shadow.

This is a remarkable ending to a remarkable document. The Zapatistas have written often recently of the need to be "from below and to the left." Here Marcos gives the meaning, the significance, of this concept. The Zapatistas draw a *key* from below and to the left. The key is not to open a door of an already existing house. It is not a "tool," "the answer" to "solve our problems." Rather, with this "key" of being from below and to the left, we can figure out what kind of houses and doors to construct so that "from below and to the left" will have "a purpose and a destiny": from a concept, an idea, to the active creating of a new world in the future—"this house will have all colors and all sounds."

•••

Why have we sought to explore the resonance between the practice and theory of the Zapatistas as found in their three decades of existence, there two decades of open struggle for autonomy 1994 to the present, ("freedom according to the Zapatistas"), their decade of the Good Government Councils [*Juntas de Buen Goberino*] *and* the dialectic as forged by Hegel and then again by Marx?

Because counter-revolution has so quickly following many of the revolutions of the 20th and now the 21st century, and in fact such counter-revolution is often found *within* revolutionary transformations, it is necessary to explicitly explore the relationship between the dialectic in life and the dialectic in thought, between philosophy and revolution, between action and thought. It is crucial to discern the threads between the rebellions and revolutionary beginnings of the here and now, as seen so explicitly in the Zapatistas, and the philosophy of human emancipation that Hegel and then Marx constructed. When we grasp and practice this dialectic of absolute negativity, negation of the negation—the positive (the "yes") inside the negative (the "no")—we can reach toward new human beginnings, the creation of a world that contains within the place/space for the many worlds that humanity *is* in its very being. A revolution in thought is as needed as a revolution in practice.

This dialectic is not a static entity, imposed externally as "the answer." Rather, it is a way of thinking and doing, "the power of negativity" that comes alive again and again, when human beings, rebels and revolutionaries, the vast social movements from below, re-create it in their practices and thinking. Working out for our day such a historically grounded world view of freedom goes hand in hand with having our eyes and ears, our energies and efforts, on the ongoing movements from below. It is the voices and actions in these movements that are the source of emancipatory change, as it is the methodology of the revolutionary dialectic that gives us the ability to comprehensively grasp the significance of the movements from below. The two labors, discerning the meaning of emancipatory philosophy and the meaning of liberation action, are not two separate tasks, but one and the same.

To recover and recreate the dialectic is to root ourselves in what has been the *praxis* of humanity throughout history. It is this practice, this method that the rulers strive to keep hidden from us. As well, many activists seeking revolutionary change have, unfortunately, ignored, or mystified emancipatory philosophy. To become practicing dialecticians, is not to possess "the word" in any elitist, vanguardist manner. Rather, it is to bring together as one, humanity's historical struggles for freedom expressed as method and the here and now of our determination to uproot the old and create the new: Utopia and the dialectic in fusion.

The Zapatistas, and many, many others, are the ones who make the dialectic alive for our day. Our obligation is to join them in thought and action. Forging the dialectic anew in thought and in life—that is, creating a new, human world—is the challenge we all face.

CHAPTER 14

Marx, Hegel and Dunayevskaya—Toward a Dialectic of Philosophy and Organization in the Context of Latin American Liberation

1 Marx and the Present Moment in Latin America

Twenty-first century capitalism in Latin America is a dysfunctional monster. It despoils our land, pollutes our waters, and contaminates the very air we breathe. It exploits and degrades the lives of our people. If we are "lucky" enough to have a job, we are reduced to "abstract labor," measured as "socially necessary labor time" wherein, "time is everything, *man is nothing*; he is, at the most, *time's carcass*" (Marx). The opposite side of the same coin is capitalism's inability to provide work. The informal economy is in fact the "real" economy for tens of millions who cannot find employment and who must scramble in thousands of different ways to survive. What Eduardo Galeano wrote of so profoundly four decades ago in *Open Veins of Latin America* (1997)—our "meshing... into the universal gearbox of capitalism," (12)—has become further intensified in the twenty-first century. If speculative, financial capitalism brought forth the recent crisis in United States and Europe, *extractive capitalism*—pillaging our natural resources and prostituting our lands to raise crops for the international market—has been our Latin American fate. The extraction of value and surplus value from sweated labor in mine, field and factory, makes its appearance in the exchange value accumulated in the pockets of the bosses residing in Latin America, in the U.S. and in Europe. In our pockets a few crumbs, in our lives poverty and hunger. Marx, writing a century and a half ago, put his finger on the pulse of this central contradiction of capitalism:

> In our days, everything seems pregnant with its contrary: Machinery, gifted with the wonderful power of shortening and fructifying human labor, we behold starving and overworking it. The newfangled sources of wealth, by some strange weird spell, are turned into sources of want... At the same pace that mankind masters nature, man seems to become enslaved to other men or to his own infamy. Even the pure light of science seems unable to shine but on the dark background of ignorance. All our invention and progress seem to result in endowing material forces with intellectual life, and in stultifying human life into a material force. This antagonism between modern industry and science on the one hand, modern misery and dissolution on the other hand; this antagonism

> between the productive powers and the social relations of our epoch is a fact, palpable, overwhelming, and not to be controverted.
>
> Speech at the anniversary of the *People's Paper,* April 19, 1856

At the same time, today there is something deeply stirring on our lands. In the Americas, south of the behemoth of the North, rage is brewing. At times it is present as a quiet dignity. But make no mistake. It can come forth as well in a deafening and earthshaking roar. What one perceives is the *permanence* of resistance and rebellion. How can our rage reach the form of uprooting social change, the fullness of revolution?

This, of course, rests in the hands of tens upon tens of millions, women and men, *the wretched of the earth,* the revolutionary subjects who proclaim "*Ya basta!,*" and who move to carry out emancipatory social transformation with their force and reason, their muscle and mind. Each historic moment calls forth new human forces specific to their circumstances. Marx wrote of the new human force that arose with industrial capitalism: "We know that to work well the new-fangled forces of society, they only want to be mastered by newfangled men—and such are the working men. They are as much the invention of modern time as machinery itself" (*People's Party* speech). In *Capital* he expressed this as "*new forces* and *new passions* [that] spring up in the bosom of society." In recent decades, the bosom of Latin American has brought forth diverse "*new forces* and *new passions*"—Indigenous, women, *campesinos,* youth and others. Without negating the revolutionary subjectivity of the proletariat, these revolutionary subjects have become crucial strands in the struggle against the rule of capital in our lands.

Again, Galeano wrote of this: "It is a big load of rottenness that has to be sent to the bottom of the sea on the march to Latin America's reconstruction. The task lies in the hands of the disposed, the humiliated, the accused. The Latin American cause is above all a social cause: the rebirth of Latin America must start with the overthrow of its masters, country by country. We are entering times of rebellion and change" (*Open Veins*).

In Mexico, Subcomandante Marcos singled out the Indigenous dimension in Chiapas: "How will this new voice make itself heard in these lands and across the country?... This wind will come from the mountains. It is already being born under the trees and is conspiring for a new world, so new that it is barely an intuition in the collective heart that inspires it." The two decades since the 1994 rebellion have manifested the concrete presence of this collective heart in the Indigenous Zapatista communities in resistance. Twenty-first century capitalism has indeed brought forth its own many gravediggers. As we have examined in this study, we have no lack of revolutionary subjectivity in the Latin America world.

And yet we still live under the rule of capital in its diverse forms and horrors, not excluding the threat of humanity's complete destruction. Why? A central reason is certainly the power of capital itself. Even in crisis, it remains a monstrous power, gorging itself on everything within its reach. Marx's description of capitalism's logic—"accumulation for accumulation's sake, production for production's sake"—has yielded disastrous consequences for the environment—including the ongoing climate change whose effects we have barely begun to experience—and for all of humanity. We need not rehearse its everyday consequences in terms of the destruction, the immiseration of human life.

At the same time, there has been the failure of many revolutionaries to come to grips both with the fullness of Marx's critique of capitalism—how deep an uprooting he discerned as necessary—and with the totality of the emancipatory vision this "philosopher of revolution in permanence" posed: his "new humanism."

The near century and a half since *Capital's* publication has witnessed perverse miss-interpretations, and crude vulgarizations of Marx's Marxism. The most grievous manifestation of this was the transformation of the Russian Revolution into a state-capitalist monstrosity under Stalin in the name of "Marxism." For very concrete class reasons, ruler and ruled, Stalinist theoreticians sought to vulgarize and hide the profound analysis of capitalist production found in *Capital*. In the Soviet Union, many workers certainly recognized Marx's analysis of the split to the category of labor into concrete and abstract labor in their own lives that was at the heart of this "workers' paradise." But many Marxist intellectuals and revolutionaries outside Russia were taken in by this deliberate obfuscation of Marx's thought.

It was not only mistaken interpretations of Marx's analysis of capitalism that were manifest in the 20th century. As well, there was the failure to comprehend Marx not alone for his profound analysis of capital, but as the revolutionary activist-thinker working out ideas and practices to help birth a new, human society—*Marx as "philosopher of revolution in permanence."* We will return to this subject in Section III below.

II Hegel's Revolution in Philosophy—From Master Slave to Absolute Negativity

The concept of Spirit in *Phenomenology of Spirit* is one of *liberation*.[1] The section on master–slave—in the transition from consciousness to self-consciousness—

1 Refer back to Chapter 2 of the present study for my discussion of Spirit. See also Chapter 1 in Gogol (2002).

is a manifestation of this movement toward liberation. It has been subject to numerous commentaries and interpretations. Its origins were often attributed to slavery in Greek times. However, *Phenomenology* was written during the time of the Haitian Revolution, and recent scholarship argues that the Hegel's master–slave dialectic was created under its impact.[2]

Among the interpretations of master–slave are ones that seek to read this dialectic with eyes of the last half of 20th century and the early 21st century. Simone de Beauvoir wrote in the *Second Sex* that "Certain passages in the argument employed by Hegel in defining the relation of master to slave apply much better to the relation of man to woman" (See also Mills 1996). Frantz Fanon in *Black Skin White Masks* explored "Hegel and the Negro," asking what happens to the dialectic when the slave is black and the master white. The master–slave dialectic has as well been commented upon in relation to the capitalist and the worker. In Latin American thinkers have seen master–slave in the relation of Latin America (as slave) to Europe and the U.S. (as master).[3]

The richness of Hegel's dialectic has thus given birth to many creative readings. And surely new ones will arise as the Hegelian dialectic is constantly being born anew within the world of here and now. My focus here will not be an analysis of any of these readings. Rather, I want to speak to the needed *fullness* of any reading: How to create the concretization of master–slave for a given historic moment and place, *while at the same time grasping the universal dimension of the Hegelian emancipatory dialectic?* The challenge is one of constructing *concrete universals*. This, even when some of Hegel's own attempts at concretizations—see his *Lectures on World History*, his *Philosophy of Right*—, failed to create concrete universals that were true to the emancipatory spirit of his dialectic in *Phenomenology of Spirit*.

With the important exception of Fanon, the primary focus of most post-Hegel commentaries has been on the dimension of domination within the master–slave dialectic. As important and necessary as have been such readings, does a focus primarily on domination end up as self-limiting, even while yielding important illuminations? Clearly, the Hegelian dialectic of master–slave brings forth the dimension of domination. At the same time, it does so within the context of a "voyage of discovery," the existence and development of the Hegelian concept of *spirit*, that is, of liberation. This voyage, the Hegelian "labor, patience and suffering of the negative" that reaches for absolute negativity, is the positive within the negative. The fullness of the dialectic reaches

2 See Chapter 4 "Haiti, 1986–1993: The Uprooting (*Dejoucki*), the Flood (*Lavalas*) and the Repression," for my commentary on this.

3 For my commentary on this theme, see Gogol (2002). One Latin American thinker who has written recently on the master–slave dialectic is Jorge Veraza (2005).

from master–slave to absolute knowing, and this absolute negativity is the voyage of overcoming domination through liberation.

The dialectic of master–slave concretely reveals the reality of domination *inseparable* from the reaching for liberation. Hegel expressed this as the slave gaining of mind of his [her] own. If his dialectic stopped at only revealing domination, there could have been no movement to mind. However, in moving from consciousness to self-consciousness we do not stop with consciousness of the master's dominance, but reach beyond toward a future free of domination—the liberated slave practicing with his/her mind.

The master–slave dialectic is thus not alone one of domination, but of resistance and rebellion. It is where the uniqueness of the dialectic as *both* negation (against domination) *and* negation of the negation (constructing liberation) emerges. "Gaining a mind of one's own" is not the end of the dialectic. Rather, a negation of this negation, the beginning of the possibility of a deeper liberation is present.

At the same time, Hegel demonstrated the pitfalls that are present when practicing with one's mind. He argued that the slave with his/her newly gained self-consciousness, must now face the totality of objectivity, the whole world, with its contradictions, its barriers to full freedom. The first of those pitfalls, seen as stages of thought, are skepticism, stoicism and unhappy consciousness. Thus dialectic was not only against the external other who dominated, the master, but was a dialectic in which one must confront not only the external barriers, but the internal ones that stop the slave from fully practicing with a mind of one's own—that is, incomplete attitudes to objectivity. We will not here follow Hegel's voyage through to *Phenomenology's* final chapter, Absolute Knowing. Though master–slave is an early moment within the Hegelian dialectic, the methodology of negation and negation of the negation, is present there in embryo, as the pathway toward absolute liberation.

It was this methodology, a revolution in philosophy, which Marx grasped and re-created as a philosophy of revolution. The great divide between Hegel and Marx was not on the question of idealism verses materialism. Marx wrote of his philosophy as a thoroughgoing naturalism or humanism that was neither idealism nor materialism but the unity of the two. The Hegelian dialectic was not rejected by Marx, but forged anew with a living revolutionary subject. Marx's great separation and critique of Hegel was a refusal to accept a dehumanized dialectic, a dialectic of spirit outside the corporal presence of humanity. The Marxian dialectic put humanity as its center. It was not a rejection of, but a fulfillment of, the emancipatory core of the Hegelian dialectic.

III Dunayevskaya's Reading of the Dialectic in Marx—Its Significance for Today[4]

The four decades-long thought-dive of Dunayevskaya into Marx's Marxism in relation to the objective-subjective situation in the post-World War II world yielded a vast corpus of work on the significance of Marx for the second half of 20th century.[5] Indeed, her explorations help us grasp the significance of Marx for our century. Here, I want to take up two categories that she created in her exploration of Marx that can provide vantage points for exploring the importance of Marx in Latin America at the present moment: 1) Marx as Philosopher of Permanent Revolution; 2) Post-Marx Marxists as Category of Critique.

A *Marx as Philosopher of Permanent Revolution*

In tracing out Marx's concept of revolution-in-permanence, Dunayevskaya was not seeking to be encyclopedic in locating Marx's every use of this term. Rather, she was exploring the significance, the meaning(s), of this concept for Marx. She arrived at the conclusion that revolution in permanence summed up the trajectory of Marx's thought and practice, and used the expression Marx as Philosopher of Revolution in Permanence. Dunayevskaya not only discussed Marx's most well known use of the term in his March 1850 Address to the Communist League, but showed its presence in the young Marx of 1843, when he was in the process of breaking totally with bourgeois society. Most crucially, she showed the presence of this *concept* even when the words "permanent revolution," were not used, whether in his studies of "economics" in the 1850s and 1860s, or his probing of revolutionary subjects outside of the West European world in the last decade of his life. We will briefly trace Dunayevskaya's tracing of these different moments, finding the concept of a philosophy of revolution in permanence as a continual thread within Marx, a tracing which she titled "Marx's Theory of Permanent Revolution, 1843–83," when writing of it in her *Rosa Luxemburg, Women's Liberation, and Marx's Philosophy of Revolution.* Dunayevskaya cited Marx's first discussion of the concept writing:

> [I]n the very first year he broke with bourgeois society, 1843, and even when he was writing on a 'mere' individual subject like the "Jewish

4 For Dunayevskaya's reading of the dialectic in Hegel see Chapter 2 of the present study.

5 See her "Trilogy of Revolution": *Marxism and Freedom, Philosophy and Revolution,* and *Rosa Luxemburg, Women's Liberation, and Marx's Philosophy of Revolution,* as well as her documents in *The Raya Dunayevskaya Collection.*

> Question," Marx refused to leave it merely 'being for' civil rights for Jews. Rather, he insisted that the question revolved around the inadequacy of any bourgeois rights. And because his vision from the start was for totally new human relations, he there, for the first time projected the concept of permanent revolution. (1982, 159)

The most often quoted use of this term in Marx is found in his March 1850 Address to the Communist League: "The relationship of the revolutionary workers' party to the petty-bourgeois democrats is this: it cooperates with them against the party which they aim to overthrow; it opposes them wherever they wish to secure their own position. ... Their battle-cry must be: *The Permanent Revolution.*" Many, including some Marxist revolutionaries post-Marx, have interpreted this as Marx having illusions that the revolution could quickly be reignited. Dunayevskaya read the Address in a different manner:

> Marx... was grounded in a philosophy of revolution in permanence as far back as 1843, and kept developing the concept and the activities in revolutionary struggles culminating in the 1849–49 Revolution, after which he worked it out not just in passing, but in full in his March 1850 *Address to the Communist League.*
>
> In reviewing 'the two revolutionary years, 1848–49' and the activities of the League 'in the movement, in all places, in the press, on the barricades, and on the battlefields,' Marx's report to the League stresses in the very next sentence that it was rooted in 'the conception of the movement as laid down in the circulars of the congress and of the Central Committee of 1847 as well as in the *Communist Manifesto...*' In a word, not a single element of this Address to the League—whether it concerned the need for 'reorganization' in a centralized way because 'anew revolution is impending, when the workers' party, therefore, must act in the most organized, most unanimous and most independent fashion,' or whether it concerned the outright declaration 'Revolution in Permanence'—is in any way separated for the total conception of philosophy *and* revolution.
>
> ... Far from the Address being something "Blanquist" [Blanquism refers to a conception of revolution generally attributed to Louis Auguste Blanqui, which held that socialist revolution should be carried out by a relatively small group of highly organized and secretive conspirators] that Marx discarded afterward, it was followed with another Address in June, in which Marx reviewed the concrete activities in five of the countries—Belgium, German, Switzerland, France, and England. And the Minutes of the Central Committee meeting of 15 September 1850 pointed

to the possibility of defeats. There was no letting go of what was needed for total uprooting of this society, even if it needed '15, 20, 50 years of civil war to go through in order to change society...'

It wasn't the phrase 'Permanent Revolution' that was the proof of the concept, but the fact that in the constant search for revolutionary allies the vision of the revolution to come was in no way changed. Thus— whether it was a question of the organization itself, i.e., the Communist League which was in fact disbanded in 1852 (and Marx kept referring to the party 'in the eminent historical sense'); or whether it was the search for historic roots and with it the projection of a revolutionary role for the peasantry (and Engels in that very same period wrote the magnificent work *The Peasant War in Germany*) – Marx was concluding: 'The whole matter in Germany will depend upon the possibility of supporting the proletarian revolution with a sort of second edition of the peasant war. Then the thing will be excellent.'

Letter to Engels, 16 April 1856, quoted in DUNAYEVSKAJA, 161

Dunayevskaya saw that Revolution in Permanence for Marx meant both new geographies, and new revolutionary subjects. She cited the *Grundrisse,* where Marx wrote of "epoch of social revolution" and called attention to his "new appreciation of the Asiatic mode of production and the Oriental society's resistance to British imperialism" (Dunayevskaya 1982, 161). She referred to Marx's writings on the abolitionists and the Civil War and the uprising of slaves in the U.S. As well, she noted Marx's citing of the role of women in the Paris Commune.

Finally, Dunayevskaya called attention to the last decade of Marx's life, where he looked at humanity's development in what became known as his *Ethnological Notebooks*, as well as Marx's study of the possibility of a different revolutionary pathway in Russia based on its peasant collective, and his 1882 Preface of the Russian Edition of the *Communist Manifesto* that noted the possible relationship between revolution in Russia and in the West. In sum, Dunayevskaya's category of Marx as philosopher of revolution in permanence created a significant way of viewing the totality of Marx.

B *Post-Marx Marxists as a Category of Critique*

In the third of her "Trilogy of Revolution," *Rosa Luxemburg, Women's Liberation, and Marx's Philosophy of Revolution,* Dunayevskaya developed the category of "post-Marx Marxists." Its focus was not simply a chronological one, but centered on these Marxists' relation to Marx's methodology, to his dialectic. She argued that *beginning with Engels,* Marx's closed collaborator, who live a dozen years after Marx's death, Marxist revolutionaries had failed to fully come to grips with

Marx as *philosopher* of revolution. In the Index of her book these post-Marx Marxists included, in addition to Engels, Lenin, Luxemburg, Trotsky and David Ryazanov, (the great Russian Marxist archivist responsible for unearthing and preparing for publication numerous of Marx's unknown writings.) These were all serious revolutionaries; none were in any sense betrayers. So what was at stake in her creating the category? What was the center of the critique?

For Dunayevskaya it was crucial for revolutionaries to have before them a comprehension of the *totality* of Marx's Marxism in order to be full continuators. The reason for the failure of many post-Marx Marxists to meet this challenge was both objective and subjective. On the one hand, a huge number of Marx's writings were unavailable to the first generations of Marxists after Marx's death. Engels himself was not acquainted with a significant part of Marx's work before Marx's death. Neither Lenin nor Luxemburg had access to writings such as the *Grundrisse* from 1857–58, the *1844 Economic-Philosophic Manuscripts*, or the *Ethnological Notebooks* of Marx's last years.

At the same time there were crucial subjective factors, different for each of these revolutionaries. Questions of building revolutionary organization, analyzing capitalist accumulation, searching for revolutionary subjects who could bring down capitalism, studying the appearance of imperialism—were all concrete questions that new generations of Marxists had to confront. However, they often did so without rooting themselves fully in Marx's Marxism. This led to a *fragmentation* from that *totality* that Dunayevskaya viewed as essential to recreating Marxism for a new moment, a new geography. By totality, we are not referring to a quantitative listing of the vast array of subjects that Marx took up in his writing. Rather, what allowed the totality to be a true unity with diverse subjects was the question of methodology, of the dialectic, and with it, a question of revolution. Marx held as one, philosophy (the dialectic as he forged it) and revolution, which he participated in and which he searched for in the world throughout his life.

Dunayevskaya asked "Is the revolutionary act sufficient to reestablish for our age the Marxism of Marx?" (ibid., 121), or, is something more needed? She questioned "Luxemburg's judgment of Marx's new continent of thought as just 'a weapon in the class struggle,' 'a method of research,' and 'an instrument of intellectual culture' needed by the 'party of practical fighters;—as if all that was needed was practice, practice, practice," noting that "was the near-fatal error of all Marxists after the death of Marx." She continued,

> It is necessary to begin at the beginning, directly with Marx's closest collaborator, without whom we would not have had either volumes 2 or 3 of *Capital*—Fredrick Engels. Here is a Marxist who did not, at least not

> when he spoke of Marxism in general and not in specifics, delimit Marx's contribution to 'method of research.' Here is Marx's closest collaborator, who could be considered, in some fundamental respects, a co-founder of Historical Materialism. He was certainly the most devoted of Marx's colleagues, and consciously tried only to follow Marx's bequests... And yet, and yet, and yet. [After Marx's death] first came Engels' own work, *The Origin of the Family, Private Property and the State* [not Volume 2 of *Capital*,] which he considered the fulfilling of a 'bequest of Marx.'
>
> Ibid., 119–120

Dunayevskaya argued that this work of Engels was far away from Marx's methodology. Yet, we are faced with many a Marxists and socialist feminists who assume that the view of Engels was as well that of Marx. For many post-Marx Marxists there is a strong tendency to consider Marx and Engels as one.

Even the greatest practicing Marxist post-Marx, Lenin—who did dig profoundly into the Hegelian dialectic in his *Philosophic Notebooks* and concretized dialectical Marxism in the Russian Revolution of 1917—was viewed in both an appreciative and a critical manner by Dunayevskaya. She wrote of Lenin's "philosophic ambivalence," even after his constructing a Great Divide for revolutionary Marxism, because of his failure to share with his Bolshevik colleagues the dialectical rethinking of Marxism found in his *Philosophic Notebooks*, and thus not subjecting the Party, his party, to the same kind of profound dialectic reorganization he had undergone.

Trotsky was seen as part of post-Marx Marxists as critique precisely at his strongest theoretical point—his Theory of Permanent Revolution, which, Dunayevskaya argued, lacked a revolutionary human subject in Trotsky's dismissal of an independent revolutionary role for the peasantry. Trotsky methodology for permanent revolution, she saw as distant from Marx's concept of revolution in permanence.

Riazanov, the Russian scholar and revolutionary, who did so much to bring Marx's Archives to life post the Russian Revolution, was at the same time critiqued by Dunayevskaya because of his facile acceptance of the view that Marx, in his last years, "lost his ability for intensive, independent intellectual creation," calling Marx's notebook summaries "inexcusable pedantry."

The question here is not alone Dunayevskaya's insistence on examining the thought and practice of these important revolutionaries visa via the totality of Marx's Marxism, his refusal to separate philosophy and revolution. It was also her view that numerous other Marxists post-Marx, who could not at all measure up to these giant revolutionaries, have contributed to the distortion and fragmentation of Marx's Marxism in the 20th century.

The stakes are huge: It is not a question of preserving the "legacy" of Marx, but of the failure to develop Marxism anew for our day, and thus not setting forth the theoretical ground needed for destroying root and branch capitalist value-production with its degrading of humanity in all its aspects, as well as its of despoiling nature itself. We who live in the 21st century live under this shadow, and have the challenging task of recovering the totality of Marx's Marxism for our day, not of course as a recipe, but as a revolutionary philosophic vision, a life in thought and practice of permanent revolution.

IV Conclusion: Toward a Dialectic of Organization and Philosophy

What can bring together the threads between utopian ideas, spontaneous freedom movements from below, and the emancipatory power of dialectical philosophy that we have been exploring in the present study? Can revolutionary organization be a crucial mediation to weave together these threads?

In a previous study, *Toward a Dialectic of Philosophy and Organization* (Gogol 2012), I explored the relation between philosophy and organization in the 19th and 20th centuries. Before discussing this question in terms of Latin American liberation today, I would like to quote from the Introduction of this previous work, beginning from Section II, "The Project of Dunayevskaya: Dialectics of Organization and Philosophy":

> Over half a century ago, Raya Dunayevskaya, then a member of a small Marxist grouping, sought to explore the relation between revolutionary organization and dialectical philosophy by examining the Absolute Idea chapter of Hegel's *Science of Logic*: "I am concerned only with the dialectic... of the *type* of grouping like ours, be it large or small, and *its* relation to the mass." (Dunayevskaya 2002, 16) This was the vantage point for a breakthrough on Hegel's Absolutes that she experienced with her May 12 and 20 Letters on Hegel's Absolute Idea and Absolute Mind (Spirit).
>
> "Whatever it was that was driving me in 1953 to write those letters of May 12 and May 20, it suddenly became the whole of Hegel's work. ... What had begun as 'the dialectic of the Party' as well as the contradictions in the Absolute Idea itself, resulted in my seeing what I called 'the new society,' i.e. the end of the division between mental and manual." (Dunayevskaya, 1988: 11, 12)

That 1953 "philosophic moment of Marxist-Humanism" would catalyze Dunayevskaya's journey of philosophic probing and organizational practice over a span of more than three decades. The philosophy of Marxist-Humanism, with American roots and world historic connections, was thus born and developed from 1953 to the end of her life in 1987. Its organizational expression was News and Letters Committees, founded in 1955.

> A direct theoretical probing of the relationship between dialectical philosophy and revolutionary organizational practice was not taken up by her in and of itself immediately following the 1953 Letters. To be sure, many aspects of the relationship were touched upon in her philosophic-political-organizational labors during the three decades following her Letters on Hegel's Absolute. It was only in the mid-1980s, however, that she decided to undertake a new theoretical/philosophic work focused directly on the subject, one which came to be tentatively titled "Dialectics of Organization and Philosophy: 'The Party' and Forms of Organization Born Out of Spontaneity." It was a project that was rooted in a return to her 1953 Letters on Hegel's Absolutes, while at the same time drawing upon the decades of "Marxism-Humanism emerging out of Marxism-Humanism," as seen in her major philosophic writings and her organizational practice in News and Letters Committees.
>
> She began to explore the historic roots of revolutionary organization from Marx's day through much of the 20th century, while at the same time, further probing what she saw as the philosophical foundation for revolutionary organization in News and Letters Committees. In October 1986, she articulated the relation between dialectic in philosophy and dialectic in organization that she was exploring for her new book as follows: "What I'm driving at, is that unless we work out the dialectic in philosophy itself, the dialectic of organization, whether it is from the vanguard party or that born from spontaneity, would be just different forms of organization, instead of an organization that is so inseparable from its philosophic ground that form and content are one." (Dunayevskaya 1981, # 10789)

Dunayevskaya's project "Dialectics of Organization and Philosophy: 'The Party' and Forms of Organization Born Out of Spontaneity" was unfinished at the time of her death. My writing of *Toward a Dialectic of Philosophy and Organization* was deeply indebted to Dunayevskaya's labors, but was not an attempt to "complete" her unfinished work. In the Introduction to *Toward a Dialectic of Philosophy and Organization* I sketched the form of the work:

The Prologue is a discussion of the centrality of the Dialectic in Philosophy Itself and sets the ground for the study. It seeks to explore crucial themes in the Hegelian dialectic—his concept of Spirit, the significance of negation of the negation, the Absolutes As New Beginnings—that I believe speak to a Dialectic of Organization for our day.

Part I, "On Spontaneous Forms of Organization vs. Vanguard Parties," begins with Marx's concept of organization, from the 1840s to the first years of the Workingman's International. Forms of organization arising from below are examined in chapters on the 1871 Paris Commune, the Russian Soviets of 1905, the factory committees and Soviets of 1917 Russia, the Spanish Revolution of the mid-1930s, and the Hungarian Revolution of 1956. As well, the ideas of Lassalle, Engels, Lenin, Luxemburg, Trotsky and Pannekock are taken up in relation to Party organizational forms and mass organizations.

Part II, "Hegel and Marx," begins with a chapter on Hegel's Absolute Knowing in relation to a dialectic of philosophy and organization. Within, is an examination of Marx's critique and indebtedness to the Hegelian dialectic, of Lukacs' view of the ending of the *Phenomenology*, and of Dunayevskaya's reading of Absolute Knowing. A second chapter examines Marx's *Critique of the Gotha Program* in relation to revolutionary organization then and now.

Part III, "Lenin and Hegel," explores the limitations of Lenin's crucial philosophic reorganization with respect to organization in the period of the First World War and the Russian Revolution. A second chapter probes Dunayevskaya's organizational reading of Hegel's Third Attitude to Objectivity.

Part IV, "Dialectics of Organization and Philosophy in Post-World War II World," details Dunayevskaya's *praxis* of organization and philosophy in the founding and first three decades of the News and Letters Committees, a Marxist-Humanist group.

In the concluding Part V, I ask as part of a battle of ideas: "What Philosophic-Organizational Vantage Point Is Needed?" Here I explore the vantage points of Holloway and Adorno, Hardt and Negri, as well as Mészáros, Postone, and Lebowitz. This concluding chapter returns to Hegel's Dialectic of Negativity, to Marx, and to Dunayevskaya, in posing the challenge of forging anew dialectics of philosophy and revolutionary organization at the end of the first decade of the 21st century.

•

Here in *Utopia and Dialectic in Latin American Liberation* I have sought to extend that work within a Latin American context, as well as continue the discussion I had launched in my earlier *The Concept of Other in Latin America Liberation.* I want to conclude this present study by briefly discussing three types of organization in a Latin American context: 1. Spontaneous forms of organization created from below; 2. Organization as small groups of revolutionary thinker-activists; 3. Organization as organization of thought, at its highest level a philosophy of revolution.

Spontaneous Forms of Organization from Below

In the second and third parts of this book we have examined these forms within Latin America. We began with the Haitian masses in the opposition to the Duvalier regime. Peasant organizations and *Ti Legliz*, the little church, as well as other organizations were infused with the actions of thousands of peasants, especially peasant women. Youth in the cities became the active motor of the little church. In Argentina, when the economy collapsed tens of thousands took to the streets to demand *Que se vayan todos!* (All must go!) and new organizational forms arose from below—neighborhood assembles, the *piqueteros* (protesters who stood on corners or marched in street actions on specific issues), occupied factories often abandoned by their owners and taken over by the workers who began to run self-organized, self-governed factories. In Bolivia, we saw the massive organizations in the city and in the countryside: The water-war in Cochabamba with the organization of the *Co-ordinadora* organizing huge protests, followed later by the gas-war; the massive road blocks organized in the countryside by Indigenous groups; the uprising in the primarily Aymara city of El Alto, where thousands upon thousands would march into La Paz and succeed in throwing out the government—all creating their own forms of struggle, including popular education. In Colombia, we witnessed Indigenous struggles in Cauca and youth actions in urban Medellin In Chile, massive continuous actions by high school and university students opened new space that earlier elections had failed to create in the post-Pinochet period. In Mexico, movements and struggles for autonomy by Indigenous groups and others in Cherán, in Guerrero, in Oaxaca, and of course two decades of the struggle for autonomy—Freedom according to the Zapatistas— brought forth new organizational forms from below. This list is but the briefest glance and the creativity and power of social movements in Latin America.

There is no substitute for these spontaneous, self-organized movements from below. Without this resistance and rebellion, no fundamental social transformation would be possible. At the same time, there is another type of organization, which, I would argue, is crucial for uprooting social change as well.

Organization as Small Groups of Revolutionary Thinker-activists

> ... I wasn't interested either in the mass party, which the masses will build, or in the elitist party, which we definitely oppose, but in what happens to a small group 'like us' [revolutionary Marxist colleagues in organization] who know that nothing can be done without the masses, and are with them, but they (small groups) are theoreticians and they always seem to be around too. So, what is the objectivity which explains their presence, as the objectivity explains the spontaneous outburst of the masses? In a word, I was looking for the objectivity of subjectivity.
>
> RAYA DUNAYEVSKAYA, 1981: Vol. XII—Presentation of June 1, 1987, "Dialectics of Organization and Philosophy"

One of the great difficulties we face on the question of organization is the contradictory history of revolutionary organization in the 20th and now 21st centuries. Contradictory in the sense that while revolutionary organizations have played a key part in social transformation, they have also halted revolutionary processes after the destruction of the old, not allowing the creation of the new to freely flow. Instead, new forms of the old domination were put in place, via "the Party." Counter-revolution *within* the revolution has emerged via the "revolutionary party."

Furthermore, "What Happens After Taking Power,"—the question of the incompleteness of social revolutions, of the danger of transformation into opposite—is not just an historical problem in a faraway land. It is also a Latin American question, a reality of the here and now: Cuba's Latin American great divide with its 1959 revolution certainly challenged U.S. imperialism. But the half-century since has raised many questions and contradictions with a single party in power, its single leader—all in the name of "socialism." To this could be added the Sandinistas in power Nicaragua, the FMLN governing in El Salvador. We have already taken up the attempt to construct socialism for the 21st century in Venezuela, and in Bolivia. None of this is to deny the overwhelmingly reactionary role of the U.S. in blocking revolutionary change. But it is to say that the contradictions *within* the revolutionary process, including especially the role of the revolution organization, especially in power, needs to be examined as well.

The point here is not so much to review this history, but rather to face the reality that at the present moment *there is a near void in the presence of small groups of the revolutionary thinker-activists* that Dunayevskaya wrote of in the quote cited immediately above. (Are the Zapatistas, particularly the Indigenous Revolutionary Clandestine Committee [El *Comité Clandestino Revolucionario Indígena, CCRI*] an important exception to this void?)

In relationship to would-be revolutionary organizations, social movements in Latin America, often spontaneous in origin, frequently face the threat of diversion from "progressive" political parties seeking to take them over and use them for electoral purposes. Brazil and Argentina, as well as Bolivia and Ecuador, come to mind. The small groups that do exist are often vanguardist-elitist in conception, as well seeking to take over or ride the waves of social movements.

In Latin America today there is a tendency toward non-party-ism, a distrust of any organizations from outside of the social movements themselves. Perhaps the history of the Left parties in Latin America provides amble reason for this distrust. However, this still does not answer the question of revolutionary organization as a needed mediation in social transformation.

What was Dunayevskaya seeking in exploring the role of "a small group 'like us'"? It was not to privilege revolutionary organization over the creativity of the masses' self-activity. She was focused on the *relation* of masses and thinker-activists, theoreticians, in revolutionary transformation. That was what she meant by looking at "the objectivity of subjectivity," in terms of revolutionary organization. What was objective about these small groups, seemingly only subjective? This brings us to Organization as Organization of Thought.

Organization as Organization of Thought—the Objectivity of Subjectivity

After the bitter experiences of elitist vanguard groups in practice, after the betrayal of mass "socialist, progressive" organizations in and out of power, the question of form of organization is no minor matter. Decentralized, non-vanguardist forms *are* important. However, form of organization alone does not answer the question "What philosophy of organization?" Dunayevskaya's book title: "Dialectics of Organization and Philosophy: 'The Party' and Forms of Organization Born Out of Spontaneity" is revealing. To put together Dialectics of Organization and Philosophy, and only then pose those two opposite forms of organization, 'The Party' and Forms of Organization Born Out of Spontaneity, meant that philosophy and organization, the dialectic and revolutionary organization, became the crucial relation to work out. Yes, the vanguard party and forms of organization born out of spontaneity were opposites, but not absolute opposites. Only when one was able to put together emancipatory philosophy and organization, could a non-elitist form of organization reach for its full potential. Without that, the question of organization revolved around the form and not about the emancipatory content, freedom. As Dunayevskaya wrote:

> What I'm driving at, is that unless we work out the dialectic in philosophy itself, the dialectic of organization, whether it is from the vanguard party

> or that born from spontaneity, would be just different forms of organization, instead of an organization that is so inseparable from its philosophic ground that form and content are one.—Oct. 6, 1986
>
> DUNAYEVSKAYA, 1981: #10789

Why do we face these extreme difficulties on revolutionary organization, be it so-called progressive political parties using social movements for their own purposes, or vanguard groups seeking to "lead the revolution," or those who reject both types of organizational forms saying the movement from below is sufficient? The unifying thread in these contradictory positions, I would argue, is the failure of all these tendencies and others to grapple with the challenge of recognizing the need for and the development of a philosophy of revolution in permanence *for our day* in the spirit of Marx. Because of a failure to work out a philosophy of revolution, these would-be revolutionaries see no need to concretize such a philosophy within organization—a dialectic of organization and philosophy, which would mean a new type of revolutionary organization. It is these types of organization—philosophic action groups that could authentically unite with the masses' struggle, and not simply supposedly "give consciousness to the masses," and thus manipulate them—that need to be built. We need organizations of thinker-activists steeped in dialectics, who could assist the masses in coming to the full realization of their own powers, their own creativity, their own working out of a vision of a new human society. This, precisely this, was at the center of Marx's concept of organization. How can we put it into practice?

In the present study I have sought to extend that discussion to Latin America by looking at the organization of thought of the Zapatistas, who project a way of practice, from below and to the left, that is sharply different from the old Left, and at the same time, is more than a question of form, horizontal-ism. Unseparated from participatory practice in the Indigenous communities building autonomy, is a way of doing theory that is dialectical. Is this a philosophy of rebellion, of revolution in the sense of Marx? It is not yet the fullness of a philosophy of revolutionary transformation, but it is on that pathway: a planting of seeds, a growing and cultivating of them; an exploring in practice and theory that can help us in the construction of such a philosophic vision of permanent social transformation. It is a challenge and a labor not alone of and for the Zapatistas, but of and for all of us reaching toward a new society, a new world, a Latin American liberation in fullness.

Bibliography

Achtenberg, Emily. 2013. Contested development: The geopolitics of Bolivia's TIPNIS conflict. *NACLA Report on the Americas* 4 (2). https://nacla.org/article/contested-development-geopolitics-bolivia%E2%80%99s-tipnis-conflict (accessed September 17, 2014).

Almeyra, Guillermo. 2012. "El estado 'de arriba' y el estado 'de abajo'." *La Jornada,* February 26. http://www.jornada.unam.mx/2012/02/26/opinion/020a2pol (accessed September 17, 2014).

Anderson, Kevin. 1995. *Lenin, Hegel and Western Marxism.* Champaign: University of Illinois Press.

Aristide, Jean-Bertrand. 1990. *In the parish of the poor.* New York: Orbis Books.

Aristide, Marx V., and Laurie Richardson. 1994. "Haiti's Popular Resistance." *NACLA Report on the Americas* 27 (4). https://nacla.org/article/haitis-popular-resistance (accessed September 17, 2014).

Baldwin, James. 1979. "If black english isn't a language, then tell me, what is?" *New York Times,* July 29. http://www.nytimes.com/books/98/03/29/specials/baldwin-english .html (accessed September 17, 2014).

Bell, Beverly. 2001. *Walking on fire—Haitian woman's stories of survival and resistance.* Cornell: Cornell University Press.

Blanco, Hugo. 1972. *Land or death: The peasant struggle in Peru.* Georgia: Pathfinder.

———. 2008. Interview in *Mariátegui,* 09/09/08, Yásser Gómez.

———. 2009. Interview in *World War 4 Report August,* 28. 9 de julio.

———. 2014. Director of *Lucha Indígena,* http://www.luchaindigena.com/

Buck-Morss, Susan. 2009. *Hegel, Haití and universal history.* Pittsburg: University of Pittsburg Press.

Burt, Jo-Marie. 2009. *Violencia y autoritarismo en el Perú: bajo la sombra de Sendero y la dictadura de Fujimori.* Lima: Instituto de Estudios Peruanos-Servicios Educativos Rurales.

Cerutti Guldberg, Horacio. 1989a. *Ensayos de utopía* (*I y II*). Toluca: Universidad Autónoma del Estado de México.

———. 1989b. *La utopía de Nuestra América* (*De Varia Utópica*). *Ensayos de utopía III.* Bogotá: Universidad Central de Bogotá.

———. 2007. *Presagio y tópica del descubrimiento. Ensayos de utopía IV.* México: Centro Coordinador y Difusor de Estudios Latinoamericanos, UNAM.

———. 2010. *Utopía es compromiso y tarea responsable. Ensayos de utopía V.* Monterrey: CECyTE-CAEIP.

Cerutti Guldberg, Horacio, and Carlos Mondragón. 2006. *Religión y política en América Latina: la utopía como espacio de resistencia social.* México: UNAM.

Chirix, García, and Emma Delfina. 2003. *Afectividad de las mujeres mayas. Ronojel kajowab'al ri mayab' taq ixoqi.* Guatemala: Grupo de Mujeres Mayas Kaqla.

Cliff, Tony. 2004. *All Power to the Soviets: Lenin, 1914–1917*. Chicago: Haymarket Books.

Contreras Baspineiro, Alex. 2011. "¿Éste es el proceso de cambio? Gobierno indígena contra marcha indígena." *Alainet*, October 11. http://alainet.org/active/50055&lang=es (accessed September 17, 2014).

Corbett, Bob. http://www2.webster.edu/~corbetre/index/index.html.

Cuevas, Rafael. 2011. "Bolivia. Mandar obedeciendo." *Alainet*, October 8. http://alainet.org/active/50045 (accessed September 17. 2014).

Danner, Mark. 2010. "To heal Haiti, look to history, not nature." *New York Times*, January 21. http://www.nytimes.com/2010/01/22/opinion/22danner.html?pagewanted=all&_r=0 (accessed September 17, 2014).

deBeauvoir, Simone. 1952 (reprinted 1989). *The Second Sex*. Vintage Books (Random House) "On the Master–slave Relation," http://www.marxists.org/reference/subject/ethics/de-beauvoir/2nd-sex/ch05.htm.

Desinformados. http://desinformemonos.org.

Dri, Rubén. 2006. *Revolución de las asambleas*. Buenos Aires: Ediciones Diaporías.

Dubos, Laurent. 2004. *Avengers of the new world—The story of the Haitian revolution.* Cambridge: Belknap Press.

———. 2011. *Haiti: The aftershocks of history*. London: Macmillan.

Dunayevskaya, Raya. 1958. *Marxism and freedom.* New York: Bookman.

———. 1963. *American civilization on trial.* Chicago: News & Letters.

———. 1973. *Philosophy and revolution.* New York: Delacort.

———. 1981. *The Raya Dunayevskaya Collection – Marxist-Humanist Archives.* Michigan: Wayne State University. Full collection available at http://rayadunayevskaya.org/.

———. 1982. *Rosa Luxemburg, women's liberation, and Marx's philosophy of revolution.* New Jersey: Humanities Press.

———. 1985. *Women's liberation and the dialectics of revolution.* New Jersey: Humanities Press.

———. 2002. *Power of negativity*. Maryland: Lexington.

Dupuy, Alex. 2007. *The prophet and power.* Maryland: Rowman and Littlefield.

Ejército Zapatista de Liberación Nacional (EZLN). Comunications of Subcomandante Insurgente Marcos and others, of the Comité Clandestino Revolucionario Indigena-Comandancia General del EZLN (CCRI-CG del EZLN), y de Juntas de Buen Gobierno. http://enlacezapatista.ezln.org.mx/.

Libertario El, Venezuela. http://www.nodo50.org/ellibertario/.

Enlace Zapatista (Communications of the Zapatistas). http://enlacezapatista.ezln.org.mx/.

Escuelita Zapatista (Zapatista Little School). 2013. The 4 books: *Gobierno autónomo I; Gobierno autónomo II; Participación de las mujeres en el gobierno autónomo;*

Resistencia autónoma. http://seminariodefeminismonuestroamericano.blogspot.mx/2013/09/participacion-de-las-mujeres-en-el.html. Available in English at: http://escuelitabooks.blogspot.co.uk/.

Falquet, Jules. 2001. "La costumbre cuestionada por sus fieles celadoras: reivindicaciones de las mujeres indígenas zapatistas." *Debate Feminista* 12 (24). http://www.debatefeminista.com/articulos.php?id_articulo=583&id_volumen=18 (accessed September 17, 2014).

Freire, Paulo. 1993. *Política y educación*. Madrid: Siglo XXI.

Fuentes, Federico. 2005. "Venezuela: land reform battle deepens." *Green Left Weekly*, October 12. https://www.greenleft.org.au/node/35858 (accessed September 17, 2014).

García Linera, Álvaro. 2004. *Sociología de los movimientos sociales en Bolivia.* La Paz: Oxfam-Diaconía.

———. 2011. *El "oenegismo," enfermedad infantil del derechismo.* Bolivia: Vicepresidencia del Estado Plurinacional. http://www.vicepresidencia.gob.bo/IMG/pdf/el-oenegismo.pdf (accessed September 17, 2014).

———. 2012. *Geopolítica de la Amazonía, poder hacendal-patrimonial y acumulación capitalista.* Bolivia: Vicepresidencia del Estado Plurinacional. http://www.vicepresidencia.gob.bo/IMG/pdf/geopolitica_de_la_amazonia.pdf (accessed September 17, 2014).

Galeano, Eduardo. 1997. *Open veins of Latin America.* New York: Monthly Review Press.

Gargallo, Francesca. 2012. *Feminismos desde Abya Yala. Ideas y proposiciones de las mujeres de 607 pueblos en nuestra América.* Bogotá: Desde Abajo.

Gogol, Eugene. 1994. *Mariátegui y Marx: La transformación social en los países en vías de desarrollo.* México: Centro Coordinador y Difusor de Estudios Latinoamericanos, UNAM.

———. 2002. *The concept of other in Latin America liberation.* Maryland: Lexington Press.

———. 2004. *Raya Dunayevskaya: Philosopher of Marxist-Humanism.* Oregon: Resource Publications.

———. 2012. *Toward a dialectic of philosophy and organization.* Chicago: Haymarket Books.

———. 2014. *Ensayos sobre Zapatismo.* México: Juan Pablos.

Guerrero, Modesto. 2009. "Emergencias y desafíos de las asambleas barriales." *Revista Herramienta* 19. http://www.herramienta.com.ar/revista-herramienta-n-19/emergencia-y-desafios-de-las-asambleas-barriales (accessed September 17, 2014).

Gutiérrez Aguilar, Raquel. 2008. *Los ritmos del Pachakuti. Movilización y levantamiento indígena-popular en Bolivia (2000–2005).* Buenas Aries: Tinta Limón.

Gutiérrez, Gustavo. 1988. *Theology of liberation.* New York: Orbis.

Hallward, Peter. 2007. *Damning the floor: Haiti, Aristide, and the politics of containment.* London: Verso.

Hardt, Michael, and Antonio Negri. 2000. *Empire*. Cambridge: The Belknap Press.

———. 2004. *Multitude*. New York: The Penguin Press.

———. 2009. *Commonwealth*. Cambridge: The Belknap Press.

Harnecker, Marta. 2002. *Hugo Chávez Frías: Un hombre, un pueblo* (entrevista). Colombia: Desde Abajo.

———. 2005. *Understanding the Venezuelan Revolution*. New York: Monthly Review Press.

Hegel, G.W.F. 1894. *Logic. Encylopedia of philosophical sciences*. London: Oxford University Press.

———. 1929. *Science of Logic*. London: George Allen & Unwin. Johnson and Struthers translation. 1969. New York: Humanities Press. Miller translation.

———. 1966. *Phenomenology of Mind (Spirit)*. New York: Humanities Press. Baillie translation.

———. 1971. *Philosophy of Mind*. Oxford: Oxford University Press.

———. 2005. *Philosophy of Right*. New York: Dover Publications.

Holloway, John. 2002. *Change the world without taking power*. London: Pluto Press.

Hylton, Forrest, and Sinclair Thomson. 2008. *Revolutionary horizons: Past and present in Bolivian politics*. London: Verso.

James, C.L.R. 1989. *Black Jacobins: Toussaint L'Ouverture and the San Domingo revolution*. New York: Vintage.

Janicke, Kiraz. 2007. "Without workers management there can be no socialism." *venezuelanalysis.com*, October 30. http://venezuelanalysis.com/analysis/2784 (accessed September 17, 2014).

Janicke, Kiraz, and Federico Fuentes. 2008. "Venezuela's labor movement at the crossroads." *Venezuelaanalysis.com*, April 29. http://venezuelanalysis.com/analysis/3398 (accessed September 17, 2014).

Lander, Edgardo, and Pablo Navarrete. 2007. "La política económica de la izquierda latinoamericana en el gobierno: Venezuela." Transnational Institute, November 24. http://www.tni.org/es/briefing/la-pol%C3%ADtica-econ%C3%B3mica-de-la-izquierda-latinoamericana-en-el-gobierno-venezuela (accessed September 17, 2014).

Lenin, V.I. 1961. *Philosophic notebooks*, Vol. 38 *Collected Works*. Moscow: Foreign Language Publishing House.

Lenin, V.I. 1902 *What is to be done?* Marxist Internet Archives. http://www.marxists.org/archive/lenin/works/1901/witbd/index.htm (accessed September 17, 2014).

Lerner, Josh. 2007. "Communal councils in Venezuela: Can 200 families revolutionize democracy?" *Z Magazine* 20 (3). http://venezuelanalysis.com/analysis/2257 (accessed September 17, 2014).

Lih, Lars. 2006. *Lenin rediscovered: What is to be done? In context*. Leiden: Brill.

Lindsay, Reed. 2006. "What future for Haiti? Interview with Patrick Elie." *NACLA*, August 6. https://nacla.org/news/2007/8/24/what-future-haiti-interview-patrick-elie (accessed September 17, 2014).

López Bárcenas, Francisco. 2008. *San Juan Cópala: dominación política y resistencia popular, de la rebelión de Hilarión a la formación del municipio autónomo.* México: UAM Xochimilco. http://desinformemonos.org/wp-content/uploads/2009/08/triquisversionparaimpresion.pdf (accessed September 17, 2014).

Magnani, Esteban. 2003. *El cambio silencioso. Empresas y fábricas recuperadas por los trabajadores en Argentina.* Buenos Aires: Editorial Prometeo.

Mariátegui, José Carlos. 1928. *7 Interpretive essays on Peruvian reality.* http://www.marxists.org/archive/mariateg/works/1928/index.htm (accessed September 17, 2014).

Márquez-Fernández, Álvaro B. 2005. "Diez años más para filosofar desde la praxis utopista en América Latina'." *Utopía y Praxis Latinoamericana. Revista Internacional de Filosofía Iberoamericana y Teoría Social* 31.

Marx, Karl. 1843. *Critique of Hegel's Philosophy of Law.* Marxist Internet Archives. http://www.marxists.org/archive/marx/works/1843/critique-hpr/.

———. 1875. *Critique of the Gotha program.* http://www.marxists.org/archive/marx/works/1875/gotha/ (accessed September 17, 2014).

———. 1909. *Capital, Vol. 1.* Chicago: Charles H. Kerr.

———. 1975. *Economic-philosophic manuscripts of 1844.* In *Marx-Engels Collected Works*, Vol. 3. New York: International Publishers.

Mehring, Frantz. 1918. *Karl Marx: The story of his life.* http://www.marxists.org/archive/mehring/1918/marx/ (accessed September 17, 2014).

Mills, Patricia J. 1996. *Feminist interpretations of G.W.F. Hegel.* Pennsylvania: Pennsylvania State University Press.

Mujeres Creando/La Virgen de los Deseos. 2009. "Constitución política feminista del estado." *Mujer pública. Revista de discusión feminista* 1.

Mujeres Indígenas Hoy. 2010. "Ecuador–Mónica Chuji: 'Las mujeres van abriéndose espacios paulatinamente'." Interview with Mónica Chuji. *Mujeres Indígenas Hoy*, June 14. http://bartolinas.blogspot.ca/2010/06/ecuador-monica-chuji-las-mujeres-van.html (accessed September 18, 2014).

Muñoz Ramírez, Gloria, Luis Hernández, and Trinidad Ramírez. 2011. *Yo Soy #132, voces del movimiento.* México: Bola de Cristal. http://desinformemonos.org/2012/11/presentacion-libro/ (accessed September 17, 2014).

News and Letters. http://newsandletters.org/.

Olivera, Oscar. 2004. *Cochabamba! Water war in Bolivia.* Boston: South End Press.

Paredes, Julieta. 2006. "Para que el sol vuelva a calentar." In *No pudieron con nosotras: El desafío del feminismo autónomo de Mujeres Creando*, ed. Elizabeth Monasterios Pérez, 61–96. La Paz: Plural editores.

Quijano, Aníbal. 1990. *Modernidad, identidad y utopía en América Latina.* Lima: El Conejo.

———. 1991. "Recovering utopía." *NACLA Report on the Americas* 24 (5): 34–38.

Ramírez F., María del Rayo. 2012. *Utopología desde nuestra América.* Colombia: desde abajo.

Rodas Morales, Raquel. 2002. *Muchas voces, demasiados silencios. Los discursos de las lideresas del movimiento de mujeres del Ecuador.* Quito: Fondo para la Igualdad de Género de ACDI.

Salazar Bondy, Augusto. 1965. *Historia de las ideas en el Perú contemporáneo, t. 2.* Peru: Francisco Moncloa Editores.

———. 1969. *Sentido y problema del pensamiento filosófico Hispanoamericano. The meaning and problem of Hispanic Amerian philosophic thought.* Occasional Publications 16. Lawrence, KA: Center of Latin American Studies, University of Kansas.

———. 1974. *América Latina: filosofía y liberación.* Buenos Aires: Editorial Bonum.

———. 1976. *Existe una filosofía de nuestra América.* México: Siglo XXI editores.

Sayers, Sean. 2011. *Marx & alienation: Essays on Hegelian themes.* London: Palgrave Macmillan.

Sitrin, Marina. 2005. *Horizontalidad: Voces de poder popular* in *Argentina.* Buenos Aires: Chilavert.

Sotelo, Adrián. 2013. "El nefasto sexenio calderonista y la irrupción del nuevo liberalismo del PRI." *Rebelión,* January 2. http://rebelion.org/noticia.php?id=161668 (accessed September 17, 2014).

Soto Santiesteban, Gustavo. 2011. "Una mirada macroscópica al conflicto del TIPNIS." *America Latina En Movimiento* (Sept–Oct.): 44–46. http://alainet.org/publica/alai468-9.pdf (accessed September 17, 2014).

Suárez Y., Amparito. 2001. "La escuela de formación de mujeres indígenas tras un nuevo sueño." *Rikcharishun, Periódico Bilingüe de la Confederación de Pueblos de la Nacionalidad Kichwa del Ecuador* 29 (5). Ecuador: Runakunapak Rikcharimui.

Svampa, Maristella. 2004. Las organizaciones piqueteras: actualización, balance y reflexiones (2002–2004). http://www.maristellasvampa.net/publicaciones-ensayos.shtml (accessed September 17, 2014).

Tabah, Mehmet. 2012. *Dialectics of Human Nature in Marx's Philosophy.* New York: Palgrave Macmillan.

Tapia, Luis. 2012. "Los pueblos de tierras bajas como minoría plural consistente." In *La victoria indígena del TIPNIS,* [autor query: page nos?]. La Paz: Autodeterminación.

Thompson, Frank. 2006. "Reconsidering Cuban economic performance in retrospect." Paper delivered at the conference *The Measure of a Revolution: Cuba 1959–2009.* Queen's University, Kingston, Canada, May 7–9.

Trinchero, Hugo, 2007. "Economía política de la exclusión. Para una crítica desde la experiencia de las empresas recuperadas por sus trabajadores (ERT)." *Cuadernos de Antropología Social* 26, 41–67.

Vallejo, Camila. 2012. *Podemos cambiar el mundo.* México: Ocean Sur.

Veraza, Jorge. 2005. *Para pensar la opresión y la emancipación desde la posmodernidad. Crítica a la dialéctica del amo y el esclavo en Hegel.* México: Ítaca.

Villa Arreola, Yamilet. 2009. "Narran casos de muertes de indígenas por golpizas y abusos. Los usos y costumbres en aldeas nahuas, prácticas que generan violencia de género." *La Jornada Guerrero*, March 9. http://www.lajornadaguerrero.com.mx/2009/03/09/index.php?section=sociedad&article=007n2soc (accessed September 17, 2014).

Wanderley, Fernanda. 2011. "El TIPNIS somos todos. Otro desarrollo es posible." *Fernanda Wanderley.* http://fernandawanderley.blogspot.ca/2011/09/el-tipnis-somos-todos-otro-desarrollo.html (accessed September 17, 2014).

Warren, Mary Anne. 1985. *Gendercide: The implications of sex selection.* Maryland: Rowman and Littlefield.

Webber, Jeffery. 2010. "Carlos Mesa, Evo Morales, and a divided Bolivia, 2003–2005." *Latin American Perspectives* 37 (3): 51–70.

———. 2011. *From rebellion to reform in Bolivia.* Chicago: Haymarket Books.

Wilentz, Amy. 2013. *Farewell, Fred Voodoo.* New York: Simon & Schuster.

Wilpert, Gregory. 2007. *Changing Venezuela by taking power.* United Kingdom: Verso.

Zapatista Army of National Liberation. 2005. *Sixth declaration of the selva lacandona* http://enlacezapatista.ezln.org.mx/sdsl-en/ (accessed September 17, 2014).

Zibechi, Raúl. 2009. "La crisis nuestra de cada día." *La Jornada*, May 8. http://www.jornada.unam.mx/2009/05/08/index.php?section=opinion&article=042a1pol (accessed September 17, 2014).

———. 2012a. *Dispersing power: Social movements as anti-state forces.* California: AK Press.

———. 2012b. *Territories in resistance: A cartography of Latin American social movements.* California: AK Press.

Index